Sparks

The Confederate
Raider *Alabama*

The Kearsarge versus *The Alabama*

The Confederate Raider *Alabama*

Selections from *Memoirs of*
Service Afloat During the
War Between the States

By Her Commander

RAPHAEL SEMMES

Edited, with an Introduction, by

PHILIP VAN DOREN STERN

Civil War Centennial Series

INDIANA UNIVERSITY PRESS

Bloomington

The Confederate Raider Alabama comprises selected chapters from *Memoirs of Service Afloat During the War Between the States* by Raphael Semmes
First cloth-bound edition 1962
Manufactured in the United States of America

Contents

20297

Chapter 21—*1863*

The Alabama at Singapore—Panic among the enemy's shipping in the China Sea—The multitude flock to see the Alabama—A curious rumor concerning a portion of her crew—The author rides to the country and spends a night—The Chinese in possession of all the business of the place—The Alabama leaves Singapore—Capture of the Martaban, alias Texan Star—The Alabama touches at Malacca—Capture of the Highlander and Sonora—The Alabama once more in the Indian Ocean . . . .

Chapter 22—*1864*

The Alabama crosses the Bay of Bengal—The Pilgrims to Mecca and the Black Giants—Burning of the Emma Jane—The town of Anjenga and the Hindoos—The great deserts of Central Asia and the cotton crop of Hindostan—The Alabama crosses the Arabian Sea—The animalculæ of the sea—The Comoro Islands—Johanna and its Arab population—The Yankee whaler at Johanna—The Alabama passes through the Mozambique Channel and arrives at the Cape of Good Hope . . . .

Chapter 23—*1864*

The Alabama again in Cape Town—The seizure of the Tuscaloosa—Final action of the Home Government and release of the Tuscaloosa . . . .

Chapter 24—*1864*

The Alabama at the Cape of Good Hope—Leaves on her return to Europe—Capture of the Rockingham and of the Tycoon—Crosses the equator into the Northern Hemisphere and arrives and anchors at Cherbourg—The engagement between the Alabama and the Kearsarge . . . . . .

Chapter 25—*1864*

Other incidents of the battle between the Alabama and the Kearsarge—The rescue of a portion of the officers and seamen by the English steam yacht Deerhound—The United States Government demands that they be given up—The British Government refuses compliance—The rescued persons not prisoners—The inconsistency of the Federal Secretary of the Navy . . . .

Illustrations

Introduction

THE *Alabama* was one of the most remarkable warships that ever roamed the seas under an American flag. (It must be remembered that the Confederate flag was American.) And Raphael Semmes, the captain who sailed her halfway around the world to destroy Northern merchant vessels, was as remarkable as his ship.

Born in Maryland in 1809 and brought up in Georgetown after his parents died, Semmes received enough education to qualify as a midshipman. He was appointed in 1826. The Academy at Annapolis had not yet been founded, and the United States Navy trained its midshipmen at sea. It was a long, hard route in those days to rise to a position of command, and promotion to any grade was exceedingly slow, especially in peacetime. But the young men who survived the rigorous training period came to know the wooden sailing ships of the day by getting actual experience on board them. And those big square-riggers were exceedingly complicated; just to learn the names and functions of the numerous pieces of wood, metal, and cordage that controlled them took a great deal of time.

Semmes was a studious lad who was interested not only in seamanship but also in maritime and international law. He was born to command, and there was never any doubt of his fitness for his chosen work. He was first in his class when he became a Passed Midshipman in 1832.

After spending six years on several ships, he was sent to the naval base at Norfolk to maintain the many chronometers belonging to the fleet. While there, he continued his law studies and was admitted to the bar.

Three years later he was back at sea again, this time on a ship which is still afloat. (This was the U. S. *Constellation*, now reduced to a hulk, but she is being restored to her original condition as a sailing frigate.) In 1837, Semmes became a lieutenant; he promptly married a New Jersey girl named Anne Elizabeth Spencer.

During the early years of their marriage, the young couple were able to be together for quite a while. In 1841 Semmes was sent to the Pensacola Navy Yard in Florida. While there he became a citizen of nearby Alabama. Then he was given command of one of the first steamships in the United States Navy, the little *Poinsett*. After commanding several other ships, Semmes was assigned to one with an unhappy history, the notorious brig *Somers*. When a threatened mutiny on board her had been detected in 1842, three of the plotters were hanged at the main yardarm. Semmes took command of her in 1846 after the war with Mexico had begun. The *Somers* was a bad-luck ship destined for an early and disastrous end. She capsized in a squall while too lightly ballasted and sank with a loss of many of her crew. But Semmes was acquitted by a Court of Inquiry and then sent to Mexico City where he worked with the Army while attached to the staff of General William J. Worth.

The years after the Mexican War were inactive ones for Semmes. He spent most of them in Mobile, which was to be his family's permanent home. While waiting for promotion and a return to active service, he devoted himself to the law. In 1855 he was made a commander and then became an official Lighthouse Inspector. He was stationed in Washington as Secretary of the Lighthouse Board in 1858 and was still there when the Southern States began to leave the Union. He resigned from the United States Navy on February 15, 1861, after Alabama had seceded. Semmes offered his services to the newly organized Confederacy and was one of the first naval officers to reach its capital, then at Montgomery, Alabama.

He was immediately sent into the Northern States to buy munitions and ships and hire skilled mechanics. By April 4 (before Fort Sumter was fired on), he was back in Montgomery, where he found that he was again in the lighthouse service, this time for the Confederacy. When war began a few days later, he quickly wangled his way out of such work and was given command of a mail steamer, the *Habana*, which had been running between New Orleans and Cuba. Semmes refitted the little ship and made her into a man-of-war renamed the *Sumter*. She was the first Confederate raider.

On June 18, the hastily converted cruiser steamed down the Mississippi to watch for a chance to run past the Federal warships blockading the mouths of the great river. Semmes had to wait for days until conditions seemed right. On June 30, the *Sumter* sailed into the Gulf and was immediately pursued by the much more powerful U. S. *Brooklyn*. After a lively chase, Semmes succeeded in outsailing the bigger and reputedly faster ship. On July 3, he took his first prize, a fine Yankee bark named *The Golden Rocket*, which he burned at sea.

The destruction of unarmed merchant vessels was an unpleasant task which no one liked to do, but it had to be done as an act of war to discourage enemy commerce. Semmes and his fellow Confederate captains were so good at their work that before long the flag of the United States was seldom seen on a merchant vessel. Ships by the hundreds were sold or transferred to other flags to escape capture and destruction. What the raiders did paralysed United States commercial shipping for several generations. George W. Dalzell, in *The Flight from the Flag* (Chapel Hill, 1940), says that

more than half of the total American merchant fleet was lost to the flag during the Civil War. The cruisers burned or sank 110,000 tons of it; 800,000 tons were sold to foreign owners. In addition, there was a considerable loss of tonnage, for which figures are not available by reason of the fact that some foreign powers, notably Portugal, issued licenses to American owners by which vessels were placed under the registry and protection of the foreign government under an arrangement which was intended to be temporary but in fact became permanent. The

ships that were left under the American flag were the
ones the foreigners did not want—old, obsolete, and
nearly worthless craft.

Since most of the Confederate raiders had been built or
purchased in England, a great deal of animus was felt toward
that country by the people of the North. After the war was
over, an elaborate legal suit was instituted against the British
government for damages done to American shipping. An
international tribunal sitting in Geneva settled the so-called
"Alabama Claims" in 1872 by awarding the United States
$15,500,000 in gold.

Semmes' first ship, the *Sumter*, which was originally designed to carry mail and passengers for short runs, made a poor
ship of war. She had to put into Gibraltar for repairs on
January 18, 1862, after taking eighteen ships and burning
seven valued at more than a million dollars. She was blockaded at Gibraltar by several United States naval vessels and
could not get out. On April 11, Semmes left her in charge
of a skeleton crew and went to England and then to Nassau.

Meanwhile, secret agents of the Confederate Government
headed by shipping expert James Dunwoody Bulloch had
succeeded in getting a ship intended for warlike purposes
built in the Laird yard at Birkenhead. This was the trim-
looking raider that was to win world fame as the *Alabama*.
British law forbade her being taken to sea as an armed
cruiser but said nothing about guns and equipment being
placed on board outside British waters. Semmes got orders
from Richmond to go from Nassau to Liverpool. He and
Bulloch sailed from there in the steamer *Bahama* to join the
Alabama, which was waiting for them in the Azores, where
her guns had been brought out by a smaller ship.

Semmes' own account of his exploits on the most celebrated of all Confederate sea raiders begins at this point. His
book, *Memoirs of Service Afloat During the War Between
the States*, first published in 1869, deals with both the
Sumter and the *Alabama*. His story of his cruise on the *Sumter*
was reissued in 1948 under the title *Rebel Raider*, edited by
Harpur Allen Gosnell (University of North Carolina Press).
The present book carries on that story from the time Semmes

Captain Raphael Semmes

Semmes' resignation from the
United States Navy

first saw the *Alabama* until the war ended. He served again with the Army when the Confederate ships on the James River had to be destroyed when Richmond was abandoned in April 1865. Already an admiral, he was temporarily made a general while he led his naval brigade south to join Jefferson Davis and the Confederate Cabinet at Danville.

Semmes was arrested in Mobile on December 15, 1865, and held without trial until April 7, 1866, when he was released because the Government could not make out a case against him. After that he taught for a short while at what is now Louisiana State University. He also worked in Memphis as a newspaper editor. But he spent most of his time in Mobile writing, lecturing, and practising law. He died there on August 30, 1877, at the age of 68.

The modern reader will enjoy Semmes' story of his adventures at sea. If he is scientifically minded he will be interested in the doughty old sailor's speculations about the mysteries of wind, current, tide, weather, and marine biology. But he may be puzzled to find that a man who was so advanced in his thinking about physical phenomena was so blindly prejudiced in his attitude toward racial and political problems. But Semmes was the product of his time and place. Like most of his fellow Confederates, he remained an unreconstructed rebel for the rest of his life. He was liberal enough in his religious opinions. Brought up as a Catholic, he married a Protestant and did not object when some of his children became Episcopalians.

He was vain, arrogant, hot-tempered, and outspoken. But he was an extraordinarily able and daring naval commander who was considerate of his prisoners and was the epitome of old-fashioned courtesy toward women. He was a strict disciplinarian, but he had to be, for his crews were made up of hard-bitten, hard-drinking seamen from the waterfronts and backstreets of the world. His men fondly called him "Old Beeswax" because of his sharply pointed mustaches. His enemies called him "pirate" and threatened to hang him, but they never had a chance to do so, for he roamed the seas for years during the war and always gave his pursuers the slip when they seemed to have him cornered. Even when he lost the *Alabama* when she was sunk off Cherbourg by the U. S.

Kearsarge, he and most of his officers escaped on an English yacht that happened to be near by. Semmes was popular with the British, and they lionized him when he stepped jauntily ashore at Southampton.

But let him tell his own tale, which he is very well able to do.

PHILIP VAN DOREN STERN

EDITOR'S NOTE: *Spelling and punctuation have been modernized. Semmes' long and ponderous passages about international law and historical precedent have been eliminated as have many of his numerous asides to the reader.*

CHART OF THE CRUISE OF THE "ALABAMA."

NOTE: of the 66 captures, given on this chart, 52 were burned; 10 were released on bond, namely, the *Emily Farnum, Tonawanda, Baron de Castine, Union, Ariel, Washington, Bethia Thayer, Punjaub, Morning Star,* and *Justina*; of the 4 not accounted for above, the *Hatteras* was sunk in action; the *Conrad* was named the *Tuscaloosa* and became a cruiser, or "tender to the *Alabama*"; the *Sea Bride* was sold; the *Martha Wenzell,* captured in neutral waters, was released.

The Author's Preface

The *Alabama* was the first steamship in the history of the world—the defective little *Sumter* excepted—that was let loose against the commerce of a great commercial people. The destruction which she caused was enormous. She not only alarmed the enemy, but she alarmed all the other nations of the earth which had commerce afloat as they could not be sure that a similar scourge, at some future time, might not be let loose against themselves. The *Alabama*, in consequence, became famous. It was the fame of steam. . . .

The cruise of a ship is a biography. The ship becomes a personification. She not only

"Walks the waters like a thing of life,"

but she speaks in moving accents to those capable of interpreting her. But her interpreter must be a seaman and not a landsman. He must not only be a seaman, he must have made the identical cruise which he undertakes to describe. It will be seen, hence, that the career of the author was a sealed book to all but himself. A landsman could not even interpret his journals, written frequently in the hieroglyphics of the sea. A line, or a bare mark made by himself, which to other eyes would be meaningless would for him be fraught with the inspiration of whole pages.

Besides, the *Alabama* had an inside as well as an outside life. She was a microcosm. If it required a seaman to interpret her as to her outside life, much more did it require one to give an intelligible view of the world that she carried in her bosom. No one but an eyewitness, and that witness himself a sailor, could unveil to an outside world the domestic mysteries of the everyday life of Jack and portray him in his natural colors as he worked and as he played. The following pages may, therefore, be said to be the first attempt to give anything like a truthful picture of the career of the author upon the high seas during the late war to the public. In their preparation the writer has discarded the didactic style of the historian and adopted that of memoir writing as better suited to his subject. This style gave him more latitude in the description of persons and events and relieved him from some of the fetters of a mere writer of history. There are portions of the work, however, purely historical, and these have been treated with the gravity and dignity which became them. In short, the author has aimed to produce what the title of his book imports—an historical memoir of his services afloat during the war. . . .

A word now as to the feeling with which the author has written. It has sometimes been said that a writer of history should be as phlegmatic and unimpassioned as the judge upon the bench. If the reader desires a dead history—in other words, a history devoid of the true spirit of history, the author assents to the remark. But if he desires a living, moving, breathing picture of events—a *personam* instead of a *subjectam*, the picture must not be undertaken by one who does not feel something of that which he writes. Such a terrible war as that through which we have passed could not be comprehended by a stolid, phlegmatic writer whose pulse did not beat quicker while he wrote. . . . All passions blind us if we give free rein to them; but when they are held in check, they sharpen instead of obscuring the intellect. In a well-balanced mind, feeling and judgment aid each other; and he will prove the most successful historian who has the two in a just equipoise. But though the author has given vent occasionally to a just indignation, he has not written in malice. He does not know the meaning of the word. He has simply written as a Southern man might be supposed to think and feel, treading upon the toes of his enemies as tenderly as possible. If he has been occasionally plain-spoken, it is because he has used the English language which calls a rogue a rogue notwithstanding his disguises. When the author has spoken of the Yankee and his "grand moral ideas," he has spoken rather of a well-known type than of individual men. If the reader will bear these remarks in mind as he goes along, he will find them a key to some of the passages in the book. In describing natural phenomena, the author has ventured upon some new suggestions. He submits these with great diffidence. Meteorology is yet a new science, and many developments of principles remain to be made.

ANCHORAGE, NEAR MOBILE, ALA.
December, 1868

Chapter One—*1862*

A brief resumé of the history of the war between the commissioning of the Sumter and the commissioning of the Alabama . . . Secretary Mallory and the difficulties by which he was surrounded . . . The reorganization of the Confederate States Navy

Although I design only to write a history of my own proceedings during the war yet it will be necessary, to enable the reader to understand these proceedings correctly, to run a thread of the general history of the war parallel with them. . . . I shall do this very briefly, barely enumerating the principal military events without attempting to describe them and glancing very cursorily at the naval events.

We ran the blockade of the Mississippi in the *Sumter* on the 30th of June, 1861. In July of that year the first great battle of Manassas was fought. This battle gave us great prestige in Europe and contributed very much to the respect with which the little *Sumter* had been received by foreign powers. A long military pause now ensued. The enemy had been so astonished and staggered by this blow that it took him some time to recover from its effects. He, however, turned it to useful account and set himself at work with great

23

patience and diligence to collect and thoroughly drill new troops. The victory, on the other hand, had an unfavorable effect upon our own people in giving them an undue impression of their superiority over their enemy and lulling them into supineness

During the summer of 1861, two naval expeditions were fitted out by the enemy and sent to operate against our coast. The first of these expeditions, under command of Commodore Stringham, captured two hastily constructed, and imperfect earthworks at Hatteras Inlet on the coast of North Carolina, and made a lodgement on Pamlico Sound. The capture of these works is no otherwise remarkable, in a naval point of view, than for the circumstance that a Confederate States naval officer fell into the hands of the enemy for the first time during the war. Commodore Samuel Barron, of the Confederate States Navy, commanded the forts and surrendered after a gallant resistance to the overwhelming force which assaulted him on condition that he should be treated as a prisoner of war. The battle of Manassas had occurred to humble the pride and appeal to the fears of the enemy, and the condition named by Barron was readily assented to. The other naval expedition, under command of Commodore Dupont, captured Port Royal, South Carolina. The "Trent Affair" came off in November 1861, and Commodore Hollins' attack upon the enemy's fleet at the mouths of the Mississippi . . . in October of the same year. This brings us to the close of the first year of the war.

The year 1862 was big with events, which we will merely string on our thread. The Confederates in the beginning of the year occupied a position at Bowling Green, Kentucky, which was seemingly a strong position, with railroad communication in their rear with all parts of the South, but they could not hold it for the simple reason that the enemy, having command of the western rivers by means of his superior naval force, penetrated into their rear and thus compelled a retreat. When the enemy, by means of his gunboats, could send armies up the Cumberland and Tennessee Rivers to the heart of Tennessee and Alabama, it was folly to think of holding Bowling Green with our limited forces. Our army fell back to Nashville and even abandoned that city after the fall of Forts Henry and Donelson which were captured by the Federal forces in February 1862.

The evacuation of all these points one after another, and afterward the loss of Island No. 10 on the Mississippi, and New Madrid, were serious blows for us. But our disasters did not end here. The battle of Shiloh followed, in which we were defeated, and compelled to retreat, after we had, to all appearance, gained a victory almost complete on the first day of the fight. Naval disasters accompanied or followed our disasters upon the land. Early in 1862, a naval expedition of the enemy, under the command of Commodore Goldsborough, entered Pamlico Sound and captured Roanoke Island. Commodore Lynch, of the Confederate States Navy, with six or seven small, ill-armed gunboats, which had been improvised from light and frail river steamers, assisted in the defence of the island, but was obliged to withdraw before the superior forces of the enemy. The enemy, pursuing his advantages, followed Lynch's retreating fleet to Elizabeth City, North Carolina, where he captured or destroyed it.

The enemy was now not only in possession of the western waters—Vicksburg and Port Hudson alone obstructing his free navigation of the Mississippi as far down as New Orleans—but Pamlico and Albemarle Sounds, in North Carolina, and the bay of Port Royal in South Carolina and Georgia, were open to him. To complete the circle of our disasters, New Orleans was captured by Farragut and Porter in April—the small Confederate fleet under Commodore John K. Mitchell making a gallant but disastrous defence in which it was totally destroyed with great loss of life of both officers and men.

Let us turn now to a more pleasing picture; for all was not disaster for the Confederates during the year 1862. In March of that year, the memorable naval engagement occurred in Hampton Roads between the Confederate States ironclad steamer *Virginia* and the enemy's fleet, resulting in the destruction by the *Virginia* of two of the enemy's wooden frigates. Great consternation and alarm were produced in the enemy's fleet and at Fortress Monroe by Admiral Buchanan and his armored ship, as well there might be, for the ship was perfectly invulnerable, and but for her great draft of water might have destroyed or driven off the whole Federal fleet. Our people were greatly elated by this victory, coming as it did, in the midst of so many disasters. It attracted great attention in Europe, also, as being decisive of the fate of all the old-time wooden ships, which had . . . composed the navies of the world. It so happened that the Federals had completed the first of their monitors at this very time, and this little iron ship, arriving opportunely, engaged the Virginia on the second day of the fight. Like her great antagonist, she, too, was invulnerable, and the result was a drawn battle. From this time onward, the enemy multiplied his armored ships very rapidly, and it is scarcely too much to say that he is almost wholly indebted to them for his success in the war.

Another very creditable affair for the Confederates came off on the 15th of May [1862]. In the interval between the fight of the Virginia with the enemy's fleet in Hampton Roads and the day last named, Norfolk had been evacuated, and the Virginia, which had passed under the command of Commodore Tatnall, was blown up. The consequence was that the James River was open to the navigation of the enemy. Taking advantage of this state of things, five of the enemy's gunboats, two of which were ironclad, ascended the river with intent to reach and shell Richmond. They met with no serious obstruction or any opposition until they reached Drury's Bluff. Here the river had been obstructed, and a Confederate earthwork erected. The earthwork was commanded by Captain Eben Farrand of the Confederate States Navy, who had some sailors and marines under him. The Federal fleet having approached within 600 yards, opened fire upon the fort, which it kept up for the space of three hours. It was so roughly handled, however, by Farrand and his sailors that at the end of that time it was obliged to retire with several of its vessels seriously damaged. No further attempt was made during the war to reach Richmond by means of ironclads; the dose which Farrand had given them was quite sufficient.

But the greatest of all the triumphs which crowned the Confederate arms during this year of 1862 were the celebrated campaigns of Stonewall Jackson in the Shenandoah Valley and the seven days' fighting before Richmond. . . . Banks, Fremont, and Shields, of the enemy, were all operating in this valley with forces greatly outnumbering those of Jackson. . . .

The enemy, after his defeat at Manassas, put General McClellan in command of the Army of the Potomac, and the balance of the year 1861 was devoted by this officer to the collecting and drilling of troops. In the spring of 1862 he landed at Fortress Monroe with a splendidly appointed army of 90,000 men, provided with 55 batteries of artillery consisting of 350 fieldpieces. Magruder held him in check for some time with 11,000 men, which enabled the Confederate commanders to gather together their forces for the defence of Richmond. He moved at length, was checked a while at Williamsburg by Longstreet, but finally deployed his immense forces on the banks of the Chickahominy.

A series of battles now took place commencing on the 30th of May and extending through the month of June, which resulted in the raising of the siege and the total rout and precipitate retreat of the Federal commander. I will barely enumerate these battles as follows: Seven Pines; Mechanicsville and Beaver Dam; Gaines' Mills; Savage Station; Frazer's Farm; and Malvern Hill—names sufficient alone to cover the Confederate cause with immortal glory . . . on those fields destined to become classic in American annals.

Following up the defeat of McClellan by Johnston and Lee, [Lee and] Stonewall Jackson gained the splendid victory of the Second Manassas over Pope, defeating him with great loss and driving him . . . to the gates of Washington. Thus, notwithstanding our disasters in the West and South, an entirely new face had been put upon the war in Virginia. The enemy's capital, instead of Richmond, was in danger, and McClellan was hastily withdrawn from Fortress Monroe for its defence.

We must now pause, for we have brought the thread of the war down to the commissioning of the *Alabama*, and the reader will see with what forebodings as well as hopes we took the sea in that ship. The war may be said now to have been at its height. Both belligerents were thoroughly aroused, and a few blows well struck on the water might be of great assistance. I resolved to attempt to strike these blows.

A few words, now, as to the *status* of the Confederate States Navy. The Confederate States had no navy at the beginning of the war, and the South being almost entirely agricultural with few or no ships and but little external commerce, except such as was conducted in Northern bottoms, had but very indifferent means of creating one. Whilst the North was one busy hive of manufacturing industry with its shipyards and workshops resounding by night and by day with the busy strokes of the hammer, the adze, and the caulking iron; whilst its steam mills and foundries were vomiting forth their thick smoke from their furnaces and deafening the ears of their workmen by the din of the trip-hammer and the whirr of the lathe; and whilst foreign material of every description was flowing into open ports, the South had neither shipyards nor workshops, steam mills nor foundries, except on the most limited scale, and all her ports were as good as hermetically sealed so far as the introduction of the heavy materials of which she stood in need was concerned.

It will be seen what a difficult task the Secretary of the Navy had before him, and how unjust are many of the censures that were cast upon him by persons unconversant with naval affairs. Indeed, it is rather a matter of surprise that so much was accomplished with our limited means. Workshops and foundries were improvised wherever it was possible to establish them; but the great difficulty was the want of the requisite heavy machinery. We had not the means in the entire Confederacy of turning out a complete steam engine of any size, and many of our naval disasters are attributable to this deficiency. Well-constructed steamers that did credit to the Navy Department and its agents were forced to put to sea and to move about upon our sounds and harbors with engines disproportioned to their size, and incapable of driving them at a speed greater than five miles the hour.

The casting of cannon and the manufacture of small arms were also undertaken by the Secretary under the direction of skilful officers and prosecuted to considerable efficiency. But it took time to accomplish all these things. Before a ship could be constructed it was necessary to hunt up the requisite timber and transport it considerable distances. Her armor—if she was to be armored—was to be rolled also at a distance and transported over long lines of railroad piecemeal; her cordage was to be picked up at one place, and her sails and hammocks at another. I speak knowingly on this subject, as I had had experience of many of the difficulties I mention in fitting out the *Sumter* in New Orleans. I was two months in preparing this small ship for sea, practising all the while every possible diligence and contrivance. The Secretary had other difficulties to contend with. By the time he had gotten many of his shipyards well established, and ships well on their way to completion, the enemy would threaten . . . by land, and either compel him to attempt to remove everything movable in great haste and at great loss, or destroy it to prevent it from falling into the hands of the enemy. Many fine ships were in this way burned on the very eve of completion.

It must be recollected, too, that in the early days of the war we had no finances. These were to be improvised along with other things. . . . If we had had plenty of funds in the beginning of the war, it is possible that we might have accomplished more than we did in Europe in the matter of getting out ships to prey upon the enemy's commerce—that is, in the way of purchase, for it soon became evident from the experience we had had in building the *Alabama* and other ships contracted for by the Navy Department that we could not rely upon constructing them. The neutral powers became too watchful and were too much afraid of the Federal power. When the Government did put the Secretary in funds, several months had elapsed, the war had begun, the coast was blockaded, and all the nations of Europe were on the alert.

With reference to the *personnel* of the Navy, a few words will describe the changes which had taken place in its organization. . . . [In the beginning] it consisted of but four captains, four commanders, and about thirty lieutenants. . . . A considerable accession was made to the navy list as Virginia, North Carolina, and other states seceded and joined their fortunes with those of their more impulsive sisters, the Cotton States. A number of old officers, past service, disdaining to eat the bread of ignoble pensioners upon the bounty of the Northern States . . . came South, bringing with them nothing but their patriotism and their gray hairs. These all took rank according to the positions they had held in the old service. These old gentlemen, whilst they would have commanded with great credit fleets and squadrons of well-appointed and well-officered ships, were entirely unsuited for such service as the Confederacy could offer them. It became necessary, in consequence, to reorganize the Navy; and although this was not done until May 1863, some months after the *Alabama* was commissioned, I will anticipate the subject here to avoid the necessity of again referring to it.

I had been promoted to the rank of captain in the Regular Navy in the summer of 1862. The Act of May 1863 established what was called the Provisional Navy; the object being, without interfering with the rank of the officers in the Regular Navy, to cull out from that navy list younger and more active men and put them in the Provisional Navy with increased rank. The Regular Navy became a kind of retired list, and the Secretary of the Navy was enabled to accomplish his object of bringing forward younger officers for active service without wounding the feelings of the older officers by promoting their juniors over their heads on the same list. As late as December 1861 we had had no admirals in our Navy. On the 24th of that month, the Act organizing the Navy was so amended as to authorize the appointment of four officers of this grade. There was but one of these admirals appointed up to the time of which I am writing—[Franklin] Buchanan, who was promoted for his gallant fight in the *Virginia* with the enemy's fleet in Hampton Roads. Buchanan, being already an admiral in the Regular Navy, was now transferred to the Provisional Navy with the same rank; and the captains' list of this latter Navy was so arranged that Barron stood first on it, and myself second. I was thus the third in rank in the Provisional Navy soon after I hoisted my pennant on board the *Alabama*. In reviewing these matters, my only regret now is that the older officers of whom I have spoken, and who made so many sacrifices for principle—sacrifices that have hastened several of them to the tomb—were not made admirals on the regular or retired list. The honors would have been barren, it is true, as no commands commensurate with the rank could have been given them, but the bestowal of the simple title would have been a compliment no more than due to veterans who had commanded squadrons in the old service and who had abandoned all for the sake of their states. . . .

Chapter Two—*1862*

---

*The author leaves Liverpool to join the Alabama . . .
Arrival at Terceira . . . Description of the Alabama . . .
Preparing her for sea . . . The Portuguese authorities
. . . The commissioning of the ship . . . A picture of
her birth and death . . . Captain Bulloch returns to
England . . . Author alone on the high seas*

I was . . . in Liverpool . . . having just arrived there in the
steamer *Bahama* from Nassau. The *Alabama*, then known as
the 290, had proceeded a few days before to her rendezvous,
the island of Terceira, one of . . . the Azores. The name 290
may need a word of explanation. The newspapers of the
enemy have falsely charged that the *Alabama* was built by
290 Englishmen of "rebel" proclivities, and hence, they say,
the name. . . . The fact is . . . that the *Alabama* was built by
the Messrs. Laird of Birkenhead under a contract with the
Confederate States, and was paid for out of the Confederate
Treasury. She happened to be the 290th ship built by those
gentlemen, and hence the name.

The *Alabama* had been built in perfect good faith by the
Lairds. When she was contracted for, no question had been
raised as to the right of a neutral to build and sell to a bel-

31

ligerent such a ship. . . . The Federal Secretary of the Navy
himself had endeavored not only to build an *Alabama* but
ironclads in England. But as the war progressed, the United
States, foreseeing the damage which a few fast steamers
might inflict on their commerce, took alarm and began to
insist that neutrals should not supply us even with unarmed
ships. The laws of nations were clearly against them. Their
own practice in all former wars in which they had been
neutrals was against them. And yet they maintained their
ground so stoutly and defiantly, threatening war if they were
not listened to, that the neutral powers, and especially Great
Britain, became very cautious. They were indeed bullied—
for that is the word—into timidity. To show the good faith
which the Lairds had practiced throughout, I quote again
from the speech made by the senior partner, in the House of
Commons:

I can only say from all I know, and from all I have heard,
that from the day the vessel was laid down, to her completion
everything was open and aboveboard in this country. I also
further say that the officers of the Government had every
facility afforded them for inspecting the ship during the
progress of building. When the officers came to the builders,
they were shown the ship, and day after day the customs
officers were on board, as they were when she finally left, and
they declared that there was nothing wrong. They only left
her when the tug left, and they were obliged to declare that
she left Liverpool a perfectly legitimate transaction.

Notwithstanding this practice of good faith on our part,
and our entire innocence of any breach of the laws of nations
or of the British Foreign Enlistment Act, Lord John Russell
had been intimidated to such an extent that the ship came
within an ace of being detained. But for the little ruse . . .
of going on a trial trip with a party of ladies and the customs
officers . . . on board, and not returning but sending our
guests back in a tug, there is no doubt that the *Alabama*
would have been tied up . . . in court. She must have been
finally released, it is true, but the delay itself would have been
of serious detriment to us.

After a few busy days in Liverpool, during which I was
gathering my old officers of the *Sumter* around me and making my financial arrangements for my cruise with the house of

The original shipbuilder's model of *The Alabama*

Above: A contemporary sketch of *The Alabama*

Below: The Alabama drawn from a description given
by a sea captain who saw her

Frazer, Trenholm & Co., I departed on the 13th of August,
1862, in the steamer *Bahama* to join the *Alabama*. Captain
James D. Bulloch*, of the Confederate States Navy, a Georgian
who had been bred in the old service but who had retired
from it some years before the war to engage in the steam-
packet service, accompanied me. Bulloch had contracted for
and superintended the building of the *Alabama* and was now
going with me to be present at the christening of his bantling.
I am indebted to him as well the Messrs. Laird for a very
perfect ship of her class.

She was of about 900 tons burden, 230 feet in length, 32
feet in breadth, 20 feet in depth, and drew when provisioned
and coaled for a cruise, 15 feet of water. Her model was of
the most perfect symmetry, and she sat upon the water with
the lightness and grace of a swan. She was barkentine rigged
with long lower masts which enabled her to carry large fore-
and-aft sails, as jibs and try-sails, which are of so much importance to a steamer in so many emergencies. Her sticks
were of the best yellow pine that would bend in a gale like
a willow wand without breaking, and her rigging was of the
best of Swedish iron wire. The scantling of the vessel was
light compared with vessels of her class in the Federal Navy,
but this was scarcely a disadvantage as she was designed as a
scourge of the enemy's commerce rather than for battle. She
was to defend herself if defence should become necessary.
Her engine was of three hundred horsepower, and she had
attached an apparatus for condensing from the vapor of sea
water all the fresh water that her crew might require. She was
a perfect steamer and a perfect sailing ship at the same time,
neither of her two modes of locomotion being at all dependent
upon the other.... The *Sumter*, when her fuel was exhausted
was little better than a log on the water because of her in-
ability to hoist her propeller, which she was compelled to
drag after her. The *Alabama* was so constructed that in fifteen minutes her propeller could be detached from the
shaft and lifted in a well contrived for the purpose sufficiently
high out of the water not to be an impediment to her speed.
When this was done, and her sails spread, she was to all
intents and purposes a sailing ship. On the other hand, when

---

*Bulloch was the chief Confederate naval agent in Europe. His
book, *The Secret Service of The Confederate States in Europe*, tells
how the cruisers were obtained. ED.

I desired to use her as a steamer I had only to start the fires, lower the propeller, and if the wind was adverse, brace her yards to the wind, and the conversion was complete. The speed of the *Alabama* was always greatly overrated by the enemy. She was ordinarily about a ten-knot ship. She was said to have made eleven knots and a half on her trial trip, but we never afterward got it out of her. Under steam and sail both we logged on one occasion thirteen knots and a quarter, which was her utmost speed.

Her armament consisted of eight guns; six 32-pounders in broadside, and two pivot-guns amidships; one on the fore-castle and the other abaft the main-mast—the former a 100-pounder rifled Blakeley, and the latter a smoothbore eight-inch. The Blakeley gun was so deficient in metal compared with the weight of shot it threw that after the first few discharges, when it became a little heated, it was of comparatively small use to us—to such an extent were we obliged to reduce the charge of powder on account of the recoil. The average crew of the *Alabama* before the mast was about 120 men; and she carried twenty-four officers: A captain, four lieutenants, surgeon, paymaster, master, marine officer, four engineers, two midshipmen, and four master's mates, a captain's clerk, boatswain, gunner, sailmaker, and carpenter. The cost of the ship, with everything complete, was $250,000.

On the morning of our departure from Liverpool, the *Bahama* had dropped some distance down the Mersey, and we joined her by tug. She had her steam up and was ready to trip her anchor the moment we arrived, and in a few minutes after getting on board we were under way. The tug cheered us as she turned to steam back to the city, and the cheer was answered lustily by our crew. We were a week on the passage from Liverpool to Terceira; our old friend, Captain Tessier of the *Bahama*, with whom I had made the passage from Nassau to Liverpool, rendering our time very comfortable. On the morning of the 20th of August, we were on the look-out at an early hour for the land, and it was not long before we discovered the island, looking at first hazy and indistinct in the distance, but gradually assuming more form and consistency. After another hour's steaming, Porto Praya, our place of rendezvous, became visible, with its white houses dotting the mountain side, and we now began to turn our glasses

upon the harbor with no little anxiety to see if our ships—
for a sailing ship* with the *Alabama's* battery and stores had
preceded her some days and should now be with her—were
all right. We first caught sight of their spars, and pretty
soon, raising their hulls sufficiently for identification, we felt
much relieved. Our secret had been well kept, and the enemy,
notwithstanding his fine "smelling qualities," had not scented
the prey.

In the meantime, our own approach was watched with
equal anxiety from the deck of the *Alabama*. We might be,
for aught she knew, an enemy's steamer coming in pursuit of
her; and as the enemy was in the habit of kicking all the small
powers that had not the means of kicking back, a neutral port belonging to effete old Portugal would not afford her
the least protection. At half-past eleven A.M. we steamed
into the harbor and let go our anchor. I had surveyed my
new ship . . . with no little interest as she was to be not only
my home, but my bride for the next few years, and I was
quite satisfied with her external appearance. She was a
beautiful thing to look upon. The store ship was already
alongside her, and we could see that the busy work of transferring her cargo was going on. Captain [Matthew J.]
Butcher, an intelligent young English seaman who had been
bred in the mail-packet service and who had taken the
Alabama out from Liverpool on that trial trip of hers . . .
now came on board of us. He had had a rough and stormy
passage from Liverpool, during which he had suffered some
little damage and consumed most of his coal. Considerable
progress had been made in receiving on board from the transport the battery and stores, and a few days more would suffice
to put the ship in a condition for defence.

The harbor of Porto Praya lies open to the eastward, and
as the wind was now from that quarter and blowing rather
freshly, a considerable sea had been raised, which rendered it
inconvenient, if not unsafe, for the transport and the *Alabama*
to continue to lie alongside each other; which was neverthe-
less necessary for the transfer of the remainder of the heavy
guns. I therefore directed Captain Butcher to get up his anchors immediately and follow me around to Angra Bay on
the west side of the island, where we should find a lee and

* The *Agrippina*. Ed.

smooth water. This was done, and we arrived at Angra at four o'clock on the same afternoon. Here the transshipment of the guns and stores was renewed, and here for the first time I visited the *Alabama*. I was as much pleased with her internal appearance and arrangements as I had been with her externally, but everything was in a very uninviting state of confusion—guns, gun ·carriages, shot, and shell, barrels of beef and pork, and boxes and bales of paymaster's, gunner's and boatswain's stores lying promiscuously about the decks, sufficient time not having elapsed to have them stowed in their proper places. The crew, comprising about sixty persons who had been picked up promiscuously about the streets of Liverpool were as unpromising in appearance as things about the decks. What with faces begrimed with coal dust, red shirts, and blue shirts, Scotch caps, and hats, brawny chests exposed, and stalwart arms naked to the elbows, they looked as little like the crew of a man-of-war as one can well conceive. Still there was some *physique* among these fellows, and soap and water and clean shirts would make a wonderful difference in their appearance. As night approached, I relieved Captain Butcher of his command, and removing my baggage on board, took possession of the cabin in which I was to spend so many weary days and watchful nights. I am a good sleeper and slept soundly. This quality of sleeping well in the intervals of harassing business is a valuable one to the sailor, and I owe to it much of that physical ability which enabled me to withstand the four years of excitement and toil to which I was subjected during the war.

There are two harbors called Angra, in Terceira—East Angra and West Angra. We were anchored in the latter, and the authorities notified us the next morning that we must move round to East Angra, that being the port of entry and the proper place for the anchorage of merchant ships. We were *playing* merchant ship as yet, but had nothing to do, of course, with ports of entry or custom houses; and as the day was fine and there was a prospect of smooth water under the lee of the island, I got under way and went to sea, the *Bahama* and the transport accompanying me. Steaming beyond the marine league, I hauled the transport alongside, and we got on board from her the remainder of our armament and stores. The sea was not so smooth as we had expected, and there was some little chafing between the ships, but we accomplished our object without serious inconvenience. This occupied us all day, and after nightfall we ran into East Angra and anchored.

As we passed the fort, we were hailed vociferously in very bad English or Portuguese—we could not distinguish which. But though the words were unintelligible to us, the manner and tone of the hail were evidently meant to warn us off. Continuing our course and paying no attention to the hail, the fort presently fired a shot over us; but we paid no attention to this either and ran in and anchored—the bark accompanying us, but the *Bahama* hauling off seaward, and lying off and on during the night. There was a small Portuguese schooner of war at anchor in the harbor, and about midnight I was aroused from a deep sleep, into which I had fallen after a long day of work and excitement, by an officer coming below and informing me very coolly that the Portuguese man-of-war was firing into us!

"The d—l she is," said I; "how many shots has she fired at us?"

"Three, sir," replied the officer.

"Have any of them struck us?"

"No, sir, none of them have struck us—they seem to be firing rather wild."

I knew very well that the little craft would not dare to fire *into* us, though I thought it probable that after the fashion of the Chinese, who sound their gongs to scare away their enemies, she might be firing *at* us to alarm us into going out of the harbor. I said therefore to the officer, "Let him fire away; I expect he won't hurt you," and turned over and went to sleep. In the morning it was ascertained that it was not the schooner at all that had been firing, but a passing mail steamer which had run into the anchorage and fired three signal guns to awaken her sleeping passengers on shore—with whom she departed before daylight.

We were not further molested from this time onward but were permitted to remain and coal from the bark; though the custom-house officers, accompanied by the British Consul, paid us a visit and insisted that we should suspend our operation of coaling until we had entered the two ships at the custom house. This I readily consented to do. I now called the *Bahama* in by signal, and she ran in and anchored near us. Whilst the coaling was going forward, the carpenter and

gunner, with the assistance of the chief engineer, were busy
putting down the circles or traverses* for the pivot guns; and
the boatswain and his gang were at work fitting side and
train tackles for the broadside guns. The reader can understand how anxious I was to complete all these arrangements.
I was perfectly defenceless without them and did not know at
what moment an enemy's ship might look in upon me. The
harbor of East Angra, where we were now anchored, was quite
open, but fortunately for us the wind was light and from the
S. W., which gave us smooth water, so our work went on
quite rapidly. . . .

I was charmed with the appearance of Terceira. Every
square foot of the island seemed to be under the most elaborate
cultivation, and snug farmhouses were dotted so thickly over
the hillsides as to give the whole the appearance of a ram-
bling village. The markets were most bountifully supplied
with excellent beef and mutton, and the various domestic
fowls, fish, vegetables, and fruits. My steward brought off
every morning . . . a most tempting assortment of the
latter; for there were apples, plums, pears, figs, dates, oranges,
and melons all in full bearing at Terceira. The little town
of Angra, abreast of which we were anchored, was a perfect
picture of a Portuguese-Moorish town, with its red-tiled roofs,
sharp gables, and parti-colored verandas, and veranda cur-
tains. And then the quiet and love-in-a-cottage air which
hovered over the whole scene, so far removed from the highways of the world's commerce and the world's alarms, was
charming to contemplate.

I had arrived on Wednesday, and on Saturday night, we
had, by the dint of great labor and perseverance, drawn order
out of chaos. The *Alabama*'s battery was on board and in
place, her stores had all been unpacked and distributed to the
different departments, and her coal bunkers were again full.
We only awaited the following morning to steam out upon
the high seas and formally put the ship in commission. Saturday had been dark and rainy, but we had still labored on
through the rain. Sunday morning dawned bright and beautiful, which we hailed as a harbinger of future success. All
hands were turned out at early daylight, and the first lieutenant

*Curved iron tracks for the wheels of the heavy guns to run on
as they were swung around. Ed.

and the officer of the deck took the ship in hand to prepare
her for the coming ceremony. She was covered with coal dust
and dirt and rubbish in every direction, for we had hitherto
had no time to attend to appearances. But by dint of a few
hours of scrubbing inside and out, and of the use of that well-
known domestic implement, the holy-stone, that works so
many wonders with a dirty ship, she became sweet and clean,
and when her awnings were snugly spread, her yards squared,
and her rigging hauled taut, she looked like a bride with the
orange wreath about her brows ready to be led to the altar.

I had as yet no enlisted crew, and this thought gave me
some anxiety. All the men on board the *Alabama*, as well as
those who had come out with me on board the *Bahama*, had
been brought thus far under the articles of agreement that were
to be no longer obligatory. Some of them had been shipped
for one voyage and some for another, but none of them for
service on board a Confederate cruiser. This was done to avoid
a breach of the British Foreign Enlistment Act. They had,
of course, been undeceived from·the day of our departure
from Liverpool. They knew that they were to be released
from the contracts they had made, but *I* could not know how
many of them would engage with me for the *Alabama*. It is
true I had had a talk with some of the leaders of the crew who
had promised to go with me and to influence others, but no
creature can be more whimsical than a sailor until you have
bound him past recall—unless indeed it be a woman.

The ship having been properly prepared, we steamed out
on this bright Sunday morning, under a cloudless sky with a
gentle breeze from the southeast scarcely ruffling the surface
of the placid sea, and under the shadow of the smiling and
picturesque island of Terceira, which nature seemed to have
decked specially for the occasion, so charming did it appear
in its checkered dress of a lighter and darker green, composed
of corn fields and orange groves, the flag of the new-born
Confederate States was unfurled for the first time from the
peak of the *Alabama*. The *Bahama* accompanied us. The ceremony was short but impressive. The officers were all in full
uniform, and the crew neatly dressed, and I caused all hands
to be summoned aft on the quarter-deck, and mounting a gun-
carriage, I read the commission of Mr. Jefferson Davis appoint-
ing me a captain in the Confederate States Navy, and the
order of Mr. Stephen R. Mallory, the Secretary of the Navy,

directing me to assume command of the *Alabama*. Following
my example, the officers and crew had all uncovered their
heads in deference to the sovereign authority, as is customary
on such occasions; and as they stood in respectful silence and
listened with rapt attention to the reading and to the short
explanation of my object and purposes in putting the ship in
commission which followed, I was deeply impressed with the
spectacle. Virginia, the grand old mother of many of the
states, who afterward died so nobly; South Carolina, Georgia,
Alabama, and Louisiana were all represented in the persons of
my officers, and I had some of as fine specimens of the daring
and adventurous seaman as any ship of war could boast.

While the reading was going on, two small balls might
have been seen ascending slowly, one to the peak and the
other to the main-royal mast-head. These were the ensign
and pennant of the future man-of-war. These balls were so
arranged that by a sudden jerk of the halliards by which
they had been sent aloft, the flag and pennant would unfold
themselves to the breeze. A curious observer would also
have seen a quartermaster standing by the English colors,
which we were still wearing, in readiness to strike them, a
band of music on the quarter-deck, and a gunner (lock-string
in hand) standing by the weather-bow gun. All these men
had their eyes upon the reader; and when he had concluded,
at a wave of his hand the gun was fired, the change of flags
took place, and the air was rent by a deafening cheer from
officers and men; the band at the same time playing "Dixie,"—
that soul-stirring national anthem of the new-born government.
The *Bahama* also fired a gun and cheered the new flag. Thus,
amid this peaceful scene of beauty, with all nature smiling
upon the ceremony, was the *Alabama* christened; the name
290 disappearing with the English flag. This had all been
done upon the high seas more than a marine league from the
land where Mr. Jefferson Davis had as much jurisdiction as
Mr. Abraham Lincoln. Who could look into the horoscope
of this ship—who anticipate her career? Many of these brave
fellows followed me unto the close.

From the cradle to the grave there is but a step; and that I
may group in a single picture the christening and the burial
of the ship, let the reader imagine some two years to have
rolled over—and such a two years of carnage and blood as
the world had never before seen—and, strangely enough,

another Sunday morning, equally bright and beautiful, to have dawned upon the *Alabama*. This is her funeral morning! At the hour when the churchgoers in Paris and London were sending up their orisons to the Most High, the sound of cannon was heard in the British Channel, and the *Alabama* was engaged in her death struggle. Cherbourg, where the *Alabama* had lain for some days previously, is connected with Paris by rail, and a large number of curious spectators had flocked down from the latter city to witness, as it proved, her interment. The sun rose, as before, in a cloudless sky, and the sea-breeze has come in over the dancing waters, mild and balmy. It is the nineteenth day of June, 1864. The *Alabama* steams out to meet the *Kearsarge* in mortal combat, and before the sun has set, she has gone down beneath the green waters and lies entombed by the side of many a gallant craft that had gone down before her in that famous old British Channel; where from the time of the Norseman and the Danish sea king to our own day, so many naval combats have been fought, and so many of the laurel crowns of victory have been entwined around the brows of our naval ancestors. Many of the manly figures who had stood with uncovered heads and listened with respectful silence to the christening went down in the ship and now lie buried with her, many fathoms deep, with no other funeral dirge than the roar of cannon and the howling winds of the North Sea. Such were the birth and death of the ship whose adventures I propose to sketch.

My speech, I was glad to find, had produced considerable effect with the crew. I informed them in the opening that they were all released from the contracts under which they had come thus far, and that such of them as preferred to return to England could do so in the *Bahama* without prejudice to their interests, as they would have a free passage back, and their pay would go on until they were discharged in Liverpool. I then gave them a brief account of the war and told them how the Southern States, being sovereign and independent, had dissolved the league which had bound them to the Northern States, and how they were threatened with subjugation by their late confederates, who were the stronger. They would be fighting, I told them, the battles of the oppressed against the oppressor, and this consideration alone should be enough to nerve the arm of every generous sailor.

Coming nearer home, for it could not be supposed that

English, Dutch, Irish, French, Italian, and Spanish sailors could understand much about the rights or wrongs of nations, I explained to them the individual advantages which they might expect to reap from an enlistment with me. The cruise would be one of excitement and adventure. We had a fine ship under us; one that they might fall in love with as they would with their sweethearts about Wapping. We should visit many parts of the world where they would have liberty given them on proper occasions; and we should no doubt destroy a great many of the enemy's ships in spite of the enemy's cruisers. With regard to these last, though fighting was not to be our principal object, yet if a favorable opportunity should offer of our laying ourselves alongside a ship that was not too heavy for us, they would find me disposed to indulge them.

Finally I came to the finances, and like a skilful Secretary of the Treasury, I put the budget to them in its very best aspect. As I spoke of good pay and payment in gold, "hear! hear!" came up from several voices. I would give them, I said, about double the ordinary wages to compensate them for the risks they would have to run, and I promised them lots of prize-money to be voted to them by the Confederate Congress for the ships of the enemy that they would be obliged to destroy. When we piped down, that is to say when the boatswain and his mates wound their "calls" three times as a signal that the meeting was over and the crew might disperse, I caused the word to be passed for all those who desired to sign the articles to repair at once to the paymaster and sign. I was anxious to strike whilst the iron was hot. The *Alabama* had brought out from the Mersey about sixty men, and the *Bahama* had brought about thirty more. I got eighty of these ninety men and felt very much relieved in consequence.

The democratic part of the proceedings closed as soon as the articles were signed. The public meeting just described, was the first and last ever held on board the *Alabama*, and no other stump speech was ever made to the crew. When I wanted a man to do anything after this I did not talk to him about "nationalities," or "liberties," or "double wages," but I gave him a rather sharp order, and if the order was not obeyed in double quick, the delinquent found himself in limbo. Democracies may do very well for the land, but monarchies— and pretty absolute monarchies at that—are the only successful governments for the sea. There was a great state of confusion on board the ship, of course, during the remainder of this day and well into the night. Bulloch and Butcher were both on board assisting me, and we were all busy, as well as the paymaster and clerk, making out half-pay tickets for the sailors' wives and sweethearts, drawing drafts for small amounts payable to relatives and dependents in different parts of England for such of the sailors as wanted them, and paying advance wages to those who had no pay tickets to leave or remittances to make. I was gratified to find that a large proportion of my men left half their pay behind them. "A man who has children hath given hostages to fortune," and you are quite as sure of a sailor who sends half his pay to his wife or sweetheart.

It was eleven P. M. before my friend Bulloch was ready to return to the *Bahama* on his way back to England. I took an affectionate leave of him. I had spent some days with him at his quiet retreat in the little village of Waterloo near Liverpool, where I met his excellent wife, a charming Southern woman with whom hospitality was a part of her religious faith. He was living in a very plain, simple style, though large sums of public money were passing through his hands, and he has had the honor to come out of the war poor. He paid out moneys in good faith to the last, even when it was quite evident that the cause had gone under and there would be no accounts to settle with an auditor of the Treasury. I had not only had the pleasure of his society during a number of anxious days, but he had greatly assisted me by his counsel and advice, given with that modesty and reserve which always mark true ability. As soon as the *Bahama* had steamed away and left me alone, I turned my ship's head to the northeast, set the fore-and-aft sails, and directed the engineer to let his fires go down. The wind had freshened considerably, and there was some sea on. I now turned into an unquiet cot, perfectly exhausted after the labors of the day, and slept as comfortably as the rolling of the ship and a strong smell of bilgewater would permit.

Chapter Three—*1862*

The Alabama a ship of war and not a privateer . . .
Sketch of the personnel of the ship . . . Putting the
ship in order for service . . . Sail and steam . . . The
character of the sailor . . . The first blow struck at the
whale fishery . . . The habitat and habits of the whale
. . . The first capture

The *Alabama* is at length upon the high seas as a commissioned ship of war of the Confederate States, her commission having been signed by Mr. Jefferson Davis, who had all the *de facto* right and much more of the *de jure* right to sign such a commission than John Hancock, who signed Paul Jones' commission. The *Alabama*, having been built by the Government of the Confederate States and commissioned by these states as a *ship of war*, was in no sense of the word a *privateer*, which is a private armed ship belonging to individuals and fitted out for purposes of gain. And yet, throughout the whole war and long after the war, when she was not called a "pirate" by the Northern press, she was called a *privateer*. Even high Government officials of the enemy so characterized her. Many of the newspapers erred through ignorance, but this misnomer was sheer malice—and very petty malice, too, on the part of

44

those of them who were better informed, and on the part of
the Government officials, all of whom, of course, knew better.
Long after they had acknowledged the war, as a war, which
carried with it an acknowledgment of the right of the Confederate States to fit out cruisers, they stultified themselves
by calling her "pirate," and "privateer." They were afraid to
speak the truth in conformity with the facts, lest the destruction of their property, for which they hoped ultimately to be
paid, should seem to be admitted to have been done under
the sanction of the laws of nations. They could as logically
have called General Robert E. Lee a *bandit* as myself a *pirate;*
but logic was not the *forte* of the enemy, either during or
since the late war.

Before we commence operations, a glance at the *personnel*
of the ship may not be uninteresting. . . . Of the lieutenants,
only one of my old set followed me. Accident separated the
rest from me, very much to my regret, and we afterward
played different *roles* in the war. . . . I took with me to the
Alabama . . . my old and well-tried First Lieutenant [John Mc-
Intosh] Kell. He became the first lieutenant of the new ship.
Lieutenant Richard F. Armstrong of Georgia, whom I had
left at Gibraltar in charge of the *Sumter.* . . . became second
lieutenant. Armstrong was a young gentleman of intelligence
and character and had made good progress in his profession.
He was a midshipman at the Naval School at Annapolis when
the war broke out. Though still a mere boy, he resigned his
appointment without hesitation and came South. . . . Midshipman Joseph D. Wilson of Florida, also an *élève* of Annapolis, and who, like Armstrong, had made the cruise with
me in the *Sumter* and been promoted. . . . became third
lieutenant. My fourth lieutenant . . . was Mr. Arthur Sinclair, who, though not bred in the old service, belonged to one
of the old naval families of Virginia, both his father and grand-
father having been captains in the United States Navy. These
two young gentlemen were also intelligent, and for the short
time they had been at sea, well informed in their profession.
My fifth lieutenant was Mr. John Low of Georgia, a capital
seaman and excellent officer.

[Dr. Francis L.] Galt, my old surgeon, had accompanied
me, as did also First Lieutenant [Beckett K.] Howell of the
marines. [Henry] Myers, the paymaster of the *Sumter,* was,
unfortunately for me, in prison in Fort Warren when the

Alabama was commissioned. . . . In his place I was forced to content myself with a man as paymaster who shall be nameless in these pages,* since he afterward, upon being discharged by me for his worthlessness, went over to the enemy and became one of Mr. Adams' hangers-on and paid witnesses and spies about Liverpool and the legation in London. As a preparatory step to embracing the Yankee cause, he married a mulatto woman in Kingston, Jamaica, (though he had a wife living) whom he swindled out of what little property she had and then abandoned. I was quite amused when I saw afterward in the Liverpool and London papers that this man, who was devoid of every virtue and steeped to the lips in every vice, was giving testimony in the English courts in the interest of the nation of "grand moral ideas." This was the only recruit the enemy ever got from the ranks of my officers.

To complete the circle of the wardroom, I have only to mention Mr. Miles J. Freeman, the chief engineer of the *Sumter*, who was now filling the same place on board the *Alabama*. Dr. [David Herbert] Llewellyn, an Englishman from Wiltshire, who having come out in the *Alabama* as surgeon when she was yet a merchant ship, had been retained as assistant surgeon; and Acting Master [Irvine D.] Bulloch, [half-] brother of the captain already named in these pages. My "steerage officers," who are too numerous to be named individually, were a capital set of young men, as were the "forward officers." . . .

I must not forget to introduce to the reader one humble individual of the *Alabama*'s crew. He was my steward, and my household would not be complete without him. When I was making the passage from Nassau to Liverpool in the *Bahama*, I noticed a pale, rather delicate, and soft-mannered young man, who was acting as steward on board. He was an obedient, respectful, and attentive major-domo, but unfortunately was rather too much addicted to the use of the wine which he set on the table every day for the guests. Poor Bartelli—I thus designate him, because of his subsequent sad fate—did not seem to have the power of self-restraint, especially under the treatment he received, which was not gentle. The captain was rough toward him, and the poor fellow seemed very much cowed and humbled, trembling

*Clarence R. Yonge

when spoken to harshly. His very forlornness drew me toward
him. He was an Italian, evidently of gentle blood, and as with
the Italians, drinking to intoxication is not an ineradicable
vice, I felt confident that he could be reformed under proper
treatment. And so, when we arrived at Terceira, I asked
Bartelli how he would like to go with me as steward on board
the *Alabama*. He seemed to be delighted with the proposal.
"There is one understanding, however," I said to him, "which
you and I must have: you must never touch a drop of liquor
on board the ship on duty. When you go on shore on liberty,
if you choose to have a little frolic that is your affair, provided
always you come off sober. Is it a bargain?"

"It is, Captain," said he; "I promise you I will behave myself like a man, if you will take me with you."

The captain of the *Bahama* had no objection, and Bartelli
was duly installed as my steward. I found him, as I had expected, a capital servant. He was faithful and became attached
to me, and kept his promise under strong temptation; for there
was always in the cabin lockers of the *Alabama* the best of
wines and other liquors. He took care of my linen like a
woman, washing it himself when we were at sea and sending
it to some careful laundress when in port. I shall perhaps
astonish a great many husbands and heads of families when I
tell them that every shirt button was always in its place, and
that I never had to call for needle and thread under difficulties! My mess affairs never gave me the least trouble. My table
was always well supplied, and when guests were expected, I
could safely leave the arrangements to Bartelli; and then it
was a pleasure to observe the air and grace of manner and
speech with which he would receive my visitors and conduct
them into the cabin. Poor Bartelli!

The day after the *Bahama* left us was cloudy and cheerless
in aspect, with a fresh wind and a rough sea. The ship was
rolling and tumbling about to the discomfort of everyone,
and confusion still reigned on board. Below decks everything
was dirt and disorder. Nobody had as yet been berthed or
messed, nor had any one been stationed at a gun or a rope.
Spare shot boxes and other heavy articles were fetching way,
and the ship was leaking considerably through her upper
works. She had been put together with rather green timber,
and, having been caulked in England in winter, her seams
were beginning to gape beneath the ardent heats of a semi-

tropical climate. I needed several days yet to put things to rights, and mold the crew into a little shape. I withdrew, therefore, under easy sail from the beaten tracks of commerce; and my first lieutenant went to work berthing, and messing, and quartering, and stationing his men. The gun equipments were completed, and such little alterations made as were found necessary for the easy and efficient working of the battery, and the guns were sealed with blank cartridges and put in a proper condition for being loaded promptly. We now devoted several days to the exercise of the crew, as well at general, as division quarters. Some few of the guns' crews had served in ships of war before and proved capital drill-sergeants for the rest. The consequence was that rapid progress was made, and the *Alabama* was soon in a condition to plume her wings for her flight. It only remained to caulk our upper works, and this occupied us but a day or two longer.

I was much gratified to find that my new ship proved to be a fine sailer under canvas. This quality was of inestimable advantage to me, as it enabled me to do most of my work under sail. She carried but an eighteen days' supply of fuel, and if I had been obliged because of her dull sailing qualities to chase everything under steam, the reader can see how I should have been hampered in my movements. I should have been half my time running into port for fuel. This would have disclosed my whereabouts so frequently to the enemy that I should have been constantly in danger of capture, whereas I could now stretch into the most distant seas and chase, capture, and destroy, perfectly independent of steam. I adopted the plan, therefore, of working under sail in the very beginning of my cruise and practised it unto the end. With the exception of half a dozen prizes, all my captures were made with my screw hoisted and my ship under sail; and with but one exception, I never had occasion to use steam to escape from an enemy.

This keeping of the sea for three and four months at a time had another great advantage—it enabled me to keep my crew under better drill and discipline, and in every way better in hand. Nothing demoralizes a crew so much as frequent visits to port. The sailor is as improvident and incapable of self-government as a child. Indeed he is regarded by most nations as a ward of the state, and that sort of legislation is thrown around him which is thrown around a ward in chan-

cery. The moment a ship drops her anchor in a port, like
the imprisoned bird he begins to beat the bars of his cage if
he is not permitted to go on shore and have his frolic; and
when on shore, to carry our simile still further, he is like the
bird let out of the cage. He gives a loose rein to his passions
and sometimes plunges so deeply into debauchery that he
renders himself unfit for duty for days and sometimes weeks
after he is hunted up and brought on board by the police,
which is most frequently the manner in which his captain
again gets possession of him. Such is the reckless intemperance into which some of the regular old salts plunge that I
have known them to go on shore, make their way straight to
a sailor boardinghouse, which is frequently a dance house
and always a grog shop, give what money they have about
them to the landlord, and tell him to keep them drunk
as long as it will last, and when they have had the worth of
it in a *good, long, big* drunk, to pick them up and send them
off to their ship! The very devil is to pay, too, when a lot
of drunken sailors is brought on board, as every first lieutenant
knows. Frequently they have to be knocked down, disarmed
of the dangerous sheath knives which they wear, and confined
in irons until they are sober. When that takes place, Jack
comes out of the Brig, very much ashamed of himself; generally with a blackened eye or two, if not with a broken nose,
and looking very seedy in the way of apparel, as the chances
are that he has sold or exchanged the tidy suit in which he
went on shore for some 'long-shore toggery, the better to
enable him to prolong that delightful drunk of his. It was
quite enough to have such scenes as these repeated once in
three or four months.

When I had put my ship in a tolerable state of defence and
given a little practice at the guns to my crew, I turned her
head toward her cruising ground. . . . I resolved to strike a
blow at the enemy's whale fishery off the Azores. There is a
curious and beautiful problem—that of Providence feeding
the whale—connected with this fishery, which I doubt not
will interest the reader, as it did the writer of these pages,
when it first came under his notice. It is because of that
problem that the Azores are a whaling station. The food
which attracts the whale to these islands is not produced in
their vicinity but is carried thither by the currents—the currents of the ocean performing the same functions for the

finny tribe that the atmosphere does for the plants. The fishes of the sea in their kingdom beneath the waters have thus their highways and byways as well as the animals upon the land, and are always to be found congregated where their great food bearers, the currents, make their deposits. Animalculæ, infusoria, small fishes, minute crustacea, and shellfish found on the algæ, or floating sea weed, sea nettles, and other food, are produced in the more calm latitudes, where the waters are comparatively still, taken up by the currents and transported to the more congenial feeding grounds of the whales and other fishes.*

Much of this food is produced in the tepid waters of the sea, into which some descriptions of whales cannot enter. The equatorial belt of waters surrounding the earth between the tropics, whose temperature is generally 80° of Fahrenheit, is as a sea of fire to the "right" whale. It would be as certain death for this species of whale to attempt to cross these waters as for a human being to plunge into a burning lake. The proof of this is that the "right" whale of the northern hemisphere is never found in the southern hemisphere, or e converso. It is a separate and distinct species. See how beneficent, therefore, the arrangement is, by which the food for these monsters of the deep is transported from the tepid waters into which they cannot enter in pursuit of it, to the cooler waters in which they delight to gambol.

The Gulf Stream is the great food carrier for the extra-tropical whales of the northern hemisphere. An intelligent sea captain, writing to Superintendent [Matthew Fontaine] Maury of the National Observatory some years before the war, informed him that in the Gulf Stream off the coast of Florida, he fell in with "such a school of young sea nettles as had never before been heard of." The sea was literally covered with them for many square leagues. He likened them in appearance to acorns floating on the water, but they were so thick as completely to cover the sea. He was bound to England and was five or six days in sailing through them. In about sixty days afterward, on his return voyage, he fell in with the same school off the Azores, and here he was three or four days in passing them again. He recognized them as the same, for

* The whale of course, is not a fish but a mammal, as Semmes well knew. Eᴅ.

he had never before seen any quite like them; and on both occasions he frequently hauled up buckets full and examined them. In their adventurous voyage of sixty days, during which they must have been tossed about in several gales of wind, these little marine animals had grown considerably, and already the whales had begun to devour them; for the school was now so much diminished in size that the captain was enabled to sail through it in three or four days, instead of the five or six which it had formerly taken him. We see, thus, that the fishes of the sea have their seed time and harvest; that the same Beneficent Hand that decks the lilies of the field in garments more superb than those of Solomon, and feeds the young raven, seeds down the great equatorial belt of waters for the fishes; and that when the harvest time has come, He sends in his reapers and gleaners, the currents, which bind up the sheaves and bear them off three thousand miles to those denizens of the great deep, which, perhaps, but for this beautiful and beneficent arrangement, would die of inanition.

The whaling season ends at the Azores about the first of October, when the first winter gales begin to blow and the food becomes scarce. The whales then migrate to other feeding grounds, and the adventurous whaler follows them. As we were now in the first days of September, we had but a few weeks left in which to accomplish our purpose of striking a blow at the enemy's whale fishery. In the afternoon of September 4th, the weather being fine and clear, we made Pico and Fayal, and reducing sail to topsails, lay off and on during the night. The next day, the weather being cloudy, and the wind light from the eastward, we made our first prize without the excitement of a chase. A ship having been discovered lying to with her foretopsail to the mast, we made sail for her, hoisting the United States colors, and approached her within boarding distance, that is to say within a few hundred yards, without her moving tack or sheet. She had shown the United States colors as we approached, and proved to be a whaler with a huge whale made fast alongside and partially hoisted out of the water by her yard tackles. The surprise was perfect and complete. . . .

The captured ship proved to be the *Ocmulgee* of Edgartown, Massachusetts, whose master was a genuine specimen of the Yankee whaling skipper; long and lean, and as elastic apparently as the whalebone he dealt in. Nothing could ex-

ceed the blank stare of astonishment that sat on his face as the
change of flags took place on board the *Alabama*. He had
been engaged up to the last moment with his men, securing
the rich spoil alongside. The whale was a fine "sperm," and
was a "big strike," and had already been denuded of much of
its blubber when we got alongside. He naturally concluded,
he said, when he saw the United States colors at our peak that
we were one of the new gunboats sent out by Mr. [Gideon]
Welles to protect the whale fishery. It was indeed remarkable
that no protection should have been given to these men by
their Government. Unlike the ships of commerce, the whalers
are obliged to congregate within small well-known spaces of
ocean and remain there for weeks at a time whilst the whaling
season lasts. It was the most obvious thing in the world that
these vessels, thus clustered together, should attract the attention of the Confederate cruisers and be struck at. There are
not more than half a dozen principal whaling stations on the
entire globe, and a ship of size and force at each would have
been sufficient protection. But the whalers, like the commerce
of the United States generally, were abandoned to their fate.
Mr. Welles did not seem capable of learning by experience
even; for the *Shenandoah* repeated the successes of the *Alabama* in the North Pacific toward the close of the war.
There were Federal steam gunboats and an old sailing hulk
cruising about in the China seas, but no one seemed to think
of the whalers until Waddel [of the *Shenandoah*] carried
dismay and consternation among them.

It took us some time to remove the crew of the *Ocmulgee*,
consisting of thirty-seven persons, to the *Alabama*. We also
got on board from her some beef and pork and small stores,
and by the time we had done this it was nine o'clock at night;
too late to think of burning her, as a bonfire by night would
flush the remainder of the game which I knew to be in the
vicinity; and I had become too old a hunter to commit such an
indiscretion. With a little management and caution, I might
hope to uncover the birds no faster than I could bag them.
And so, hoisting a light at the peak of the prize, I permitted
her to remain anchored to the whale, and we lay by her until
the next morning, when we burned her; the smoke of the
conflagration being no doubt mistaken by vessels at a distance
for that of some passing steamer.

To those curious in such matters, I may state that a large sperm whale will yield twenty-five barrels of oil from the head alone. The oil is found in its liquid state and is baled out with buckets from a hole cut in the top of the head. What can be the uses in the animal economy to which this immense quantity of oil in the head of the fish is applied? They are probably twofold. First, it may have some connection with the sustenance of the animal in seasons of scarcity of food, and secondly, and more obviously, it appears to be a provision of nature, designed on the same principle on which birds are supplied with air cells in their bones. The whale, though very intelligent, and with an affection for its "calf" almost human, has but a small brain, the great cavity of its skull being filled as described. As the specific gravity of oil is considerably less than that of water, we can be at no loss to conjecture why the monster has so bountiful a supply, nor why it is that it carries the supply in its head. As is well known, the whale is a warm-blooded mammal, as much so as the cow that roams our pastures, and cannot live by breathing the water alone. Instead of the gill arrangement of fishes, which enables them to extract from the water sufficient air to vitalize the blood, it has the lungs of the mammal and needs to breathe the atmosphere. The oil in the head, acting on the principle of the cork, enables it to ascend very rapidly from great depths in the ocean when it requires to breathe or "blow." See how beautiful this oil arrangement is, too, in another aspect. It enables the monster, when it requires rest, to lay its head on the softest kind of a pillow, an ocean wave, and sleep as unconcernedly as the child does upon the bosom of its mother.

On the day after the capture of the *Ocmulgee*, we chased and overhauled a French ship bound to Marseilles. After speaking this ship and telling her that we were a United States cruiser, we bore away north, half west, and in a couple of hours made the island of Flores, the westernmost of the Azores, and a favorite island to be sighted by the whalers for the correction of their chronometers. Approaching it just at nightfall, we shortened sail and lay off and on during the night.

This island is an exceedingly picturesque object. It rises like a huge mountain from the depths of the sea with the bluest and deepest of water all around it. It is rock-bound, and there is scarcely any part of it where a ship might not haul alongside

of the rocks and make fast to the shore. It rises to the height
of a thousand feet and more and is covered with a luxuriant
vegetation, the substratum of rock being overlaid with a generous soil. The climate is genial for three-fourths of the year,
but almost a perpetual gale howls over it in winter. At a distance, the island appeared like an unbroken mountain, but as
we approached it, many beautiful valleys, and gaps in the
mountain presented themselves with the neat white farmhouses of the lonely dwellers peeping out from beneath the
dense foliage. It was indeed a beautiful scene to look upon,
and such was the air of perfect repose and peace that per-
vaded it, that a ship of war seemed out of place approaching its quiet shores.

The next day, Sunday, dawned beautiful and bright, and the
Alabama having approached this semi-tropical island sufficiently near to inhale the fragrance of its shrubs and flowers,
mustered her crew for the first time. When we speak of "muster" on board a ship of war, we do not mean simply the calling
of the roll but a ceremony of dress and inspection. With
clean, white decks, with the brass and ironwork glittering like
so many mirrors in the sun, and with the sails neatly trimmed,
and the Confederate States flag at our peak, we spread our
awnings and read the Articles of War to the crew. A great
change had taken place in the appearance of the men since I
made that stump speech to them. Their parti-colored garments
had been cast aside, and they were all neatly arrayed in duck
frocks and trousers, well-polished shoes, and straw hats. There
was a visible improvement in their health, too. They had been
long enough out of Liverpool to recover from the effects of
their debauches and regain their accustomed stamina. This
was the first reading of the Articles of War to them, and it was
curious to observe the attention with which they listened to
the reading, occasionally eying each other as they were struck
by particular portions of them. These Articles, which were
copied from similar Articles for the "better government of
the Navy of the United States," were quite severe in their
denunciations of crime. The penalty of death frequently occurred in them, and they placed the power of executing this
penalty in the hands of the captain and a court-martial.

Jack had already had a little foretaste of discipline in the
two weeks he had been on board; the first lieutenant having
brought several of them to the mast, whence they had been

sent into confinement by me for longer or shorter intervals according to the grade of their offences; and he now began more distinctly to perceive that he had gotten on board a ship of war instead of the privateer he had supposed the *Alabama* to be, and that he would have to toe a pretty straight mark. It is with a disorderly crew, as with other things, the first blows are the most effective. I had around me a large staff of excellent officers who always wore their side arms and pistols when on duty, and from this time onward we never had any trouble about keeping the most desperate and turbulent characters in subjection. My code was like that of the Medes and Persians—it was never relaxed. The moment a man offended, he was seized and confined in irons, and if the offence was a grave one, a court-martial was sitting on his case in less than twenty-four hours. The willing and obedient were treated with humanity and kindness; the turbulent were jerked down with a strong hand and made submissive to discipline. I was as rigid with the officers as with the crew, though, of course, in a different way, and both officers and men soon learned what was required of them, everything went on on board the *Alabama* after the first few weeks as smoothly and with as little jarring as if she had been a well-constructed and well-oiled machine.

Chapter Four—*1862*

Capture of the Starlight, Ocean Rover, Alert, Weathergauge . . . A race by night . . . Capture of the Altamaha, Virginia, and Elisha Dunbar . . . A rough sea, toiling boats, and a picturesque burning of a ship in a gale

While the muster described in the last chapter was going on we were running in for the little . . . seaside village of Lagens on the south side of the island of Flores, and having approached the beach quite near, we hove the ship to, and hauling alongside . . . the whaleboats of the captured ship, which we had brought . . . for this purpose, we paroled our prisoners and . . . shoved them off for the shore. I had two motives in thus landing my prisoners in their own boats. . . . It saved me the trouble of landing them myself; and, as the boats were valuable, and I permitted the prisoners to put in them as many provisions as they desired and as much other plunder as they could pick up about the decks of their ships—excepting always such articles as we needed on board the *Alabama*—the sale of their boats and cargoes to the islanders gave them the means of subsistence until they could communicate with their consul in the neighboring island of Fayal.

We had scarcely gotten through with the operation of

landing our prisoners before the cry of "Sail ho!" came to us from the mast-head; and we made sail in chase of a schooner which was approaching the island, hoisting the English colors to throw the stranger off his guard. As the two vessels were sailing toward each other, they approached very rapidly, and in the course of an hour we were within a mile of each other. Still the schooner did not show any colors. The reason was quite plain; she was American in every feature and could show us no other colors than such as would subject her to capture in case we should prove to be her enemy—of which she seemed to be suspicious. Indeed, the gallant little craft with every stitch of canvas set, sails well hoisted, and sheets a little eased, was now edging off a little from us and endeavoring to gain the shelter of the well-known marine league, the land being distant only about five miles. Perceiving her object and seeing that I had only a couple of miles to spare, I kept my own ship off, the better to throw myself across the stranger's path, changed my colors, and fired a blank cartridge to heave her to. But she neither hove to, nor showed colors, being evidently intent upon giving me a race. Although I already had the little craft under my guns, I humored her for a few minutes just to show her that I could beat her in a fair trial of speed, and when I had proved this by gaining rapidly upon her, I sent a round shot from one of the bow guns between her masts, a few feet only over the heads of her people. If the reader has heard a 32-pounder whistle in such close proximity, he knows very well what it says, to wit, that there must be no more trifling. And so the captain of the schooner understood it, for in a moment afterward we could see the graceful little craft luffing up in the wind, brailing up her foresail, and hauling her jib sheet to windward. The welcome stars and stripes fluttered soon afterward from her peak. The master being brought on board with his papers, the prize proved to be the schooner *Starlight* of Boston, from Fayal bound to Boston by the way of Flores, for which island she had some passengers, several ladies among the number.

The crew consisted of seven persons—all good Yankee sailors. Having heard by this time full accounts of the shameful treatment of my paymaster of the *Sumter** . . . I resolved

---

*He had been seized at Tangier at the direction of the U. S. Consul there and had then been imprisoned at Fort Warren in Boston Harbor. Ed.

to practise a little retaliation upon the enemy and ordered the crew of the *Starlight* put in irons. I pursued this practice, painful as it was, for the next seven or eight captures, putting the masters and mates of the ships, as well as the crews, in irons. The masters would frequently remonstrate with me, claiming that it was an indignity put upon them; and so it was, but I replied to them that their countrymen had put a similar indignity upon an officer and a gentleman who had worn the uniform of the navies of both our countries. By the time that the capture of the *Starlight* had been completed, the sun was near his setting, and it was too late to land the passengers. I therefore sent a prize crew on board the captured ship, directing the prize-master to lie by me during the night, and giving him especial charge to inform the passengers that they should be safely landed in the morning, and, in the meantime, to quiet the fears of the ladies, who had been much alarmed by the chase and the firing, we hoisted a light at the peak of the *Alabama* and lay to all night in nearly a calm sea. There were some dark clouds hanging over the island, but they had apparently gone there to roost, as no wind came from them. Among the papers captured on board the *Starlight* were a couple of dispatches from the Federal Consul at Fayal to the Sewards—father and son—in which there was the usual amount of stale nonsense about "rebel privateers" and "pirates."

The weather proved fine the next morning, and standing in within a stone's throw of the little town of Santa Cruz, we landed both passengers and prisoners, putting the latter as usual under *parole*. In the meantime, the Governor of the island and a number of the dignitaries came off to visit us. They were a robust, farmer-looking people, giving evidence, in their persons, of the healthfulness of the island, and were very polite, franking to us the ports of the island, and informing us that supplies were cheap and abundant. Their visit was evidently one of curiosity, and we treated his Excellency with all due ceremony, notwithstanding the smallness of his dominions. We talked to him, however, of bullocks, and sheep, fish and turtles, yams and oranges, rather than of the War between the States and the laws of nations. Bartelli made the eyes of the party dance with flowing goblets of champagne, and when I thought they had remained long enough, I bowed them out of the cabin with a cigar all round and sent them on shore with rather favorable impressions, I do not doubt, of the "pirate."

Hauling off, now, from the island and running seaward for a space, we chased and overhauled a Portuguese whaling brig. Seeing by her boats and other indications that she was a whaler, I thought at first that I had a prize and was quite disappointed when she showed me the Portuguese colors. Not being willing to trust to the verity of the flag, I sent a boat on board of her and invited the master to visit me with his papers, which he did. The master was himself a Portuguese, and I found his papers to be genuine. Thanking him for his visit, I dismissed him in a very few minutes. I had no right to command him to come on board of me—he being a neutral, it was my business to go on board of him if I desired to examine his papers, but he waived ceremony, and it was for this that I had thanked him. I may as well remark here, in passing, that this was the only foreign whaling ship I ever overhauled; the business of whaling having become almost exclusively an American monopoly—the monopoly not being derived from any sovereign grant but resulting from the superior skill, energy, industry, courage, and perseverance of the Yankee whaler, who is perhaps the best specimen of a sailor the world over.

Later in the same afternoon, we chased a large ship, looming up almost like a frigate in the northwest, with which we came up about sunset. We had showed her the American colors, and she approached us without the least suspicion that she was running into the arms of an enemy; the master crediting good old Mr. Welles, as the master of the *Ocmulgee* had done, with sending a flashy-looking Yankee gunboat to look out for his whalebone and oil. This large ship proved to be, upon the master being brought on board with his papers, the *Ocean Rover* of New Bedford, Massachusetts. She had been out three years and four months, cruising in various parts of the world, had sent home one or two cargoes of oil, and was now returning herself with another cargo of eleven hundred barrels. The master, though anxious to see his wife, and dandle on his knee the babies that were no longer babies, with true Yankee thrift thought he would just take the Azores in his way home and make another "strike" or two to fill up his empty casks. The consequence was . . . a little disappointment. I really felt for the honest fellow, but when I came to reflect for a moment upon the diabolical acts of his countrymen of New England, who were out-heroding Herod in carrying on against us a vindictive war, filled with hate and vengeance, the milk of human kindness which had begun to well up in my heart disappeared, and I had no longer any spare sympathies to dispose of.

It being near night when the capture was made, I directed the prize to be hove to in charge of a prize crew until morning. In the meantime, however, the master, who had heard from some of my men that I had permitted the master of the *Ocmulgee*, and his crew, to land in their own boats, came to me and requested permission to land in the same manner. We were four or five miles from the land, and I suggested to him that it was some distance to pull.

"Oh! that is nothing," said he, "we whalers sometimes chase a whale on the broad sea, until our ships are hull-down and think nothing of it. It will relieve you of us the sooner and be of some service to us besides."

Seeing that the sea was smooth, and that there was really no risk to be run, for a Yankee whale boat might be made with a little management to ride out an ordinary gale of wind, I consented, and the delighted master returned to his ship to make the necessary preparations. I gave him the usual permission to take what provisions he needed, the whaling gear belonging to his boats, and the personal effects of himself and men. He worked like a beaver, for not more than a couple of hours had elapsed before he was again alongside of the *Alabama* with all his six boats, with six men in each, ready to start for the shore. I could not but be amused when I looked over the side into these boats at the amount of plunder that the rapacious fellow had packed in them. They were literally loaded down with all sorts of traps, from the seamen's chests and bedding to the tabby cat and parrot. Nor had the "main chance" been overlooked, for all the "cabin stores" had been secured, and sundry barrels of beef and pork, besides.

I said to him, "Captain, your boats appear to me to be rather deeply laden; are you not afraid to trust them?"

"Oh! no," he replied; "they are as buoyant as ducks, and we shall not ship a drop of water."

After a detention of a few minutes, during which my clerk was putting the crew under *parole*, I gave the master leave to depart.

The boats, shoving off from the side one by one and falling into line, struck out for the shore. That night landing of this whaler's crew was a beautiful spectacle. I stood on the horse-block watching it, my mind busy with many thoughts. The moon was shining brightly, though there were some passing clouds sailing lazily in the upper air, that fleckered the sea. Flores, which was sending off to us even at this distance her perfumes of shrub and flower, lay sleeping in the moonlight with a few fleecy, white clouds wound around the mountain-top, like a turban. The rocky islets that rise like so many shafts out of the sea, devoid of all vegetation and at different distances from the shore, looked weird and unearthly, like sheeted ghosts. The boats moving swiftly and mysteriously toward the shore might have been mistaken, when they had gotten a little distance from us, for Venetian gondolas with their peaked bows and sterns, especially when we heard coming over the sea, a song sung by a powerful and musical voice and chorussed by all the boats. Those merry fellows were thus making light of misfortune and proving that the sailor after all is the true philosopher. The echo of that night song lingered long in my memory, but I little dreamed as I stood on the deck of the *Alabama* and witnessed the scene I have described, that four years afterward it would be quoted against me as a violation of the laws of war! And yet so it was. It was alleged by the malice of my defamers, who never have and never can forgive me for the destruction of their property, that miles away at sea, in rough and inclement weather, I *compelled* my prisoners to depart for the shore in leaky and unsound boats at the hazard of their lives, designing and desiring to drown them! And this was all the thanks I received for setting some of these fellows up as nabobs among the islanders. Why, the master of the *Ocean Rover* with his six boats and their cargoes was richer than the Governor when he landed in Flores, where the simple islanders are content with a few head of cattle, a cast net, and a canoe.

The *Alabama* had now two prizes in company with which she lay off and on the island during the night, and she was destined to secure another before morning. I had turned in and was sleeping soundly, when about midnight an officer came below to inform me that there was another large ship close on board. of us. I was dressed and on deck in a few minutes. The stranger was plainly visible, being not more

than a mile distant. She was heading for the island. I wore
ship as quietly as possible and followed her, but she had in
the meantime drawn some distance ahead; an exciting chase
now ensued. We were both close-hauled on the starboard tack,
and the stranger, seeing that he was pursued, put every rag
of sail on his ship that he could spread. I could but admire
her, with her square yards and white canvas, every sheet
home, and every leach taut. For the first half hour it was
hard to tell which ship had the heels of the other, but at the
end of that time we began to head-reach the chase very perceptibly, though the latter rather "eat us out of the wind,"
or, to speak more conformably with the vocabulary of the
land, went to windward of us. This did not matter much,
however, as when we should be abreast of her, we would be
near enough to reach her with a shot. After a chase of about
four hours, day broke, when we hoisted the English ensign.
This was a polite invitation to the chase to show her colors,
but she declined to do so. We now felt sure that she was an
enemy and a prize, and as we were still gaining on her, it was
only a matter of an hour or two when she would fall into our
hands. Our polite invitation to the chase to show her colors,
not succeeding, we became a little more emphatic and fired a
blank cartridge. Still she was obstinate. She was steering for
Flores and probably, like the *Starlight,* had her eye on the
marine league. Having approached her in another half hour
within good round-shot range, I resolved to treat her as I had
treated the *Starlight* and threw a 32-pounder near enough to
her stern to give the captain a shower bath. Shower baths
are very efficacious in many cases, and we found it so in this,
for in a moment more we could see the stars and stripes
ascending to the stranger's peak, and that he had started his
tacks and sheets and was in the act of hauling up his courses.
This done, the main-yard was swung aback, and the prize had
surrendered herself a prisoner.

Bartelli now came to tell me that my bath was ready, and
descending to the cabin, I bathed and dressed for breakfast,
whilst the boarding officer was boarding the prize. She proved
to be the *Alert,* of, and from New London, and bound by the
way of the Azores and Cape de Verde Islands to the Indian
Ocean. She was only sixteen days from port, with files of late
newspapers; and besides her own ample outfit for a large crew
and a long voyage, she had on board supplies for the group

known as the Navigators' Islands in the South Indian Ocean, where among icebergs and storms the Yankees had a whaling and sealing station. This capture proved to be a very opportune one, as we were in want of just such a lot of clothing for the men, as we found on board the prize; and the choice beef, and pork, nicely put up ship bread, boxes of soap, and tobacco, and numerous other articles of seamen's supplies did not come amiss. We had been particularly short of a supply of tobacco, this being a costly article in England, and I could see Jack's eye brighten as he rolled aft and piled up on the quarter-deck sundry heavy oaken boxes of good Virginia twist. That night the pipes seemed to have wonderfully increased in number on board the *Alabama*, and the song and the jest derived new inspiration from the fragrance of the weed. We paroled the officers and crew of the *Alert* and sent them ashore in their own boats as we had done the others.

I had now three prizes on my hands, viz.: the *Starlight*, the *Ocean Rover*, and the *Alert*, with a prize crew on board of each, and as I could make no better use of them than to destroy them, thanks to the unfriendly conduct of neutrals so often referred to, it became necessary to think of burning them. They were lying at distances ranging from half a mile to three miles from the *Alabama* and were fired within a short time of each other, so that we had three funeral pyres burning around us at the same moment. The other whalers at a distance must have thought that there were a good many steamers passing Flores that day. It was still early in the afternoon, and there was more work before us ere night set in. I had scarcely gotten my prize crews on board and my boats run up, before another sail was discovered standing in for the island. We immediately gave chase, or rather . . . proceeded to meet the stranger, who was standing in our direction. The ships approached each other very rapidly, and we soon discovered the new sail to be a large schooner of unmistakable Yankee build and rig. We hoisted the United States colors, and she responded soon afterward with the stars and stripes. She came on quite unsuspiciously, as the two last prizes had done, until she arrived near enough to see that the three mysterious cones of smoke at which she had probably been wondering for some time past, proceeded from three ships on fire. Coupling this unusual spectacle with the approach toward her of a rakish-looking barkentine, she at once smelt rather a large rat and wheeled suddenly in flight. But it was too late. We were already within three miles of her, and a pursuit of half an hour brought her within effective range of our bow-chaser. We now changed colors and fired a blank cartridge. This was sufficient. She saved us the expenditure of a shot and hove to without further ado. Upon being boarded, she proved to be the *Weathergauge*, a whaler of Provincetown, Massachusetts, six weeks from the land of the Puritan, with other files of newspapers, though not so late as those captured on board the *Alert*.

In running over these files, it was wonderful to observe the glibness with which these Massachusetts brethren of ours now talked of treason and of rebels and traitors at no greater distance, in point of time, than forty-five years from the Hartford Convention; to say nothing of certain little idiosyncrasies of theirs that were developed during the annexation of Texas. There were some Sunday papers among the rest, and all the pious parsons and deacons in the land were overflowing with patriotism and hurling death and damnation from their pulpits against those who had dared to strike at the "Lord's anointed," the sainted Abraham Lincoln. But as the papers contained little or no war news, we had no time to bestow upon the crotchets of the Yankee brain, and they were promptly consigned to the waste-paper basket.

Another sail being discovered, whilst we were receiving the surrender of the *Weathergauge*, we hastily threw a prize crew on board this latter vessel, directing the prize-master to "hold on to the island of Corvo," during the ensuing night, which was now falling, until we should return, and started off in pursuit of the newly discovered sail.

Chasing a sail is very much like pursuing a coy maiden, the very coyness sharpening the pursuit. The chase, in the present instance, seemed determined to run away from us; and as she was fast, and we were as determined to overhaul her as she was to run away, she led us a beautiful night dance over the merry waters. The moon rose bright soon after the chase commenced, and striking upon the canvas of the fleeing vessel lighted it up as though it had been a snow bank. The American vessels are distinguished above all others for the whiteness of their canvas; being clothed for the most part in the fiber of our cotton fields. The cut of the sails and the taper of the spars of the chase looked American, and then the ship was cracking on every stitch of canvas that would draw in the effort to escape—she must surely be American, we thought. And so we "looked on her, to lust after her," and gave our little ship the benefit of all our skill in seamanship. The speed of the two ships was so nearly matched that for the first hour or two it was impossible to say whether we had gained on her an inch. We were both running dead before the wind, and this was not the *Alabama's* most favorable sailing point. With her tall lower masts and large fore-and-aft sails, she was better on a wind or with the wind abeam. The chase was leading us away from our cruising ground, and I should have abandoned it if I had not had my pride of ship a little interested. It would never do for the *Alabama* to be beaten in the beginning of her cruise, and that too by a merchantman; and so we threw out all our "light kites" to the wind and gave her the studding sails alow and aloft. To make a long story short, we chased this ship nearly all night and only came up with her a little before dawn; and when we did come up with her, she proved to be a Dane! She was the bark *Overman* from Bankok, Siam, bound to Hamburg. There had been no occasion whatever for this neutral ship to flee, and the long chase which she had given me was evidently the result of a little spleen; and so to revenge myself in a good-natured way, I insisted upon all my belligerent rights. Though satisfied from her reply to my hail that she was what she proclaimed herself to be, I compelled her to heave to, which involved the necessity of taking in all that beautiful white canvas with which she had decoyed me so many miles away from my cruising ground, and sent a boat on board of her to examine her papers. She thus lost more time than if she had shortened sail earlier in the chase to permit me to come up with her.

It was late next day before I rejoined the *Weathergauge* off Corvo, and I felt, as I was retracing my steps. pretty much as Music or Rover may be supposed to feel as he is limping back to his kennel after a run in pursuit of a fox that has escaped him. Bartelli failed to call me at the usual hour that morning, and I need not say that I made a late breakfast. We now landed the crew of the *Weathergauge* in their own boats with the usual store of provisions and traps, and burned her. Two days elapsed now without a capture, during which we overhauled but one ship, a Portuguese bark homeward bound.

Having beaten the "cover" of which Flores was the center pretty effectually, I now stretched away to the northwest and ran the island out of sight, intending to skirt it at the distance of forty or fifty miles. On the third day the welcome cry of "Sail ho!" again rang from the masthead, and making sail in the direction indicated by the lookout, we soon discovered that the chase was a whaler. Resorting to the usual ruse of the enemy's flag, the stranger did not attempt to escape, and in an hour or two more we were alongside of the American whaling brig *Altamaha* from New Bedford, five months out. The *Altamaha* had had but little success and was comparatively empty. She did not make so beautiful a bonfire, therefore, as the other whalers had done.

In the afternoon, we overhauled a Spanish ship. Our position today was latitude 40° 34′ N. and longitude 35° 24′ 15″ W. The barometer stood at 30.3 inches, and the thermometer at 75°; from which the reader will see that the weather was fine and pleasant. It was now the middle of September, however, and a change might be looked for at any moment. On the night after capturing the *Altamaha*, we had another night chase with more success, however, than the last. It was my habit, when there was no game up, to turn in early, usually at nine o'clock, to enable my *physique* to withstand the frequent drafts upon its energies. I was already in a sound sleep, when about half-past eleven, an old quartermaster came below, and giving my cot a gentle shake, said: "There has a large ship just passed to windward of us on the opposite tack, sir."

I sprang out of bed at once, and throwing on a few clothes, was on deck almost as soon as the quartermaster. I immediately wore ship and gave chase. My ship was under topsails, and it took us some little time to make sail. By this time the chase was from two and a half to three miles distant but quite visible to the naked eye in the bright moonlight. We were both close-hauled on the starboard tack, the chase about three points on the weather bow. The stranger, who was probably keeping a better lookout than is usual with merchant ships in consequence of the war, had discovered our movement and knew he was pursued, as we could see him setting his royals and flying jib which had been furled. The *Alabama* was now at her best point of sailing. The sailors used to say, when we drew aft the sheets of those immense trysails of hers, and got the fore-tack close aboard, that she was putting on her seven-league boots. She did, indeed, then seem

> To walk the waters like a thing of life,

and there were few sailing ships that could run away from her.

We gained from the start upon the chase, and in a couple of hours were on his weather-quarter, having both head-reached and gone to windward of him. He was now no more than about a mile distant, and I fired the accustomed blank cartridge to heave him to. The sound of the gun broke upon the stillness of the night, with startling effect, but the chase did not stir tack or sheet in obedience to it. She was evidently resolved to try conclusions with me a little farther. Finding that I had the advantage of him on a wind, he kept off a little and eased his sheets, and we could see with our night glasses that he was rigging out his studding-sail booms preparatory to setting the sails upon them. We kept off in turn, bringing the wind a little forward of the beam, and such good use did the *Alabama* make of her seven-league boots that before the stranger could get even his foretopmast studding-sail set, we had him within good point-blank range of a 32-pounder. The moon was shining very poetically, and the chase was very pretty, but it was rather after hours, and so I resolved to shift the scenes, cut short the drama an act or two, and bring it to a close. I now fired a second gun, though still unshotted, and the smoke had hardly blown away before we could see the stranger hauling up his courses and bringing his ship to the wind, as much as to say, "I see you have the heels of me, and there is no use in trying any longer." I gave the boarding-officer orders, in case the ship should prove to be a prize, of which I had but little doubt, to show me a light as soon as he should get on board of her. The oars of his boat had scarely ceased to resound before I saw the welcome light ascending to the stranger's peak and knew that another of the enemy's ships had fallen into my power. It was now nearly daylight, and I went below and finished the nap which had been so unceremoniously broken in upon. I may as well observe here that I scarcely ever disturbed the regular repose of the officers and crew during these night operations. Everything was done by the watch on deck, and all hands were never called except on emergencies.

When I came on deck the next morning, there was a fine

large ship lying under my lee, awaiting my orders. She proved to be the *Benjamin Tucker* of New Bedford, eight months out, with three hundred and forty barrels of oil. We received from her an additional supply of tobacco and other small stores. As early as ten o'clock, the crew of the *Tucker*, numbering thirty persons, were on board the *Alabama*, and the ship was on fire. The remainder of this day and the next passed without incident, except the incidents of wind and weather, which have so often been recorded. We improved the leisure by exercising the men at the guns, and caulking the decks, which were again beginning to let water enough through them to inconvenience the men in their hammocks below. Just as the sun was setting on the evening of the second day, we caught a glimpse from the masthead of the island of Flores, distant about forty miles.

The next morning dawned bright and clear with a smooth sea and summer clouds sailing lazily overhead, giving us just breeze enough to save us from the ennui of a calm. As soon as the morning mists lifted themselves from the surface of the waters, a schooner appeared in sight at no great distance. We had approached each other unwittingly during the night. We immediately gave chase, hoisting the United States colors, for the schooner was evidently Yankee. She did not attempt to escape, and when, as early as half-past seven A. M., we came near enough to fire a gun and change colors, she hove to and surrendered. She was the whaling schooner *Courser*, of Provincetown, Massachusetts. Her master was a gallant young fellow, and a fine specimen of a seaman, and if I could have separated him in any way from the "Universal Yankee Nation," I should have been pleased to spare his pretty little craft from the flames; but the thing was impossible. There were too many white-cravatted, long-haired fellows bawling from the New England pulpits, and too many house-burners and pilferers inundating our Southern land to permit me to be generous, and so I steeled my heart, as I had done on a former occasion, and executed the laws of war.

Having now the crews of the three last ships captured on board, amounting to about seventy, who were not only beginning, on account of their number and the limited accommodations of the *Alabama*, to be uncomfortable themselves, but were inconveniencing my own people and hindering more or less the routine of the ship, I resolved to run back to

Flores and land them. I had eight whaleboats in tow, which I had brought away from the burning ships for the purpose of landing these prisoners, and no doubt the islanders, as they saw my well-known ship returning with such a string of boats, congratulated themselves upon the prospect of other good bargains with the Yankees. The traffic must now have been considerable in this little island; such was the avalanche of boats, harpoons, cordage, whales' teeth, whalebones, beef, pork, tobacco, soap, and jackknives that I had thrown on shore. When we had reached sufficiently near, I shoved all the boats off at once, laden with my seventy prisoners, and there was quite a regatta under the lee of Flores that afternoon, the boats of each ship striving to beat the others to the shore. The fellows seemed to be so well pleased, that I believe with a little coaxing they would have been willing to give three cheers for the *Alabama*.

We had some sport ourselves after the prisoners had departed; for we converted the *Courser* into a target before setting fire to her, and gave the crew a little practice at her with the battery. They did pretty well for green hands, but nothing to boast of. They were now becoming somewhat familiar with the gun exercise and in the evolutions that are usually taught sailors at general quarters. Not only my excellent first lieutenant, but all the officers of the divisions took great pains with them, and their progress was quite satisfactory.

We again stood away to the northward and westward under easy sail during the night, and the next day, the weather being still fine, and the breeze moderate from the southwest, in latitude about 40° and longitude 33°, we chased a large ship which tried her heels with us—to no purpose, however—as we overhauled her in about three hours and a half. It was another American whaling ship, the *Virginia*, only twenty days out from New Bedford. She brought us another batch of late newspapers, and being fitted out like the *Alert* for a long cruise, we got on board some more supplies from her. The master of this ship expressed great surprise at the speed of the *Alabama* under sail. His own ship, he said, was fast, but he had stood no chance with the *Alabama*. It was like a rabbit attempting to run away from a greyhound. We burned the *Virginia*, when we had gotten our supplies on board and despoiled her of such cordage and spare sails as we needed and stood away to the northwest again. The torch having

been applied to her rather late in the afternoon, the burning
wreck was still visible some time after nightfall.

The next morning the weather had changed considerably.
It was cloudy and rather angry-looking, and the wind was
fresh and increasing. We overhauled a French brig, during
the day, and after detaining her no longer than was necessary
to examine her papers, permitted her to depart. We had
barely turned away from the Frenchman when a bark was
announced from the masthead. We immediately gave chase.
We had to wear ship for this purpose, and the bark, which
seemed to have descried us quite as soon as we had descried
her, observing the evolution, made all sail at once in flight.
Here was another chase, and under different circumstances
from any of those that had preceded it. It was blowing half a
gale of wind, and it remained to be proved whether the
Alabama was as much to be dreaded in rough weather as in
smooth. Many smooth-water sailers lose their quality of speed
entirely when the seas begin to buffet them. I had the wind of
the chase and was thus enabled to run down upon her with a
flowing sheet. I held on to my topgallant sails, though the
masts buckled and bent as though the sticks would go over the
side. The chase did the same. It was soon quite evident that
my gallant little ship was entirely at home in the roughest
weather. She seemed, like a trained racer, to enjoy the sport,
and though she would tremble now and then as she leaped
from sea to sea, it was the tremor of excitement, not of weakness. We gained so rapidly upon the chase that in three hours
from the time the race commenced, we had her within the
range of our guns. By way of a change, I had chased this ship
under English colors, but she obstinately refused to show any
colors herself until she was compelled by the loud-mouthed
command of a gun. She then ran up that "flaunting lie," the
"old flag," and clewed up her topgallant sails and hauled up
her courses and submitted to her fate with such resignation
as she might.

I now not only took in my topgallant sails and hauled up
my courses, but furled the latter and took a single reef in my
topsails, so fresh was the wind blowing. Indeed it was so
rough that I hesitated a moment about launching my boats;
but there was evidently a gale brewing, and if I did not take
possession of my prize, she would in all probability escape
during the darkness and tempest of the ensuing night. I had

a set of gallant, and skilful young officers around me who would dare anything I told them to dare, and some capital seamen, and with the assistance I could give them by manœuvring the ship, I thought the thing could be managed; and so I ordered two of the best boats to be launched and manned. We were lying to, to windward of the prize, and the boats had nothing to do, of course, but to pull before the wind and sea to reach her. I directed the boarding-officers to bring off nothing whatever, from the prize, in the way of property, except her chronometer and her flag, and told them when they should have gotten the prisoners on board and were ready to return, that I would run down to leeward of the prize to receive them. They would thus, still, only have to pull before the wind and the sea to regain their ship. The prize was to be fired just before leaving her. This was all accomplished successfully; but the reader may well conceive my anxiety as I watched those frail, tempest-tossed boats as they were returning to me with their human freight; now thrown high on the top of some angry wave that dashed its foam and spray over them, as though it would swamp them for daring thus to beard it, and now settling entirely out of sight in the trough of the sea. When they pulled under the lee of the *Alabama*, and we threw them a rope, I was greatly relieved. This was the only ship I ever burned before examining her papers. But as she was a whaler, and so could have no neutral cargo on board, the risk to be run was not very great. She proved to be the *Elisha Dunbar* of New Bedford, twenty-four days out.

This burning ship was a beautiful spectacle, the scene being wild and picturesque beyond description. The black clouds were mustering their forces in fearful array. Already the entire heavens had been overcast. The thunder began to roll and crash, and the lightning to leap from cloud to cloud in a thousand eccentric lines. The sea was in a tumult of rage; the winds howled, and floods of rain descended. Amid this turmoil of the elements, the *Dunbar*, all in flames and with disordered gear and unfurled canvas, lay rolling and tossing upon the sea. Now an ignited sail would fly away from a yard and scud off before the gale; and now the yard itself, released from the control of its braces, would swing about wildly as in the madness of despair and then drop into the sea. Finally the masts went by the board, and then the hull rocked to and fro for a while, until it was filled with water and the fire nearly quenched, when it settled to the bottom of the great deep, a victim to the passions of man and the fury of the elements.

Chapter Five—*1862*

The Yankee colony in the island of Flores . . . What the captains of the Virginia and Elisha Dunbar said of the Alabama, when they got back among their countrymen . . . The whaling season at the Azores at an end . . . The Alabama changes her cruising ground . . . What she saw and did

The reader has seen how rapidly we had been peopling the little island of Flores. I had thrown ashore there nearly as many Yankee sailors as there were original inhabitants. I should now have gone back with the crews of two more ships but for the bad weather. Jack, suddenly released from the labors and confinement of his ship, must have run riot in this verdant little paradise, where the law was too weak to restrain him. With his swagger, devil-may-care air, and propensity for fun and frolic when he has a drop in his eye, the simple inhabitants must have been a good deal puzzled to fix the genus of the bird that had so suddenly dropped down upon them. The history of my colony would, no doubt, be highly interesting; and I trust that some future traveller will disinter it from the archives of the island for the benefit of mankind. The police reports would be of especial interest. In due time the Federal Consul at Fayal chartered a vessel and removed the colony back to the New England States.

The gale which was described in the last chapter, did not prove to be very violent, though it blew sufficiently fresh to reduce the *Alabama* to close-reefed topsails with the bonnets off her trysails. It was but the forerunner of a series of gales, occurring about the period of the equinox. The bad weather had the effect to put an end to the whaling season a little in advance of the regular time. From the 19th to the 23d of September we were constantly under reefed sails, and the wind being from the northward, we drifted as far south as the 34th degree of latitude. We were now in a comparatively unfrequented part of the ocean, and had not seen a sail since the capture of the *Elisha Dunbar*. During the prevalence of this bad weather our prisoners necessarily suffered some inconvenience and were obliged to submit to some discomforts. I need not say that these were greatly magnified by the Northern press. The masters of the captured ships took this mode of revenging themselves upon me. The captains of the last two ships captured made long complaints against the *Alabama* when they got back to New England, and I will here give them the benefit of their own stories that the reader may see what they amount to. It is the master of the *Virginia* who speaks first—a Captain Tilton. He says:

I went on the quarter-deck with my son, when they ordered me into the lee waist with my crew, and all of us were put in irons with the exception of the two boys and the cook and steward. I asked if I was to be put in irons? The reply of Captain Semmes was that his purser had been put in irons and had his head shaved by us, and that he meant to retaliate. We were put in the lee waist with an old sail over us and a few planks to lie upon. The steamer was cruising to the west, and the next day they took the *Elisha Dunbar*, her crew receiving the same treatment as ourselves. The steamer's guns being kept run out, the side ports could not be shut, and when the sea was a little rough, or the vessel rolled, the water was continually coming in on both sides and washing across the deck where we were, so that our feet and clothing were wet all the time, either from the water below or the rain above. We were obliged to sleep in the place where we were and often waked up in the night nearly under water. Our fare consisted of beef and pork, rice, beans, tea, and coffee, and bread. Only one of my irons was allowed to be taken off at a time, and we had to wash in salt water. We kept on deck all the time, night and day, and a guard was placed over us.

The above statement is substantially correct with the exception that the prisoners were not drenched with sea water or with the rain all the time as is pretended. It is quite true that they were compelled to live and sleep on deck. We had nowhere else to put them. My berth-deck was filled with my own crew, and it was not possible to berth prisoners there without turning my own men out of their hammocks. To remedy this difficulty, we spread a tent made of spare sails, and which was quite tight, in the lee waist, and laid gratings upon the deck to keep the men and their bedding as dry as possible. Ordinarily they were very comfortable, but sometimes during the prevalence of gales they were, no doubt, a little disturbed in their slumbers by the water, as Captain Tilton says. But I discharged them all in good physical condition, and this is the best evidence I could give that they were well cared for. It was certainly a hardship that Captain Tilton should have nothing better to eat than my own crew, and should be obliged, like them, to wash in salt water, but he was waited upon by his own cook and steward, and the reader can see from his own bill of fare that he was in no danger of starving. He was, as he says, ordered off the quarter-deck. That is a place sacred to the officers of the ship, where even their own crew are not permitted to come except on duty, and much less a prisoner. He explains how he came to be put in irons. The good book says that we must have "an eye for an eye, and a tooth for a tooth." The enemy had put one of my officers in irons, and I had followed the rule of the good book. Now let us hear from Captain Gifford of the *Dunbar*. This witness says:

On the morning of the 18th of September, in latitude 39° 50', longitude 35° 20', with the wind from the southwest, and the bark heading southeast, saw a steamer on our port-quarter, standing to the northwest. Soon after, found she had altered her course and was steering for the bark. We soon made all sail to get out of her reach and were going ten knots at the time; but the steamer, gaining on us, under canvas alone, soon came up with us and fired a gun under our stern, with the St.

George's cross flying at the time. Our colors were set when she displayed the Confederate flag. Being near us, we hove to, and a boat, with armed officers and crew came alongside, and upon coming on board, stated to me that my vessel was a prize to the Confederate steamer *Alabama*, Captain Semmes. I was then ordered on board the steamer with my papers, and the crew to follow me with a bag of clothing each. On getting on board, the captain claimed me as a prize and said that my vessel would be burned. Not having any clothes with me, he allowed me to return for a small trunk of clothes; the officer on board asked me what I was coming back for and tried to prevent me from coming on board. I told him I came after a few clothes, which I took and returned to the steamer. It blowing very hard at the time and very squally, nothing but the chronometer, sextant, charts, &c., were taken, when the vessel was set fire to and burnt; there were sixty-five barrels of sperm oil on deck, taken on the passage, which were consumed. We were all put in irons and received the same treatment that Captain Tilton's officers and crew did, who had been taken the day before. While on board, we understood that the steamer would cruise off the Grand Banks for a few weeks, to destroy the large American ships to and from the Channel ports. They had knowledge of two ships being loaded with arms for the United States and were in hopes to capture them. They were particularly anxious to fall in with the clippership *Dreadnought* and destroy her, as she was celebrated for speed; and they were confident of their ability to capture or run away from any vessel in the United States. The steamer being in the track of outward and homeward-bound vessels and more or less being in sight every day, she will make great havoc among them.

Captain Gifford does not seem to have anything to complain of, in particular, except that the sailors had to put their clothes in bags, and that his trunk was small; but both he and his sailors got their clothing, which was more than some of our women and children in the South did when the gallant Sherman, and the gallant Wilson, and the gallant Stoneman, and a host of other gallant fellows were making their grand marches, and raids in the South merely for the love of "grand moral ideas." The terrible drenchings that Captain Tilton got did not seem to have made the same impression upon Captain Gifford.

Few of the masters whose ships I burned ever told the whole truth when they got back among their countrymen. Some of them forgot entirely to mention how they had implored me to save their ships from destruction, professing to be the best of *Democrats* and deprecating the war which their countrymen were making upon us! How they had come to sea, bringing their New England cousins with them to get rid of the draft, and how abhorrent to them the sainted Abraham was. "Why, Captain," they would say, "it is hard that I should have my ship burned; I have voted the *Democratic* ticket all my life; I was a *Breckinridge* man in the last Presidential contest. . . ."

"That may be all very true," I would reply; "but, unfortunately, the political rascals of whom you speak have been strong enough to get up this war, and you are in the same boat with the political rascals, whatever may be your individual opinions. Every whale you strike will put money into the Federal treasury and strengthen the hands of your people to carry on the war. I am afraid I must burn your ship."

"But, Captain, can't we arrange the matter in some way? I will give you a ransom bond, which my owners and myself will regard as a debt of honor."

I have some of these debts of honor in my possession, now, which I will sell cheap. And so they would continue to remonstrate with me until I cut short the conversation by ordering the torch applied to their ships. They would then revenge themselves in the manner I have mentioned. . . .

The whaling season at the Azores being at an end, I resolved to change my cruising ground and stretch over to the Banks of Newfoundland and the coast of the United States in quest (as some of my young officers, who had served in the China seas playfully remarked) of the great American junk fleet. In China, the expression "junk fleet" means, more particularly, the grain ships, that swarm all the seas and rivers in that populous empire in the autumn, carrying their rich cargoes of grain to market. It was now the beginning of October. There was no cotton crop available with which to freight the ships of our loving Northern brethren and conduct their exchanges. They were forced to rely upon the grain crop of the great Northwest; the political rascals having been cunning enough to wheedle these natural allies of ours into this New England war. They needed gold abroad with which to pay for arms and military supplies of various kinds, shiploads of which were, every day, passing into New York and Boston in violation of those English neutrality laws, which Mr. Seward and Mr. Adams had been so persistently contending should be enforced against ourselves. Western New York, Ohio, Indiana, Illinois, Michigan, Minnesota, and Iowa had gathered in the rich harvests from their teeming grain fields; and it was this grain, laden in Yankee ships, which it was my object now to strike at.

The change from one cruising ground to another, during which no vessels were sighted, afforded my crew a much-needed relaxation of a few days, for they had been much fagged and worn during the last month by a succession of captures. That which had been but a pleasurable excitement, in the beginning soon became a wearing and exhausting labor, and they were glad to be relieved for a time from the chasing and burning of ships, hard service in boats during all kinds of weather, and the wet jackets and sleepless nights which had sometimes been the consequences of these. I will avail myself of this comparative calm in the moral atmosphere on board the *Alabama* to introduce the reader, more particularly, to our interior life. Thus far, he has only seen the ship of war in her outward garb, engaged in her vocation. I propose to give him a sight of my military family and show him how my children played as well as worked; how I governed them and with what toys I amused them.

From the very beginning of our captures, an order had been issued that no sailor should lay his hand on any article of property to appropriate it to his own use, unless by permission of an officer; and especially that no spirituous liquors should be brought on board the *Alabama*. It was made the duty of every boarding-officer upon getting on board a prize to demand possession of the keys of the liquor lockers, and either to cause the liquor to be destroyed or thrown overboard. To the rigid enforcement of this rule, I attribute much of the good order which prevailed on board my ship. It was enforced against the officers as well the men, and no officer's mess was allowed to supply itself with liquor by purchase or otherwise, unless by my consent; and I never gave this consent to the midshipmen's mess. We burned, on one occasion, a ship whose entire cargo consisted of French brandies, champagne, and other wines, without allowing a bottle of it to be brought on board. But whilst I used these precautions, I caused a regular allowance of grog to be served out to the crew, twice in each day. I was quite willing that Jack should drink, but I undertook to be the judge of how much he should drink.

Such articles of clothing and supplies as were captured were turned over to the paymaster to be credited to the Government and duly issued and charged to the crew as if they had been purchased in the market. In spite of all these precautions, however, a sailor would now and then be brought on board from a prize, drunk, would manage to smuggle liquor to his comrades, and would be found arrayed in all sorts of strange garbs from whaler's boots and red flannel shirts and comforters, to longtailed coats and beaver hats. Notwithstanding the discipline of the ship, the gravity of the crew would sometimes give way to merriment, as one of these fellows thus ludicrously apparelled would have to be hoisted or lifted on board, being too comfortably drunk to attend to his own locomotion. Each offender knew that he would have to walk straight into the Brig upon being thus detected in the violation of these orders and that punishment would speedily follow the offence; and yet I found it one of the most difficult parts of my duty to convince some of these free-and-easy fellows, who had mistaken the *Alabama*, when they signed the articles off Terceira . . . for what Mr. Seward and Mr. Adams insisted she was, a "privateer," that everything was captured in the name of the Confederate States, and that nothing belonged to them personally. The California-bound ships frequently had on board boxes and bales of fine clothing, boots, shoes, and hats, but not a garment was allowed to be brought on board except such as the paymaster might need for issue. It seemed hard to consign all these tempting articles to the flames without permitting the sailors to help themselves, but if such license had been permitted, disorder and demoralization would have been the consequence.

I had no chaplain on board, but Sunday was always kept as a day of abstinence from labor when the exigencies of war and weather would permit, and it was my uniform practice on this day to have the ship thoroughly cleansed in every part for inspection—particularly the sleeping apartments and the engine room—and to require the officers and seamen to appear on the quarter-deck for muster; the former in their appropriate uniforms, and the latter in clean duck frocks and trousers or other clothing adapted to the latitude and climate. . . .

The boys of the ship, of whom I had quite a number on board, were placed under the special charge of the master-at-arms—a subordinate officer with police-powers in charge of the berth-deck—whose duty it was to inspect them in every morning watch with reference to personal cleanliness; turning down the collars and rolling up the trousers of the youngsters to see that they had duly performed their ablutions. These boys had been taken from the stews and haunts of vice about Liverpool and were as great a set of scamps as any disciplinarian could desire to lick into shape, but it is astonishing what a reformation soap and water and the master-at-arms effected in them in a short time. Many of them became very respectable young fellows, for which they were indebted almost entirely to the free use of soap and water.

As a hygienic precaution when we were cruising in warm latitudes, where the dews were heavy, the whole crew was required to appear every evening at sunset muster in blue flannel shirts and trousers. They could then sleep in the dews without fear of colds or rheumatisms. We were always supplied with the best of provisions, for, being at war with a provision-producing people, almost every ship we captured afforded us a greater or less supply; and all the water that was drank on board the *Alabama* was condensed by the engine from the vapor of sea water. The consequence of all this care was highly gratifying to me, as, in the three years I was afloat, I did not lose a man by disease. . . . When it is recollected that I cruised in all parts of the world, now fencing out the cold, and battling with the storms of the North Atlantic and South Indian Oceans, and now being fried and baked and stewed within the tropics and on the equator, and that, besides my own crews, some two thousand of the enemy's sailors passed through my hands . . . as prisoners, this is a remarkable statement to be able to make. My excellent surgeon, Dr. Galt, and, after him, Dr. Llewellyn, ably seconded me by their skill and experience.

On week days we mustered the crew at their quarters twice a day—at nine A. M., and at sunset, and when the weather was suitable, one division, or about one fourth of the crew, was exercised, either at the battery or with small arms. This not only gave them efficiency in the use of their weapons but kept them employed—the constant employment of my men being a fundamental article of my philosophy. I found the old adage that "Idleness is the parent of vice" as true upon the sea as upon the land. My crew were never so happy as when they had plenty to do and but little to think about. Indeed, as to the thinking, I allowed them to do very little of that. Whenever I found I had a sea lawyer among them, I got rid of him as soon as possible—giving him a chance to desert. I reserved the *quids* and *quos* and *pros* and *cons* exclusively for myself.

But though I took good care to see that my men had plenty of employment, it was not all work with them. They had their pastimes and pleasures as well as labors. After the duties of the day were over, they would generally assemble on the forecastle, and with violin, and tambourine—and I always kept them supplied with these and other musical instruments—they would extemporize a ballroom by moving the shot racks, coils of rope, and other impediments out of the way, and with handkerchiefs tied around the waists of some of them to indicate who were to be the ladies of the party, they would get up a dance with all due form and ceremony; the ladies, in particular, endeavoring to imitate all the airs and graces of the sex—the only drawback being a little hoarseness of the voice, and now and then the use of an expletive which would escape them when something went wrong in the dance, and they forgot they had the aprons on. The favorite dancing-tunes were those of Wapping and Wide Water Street, and when I speak of the airs and graces, I must be understood to mean those rather demonstrative airs and graces of which Poll and Peggy would be likely to be mistresses. On these occasions, the discipline of the ship was wont to be purposely relaxed, and roars of laughter and other evidences of the rapid flight of the jocund hours, at other times entirely inadmissible, would come resounding aft on the quarter-deck.

Sometimes the recreation of the dance would be varied, and songs and story telling would be the amusements of the evening. The sea is a wide net, which catches all kinds of fish, and in a man-of-war's crew a great many odd characters are always to be found. Broken-down gentlemen who have spent all the money they have been able to raise upon their own credit or that of their friends; defaulting clerks and cashiers; actors who have been playing to empty houses; third-class musicians and poets, are all not unfrequently found in the same ship's company. These gentlemen play a very unimportant role in seamanship, but they take a high rank among the crew when fun and frolic, and not seamanship, are the order of the day—or rather night. In the *Alabama*, we had a capital Falstaff, though Jack's capacious pouch was not often with fat capon lined; and as for sherry-sack, if he now and then got a good glass of red-eye instead, he was quite content. We had several Hals, who had defied their harsh old papas and given them the slip, to keep Falstaff company; and as for *raconteurs*, we had them by the score. Some of these latter were equal to the Italian *lazzaroni* and could extemporize yarns by the hour; and there is nothing of which a sailor is half so fond as a yarn.

It was my custom on these occasions to go forward on the bridge—a light structure spanning the deck near amidships —which, in the twilight hours, was a sort of lounging place for the officers, and smoke my single cigar and listen to whatever might be going on, almost as much amused as the sailors themselves. So rigid is the discipline of a ship of war that the captain is necessarily much isolated from his officers. He messes alone, walks the quarter-deck alone, and rarely, during the hours of duty, exchanges, even with his first lieutenant or officer of the deck, other conversation than such as relates to the ship or the service she is upon. I felt exceedingly the irksomeness of my position and was always glad of an opportunity to escape from it. On the bridge, I could lay aside the "captain," gather my young officers around me and indulge in some of the pleasures of social intercourse; taking care to tighten the reins gently again the next morning. When song was the order of the evening, after the more ambitious of the *amateurs* had delivered themselves of their *solos* and *cantatas*, the entertainment generally wound up with "*Dixie*," when the whole ship would be in an uproar of enthusiasm, sometimes as many as a hundred voices joining in the chorus; the unenthusiastic Englishman, the stolid Dutchman, the mercurial Frenchman, the grave Spaniard, and even the serious Malayan, all joining in the inspiring refrain,

Above: A practice duel on *The Alabama*

Left: *The Alabama* crew's Christmas at Arcas Keys

Below: Ordering an overtaken ship to heave to

William Fehr, Cape Town
Above: The Alabama passes Mouille Point lighthouse

Below: The Alabama in Table Bay

Parliament Library

We'll live and die in Dixie!

and astonishing old Neptune by the fervor and novelty of their music.

Eight o'clock was the hour at which the night watches were set, when, of course, all merriment came to an end. When the officer of the deck reported this hour to the captain and was told by the latter to "make it so," he put the trumpet to his mouth and sang out in a loud voice, "Strike the bell eight—call the watch!" In an instant, the most profound silence fell upon the late uproarious scene. The witches did not disappear more magically in that famous revel of Tam O'Shanter, when Tam sang out, "Weel dune, Cutty Sark!" than the sailors dispersed at this ominous voice of authority. The violinist was arrested with half-drawn bow; the *raconteur* suddenly ceased his yarn in the most interesting part of his story, and even the inspiring chorus of "Dixie" died a premature death upon the lips of the singers. The shrill call of the boatswain's whistle, followed by his hoarse voice calling "All the starboard watch!" or "All the port watch!" as the case might be, would now be heard, and pretty soon, the watch, which was off duty, would tumble below to their hammocks, and the midshipmen would be seen coming forward from the quarter-deck with lantern and watch-bill in hand to muster the watch whose turn it was to be on deck. The most profound stillness now reigned on board during the remainder of the night, only broken by the necessary orders and movements in making or taking in sail, or it may be by the whistling of the gale and the surging of the sea, or the cry of the lookouts at their posts every half hour.

To return now to our cruise. We are passing from the Azores to the Banks of Newfoundland. On the 1st of October, the following record is found upon my journal: "The gale moderated during the last night, but the weather today has been thick and rainy, with the wind from the northwest, and a confused, rough sea. No observation for latitude. The barometer, which had gone down to 29.8 is rising and stands at nine P. M. at 29.9. The ship being about two hundred miles only from the Banks of Newfoundland, we are trying the temperature of the air and water every hour. At nine P. M. we found the temperature of the former to be 63°, and of the latter 70°, indicating that we have passed into the Gulf Stream." The thick, rainy weather is almost as unerring a sign of the presence of this stream as the thermometer.

The stream into which we have now passed is literally an immense salt-water river in the sea. Coming out of the Gulf of Mexico, it has brought the temperature of the tropics all the way to the Banks of Newfoundland in the latitude of 50° north, and it has run this distance between banks, or walls of cold water, on either side, parting with very little of its warmth by the way. When it is recollected that this salt-water river in the sea is about three thousand times larger than the Mississippi River, that is to say, that it brings out of the Gulf of Mexico, three thousand times as much water as that river empties into it, and that all this great body of water is carried up into the hyperborean regions of Newfoundland at a temperature, even in mid-winter, ranging from 73 to 78 degrees, it will be seen at once what a powerful weather breeder it must be. Accordingly, no port of the world is more stormy than the Gulf Stream off the northeastern coast of the United States and the Banks of Newfoundland. Such is the quantity of heat brought daily by this stream and placed in juxtaposition with the rigors of a Northern winter that it is estimated, that if it were suddenly stricken from it, it would be sufficient to make the column of superincumbent atmosphere hotter than melted iron! With such an element of atmospheric disturbance, it is not wonderful that the most terrific gales that rage on the ocean are wont to sweep over the surface of this stream.

Indeed, this stream not only generates hurricanes of its own, it seems to attract to it such as are engendered in the most distant parts of our hemisphere; for hurricanes known to have originated near Cape St. Roque, in Brazil, have made their way straight for the Gulf Stream and followed it in its course for a thousand miles and more, spreading shipwreck and disaster broadcast in their track. The violence of these gales is inconceivable by those who have not witnessed them. The great hurricane of 1780 originated to the eastward of the island of Barbadoes and made straight for the Gulf Stream. As it passed over the West India Islands, trees were uprooted, and the bark literally blown from them. The very bottom and depths of the sea in the vicinity of some of the islands were uncovered, and rocks torn up, and new channels formed. The waves rose to such a height that forts and castles, removed, as it was thought, far out of the reach of the water, were washed away, and the storm taking hold of their heavy artillery played with it as with so many straws, throwing it to considerable distances. Houses were razed, and ships wrecked, and the bodies of men and beasts were lifted up into the air and dashed to pieces in the storm. Still, the European-bound ships defy all the bad weather so prevalent in this stream, on account of the easterly current which accelerates their passage at the rate of from two to three miles per hour. The stream, therefore, has been literally bearded by commerce, and has become one of its principal highways. It is because it is a highway of commerce that the *Alabama* now finds herself in it. Nor was she long in it before the travellers on the highway began to come along.

Early on the morning of the 3d of October, two sails were simultaneously reported by the lookout at the masthead— one right ahead, and the other on the lee-bow. As both the ships were standing in our direction, there was no necessity for a chase. We had nothing to do but await their approach. As their hulls were lifted above the horizon, we could see that they were fine, large ships, with a profusion of tapering spars and white canvas. We at once pronounced them American; and so, after a little, they proved to be. They were, in fact, the *avant courriers* of the "junk fleet," for which we had come to look. The wind was light, and they came on with all their sails set from truck to rail. We, on our part, put on an air of perfect indifference. We made no change in our sail, and it was not necessary to alter our course, as the strangers would pass sufficiently near us unless they altered their own courses, which they did not seem inclined to do. They apparently had no suspicion of our real character. We did not hoist any colors until the vessels were nearly abreast of us and only a few hundred yards distant, when suddenly wheeling, we fired a gun and hoisted the Confederate flag. The capture of these two ships must have been a perfect surprise to them, judging by the confusion that was visible on board. There was a running about the decks, and an evident indecision for a few moments as to what was best to be done; but it did not take the masters long to take an intelligent view of the situation. There was nothing to be done but surrender; and this they did by hoisting their colors and heaving to their ships.

We now shortened sail, and laying the maintopsail to the mast, lowered a couple of quarter boats and boarded the prizes. One of them proved to be the *Brilliant* from New York for London, laden with flour and grain; and the other the *Emily Farnum* from New York for Liverpool with a similar cargo. The cargo of the *Farnum* being properly documented as neutral property, I released her on ransom bond, and converting her into a cartel, sent on board of her all my prisoners, of whom I had fifty or sixty on board the *Alabama*, besides those just captured in the *Brilliant*. The latter ship was burned, and her destruction must have disappointed a good many holders of bills of exchange, drawn against her cargo, as this was large and valuable. The owners of the ship have since put in a claim in that little bill, which Mr. Seward has pressed with so little effect hitherto against the British Government for indemnity for the "depredations of the *Alabama*" for the ship alone, and the freight-moneys which they lost by her destruction to the amount of $93,000. The cargo was probably even more valuable than the ship.

I made a positive stipulation with the *Farnum* upon releasing her that she should continue her voyage to Liverpool and not put back into any American port; the master pledging me his word that he would comply with it. My object was, of course, to prevent him from giving news of me to the enemy. He had no sooner passed out of sight, however, steering his course for Liverpool, than he dodged and put into Boston and reported me. This being nothing more than a clever Yankee trick, of course there was no harm done the master's honor.

I was much moved by the entreaties of the master of the *Brilliant* to spare his ship. He was a hard-working seaman, who owned a one third interest in her. He had built her and was attached to her, and she represented all his worldly goods. But I was forced again to steel my heart. He was, like the other masters who had remonstrated with me, in the same boat with the political rascals who had egged on the war; and I told him he must look to those rascals for redress. The ship made a brilliant bonfire, lighting up the Gulf Stream for many miles around. Having been set on fire near night, and the wind falling to nearly a calm, we remained in sight of the burning wreck nearly all night.

Among the many slanders against me, to which the Northern press gave currency during the war, it was stated that I decoyed ships into my power by setting fire to my prizes at night and remaining by them in ambuscade. Of course, when seamen discover a ship on fire at sea they rush with all their manly sympathies aroused to the rescue of their comrades, who are supposed to be in danger; but if they should find, it was said, that they were waylaid and captured, none would go to the rescue in future, and thus many seamen would perish. It can scarcely be necessary for me to say that I never purposely lay by a burning ship by night or by day longer than to see her well on fire. The substantial answer to the slander is that I never captured a ship under the circumstances stated.

For the next few days we had fine, clear weather, and chased and overhauled a number of neutral ships, most of them out of New York and bound for Europe laden with grain. The English, French, Prussian, Hamburg, Oldenham, and other flags were fast monopolizing the enemy's carrying trade and enjoying a rich harvest. These were not the sort of "junks" that we were in quest of, but they compensated us somewhat for the time and labor lost in chasing and boarding them by supplying us with late newspapers of the enemy and giving us valuable information concerning the progress of the war.

On the afternoon of the 7th of October, the weather being fine and the breeze light, we chased and captured the American bark *Wave Crest* from New York, bound for Cardiff, Wales, with flour and grain. In the language of the enemy, we plundered her, that is, we received on board from her such articles as we needed, and after having made use of her for a while as a target at which to practise the men at the battery, we burned her.

Filling away, we again made sail to the northwest. We were now in about latitude 41° and longitude 54° and were working our way under easy sail toward the coasts of the United States. Just before nightfall, on the same afternoon, another sail was cried from aloft, and we made all sail in pursuit immediately, anxious to draw sufficiently near the chase before dark to prevent losing sight of her. By this time, the wind, which had been very light all day, had freshened to a stiff breeze, and the chase, soon perceiving our object, spread a

cloud of canvas with studding-sails alow and aloft in the effort
to escape. She had seen the fire of the burning *Wave Crest*
and knew full well the doom that awaited her if she were overtaken. As night threw her mantle over the scene, the moon,
nearly at the full, rose with unusual splendor and lighted up
the sea for the chase; and a beautiful, picturesque chase it was.
Although it lasted several hours, our anxiety as to the result
was relieved in a very short time, for we could see from the
first that we gained upon the fleeing ship, although her master
practised every stratagem known to the skilful seaman. As
soon as we approached sufficiently near to get a good view of
her through our excellent night glasses, which, in the bright
moonlight, brought out all her features almost as distinctly as
if we had been viewing them by the rays of the sun, we discovered that she was one of those light and graceful hermaphrodite brigs, that is, a rig between the brig and the schooner,
so peculiarly American. Her sails were beautifully cut, well
hoisted, and the clews well spread; her masts were long and
tapering, and her yards more square than usual. There was
just sea enough on to give her now and then a gentle motion
as she rose upon a wave and scudded forward with renewed
impulse. Her sails looked not unlike so many silver wings in
the weird moonlight, and with a little effort of the imagination it would not have been difficult to think of her as some
immense waterfowl which had been scared from its roost and
flown seaward for safety.

I sat astride of the hammock cloth on the weather-quarter,
and watched the beautiful apparition during the whole chase,
only taking off my eye now and then to give some order to
the officer of the deck or to cast it admiringly upon the buck-
ling and bending masts and spars of my own beautiful ship as
she sped forward with all the animation of a living thing in
pursuit. The poor little, affrighted fawn ahead of us, how its
heart must have gone pit-a-pat, as it cast its timid eyes behind
it and saw its terrible pursuer looming up larger and larger
and coming nearer and nearer! Still there might be some
hope. The pursuing vessel might be some peaceful merchant-
ship, bound on the same errand of commerce with herself and
only trying heels with her, in sport over these dancing waves
and by this bright moonlight. Alas! the hope was short-lived;
for presently in the stillness of near midnight a flash was
seen, followed by the sound of a booming gun and there could

no longer be any doubt, that the pursuer was a ship of war and most likely a Confederate. Halliards and tacks and sheets were let fly on board the brigantine, and as soon as her seamen could gather in the folds of the flapping sails and haul up clew-garnets, her helm was put down, and she rounded gracefully to the now whistling wind with fore-topsail aback. So rapidly had this been done, and so close was the *Alabama* upon the chase that we had just time to sheer clear of her by a little trick of the helm. Our own sail was now shortened, and the boarding-officer dispatched on board the prize.

She proved to be the *Dunkirk* from New York with a cargo of grain for Lisbon. There being no evidence of neutral ownership of the cargo among the papers, she was burned as soon as her crew could be transferred to the *Alabama*. We made two novel captures on board this ship—one was a deserter from the *Sumter*, a worthless sailor out of one of the Northern States, whom we afterward discharged from the Confederate Naval service in disgrace, instead of hanging him as we might have done under our Articles of War; and the other a number of very neatly put up tracts in the Portuguese language; our Northern brethren dealing in a little piety as well as trade. These tracts had been issued by that pious corporation, the American Tract Society of New York, whose fine fat offices are filled with sleek, well-fed parsons . . . whose business it is to prey upon the credulity of kind-hearted American women and make a pretence of converting the heathen! On the cover of these tracts was printed the following directions as to how the doses were to be taken: "Portuguese tracts from the American Tract Society for distribution among Portuguese passengers and to give upon the coast to visitors from the shore, &c. When in port, please keep conspicuously on the cabin table for all comers to read: but be very careful not to take any ashore as the laws do not allow it." A pen had been run through the last injunction, as though the propagandists of "grand moral ideas" had become a little bolder since the war and were determined to thrust their piety down the throats of the Portuguese whether they would or not. If there should be any attempt now on the part of poor old Portugal to seize the unlawful distributor of the tracts, a gunboat or two would set the matter right. A little farther on, on the same cover, was the following instruction: "As may be convenient, please report (by letter if necessary) anything of interest which may occur in connection with the distribution; also take any orders for Bibles and forward to John S. Pierson, Marine Agent, New York Bible Society, No. 7 Beekman Street."

Chapter Six—*1862*

Capricious weather of the Gulf Stream . . . Capture of the packet ship Tonawanda; of the Manchester and the Lamplighter . . . A cyclone

Though the month of October is remarkable for its fine weather along the American coast, yet here in the Gulf Stream we had a constant succession of changes, the wind going regularly around the compass every two or three days, and thick, rainy weather predominating. We were now, besides, experiencing a southeasterly current of about two knots, and as we were bound to the northwest and frequently had the wind as well as the current ahead, we made but slow progress. On the second day after capturing the *Dunkirk*, the familiar cry of "Sail ho!" again came ringing from the masthead, and pretty soon a large ship loomed up above the horizon. We gave chase, and, just before sunset came up with a fine packet ship, whose deck we could see was crowded with passengers. This was a somewhat unusual spectacle—a sailing ship filled with passengers for Europe during the month of October. Since the introduction of the steam packet, but few passengers, except emigrants, take passage in a sailing ship, and the current of emigration sets the other way.

Upon being boarded, the ship proved to be the *Tonawanda* of and from Philadelphia, bound to Liverpool. Some of the passengers were foreigners, fleeing from the tyranny and outrages of person and property which had overtaken them under the reign of the Puritan, in the "land of the free, and the home of the brave," and others were patriotic Puritans themselves running away from the City of Brotherly Love, to escape the draft. We captured the *Tonawanda* and the question immediately presented itself what should we do with her? There being no claim by any neutral for the cargo, both ship and cargo were good prize of war, but unfortunately we could not burn the ship without encumbering ourselves with the passengers; and thirty of the sixty of these were women and children! The men we might have disposed of without much inconvenience, but it was not possible to convert the *Alabama* into a nursery and set the stewards to serving pap to the babies. Although I made it a rule never to bond a ship if I could burn her, I released the *Tonawanda* on bond, though there was no legal impediment to her being burned. I kept her cruising in company with me, however, for a day or two, hoping that I might fall in with some other ship of the enemy that might be less valuable or might have a neutral cargo on board to which I could transfer the passengers and thus be enabled to burn her. But here again her owners were in luck, for the finest and most valuable ships with cargoes entirely uncovered would persist in crossing my path.

On the second day after the capture of the *Tonawanda*— that ship being still in our company with a prize crew on board—the weather inclining to be overcast, and the breeze light—a ship was reported, at early daylight on our weather-quarter. It was another heavy ship of the "junk fleet," and as we were lying right across her path, we had nothing to do but await her approach. She came along under a cloud of canvas, though, as the wind was light, it took her some three or four hours to come up with us. To disarm her of suspicion, I hoisted the American colors and caused my prize to do the same. She naturally concluded that the two ships were "visiting," which ships sometimes do at sea, when the wind is light, and there is not much time lost by the operation, and came on without so much as shifting her helm or stirring tack or sheet. When she had approached sufficiently near, I invited her too to visit me; my card of invitation be-

ing a blank cartridge and a change of flags. She hove to at
once, and upon being boarded, proved to be the ship *Manchester* from New York, bound to Liverpool. I now threw the
Manchester's crew together with the crews of the *Wave Crest*,
and *Dunkirk*, on board the *Tonawanda*, as being the less valuable ship of the two, and permitted the latter to depart; but
before doing so, I took from on board of her one of her passengers. This was a likely Negro lad of about seventeen years
of age—a slave until he was twenty-one under the laws of
Delaware. This little state, all of whose sympathies were
with us, had been ridden over roughshod by the Vandals
north of her (as Maryland afterward was) and was arrayed on
the side of the enemy. I was obliged, therefore, to treat her as
such. The slave was on his way to Europe in company with
his master. He came necessarily under the laws of war, and
I brought him on board the *Alabama*, where we were in
want of good servants and sent him to wait on the wardroom
mess.

The boy was a little alarmed at first, but, when he saw
kindly faces beaming upon him and heard from his new masters and the servants of the mess some words of encouragement, he became reassured, and in the course of a few days
was not only at home but congratulated himself on the exchange he had made. He became, more especially, the servant of Dr. Galt, and there at once arose between the Virginia
gentleman and the slave boy that sympathy of master and
servant which our ruder people of the North find it so impossible to comprehend. Faithful service, respect, and attach-
ment followed protection and kind treatment, and the slave
was as happy as the day was long. David soon became to
Galt what Bartelli was to me—indispensable—and the former
was really as free as the latter, except only in the circumstance
that he could not change masters. I caused his name to be
entered on the books of the ship as one of the crew and
allowed him the pay of his grade. In short, no difference was
made between him and the white waiters of the mess. His
condition was in every respect bettered; though I doubt not,
a howl went up over his capture as soon as it became known
to the pseudo-philanthropists of the North, who know as
little about the Negro and his nature, as they do about the
people of the South.

It was pleasant to regard the affection which this boy conceived for Galt and the pride he took in serving him. As he brought the doctor's camp stool for him to the bridge, placed it in the cosiest corner he could find, and ran off to bring him a light for his cigar, his eyes would dilate, and his ivories shine. Dave served us during the whole cruise. He went on shore in all parts of the world, knew that the moment he touched the shore he was at liberty to depart if he pleased and was tampered with by sundry Yankee Consuls but always came back to us. He seemed to have the instinct of deciding between his friends and his enemies.

The following correspondence took place between the Liverpool Chamber of Commerce, and Earl Russell, the British Foreign Secretary, on the occasion of the two last captures:—

TO THE RT. HON. EARL RUSSELL, ETC., ETC.:

MY LORD: I have been requested by the Council of this Chamber to inform you that they have had brought before them the facts of the destruction at sea, in one case, and of seizure and release under ransom bond in another case, of British property on board Federal vessels, (the *Manchester* and the *Tonawanda*,) by an armed cruiser sailing under the Confederate flag, the particulars of which have been already laid before your Lordship. As the question is one of serious importance to the commerce of this country, the Council wish me most respectfully to solicit the favor of your Lordship's acquainting them, for the information of the mercantile community, what, in the opinion of her Majesty's Government, is the position of the owners of such property in these and other similar cases. Submitting this question with every respect to your Lordship, I have the honor to be, my Lord, your most obedient humble servant,

THOMAS CHILTON
President Chamber of Commerce
LIVERPOOL, 8th Nov., 1862

TO THOMAS CHILTON, ESQ., CHAMBER OF COMMERCE, LIVERPOOL.

SIR: I am directed by Earl Russell to acknowledge the receipt of your letter of the 8th inst., calling attention to the recent proceedings of the armed vessel *Alabama*, with regard to British property on board the Federal vessels *Manchester* and *Tonawanda* and requesting the opinion of her Majesty's Government with regard to the position of the owners of such property in those and other similar cases which may arise; and I am to request that you will inform the Council of the Chamber of Commerce that the matter is under the consideration of her Majesty's Government.

I am, sir, your most obedient, humble servant,
E. HAMMOND
FOREIGN OFFICE, Nov. 7th, 1862

After the usual period of gestation, Earl Russell informed his questioners that British owners of property on board of Federal ships alleged to have been wrongfully captured by Confederate cruisers were in the same position as any other neutral owners shipping in enemy's bottoms during a war; they must look for redress to the country of the captor. But these British owners did what was more sensible—they withdrew in due time their freights from the enemy's ships; and British and other neutral ships soon became the carriers of the American trade. It is claimed in the above correspondence, that there was British property destroyed on board the *Manchester.* If so, it was the fault of the British owner in failing to document his property properly, for there was no certificate or other paper found on board that ship claiming that any part of the cargo belonged to neutrals.

The *Manchester* brought us a batch of late New York papers, and I was much obliged to the editors of the New York *Herald* for valuable information. I learned from them where all the enemy's gunboats were and what they were doing; which, of course, enabled me to take better care of the *Alabama* than I should otherwise have been enabled to do.

The Americans effected many reforms in the art of war during our late struggle. Perhaps this was the only war in which the newspapers ever explained beforehand all the movements of armies and fleets to the enemy.

The reader will observe that I received my mails quite regularly now from the United States. They were sometimes daily and rarely less frequent than tri-weekly. I appointed my excellent clerk, Mr. Breedlove Smith, postmaster, and he delivered the mail regularly to the officers and crew—

that is to say, the newspaper and periodical mail—the letters I considered as addressed to myself personally. They might give valuable information of the objects and designs of the enemy and throw some light upon the true ownership of cargoes, falsely documented. I therefore took the liberty, which the laws of war gave me, of breaking the seals. There were some curious developments made in some of these letters, nor were they all written on business. Sometimes, as I would break a seal, a photograph would tumble out, and the first few lines of the letter would inform me of a tender passion that was raging in the heart of the writer. These epistles, photographs and all, were always pitched with a pshaw! into the wastepaper basket and were soon afterward consigned by Bartelli to the sea. So that the fair writers—and some of the writers were fair if I might judge by their portraits—may rest satisfied that their secrets are safe. My young officers became so accustomed to their morning's newspaper as they sat down to the breakfast table that if it was not forthcoming, they would wonder "what the devil *Alabama* had been about the past night that she had not gotten hold of a mail?"

For two or three days after capturing the *Manchester*, we fell in with nothing but neutral vessels. When the nationality of these was distinctly marked, as generally it was, we forbore to chase them. The weather began now to give unmistakable signs of a general disturbance of the atmospheric machine. On the 15th of October we captured our next ship. It was blowing half a gale of wind with a thick atmosphere and rain squalls. We were lying to under topsails when she was reported. As in the case of the *Manchester*, we had only to await her approach, for we were still in the beaten track of these lone travelers upon the sea. She came along quite fast before the gale, and when within reach we hove her to with the accustomed gun. She proved upon being boarded to be the bark *Lamplighter* of Boston, from New York for Gibraltar with a cargo of tobacco. There was no attempt to cover the cargo, and when we had removed the crew to the *Alabama*, we burned her.

From the frequent mention which has been made of "uncovered cargoes," the reader will see how careless the enemy's merchants were, and how little they dreamed of disaster. They had not yet heard of the *Alabama*, except only that she had escaped from Liverpool as the "290." They looked upon her yet as a mere myth which it was not necessary to take any precautions against. But the reader will see how soon their course will change and in what demand British Consular certificates vouching for the neutrality of good American cargoes will be in the good city of Gotham toward which the *Alabama* is slowly working her way.

We captured the *Lamplighter* early in the day, and it was well for us she came along when she did. If she had delayed her arrival a few hours, we should probably not have been able to board her, so much had the gale increased and the sea risen. For the next few days we had as much as we could do to take care of ourselves without thinking of the enemy or his ships. We had a fearful gale to encounter. As this gale was a cyclone, and the first really severe gale that the *Alabama* had met with, it is worthy of a brief description. We begin, in our generation, to have some definite knowledge of the atmospheric laws. To our ancestors of only a generation or two back these laws were almost a sealed book. It is now well ascertained that all the great hurricanes which sweep over the seas are cyclones; that is, circular gales revolving around an axis or vortex, at the same time that they are traveling in a given direction. These gales all have their origin in warm latitudes, or as has been prettily said by an officer of the Dutch Navy writing on the subject, they "prefer to place their feet in warm water." They do not, however, confine themselves to the places of their origin, but passing out of the tropics sweep over large tracts of extra-tropical seas. These circular gales are the great regulators or balance-wheels, as it were, of the atmospheric machine. They arise in seasons of atmospheric disturbance and seem necessary to the restoration of the atmospheric equilibrium.

In the East Indian and China seas the cyclone is called a typhoon. It prevails there with even more destructive effect than in the western hemisphere. It takes its origin during the change of the monsoons. Monsoons are periodical winds which blow one half of the year from one direction—the northeast for example—and then change and blow the other half of the year from the opposite direction, the southwest. When these monsoons are changing, there is great disturbance in the atmospheric equilibrium. A battle of the winds, as it were, takes place; the out-going wind struggling for existence,

and the in-coming wind endeavoring to throttle it and take
its place. Calms, whirlwinds, waterspouts, and heavy and
drenching rains set in; the black, wild-looking clouds, sometimes rent and torn, sweeping with their heavy burdens of
vapor over the very surface of the sea. Now, the out-going,
or dying monsoon will recede for days together, its enemy,
the in-coming monsoon, greedily advancing to occupy the
space left vacant. The retreating wind will then rally, regain
its courage, and drive back, at least for a part of the way, the
pursuing wind. In this way, the two will alternate for weeks,
each watching the other as warily as if they were opposing
armies. It is during these struggles when the atmosphere is
unhinged, as it were, that the typhoon makes its awful appearance. Every reader is familiar with the phenomenon of the
miniature whirlwind, which he has so often seen sweep along
a street or road for a short distance and then disappear; the
want of local equilibrium in the atmosphere which gave rise
to it having been restored.

These little whirlwinds generally occur at street corners or
at cross roads and are produced by the meeting of two winds.
When these winds meet, the stronger will bend the weaker,
and a whirl will ensue. The two winds still coming on, the
whirl will be increased, and thus a whirlwind is formed, which
immediately begins to travel—not at random, of course, but
in the direction of least pressure. The meeting of two currents
of water, which form a whirlpool, may be used as another
illustration. It is just so that the typhoon is formed. It steps
in as a great conservator of the peace to put an end to the
atmospherical strife which has been going on and to restore
harmony to nature. It is a terrible scourge whilst it lasts; the
whole heavens seem to be in disorder, and that which was
only a partial battle between outposts of the aërial armies, has
now become a general engagement. The great whirl sweeps
over a thousand miles or more, and when it has ceased, nature
smiles again; the old monsoon has given up the ghost, and
the new monsoon has taken its place. All will be peace now
until the next change—the storms that will occur in the interval, being more or less local. We have monsoons in the western hemisphere, as well as in the eastern, though they are
much more partial, both in space and duration.

The cyclones which sweep over the North Atlantic are

generated to the eastward of the West India Islands—somewhere between them and the coast of Brazil. They occur in August, September, and October—sometimes, indeed, as early as the latter part of July. In these months, the sun has drawn after him into the northern hemisphere the southeast trade winds of the South Atlantic. These trade winds are now struggling with the northeast trade winds, which prevail in these seas for three fourths of the year, for the mastery. We have, thus, another monsoon struggle going on; and the consequence of this struggle is the cyclone. . . .

If the reader will pay a little attention to the diagram on page 104 it will assist him, materially, in comprehending the nature of the storm into which the *Alabama* had now entered. The outer circle represents the extent of the storm; the inner circle, the center or vortex; the arrows along the inner edge of the outer circle represent the direction, or gyration of the wind, and the dotted line represents the course traveled by the storm. The figures marked 1, 2, and 3 represent the position of the *Alabama* in the different stages of the storm as it passed over her; the arrowheads on the figures representing the head of the ship.

If the reader, being in the northern hemisphere, will turn his face toward the sun at his rising and watch his course for a short time, he will observe that this course is from left to right. As the course of the arrows in the figure is from right to left, the reader observes that the gyration of the wind in the storm is *against the course of the sun.* This is an invariable law in both hemispheres; but in the southern hemisphere the gyration of the wind is in the opposite direction from its gyration in the northern hemisphere, for the reason that to an observer in the southern hemisphere the sun appears to be moving, not from left to right, but from right to left. Whilst, therefore, the storm, in the northern hemisphere, gyrates from right to left, in the southern hemisphere, it gyrates from left to right; both gyrations being *against the course of the sun.*

This is a curious phenomenon which has thus far puzzled all the philosophers. It is a double puzzle; first, why the storm should gyrate always in the same direction, and secondly, why this gyration should be different in the two hemispheres. The law seems to be so subtle as utterly to elude investigation. There is a curious phenomenon in the vegetable world which seems to obey this law of storms, and which I do not recollect

ever to have seen alluded to by any writer. It may be well
known to horticulturists, for aught that I know, but it attracted
my attention in my own garden for the first time, since the
war. It is that all creeping vines and tendrils when they wind
themselves around a pole, invariably wind themselves from
right to left or *against the course of the sun!* I was first struck
with the fact by watching from day to day the tender unfolding
of the lima bean—each little creeper as it came forth feeling
as with the instinct of animal life for the pole and then
invariably bending around it in the direction mentioned. I
have a long avenue of these plants numbering several hundred
poles, and upon examining them all, I invariably found the
same result. I tried the experiment with some of these little
creepers of endeavoring to compel them to embrace the pole
from left to right, or *with the course of the sun,* but in vain.
In the afternoon I would gather blades of grass and tie some
of the tendrils to the poles in a way to force them to disobey
the law, but when I went to inspect them the following
morning, I would invariably find that the obedient little plants
had turned back and taken the accustomed track! What is
the subtle influence which produces this wonderful result?
May it not be the same law which rides on the whirlwind and
directs the storm?

The cyclone of which I am writing must have traveled a
couple of thousand miles before it reached the *Alabama.* Its
approach had been heralded by several days of bad weather;
and on the morning of the gale, which was on the 16th of
October, the barometer—that faithful sentinel of the seaman—began to settle very rapidly. We had been under short
sail before, but we now took the close reefs in the topsails,
which tied them down to about one third of their original
size, got up, and bent the main storm-staysail, which was
made of the stoutest No. 1 canvas and scarcely larger than a
pocket handkerchief, swung in the quarter-boats and passed
additional lashings around them; and in short made all the
requisite preparations for the battle with the elements which
awaited us. If the reader will cast his eye upon the diagram
at *Alabama,* No. 1, he will see that the ship has her head to
the eastward, that her yards are braced up on the starboard
tack, and that she took the wind as indicated by the arrows
from S. to S. S. E.

The ship is lying still, and the storm, which the reader sees by the dotted line is traveling to the northeast, is approaching her. She was soon enveloped in its folds; and the winds, running around the circle in that mad career represented by the arrows, howled and whistled and screeched around her like a thousand demons. She was thrown over, several streaks, and the waves began to assault her with sledge-hammer blows and occasionally to leap on board of her, flooding her decks, and compelling us to stand knee-deep in water. By this time, we had furled the fore-topsail; the fore-staysail had been split into ribbons; and whilst I was anxiously debating with myself whether I should hold on to the main-topsail a little longer, or start its sheets and let it blow to pieces—for it would have been folly to think of sending men aloft in such a gale to furl it—the iron bolt on the weather-quarter, to which the standing part of the. main-brace was made fast, gave way; away went the main-yard, parted at the slings, and in a trice the main-topsail was whipped into fragments and tied into a hundred curious knots. We were now under nothing but the small storm-staysail described; the topgallant yards had been sent down from aloft, there was very little top-hamper exposed to the wind, and yet the ship was pressed over and over until I feared she would be thrown upon her beam-ends or her masts swept by the board. The lee-quarter-boat was wrenched from the davits and dashed in pieces; and, as the sea would strike the ship, forward or aft, she would tremble in every fiber, as if she had been a living thing, in fear of momentary dissolution.

But she behaved nobly, and I breathed easier after the first half hour of the storm. All hands were, of course, on deck, with the hatches battened down, and there was but little left for us to do but to watch the course of the storm and to ease the ship all it was possible to ease her with the helm. Life lines had been rove fore and aft the decks by my careful first lieutenant to prevent the crew from being washed overboard, and it was almost as much as each man could do to look out for his own personal safety.

The storm raged thus violently for two hours, the barometer settling all the while until it reached 28.64. It then fell suddenly calm. Landsmen have heard of an "ominous" calm, but this calm seemed to us almost like the fiat of death. We knew at once that we were in the terrible vortex of a cyclone from which so few mariners have ever escaped to tell the tale!

Nothing else could account for the suddenness of the calm coupled with the lowness of the barometer. We knew that when the vortex should pass, the gale would be renewed as suddenly as it had ceased and with increased fury, and that the frail little *Alabama*—for indeed she looked frail and small, now amid the giant seas that were rising in a confused mass around her and threatening every moment to topple on board of her with an avalanche of water that would bury her a hundred fathoms deep—might be dashed in a thousand pieces in an instant. I pulled out my watch and noted the time of the occurrence of the calm, and causing one of the cabin doors to be unclosed, I sent an officer below to look at the barometer. He reported the height already mentioned—28.64. If the reader will cast his eye upon the diagram again—at figure No. 2—he will see where we were at this moment. The *Alabama's* head now lies to the southeast—she having come up gradually to the wind, as it hauled—and she is in the southeastern hemisphere of the vortex. The scene was the most remarkable I had ever witnessed. The ship, which had been pressed over only a moment before by the fury of the gale, had now righted, and the heavy storm staysail, which, notwithstanding its diminutive size had required two stout tackles to confine it to the deck, was not for want of wind to keep it steady jerking these tackles about as though it would snap them in pieces as the ship rolled to and fro! The aspect of the heavens was appalling. The clouds were writhing and twisting like so many huge serpents engaged in combat, and hung so low in the thin air of the vortex as almost to touch our mast heads. The best description I can give of the sea is that of a number of huge watery cones—for the waves seemed now in the diminished pressure of the atmosphere in the vortex to jut up into the sky and assume a conical shape— that were dancing an infernal reel played by some necromancer. They were not running in any given direction, there being no longer any wind to drive them, but were jostling each other like drunken men in a crowd and threatening every moment to topple one upon the other.

With watch in hand I noticed the passage of the vortex. It was just thirty minutes in passing. The gale had left us with the wind from the southwest; the ship, the moment she emerged from the vortex, took the wind from the northwest. We could see it coming upon the waters. The disorderly seas were now no longer jostling each other; the infernal reel had ended; the cones had lowered their late rebellious heads as they felt the renewed pressure of the atmosphere and were being driven like so many obedient slaves before the raging blast. The tops of the waves were literally cut off by the force of the wind and dashed hundreds of yards in blinding spray. The wind now struck us "butt end foremost," throwing the ship over in an instant . . . and threatening to jerk the little storm-sail from its bolt-ropes. It was impossible to raise one's head above the rail, and difficult to breathe for a few seconds. We could do nothing but cower under the weather bulwarks and hold on to the belaying pins (or whatever other objects presented themselves) to prevent being dashed to leeward or swept overboard. The gale raged now precisely as long as it had done before we entered the vortex—two hours—showing how accurately Nature had drawn her circle.

At the end of this time, the *Alabama* found herself in position No. 3. The reader will observe that she is still on the starboard tack, and that from east she has brought her head around to nearly west. The storm is upon the point of passing away from her. I now again sent an officer below, to inspect the barometer, and he reported 29.70; the instrument having risen a little more than an inch in two hours! This alone is evidence of the violence of the storm. During the whole course of the storm a good deal of rain had fallen. It is the rain which adds such fury to the wind. These storms come to us, as has been said, from the tropics, and the winds by which they are engendered are highly charged with vapor. In the course of taking up this vapor from the sea, the winds take up along with it a large quantity of latent heat, or heat whose presence is not indicated by the thermometer. As the raging cyclone is moving onward in its path, the winds begin to part with their burden—it begins to rain. The moment the vapor is condensed into rain, the latent heat, which was taken up with the vapor, is liberated, and the consequence is the formation of a furnace in the sky, as it were, overhanging the raging storm and traveling along with it. The more rain there falls, the more latent heat there escapes; the more latent heat there escapes, the hotter the furnace becomes; and the hotter the furnace, the more furiously the wind races around the circle and rushes into the upper air to fill the vacuum and restore the equilibrium.

In four hours and a half from the commencement of the gale, the *Alabama* was left rolling and tumbling about in the confused sea, which the gale had left behind it with scarcely wind enough to fill the sails, which, by this time, we had gotten upon her to keep her steady. Little more remains to be said of the cyclone. If the reader will take a last look at the diagram, he will see how it is that the wind which appears to him to change has not changed in reality. The wind from first to the last is traveling around the circle, changing not at all. It is the passage of the circle over the ship—or over the observer upon the land—which causes it apparently to change.

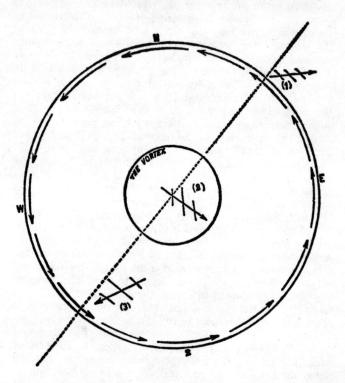

Diagram of the cyclone experienced by the *Alabama* on the 16th of October, 1862.

The *Alabama* lay still during the whole gale, not changing her position perhaps half a mile. As the circle touched her, she took the wind from S. to S.S.E., and when it had passed over her, she had the wind at northwest. In the intermediate time, the wind had *apparently* hauled first to one, and then to the other, of all the intermediate points of the compass, and yet it had not changed a hair's breadth.

The weather did not become fine for several days after the gale. On the following night, it again became thick and cloudy, and the wind blew very fresh from the southwest. The sea, though it had somewhat subsided, was still very rough, and the night was so dark that the officer of the deck could not see half the length of the ship in any direction. The southwest wind was a fair wind from the enemy's ports to Europe, and we kept a very bright lookout to prevent ourselves from being run over by some heavy ship of commerce hurrying, with lightning speed before wind and sea.

Chapter Seven—*1862*

*The physiognomy of ships . . . Capture of the Lafay-
ette . . . Decree of the Admiralty Court on board the
Alabama in her case, and in that of the Lauretta . . .
The criticisms of the New York press . . . Further
evidence of the rotary nature of the winds . . . The
Lauretta captured . . . The Crenshaw captured . . .
The New York Chamber of Commerce cries aloud
in pain . . . Capture of the Baron de Castine, and the
Levi Starbuck . . . Capture of the T. B. Wales . . .
Lady prisoners*

The day after the gale we set all hands at work repairing
damages—the carpenters fishing, and the boatswain and his
gang refitting the broken main-yard; the gunners putting their
battery in order, the sail-maker repairing sails, and the old
signal-quartermaster breaking out his signal lockers, which had
been invaded by the sea water, and airing his flags. The latter
was enabled by this time to make quite a display of Yankee
flags, from his signal-halliards—the *Alabama* having captured
seventeen ships in six weeks. As the Yankee ships now began
to wear, out of pure patriotism (though they were out of the

war and profitably chasing the honest penny) the biggest sort
of "flaunting lies," there were several bagsful of these flags.

We began now to overhaul sails again. From the 16th to
the 20th of October we chased and boarded nine, all of which
were neutral! We were in fact in an American sea—the Gulf
Stream being the thoroughfare of American and West Indian
commerce to Europe—and yet the American flag was beginning to disappear from it. Such of the Federal ships as could
not obtain employment from the Government as transports,
or be sold under neutral flags, were beginning to rot at the
wharves of the once thrifty seaports of the Great Republic.
Our nautical enterprise was beginning to tell on the enemy,
and if we had had the ability to imitate Massachusetts in the
war of the first Revolution in the way of putting forth armed
cruisers to prey upon the enemy's commerce, the said enemy
would not have had so much as a rope yarn upon the sea in
the course of twelve months. But at the time of which I am
writing the *Alabama* and the *Florida* were the only two Confederate ocean cruisers afloat.

On the 21st of October, we observed in latitude 39° 35',
and longitude 63° 26', and on that day we made our first
capture since the gale. We were lying to as usual, when a
large ship was descried in the northwest running in our
direction. Though the wind was very fresh, she had her royals
and fore-topmast studding-sails set and was in consequence
running before the wind with great speed. I shook the reefs
out of my own topsails and prepared to set the topgallant-
sails if it should be necessary and filled away and moved
toward the path of the stranger as she approached, with the
English colors at my peak. The fine, large ship, as she ran
down to us presented a beautiful picture—all the more beautiful because we knew her to be Yankee, although she had
not yet shown her colors.

We had become now very expert in detecting the nationalities of ships. I had with me a master's mate—[James] Evans—
who had a peculiar talent in this respect. He had been a pilot
out of Savannah and had sailed in the *Savannah*, privateer,
at the beginning of the war. He escaped the harsh treatment
and trial for piracy, which were the fate of the prisoners
captured in that little vessel, by being absent in a prize at the
time of her capture. He afterward joined me at Liverpool.
Whenever I had any doubt about the nationality of a ship,

I always sent for Mr. Evans and putting my telescope in his hand, I would say to him, "Look at that ship," pointing in the given direction, "and tell me to what nation she belongs." A glance of a minute or two was all he required. Lowering his glass at the end of this time, he would say to me, "She is a Yankee, sir," or, "She is not a Yankee," as the case might be; and if she was not a Yankee, he would say, "I think she is English," or French, or Dutch, or whatever other nation to which he supposed her to belong. He sometimes failed, of course, in assigning their proper nationality to neutrals, but his judgment seemed to amount to an instinct with regard to the question Yankee or no Yankee. When he pronounced a ship a Yankee, I was always certain of her. I never knew him to fail in this particular but once, and that can scarcely be said to have been a failure. He once mistook a St. John's, New Brunswick-built ship, for an enemy; and the ships built in the British Colonies on the Yankee border are such counterparts of American ships that it is very difficult to distinguish one from the other.

The ship which was now running down for us was a picture, with her masts yielding and swaying to a cloud of sail, her tapering poles shooting skyward even above her royals, and her well-turned, flaring bows—the latter a distinctive feature of New York-built ships. She came on, rolling gracefully to the sea, and with the largest kind of a "bone in her mouth." She must have suspected something from our very equivocal attitude in such weather and in such a place; but she made no change in her course and was soon under our guns. A blank cartridge brought her to the wind. If the scene was beautiful before, it was still more so now. If she had been a ship of war, full of men, and with hands stationed at sheets, halliards, and braces, she could not have shortened sail much more rapidly, or have rounded more promptly and gracefully to the wind with her main topsail aback. Her cloud of canvas seemed to shrivel and disappear as though it had been a scroll rolled up by an invisible hand. It is true nothing had been furled, and her light sails were all flying in the wind, confined to the yards only by their clew-lines, but the ship lay as snugly and conveniently for boarding as I could desire. I frequently had occasion during my cruises to admire the seamanship of my enemies. The Yankee is certainly a remarkable specimen of the *genus homo*. He is at once a duck and a chicken and takes

to the water or the land with equal facility. Providence has
certainly designed him for some useful purpose. He is ambitious, restless, scheming, energetic, and has no inconvenient
moral nature to restrain him from the pursuit of his interests,
be the path to these never so crooked. In the development of
material wealth he is unsurpassed, and perhaps this is his
mission on this new continent of ours. But he is like the
beaver, he works from instinct and is so avid of gain that he
has no time to enjoy the wealth he produces. Some malicious
demon seems to be goading him on in spite of himself to
continuous and exhausting exertion which consigns him to
the tomb before his time, leaving a pile of untouched wealth
behind him.

The prize upon being boarded proved to be the *Lafayette*
from New York, laden with grain chiefly for Irish ports. We
learned from newspapers captured on board of her that news
of our capture of the *Brilliant* and *Emily Farnum* off the
Banks of Newfoundland had reached the United States and
as was to be expected, I found, when I came to examine the
papers of the *Lafayette*, plenty of certificates to cover her
cargo. In fact, from this time onward I rarely got hold of an
enemy's ship whose cargo was not certificated all over—oaths
for this purpose being apparently as cheap as the much-
derided custom-house oaths that every ship-master is expected
to take, without the least regard to the state of the facts.
Upon examination of these certificates, I pronounced them
fraudulent and burned the ship.

As the burning of this vessel, with her cargo nicely "covered," as the shippers had hoped with British Consular seals
and certificates, seemed to warm up the Northern press and
cause it to hurl fresh denunciations of "piracy" against me,
I will detain the reader a moment from the thread of my nar-
rative to look a little into the facts. The reader has already
been told that I held a regular prize-court on board the *Sumter*.
I did the same thing on board the *Alabama*, never condemning
a ship or cargo when there was any claim of neutral property,
without the most careful and thorough examination of her
papers and giving to the testimony the best efforts of my
judgment. I had every motive not to offend neutrals. We were
hoping for an early recognition of our independence by the
principal powers of the earth and were covetous of the good
will of them all. I had, besides, the most positive instructions

from Mr. Mallory, our Secretary of the Navy, to pay the utmost attention and respect to neutral rights.

Referring to the records of "The Confederate States Admiralty Court, held on board the Confederate States steamer *Alabama* on the high seas," I find the following decree entered in the case of the *Lafayette*:

In re LAFAYETTE

The ship being under the enemy's flag and register is condemned. With reference to the cargo, there are certificates prepared in due form and sworn to before the British Consul that it was purchased and shipped on neutral account. These *ex parte* statements are precisely such as every unscrupulous merchant would prepare, to deceive his enemy and save his property from capture. There are two shipping houses in the case; that of Craig & Nicoll and that of Montgomery Bros. Messrs. Craig & Nicoll say that the grain shipped by them belongs to Messrs. Shaw & Finlay and to Messrs. Hamilton, Megault & Thompson, all of Belfast, Ireland, to which port the ship is bound, but the grain is not consigned to them, and they could not demand possession of it under the bill of lading. It is, on the contrary, consigned to the order of the shippers; thus leaving the possession and control of the property in the hands of the shipper. Farther: The shippers, instead of sending this grain to the pretended owners in a general ship on freight consigned to them, they paying freight as usual, have chartered the whole ship and stipulated themselves for the payment of all the freights. If this property had been *bona fide*, the property of the parties in Belfast named in the depositions, it would undoubtedly have gone consigned to them in a bill of lading authorizing them to demand possession of it, and the agreement with the ship would have been that the consignees and owners of the property should pay the freight upon delivery. But even if this property were purchased as pretended by Messrs. Craig & Nicoll for the parties named, still their not consigning it to them, and delivering them the proper bill of lading, passing the possession, left the property in the possession and under the dominion of Craig & Nicoll and as such liable to capture. See 3, *Phillimore on International Law*, 610, 612, to the effect that if the goods are going on account of the shipper, or subject to his order or control, they are good prize. They cannot even be sold and transferred to a neutral *in transitu*. They must abide by their condition at the time of the sailing of the ship.

The property attempted to be covered by the Messrs.
Montgomery Bros. is shipped by Montgomery Bros. of New
York and consigned to Montgomery Bros. in Belfast. Here the
consignment is all right. The possession of the property has
legally passed to the Belfast house. But when there are two
houses of trade doing business as partners, and one of them
resides in the enemy's country, the other house, though resident in a neutral country, becomes also enemy, *quoad* the
trade of the house in the enemy's country, and its share in
any property belonging to the joint concern is subject to capture equally with the share of the house in the enemy's country. To this point, see 3, *Phillimore*, 605. Cargo condemned.

This is the whole case of the *Lafayette*. As this case was
coupled in the criticisms in the Yankee papers to which I
have alluded, and which the reader will see presently, with the
case of the *Lauretta*, not yet captured, I will anticipate the
capture of this ship by a few days that the reader may have
the facts also in her case.

In re LAURETTA

The ship being under the enemy's colors and register is condemned. There are two shippers of the cargo, the house of
Chamberlain, Phelps & Co., and Mr. H. J. Burden—all the
shippers resident and doing business in the city of New York.
Chamberlain, Phelps & Co. ship 1424 barrels of flour and a
lot of pipe staves, to be delivered at Gibraltar, or Messina,
to their own order, and 225 kegs of nails to be delivered at
Messina to Mariano Costarelli. The bill of lading for the flour
and staves has the following indorsement, sworn to before a
notary: "State, city, and county of New York: Louis Con-
tencin, being duly sworn, says that he is clerk with Chamberlain, Phelps & Co., and that part of the merchandise in the
within bill of lading is the property of the subjects of the King
of Italy." This certificate is void for uncertainty. It does not
separate the property in the bill of lading and say which of it
belongs to the "subjects of the King of Italy" and which to
the enemy. For aught that appears, "the subjects" alluded to
may own no more than a single pipe-staff apiece. Indeed, they
can own nothing, as it does not appear what they own. Further: If the property was identified in the certificate, the
"subjects of the King of Italy" are not. No man—for there is
none named—could claim the property under this certificate.
It is, therefore, void for this reason. See 3, *Phillimore*, 596.

But the flour and staves are consigned to the order of the

shippers, and this alone would be sufficient to condemn them even if the articles had been identified and the proper owners pointed out in the certificate. The *possession of the property at the time of the sailing of the ship must be divested out of the enemy shipper*. See 3, *Phillimore*, 610, 612, cited in the case of the *Lafayette*.

The contingent destination of this property is another pregnant circumstance. It shows that it was intended for a market and not for any particular neutral owner. It was to be delivered at Gibraltar or Messina as the shippers might determine after the sailing of the ship—probably upon advices received by steamer. So much for the claim of Chamberlain, Phelps & Co.

The property shipped by H. J. Burden consists of 998 barrels of flour and 290 boxes of herring and is consigned to Charles R. Blandy, Esq., at Funchal, Madeira. The shipper makes the following affidavit before the British Consul in New York: "That all and singular, the goods specified in the annexed bill of lading were shipped by H. J. Burden in the bark *Lauretta* for and on account of H. J. Burden, subject of her Britannic Majesty." Mr. Burden may be a very good subject of her Britannic Majesty, but he describes himself as of 42 Beaver Street, New York City, and seems to lose sight of the fact that his domicile in an enemy's country for the purposes of trade makes him, quoad that trade, an enemy. Cargo condemned.

The reader is now in a condition to understand the following criticism from that very elegant sheet, the New York *Commercial Advertiser* and to appreciate the justice and courtesy with which I was treated by the press of New York.

THE ALABAMA
BRITISH AND ITALIAN PROPERTY DESTROYED—PORTUGAL ALSO INVOLVED

The English Authorities Acting—Important Facts—Some important facts have just been developed in relation to the operations of the rebel privateer *Alabama*, and the present and prospective action of the British and other foreign Governments whose citizens have lost property by the piracies of her commander. The depredations of the vessel involve the rights of no less than three European governments—England, Italy, and Portugal—and are likely to become a subject of special interest to all maritime nations.

Already the capture and burning of the ship *Lafayette*,

which contained an English cargo, has been the occasion of a correspondence between the British Consul at this port, Mr. Archibald, and Rear-Admiral Milne, commanding the British squadron on the American coast; and it is stated (but we cannot vouch for the truth of the statement) that the Admiral has dispatched three war-vessels in pursuit of the pirate. The Consul has also, we understand, communicated the facts of the case to the British Government and Her Majesty's Minister at Washington. What action will be taken by the British Government, remains to be seen.

The *Lafayette* sailed from this port with a cargo of grain for Belfast, Ireland. The grain was owned by two English firms of this city, and the facts were properly certified on the bills of lading under the British national seal. The *Lafayette* was, however, a Boston vessel and was commanded by Captain Saunders. The facts of the burning have been published.

But another case (that of the bark *Lauretta*) is about to be submitted for the consideration of the British authorities, as well as those of Italy and Portugal. The facts establish a clear case of piracy. The *Lauretta*, which had on board a cargo consisting principally of flour and staves, was burned by Semmes on the 28th of October. She was bound from this port for the island of Madeira and the port of Messina, Italy. Nearly a thousand barrels of flour and also a large number of staves were shipped by Mr. H. J. Burden, a British subject residing in this city, to a relative in Funchal, Madeira. The bill of lading bore the British seal affixed by the consul, to whom the shipper was personally known. The other part of the cargo was shipped by Chamberlain, Phelps & Co. to the order of parties in Messina, and this property was also covered by the Italian consular certificates.

The Portuguese consul at this port also sent a package under seal to the authorities at Madeira besides giving a right to enter the port and sending an open bill of lading.

Captain Wells' account of the manner in which Semmes disposed of these documents, and which he has verified under oath, is not only interesting but gives an excellent idea of the piratical intentions of the commander of the *Alabama*.

The papers of the bark were at the command of Semmes taken by Captain Wells on board the *Alabama*. There was no American cargo and therefore no American papers except those of the vessel. These, of course, were not inquired into. Semmes took first the packet which bore the Portuguese seal and with an air which showed that he did not regard it as of

the slightest consequence, ripped it open and threw it upon
the floor with the remark that "he did not care a damn for the
Portuguese." The Italian bill of lading was treated in a similar
manner, except that he considered it unworthy even of a
remark.

Taking up the British bill of lading and looking at the seal,
Semmes called upon Captain Wells, with an oath to explain.
It was evidently the only one of the three he thought it
worth his while to respect.

"Who is this Burden?" he inquired sneeringly. "Have you
ever seen him?"

"I am not acquainted with him; but I have seen him once
when he came on board my vessel," replied Captain Wells.

"Is he an Englishman—does he look like an Englishman?"

"Yes," rejoined the captain.

"I'll tell you what," exclaimed the pirate, "this is a damned
pretty business—it's a damned Yankee hash, and I'll settle
it,"—whereupon he proceeded to rob the vessel of whatever
he wanted, including Captain Wells' property to a considerable amount; put the crew in irons; removed them to the
Alabama; and concluded by burning the vessel.

These facts will at once be brought before the British
consul. The preliminary steps have been taken. The facts will
also be furnished the Portuguese consul, who announces his
intention of placing them before his Government; and besides
whatever action the Italian consul here may choose to take,
the parties in Messina, to whom the property lost on the
Lauretta was consigned, will of course do what they can to
maintain their own rights. The case is likely to attract more
attention than all the previous outrages of the *Alabama*, inasmuch as property rights of the subjects of other nations are
involved, and the real character of Semmes and his crew
becomes manifest.

Some interesting facts are given by Captain Wells in regard
to the *Alabama*, to which, however, we can only make a brief
allusion. The officers of the privateer are principally Southern
men, but the crew are nearly all English and Irish. They claim
that they were shipped by stratagem; that they were told the
vessel was going to Nassau, and now they are promised shares
in captured property—not only the property taken, but that
which is burned, of which Semmes says he keeps an accurate
account. The bills are to be paid by the Confederate Government, which Semmes, who enforces discipline only by terror-
ism, declares will soon achieve its independence. The men

suppose they are gaining fortunes—though some of them protest against the cheat which has been practised upon them.

The above is a fair specimen of the average intelligence of Yankee newspapers on any subject outside of the dirty pool of politics in which they habitually dabble. I was not quite sure when I burned the *Lafayette* that her cargo belonged to the shippers, British merchants resident in New York. The shippers swore that it did not belong to them but to other parties resident in Ireland on whose account they had shipped it. I *thought* they swore falsely, but as I have said, I was not quite certain. The *Advertiser* sets the matter at rest. It says that I was right. And it claims with the most charming simplicity that I was guilty of an act of piracy in capturing and destroying the property of neutral merchants *domiciled in the enemy's country and assisting him to conduct his trade!* The reader now sees what estimate to put upon all the other balderdash of the article. I presume the only thing Admiral Milne and the British Minister at Washington did was to wonder at the stupidity of the New York *Commercial Advertiser*. It is scarcely necessary to say that Captain Wells of the *Lauretta* took a custom-house oath when he swore to the account which the *Advertiser* gives of his interview with me when I burned his ship. It was a business operation with these Yankees to abuse me, and they performed it in a *businesslike manner*—with oaths and affidavits.

Having captured the Lafayette at nightfall, it was as late as ten P. M. before we got through with the business of "robbing" her—robbing her in spite of all those nicely contrived certificates and British consular seals—when we set her on fire. In a few hours, she was a mere beacon light, upon the sea, marking, as so many other fine ships had marked, the track of the "pirate."

Though I have given the reader already a pretty large dose of the meteorology of the Gulf Stream in which we are still cruising, I cannot forbear to call his attention to other proofs of the rotary character of the winds which prevail along this hot-water river in the sea. From the 2d to the 22d of October, a period of twenty days, the wind had gone nine times entirely around the compass with the regularity of clockwork. With the exception of the cyclone of the 16th, we had had no regular gale of wind; though the wind frequently blew very fresh with the barometer sometimes as low as 29.60. These rotary winds were circles of greater or less diameter, obeying the laws of storms and traveling along in the direction of the current, or about northeast. There was an interval of only a few hours between them, the barometer rising regularly as one circle or whirl departed and falling as the next approached. I was much struck with the exceeding regularity of the recurrence of this phenomenon. The received impression is that it is only the great gales, which we call cyclones or hurricanes that gyrate. From my observations in the Gulf Stream—and I lay in it, continuously, for something like a month, changing place, in all this time but a few hundred miles—gyration is the normal condition of the winds in this stream—that even the most gentle winds, when undisturbed by local causes—the proximity of the land, for instance—are gyrating winds, winding around and around their respective vortices *against the motion of the sun*, as we have seen the tendril of the vine to wind around the pole to which it clings.

On the third day after capturing the *Lafayette*, having chased and overhauled in the meantime a number of neutrals, we descried a large schooner, evidently American, bound to the southward and eastward. We gave chase at once, but as the schooner was to windward of us a considerable distance, the chase promised to be long without the aid of steam, and this I was averse to using, though we kept at all times banked fires in the furnaces, and warm water in the boilers. The stranger hugged his wind very closely, this being always the best point of sailing with schooners; but this was also the best point of sailing with the *Alabama*. The reader has seen that she always put on her seven-league boots when she had a chance of drawing aft the sheets of those immense trysails of hers. We gained perceptibly, but the wind was falling light, and it was to be feared night would overtake us before we could bring the chase within reach of our guns. She was still good four miles to windward of us when I resolved to try the effect of a solid shot from my rifled pivot on the forecastle. Elevating the gun some ten degrees, we let fly the bolt. It threw up the water in a beautiful jet within less than half a mile of her! It was enough. The schooner came to the wind with the Federal colors at her masthead and awaited our approach. Upon being boarded, she proved to be the *Cren-*

shaw, three days out from New York and bound for Glasgow, Scotland.

The *Crenshaw* was grain-laden, though rather small for a member of the "junk fleet," and there was the usual number of certificates and British consular seals on board of her, vouching upon good Yankee oaths that her cargo was neutral. It was amusing to see how these merchants clung to the British seal and appealed to the British power when their grain sacks were in danger. But it was all to no purpose. I would have respected scrupulously any *bona fide* neutral ownership of property, but I knew all these certificates to be fraudulent. Fraudulent as the transactions were, however, some of the shippers might have imposed upon me if they had only known how to prepare their vouchers. But they were such bunglers that they committed the most glaring mistakes. The New York merchant is a pretty sharp fellow in the matter of shaving paper, getting up false invoices, and "doing" the custom house; but the laws of nations, which had had little connection, heretofore, with the debit and credit side of his ledger, rather muddled his brain. The *Crenshaw's* certificates were precisely like so many others I had by this time over- hauled. They simply stated that the cargo belonged to "sub- jects of her Britannic Majesty" without naming them. To quote the certificates literally, they were in these terms: "The goods specified, in the annexed bill of lading were shipped on board the schooner *Crenshaw* for and on account of subjects of her Britannic Majesty, and the said goods are wholly and *bona fide* the property of British subjects." And when I came to look at the bills of lading, I found that the property was consigned *to the order of the shippers*. Here was evidently another of those "Yankee hashes" spoken of by the New York *Commercial Advertiser*; or, if it was not a Yankee hash, it was an English hash gotten up by some subjects of her Britannic Majesty, who were *resident merchants in the enemy's country*—whose property the aforesaid *Advertiser* so innocently thought was not subject to capture. For aught that appeared from the certificates, the "subjects" were all resident in New York. And so we did the usual amount of "plunder- ing" on board the *Crenshaw* and then consigned her to the flames.

From papers captured on board this vessel we learned that the New York Chamber of Commerce—whose leading spirit seemed to be a Mr. Low, one or two of whose ships, if I mistake not, I had burned—was in a glow of indignation. Its resolutions were exceedingly eloquent. This Chamber of Commerce was a sort of debating society, which by no means confined itself to mere commerce as its name would seem to imply, but undertook to regulate the affairs of the Yankee nation generally, and its members had consequently become orators. The words "privateer," "pirate," "robbery," and "plunder," and other blood-and-thunder expressions ran through their resolutions in beautiful profusion. These resolutions were sent to Mr. Seward, and that renowned statesman sat down forthwith and wrote a volume of dispatches to Mr. Adams in London about the naughty things the "British Pirate" was doing in American waters. The *Alabama*, said he, was burning everything right and left—even *British* property; would the Lion stand it?

Another set of resolutions was sent to Mr. Welles, the Federal Secretary of the Navy, and that old gentleman put all the telegraph wires in motion, leading to the different seaport towns; and the wires put in motion a number of gunboats which were to hurry off to the banks of Newfoundland and capture the *Alabama*. Whilst these gunboats were going from New York to cruise among the codfishermen and icebergs, the *Alabama* was jogging along under easy sail toward New York. We kept ourselves all the time in the track of commerce; what track the gunboats—some of which only mounted a couple of guns and would have been very shy of falling in with the *Alabama*,—took to look for us we never knew, as we did not see any of them.

On the day after capturing the *Crenshaw*, we observed in latitude 39° 47′ and longitude 68° 06′. Being near the edge of St. George's Bank off the coast of New England, we sounded with eighty-five fathoms of line but got no bottom. Here another gale of wind overtook us; the barometer descending as low as 29.33 at the height of the gale. On the next day, the 28th of October, the weather being still rough, we captured the bark *Lauretta* of which the veracious Captain Wells was master. The *Lauretta* was skirting St. George's Bank on her way to Madeira and the Mediterranean and literally ran into our arms. We had no other trouble than to heave her to with a gun as she approached, send a boat on board, and take possession of her; transferring her crew to the *Alabama* with as much dispatch as possible, and "robbing" Captain Wells, as he states—by which he means, probably, that we deprived him of his chronometer and nautical instruments; for the mere personal effects of a prisoner were never disturbed. We burned the ship.

On the next day, the weather being thick and rainy, and the *Alabama* being about two hundred miles from New York, we chased and captured the brig *Baron de Castine* from Bangor, Maine, and bound with a load of lumber to Cardenas in the island of Cuba. This vessel being old and of little value, I released her on ransom bond and sent her into New York with my prisoners, of whom I had now a large number on board. I charged the master of this ship to give my special thanks to Mr. Low of the New York Chamber of Commerce for the complimentary resolutions he had had passed in regard to the *Alabama*. The more the enemy abused me, the more I felt complimented, for it is "the galled jade only that winces." There must have been a merry mess in the cabin of the *Baron* that night, as there were the masters and mates of three burned ships. New York was all agog when the *Baron* arrived, and there was other racing and chasing after the "pirate," as I afterward learned.

The engineer having now reported to me that we had no more than about four days of fuel on board, I resolved to withdraw from the American coast, run down into the West Indies to meet my coal ship and renew my supply. Being uncertain, in the commencement of my career, as to the reception I should meet with in neutral ports, and fearing that I might have difficulty in procuring coal in the market, I had arranged, with my ever-attentive co-laborer, Captain Bulloch, when we parted off Terceira, to have a supply ship sent out to me from time to time, as I should indicate to him the rendezvous. The island of Martinique was to be the first rendezvous, and it was thither accordingly that we were now bound. This resolution was taken on the 30th of October, and shaping our course and making sail accordingly, we soon crossed the southern edge of the Gulf Stream and were in a comparatively desert track of the ocean. Our sinews were once more relaxed, and we had a few days of the *dolce far niente*. The weather became fine as we proceeded southward, and the sailors, throwing aside their woollen garments, were arrayed again in their duck frocks and trousers. Our mornings were spent in putting the ship in order preparatory to going into port and in exercising the crew at the battery, and the evenings were given up to amusement. Great inroads had been made by the continuous bad weather of the Gulf Stream on both duty and pleasure. Sometimes a week or ten days would elapse, during which it would not be possible to cast loose a heavy gun for exercise; and evening after evening passed in drenching rain and storm, when not so much as a note on the violin was heard or even a song. The men were, however, cheerful and obedient, were as much excited as ever by the chase and the capture, and were fast becoming a well-disciplined crew. If there was any of that discontent spoken of by Captain Wells, it was not visible to the eyes of the officers. Our numbers had been considerably increased by recruits from the enemy's ships, and we now had men enough to man all our guns, which added considerably to our sense of security. The young officers had gained much experience in the handling of their ship, and I began in consequence to sleep more soundly in my cot at night when the weather was dark and stormy.

On the 2d of November, when we were scarcely expecting it, we captured another of the enemy's ships. She was descried from the masthead about half-past eight in the morning, and we immediately gave chase. It was Sunday, and the muster hour coming on, we mustered the crew and read the Articles of War in the midst of the chase. We came up with the stranger about noon, with the United States colors at our peak, and upon firing a gun, the fugitive hoisted the same colors and hove to. She proved to be the *Levi Starbuck*, a whaler out of New Bedford, bound on a voyage of thirty months to the Pacific Ocean. Here was another store ship for us with plenty of provisions, slops, and small stores. Getting on board from her such articles as we stood in need of, and removing the crew, we burned her about nightfall.

Her New Bedford papers were only four days old with the latest news from the seat of war. The two armies were watching each other on the Potomac, and additional gunboats had been sent in pursuit of the *Alabama*. In the meantime, the *Alabama* was approaching another track of commerce, across which she intended to run on her way to Martinique —the track of the homeward-bound East India ships of the enemy.

Toward midnight of the 7th of November, we descried a schooner standing to the southward to which we gave chase. She had heels, as well as the *Alabama*, and when day dawned she was still some distance from us, though we had gained on her considerably. But fortune came to her rescue, for very soon a large ship looming up on the horizon like a frigate came in sight, steering to the northwest. She was under all sail with studding-sails and sky-scrapers set, and Evans, having been sent for, pronounced her "Yankee." The small craft was probably Yankee, too, but we were like a maiden choosing between lovers—we could not have both—and so we took the biggest prize, as maidens often do in a similar conjuncture. The large ship was standing in our direction, and we had nothing to do but await her approach. When she came sufficiently near to distinguish our colors, we showed her the stars and stripes, which she was apparently very glad to see, for she began, of her own accord to shorten sail as she neared us, evidently with the intention of speaking us, and getting, it might be, a welcome newspaper from home. The stars and stripes were by this time flying from her own peak. She was terribly astonished, as her master afterward confessed, when the jaunty little gunboat, which he had eyed with so much pleasure, believing her to be as good a Yankee as himself, fired a gun, and hauling down "hate's polluted rag," hoisted in its stead the banner of the Southern Republic.

The stranger had not much more to do in order to surrender himself a prisoner. His studding-sails had already been hauled down, and he now hauled his courses and backed his mainyard. We were once more in gentle airs and a smooth sea; and in a few minutes the boarding-officer was alongside of him. She proved to be as we had expected, an East India trader. She was the *T. B. Wales* of Boston, from Calcutta for Boston, with a cargo consisting chiefly of jute, linseed, and saltpeter. Of the latter, she had 1700 bags, sufficient to supply our pious Boston brethren, who were fighting for nothing but "grand moral ideas," with a considerable quantity of powder. . . . The jute, which she had on board, was intended as a substitute for cotton in some of the coarser fabrics; the Boston people being somewhat pressed at the period for the Southern staple.

The captain of the *Wales*, though a Northern man, had very few of the earmarks of the Yankee skipper about him. He was devoid of the rawbone angularity which characterizes most of them, and spoke very good English through his mouth, instead of his nose. His pronunciation and grammar were both good—quite an unusual circumstance among his class. He had been five months on his voyage, and, of course, had not heard of any such craft as the *Alabama*. He had quite a domestic establishment on board his ship, as, besides his own wife, who had accompanied him on the voyage, there was an ex-United States Consul with his wife and three small daughters returning with him as passengers to the New England States.

There was no attempt to cover the cargo of the *Wales*, and I was glad to find that it was consigned to, and probably owned by, the obnoxious house of the Barings in Boston, whose ship, the *Neapolitan*, I had burned in the Strait of Gibraltar. This British house had rendered itself exceedingly active during the war in the Federal interest, importing large quantities of arms and otherwise aiding the enemy; and I took especial pleasure, therefore, in applying the torch to its property. It was one of the New York *Commercial Advertiser's* pets—being a neutral house domiciled in an enemy's country for the purposes of trade. I have not heard what Admiral Milne and the British Minister at Washington did when they heard of the burning of the *Wales*, or whether the *Advertiser* invoked anew the protection of the British lion. A few hours sufficed to transfer the crew and passengers of the East-Indiaman to the *Alabama* and get on board from her some spars of which we were in want. It was found upon measurement that her main-yard was almost of the precise dimensions of that of the *Alabama*, and as ours had been carried away in the cyclone of the 16th of October and had only been fished for temporary use, we got down the yard from the *Wales* and brought it on board.

We treated the ladies—our first prisoners of the sex—with all due consideration, of course; but I was forced to restrict them in the matter of baggage and furniture for the want of room. I permitted them to bring on board their entire wardrobes without permitting it to be examined, but was forced to consign to the flames some fancy chairs and other articles of East India workmanship which they seemed to prize very highly. I dare say they thought hard of it at the time though I doubt not they have long since forgiven me.

Both ladies were gentle. The Consul's wife was an English-woman, the daughter of a general in the British Army serving in the *Mauritius,* where her husband had met and married her. She was refined and educated, of course, and her three little daughters were very beautiful children. Mr. George H. Fairchild—for such was her husband's name—though a New Englander, was apparently an unbigoted gentleman and observed all the gentlemanly proprieties during his stay on board my ship.

When I was arrested after the war by the Administration of President Johnson in violation of the contract which the Government had made with me at my surrender and threatened with a trial by one of those Military Commissions which have disgraced American civilization, on the trumped-up charge, among others of cruelty to prisoners, Mr. Fairchild was kind enough to write to me in prison and tender himself as a witness in my behalf. In the then state of New England feeling, with all the passions, and especially those of malignity, and hate running riot through the land, it required moral courage to do this; and I take this opportunity of thanking a New England man for obeying the instincts of a Christian and a gentleman.

It took us some time to despoil the *Wales* of such of her spars and rigging as we wanted, and it was near nightfall when we applied the torch to her. We had scarcely turned away from the burning prize when another sail was discovered in the fading twilight, but the darkness soon shutting her out from view, it was useless to attempt to chase. The *Wales* was one of the most useful of my captures. She not only served as a sort of shipyard in enabling me to repair the damages I had suffered in the Gulf Stream, but I received eight recruits from her, all of whom were fine, able-bodied seamen. My crew now numbered 110 men—120 being my full complement. I bestowed the ladies, with their husbands, upon the wardroom mess, consigning them to the care of my gallant friend Kell. Some of the lieutenants were turned out of their staterooms for their accommodation, but being carpet knights as well as knights of the lance, they submitted to the discomfort with becoming grace.

My *ménage* began now to assume quite a domestic air. I had previously captured another interesting prisoner, who was still on board—not having been released on parole. This prisoner was a charming little canary bird, which had been brought on board from a whaler in its neat gilded cage. Bartelli had the wonderful art, too, of supplying me with flowers —brought from the shore when this was practicable, and when not practicable, raised in his own tiny pots. When I would turn over in my cot in the morning for another nap in that dim consciousness which precedes awakening, I would listen in dreamy mood to the sweet notes of the canary, the pattering of the tiny feet of the children and their gleeful voices over my head; inhaling the while the scent of the geranium, or the jessamine, and forget all about war's alarms. "Home, Sweet Home" with all its charms would cluster around my imagination, and as my slumber deepened, putting reason to rest, and giving free wing to fancy, I would be clasping again the long-absent dear ones to my heart. Bartelli's shake of my cot, and his announcement that it was seven bells—half-past seven, which was my hour for rising—would often be a rude dispeller of such fancies whilst the Fairchilds were on board.

Chapter Eight—*1862*

---

*The calm belts and the trade winds . . . The arrival
of the Alabama at the island of Martinique . . . The
curiosity of the islanders to see the ship . . . A quasi-
mutiny among the crew and how it was quelled*

We captured the *Wales* on the 8th of November. On the
10th of the same month we observed in latitude 25°. We were
approaching the calm belt of Cancer. There are three of these
calm belts on the surface of the earth, and the phenomena
which they present to the eye of the seaman are very beautiful.
A ship coming out of New York, for instance, and bound
south, will first encounter the calm belt which the *Alabama*
is now approaching—that of Cancer. She will lose the wind
which has brought her to the belt and meet with light airs,
and calms, accompanied frequently by showers of rain. She
will probably be several days in passing through this region
of the doldrums, as the sailors expressively call it, continually
bracing her yards, to catch the "cat paws" that come, now
from one, and now from another point of the compass; and
making no more than twenty or thirty miles per day. As she
draws near the southern edge of the belt, she will receive the
first light breathings of the northeast trade wind. These will
increase as she proceeds farther and farther south, and she

will ere long find herself with bellying canvas in a settled trade. She will now run with this wind, blowing with wonderful steadiness and regularity until she begins to near the equator. The wind will now die away again, and the ship will enter the second of these belts—that of equatorial calms. Wending her way slowly and toilsomely through these, as she did through those of Cancer, she will emerge next into the southeast trade wind, which she will probably find somewhat stronger than the northeast trade. This wind will hurry her forward to the tropic of Capricorn in the vicinity of which she will find her third and last calm belt.

These three calm belts enclose two systems of trade winds. To understand something of these winds and the calms which enclose them, a brief reference to the atmospheric machine in which we live, and breathe, and have our being will be necessary. A philosopher of the East has thus glowingly described some of the beauties of this machine: "It is," says he, "a spherical shell which surrounds our planet to a depth which is unknown to us by reason of its growing tenuity, as it is released from the pressure of its own superincumbent mass. Its surface cannot be nearer to us than fifty, and can scarcely be more remote than five hundred miles. It surrounds us on all sides, yet we see it not; it presses on us with a load of fifteen pounds on every square inch of surface of our bodies, or from seventy to one hundred tons on us in all, and yet we do not so much as feel its weight. Softer than the softest down—more impalpable than the finest gossamer—it leaves the cobweb undisturbed and scarcely stirs the lightest flower that feeds on the dew it supplies; yet it bears the fleets of nations on its wings around the world and crushes the most refractory substances with its weight. When in motion, its force is sufficient to level the most stately forests and stable buildings with the earth—to raise the waters of the ocean into ridges like mountains and dash the strongest ship to pieces like toys.

"It warms and cools, by turns, the earth and the living creatures that inhabit it. It draws up vapors from the sea and land, retains them dissolved in itself, or suspended in cisterns of clouds, and throws them down again as rain or dew when they are required. It bends the rays of the sun from their path to give us the twilight of evening and of dawn; it disperses and refracts their various tints to beautify the approach and the retreat of the orb of day. But for the atmosphere, sun-

shine would burst on us and fail us at once, and at once remove us from midnight darkness to the blaze of noon. We
should have no twilight to soften and beautify the landscape;
no clouds to shade us from the scorching heat, but the bald
earth as it revolved on its axis would turn its tanned and
weakened front to the full and unmitigated rays of the lord of
day.

"It affords the gas which vivifies and warms our frames, and
receives into itself that which has been polluted by use and
thrown off as noxious. It feeds the flame of life exactly as it
does that of the fire. It is in both cases consumed and affords
the food of consumption—in both cases it becomes combined
with charcoal, which requires it for combustion and is removed
by it when this is over."

The first law of nature may be said to be *vis inertiæ*, and
the atmosphere thus beautifully described, following this
law, would be motionless if there were not causes outside of
itself to put it in motion. The atmosphere in motion is *wind*,
with which the sailor has so much to do, and it behooves him
to understand not only the causes which produce it but the
laws which control it. "Whence cometh the wind, and whither
goeth it?" It comes from heat, and as the sun is the father
of heat, he is the father of the winds. Let us suppose the
earth and atmosphere both to be created, but not yet the sun.
The atmosphere, being of equal temperature throughout the
earth, would be in equilibrium. It could not move in any direction, and there would not be the slightest breeze to fan the
brow. Now let us suppose the sun to be called into existence
and to begin to dart forth his rays. If he heated the earth and
the atmosphere in all parts alike, whilst there would be a
swelling of the atmosphere into greater bulk, there would still
be no motion which we could call wind. But the earth being
placed in an elliptical orbit and made to revolve around the
sun with its axis inclined to the plane in which it revolves,
now approaching and now receding from the sun, and now
having the sun in one hemisphere and now in another, the
atmosphere is not only heated differently in different parts of
the earth, but at different seasons of the year; and thus the
winds are engendered.

Let us imagine this heating process to be going on for the
first time. How we should be astonished! The atmosphere
having hitherto had no motion in our experience, we should

have conceived it as immovable as the hills and would be quite as much astonished to see it putting itself in motion, as to see the hills running away from us. But in what direction is the atmosphere now moving? Evidently from the north, and south poles toward the equator, because we know that the intertropical portions of the earth are more heated than the extratropical portions.

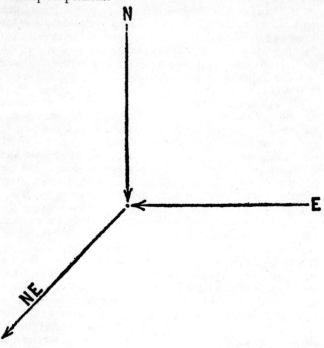

Thus far, we have not given the earth any diurnal motion around its axis. Let us give it this motion. It is revolving now from west to east at the rate of fifteen miles in a minute. If the atmosphere had been perfectly still when this motion was given to the earth, as we have supposed it to have been before the creation of the sun, the consequence would be a breeze directly from the east blowing with different degrees of strength, as it was nearer to, or further from the equator. For it is obviously the same thing whether the atmosphere stands still, and the earth revolves, or whether the earth stands still, and the atmosphere moves. In either case we have a wind.

But the atmosphere was not still when we gave the diurnal motion to the earth. There was already a breeze blowing, as we have seen, from the north and south poles towards the equator. We have thus generated two winds—a north wind and an east wind. But these two winds cannot blow in the same place at the same time; and the result will be a wind compounded of the two. Thus in the northern hemisphere we shall have a northeast wind and in the southern hemisphere we shall have a southeast wind.

These are the two trade winds, enclosed by the three calm belts which have been described to the reader. The three arrows in the diagram will illustrate the manner in which the northeast trade wind is formed by the north wind and the east wind, which our theory puts in motion.

Why it is that the trade winds do not extend all the way from the poles to the equator, but take their rise in about the thirtieth parallel of latitude, north and south, we do not know. The theory would seem to demand that they should spring up at the poles and blow continuously to the equator; in which case we should have but two systems of winds covering the entire surface of the earth. This non-conformity of the winds of the extratropical regions to our theory does not destroy it, however, but brings into the meteorological problem other and beautiful features. Having put the winds in motion our next business is to follow them and see what circuits they travel. The quantity of atmosphere carried to the equator by the northeast and southeast trade winds must find its way back whence it came in some mode or other; otherwise, we should soon have all the atmosphere drawn away from the poles and piled up at the equator. We can easily conceive this, if we liken the atmosphere to fleeces of wool and suppose an invisible hand to be constantly drawing away the fleeces from the poles and piling them up at the equator. But how to get back is the difficulty. It cannot go back on the surface of the earth within the tropics, for there is a constant surface current here toward the equator. There is but one other way, of course, in which it can go back and that is as an upper current running counter to the surface current. We may assume, indeed, we must assume, that there are two upper currents of air setting out from the equator and traveling, one of them to the 30th degree of north latitude, and the other to the 30th degree of south latitude.

What becomes of these two upper currents when they reach these parallels of latitude is not quite so certain; but there is good reason for believing that they now descend, become surface currents, and continue their journey on to the poles. It is further supposed that, when they reach the poles, they whirl about them, ascend, become upper currents again, and start back to the 30th parallel; and that when they have returned to this parallel, they descend, become a surface current again—in other words, the trade wind—and proceed to the equator as before.

But there is another and more beautiful problem still connected with these winds. It is their crossing each other at the equator, of which the proofs are so abundant that there can be but little doubt concerning it. And yet the proposition, looked at apart from the proofs, is a very startling one. One would think that when the two winds met at the equator, there would be a general intermingling and confounding of particles, and that when they ascended to form the upper currents, of which I have spoken, the northern particle would be as likely to turn back to the north as to cross the equator and go south. The figure below will illustrate the crossing. Let A represent the equator, the arrows near the surface of the circle the two trade winds, and the two cross arrows, two particles of wind in the act of crossing. The difficulty is to conceive how these particles should cross without mixing with each other and losing their identity; or why they should not turn back as well as continue their course. What law of nature is it that makes the particles of atmosphere which have come from the north pole so separate and distinct from those which have come from the south pole as to prevent the two from fusing and becoming one? Is it because the two particles, as they have gyrated around their respective poles have received a repulsive polarity? Whatever may be the reason, there can be no doubt, as remarked, that they do actually cross. One strong proof of their crossing is that we cannot conceive, otherwise, how the great atmospheric

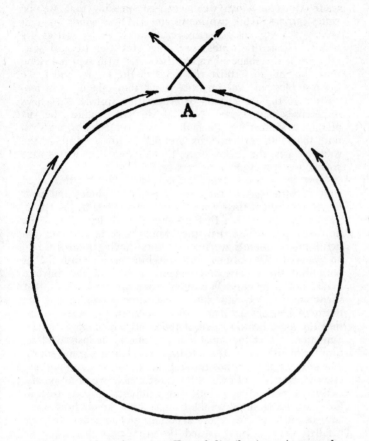

machine could perform its office of distributing rain over the earth in due proportions. The reader will recollect that there is from a fourth to a third more land than water in the northern hemisphere, and that there is from a fourth to a third more water than land in the southern hemisphere. The consequence of this unequal distribution of land and water in the two hemispheres is that the northern hemisphere requires more rain than the southern in the proportion in which it has more land to be rained upon. Now it is these mysterious trade winds of which we have been speaking that are the water carriers of the two hemispheres. These winds on their way to the equator generally reach the 30th parallel as dry winds. These dry winds, sweeping over the tropical seas, take up in the shape of vapor, the water with which in due time they are to fertilize the fields of the farmer and make the rose blossom. The quantity which they take up is in proportion to the sea surface, or evaporating surface, they have respectively passed over. Now, if we will examine the jars of these water-carriers when they reach the equator, we shall find that the northern jars are not nearly so full as the southern jars; the reason being that the northern winds have passed over less evaporating surface.

Now, if the two systems of winds with their jars thus filled were to turn back to their respective hemispheres and pour down upon them their water in the shape of rain, the consequence would be . . . that we should have less rain in the northern hemisphere than they would have in the southern hemisphere; whereas we require more, having more land to be watered. The atmospheric machine would thus be at fault. But the all-wise and beneficent ruler of the universe makes nothing faulty. We know from the evidence of that silent witness, the rain gauge, that more waters fall in the northern hemisphere than in the southern; in other words, that the more heavily laden of those jars which we examined a moment ago at the equator have come to us instead of returning to the south; the less heavily laden jars going south. The crossing of the winds thus satisfies our theory and nothing else can; which is, of course, the most conclusive of all proofs.

But we have other proofs. For a number of years past, as the East India ships would be returning home from their voyages, they would report a curious phenomenon to have befallen them as they passed the parallel of the Cape de Verde. This was the falling, or rather silting down upon their decks and rigging, of a brick dust or cinnamon-colored powder. This dust, which when rubbed between the thumb and forefinger would be impalpable, would sometimes nearly cover the entire deck and rigging. The ships would be hundreds of miles away from the land, and where could this dust come from? The fact puzzled the philosophers, but having been reported so often, it ceased to attract attention. Still it was a fact and was laid away carefully in the archives of philosophy for future use. Years passed away, and the great traveller and philosopher, Humboldt, arose to instruct and delight mankind. He traveled extensively in South America; and among other places visited the lower valley of the Orinoco. He happened there in the dry season and gives a graphic account of the wild and weird spectacle of desolation which met his eye in that season of universal drought.

All annual vegetation lay dead and desiccated on the immense pampas or plains. The earth was cracked open, gaping as it were, for rain. The wild cattle were roaming about in herds, bellowing for their accustomed food and water; many of them perishing. Even the insect world, so numerous and vivacious in all southern climates, had perished. Their tiny little organisms lay in heaps, fast disintegrating, and being reduced to powder by the scorching and baking rays of a perpendicular sun between which and the parched earth not so much as a speck of cloud appeared. The philosopher examined a number of these little organisms with his microscope. They were peculiar to the region in which he found them, and he was struck with the fact. There was another phenomenon which he observed. A number of little whirlwinds were playing their pranks about the arid waste, sporting with dead nature. These little whirlwinds, as they traveled hither and thither, would draw up into their vortices and toss high into the upper air the impalpable dust that lay everywhere and which was composed in great measure, of the decomposed and decomposing organisms of which I have spoken. The atmosphere, at times, when filled with this dust, would assume a yellowish or pale straw-colored hue.

The reader probably, by this time, sees my design of connecting the dusty remains described by Humboldt with the rain dust reported by the mariners to have fallen on the decks and rigging of their ships in the neighborhood of the Cape de Verde islands. But the "rain dust" was of brick dust or cinnamon color when collected by the masters of the ships as specimens, and the heavens, when filled with the dust thrown up by the whirlwinds as described by Humboldt, appeared to him to be of a straw color. Here is a discrepancy to be reconciled, and we must call in the aid of another philosopher, Captain M. F. Maury, later Superintendent of the National Observatory at Washington, to whom I am indebted for many of the facts here quoted. Captain Maury was struck with this discrepancy and in reconciling it with the theory here discussed makes the following statement: "In the search for spider lines, for the diaphragms of my telescopes, I procured the finest and best threads from a cocoon of a mud-red color; but the threads of this cocoon, as seen singly in the diaphragm, were of a golden color; there would seem, therefore, no difficulty in reconciling the difference between the colors of the rain dust when viewed in little piles by the microscopist, and when seen attenuated and floating in the wind by the regular traveler."

There remains but another link in the chain of evidence, to render it complete. It remains to be shown how the whirlwind dust of the valley of the lower Orinoco can be identified with the rain dust of the Cape de Verde. Ehrenberg, a German philosopher, has done this in our day. Some specimens of the rain dust having been sent him by ship captains, he brought them under his microscope, as Humboldt had done the whirlwind-dust, and to his great astonishment and delight, he found it to be the same. These facts correspond entirely with our theory of the crossing of the trade winds at the equator. The great Orinoco River disembogues near the island of Trinidad . . . in about the latitude of 9° N. The vernal equinox is the dry season here, and at this season the northeast trade wind is quite fresh. Running counter to this wind in the upper atmosphere, there is, according to our theory, a strong southwest wind blowing. Now if the reader will inspect a map, he will find that a southwest wind, starting from the mouth of the Orinoco will blow over the Cape de Verde islands. The rest is plain. The whirlwind dust is tossed high enough into the upper atmosphere to be taken in charge by the counter southwest wind, is carried to the Cape de Verde, and there silted down upon the decks and rigging of the passing ships as gently as so many snowflakes, becoming the rain dust which so long puzzled the philosophers!

We have reasoned, hitherto, on the supposition that the three calm belts, one of which the *Alabama* is now passing, and the two systems of trade winds which they enclose, are stationary within certain limits. But this is not so; the whole system of belts and winds is moved north and south as the sun passes now into one hemisphere and now into another. The calm belt of Cancer is not always in the latitude of 30° N.; nor is the calm belt of the equator always at the equator. The reader will recollect that we observed on board the *Ala-*

bama on the 10th of November in latitude 25° N. and that we were only just then entering the calm belt of Cancer. The reason is that the sun on that day was in the southern hemisphere, well advanced toward his extreme limit in that hemisphere, and that he had dragged . . . the whole system of belts and winds after him. The figures below will make this idea plain. Let the broad, dark lines in the circles represent the system of belts and winds, all in one; and in circle A let the sun be in the northern hemisphere, and in circle B let him be in the southern.

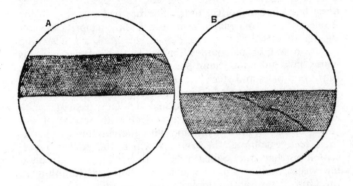

The reader will see how the sun, having hitched this system of belts and winds to his chariot wheels, has drawn it after him. The distances north and south to which they have been drawn are exaggerated in the figures, but this is only for the purpose of better illustration. The reader will see from this diagram how much farther south the *Alabama* will have to run in November to catch the northeast trade wind than she would have had to run in May. We may now return to our ship and our cruise, and when I shall mention the trade winds and the calm belts hereafter, the reader will not, I hope, regret the time I have consumed in refreshing his memory on so interesting a subject.

We spoke several English vessels after burning the *Wales*, and a couple of them bound to Demerara kept company with us through the calm belt. We sent a boat on board one of them from New York, but she had neither news nor newspapers. At length, when we had reached the parallel of about

20°, we began to receive the first gentle breathings of the trade wind. Our light sails aloft began first to belly out, and then a topsail would fill for a moment, until the ship rising on the gentle undulations of the sea and falling again, would flap the wind out of it. The zephyr—for as yet it was nothing more—visibly gained strength, however, from hour to hour, and on the 16th of November, I find the following record in my journal: "Beautiful, clear weather, with a moderate trade wind from about east by south, and the well-known fleecy trade clouds sailing leisurely over our heads."

It is Sunday and muster day, and the *Alabama* has once more been put in perfect order. She has had a coat of paint inside and out, her masts have been freshly scraped, and her rigging re-rattled and tarred down. Her guns are glistening in the new coat of composition which the gunner and his mates have put upon them; her engine room is all aglow with burnished brass and steel; her decks are white and sweet, and her awnings are spread. The muster is over, the men are lying listlessly about the decks, and our lady passengers are comfortably seated on the quarter-deck with several of the young officers around them, and with the children playing at their feet. Such was the contrast which the *Alabama* presented on that quiet Sabbath day with her former self only a few weeks back, when we had been rolling and tumbling in the Gulf Stream with crippled yards, torn sails, and her now bright sides seamed and defaced with iron rust from her corroding chains.

We were soon ready to go into port—our first port since leaving Terceira. Men and officers were all desirous of a little relaxation, and were pretty soon on the lookout for land. On the next day at two P. M., we made the island of Dominica—the same Dominica that lay so fast asleep in the gentle moonlight on the night that the little *Sumter* ran so close along it like a startled deer after her escape from the *Iroquois*. We were returning to our old cruising-ground after an interval of just one year, in a finer and faster ship, and we cared very little now about the *Iroquois* and vessels of her class. Having doubled the northeast end of Dominica during the night, at four o'clock the next morning we lowered the propeller, put the ship under steam, and ran down for the island of Martinique. We passed close enough to the harbor of St. Pierre . . . to look into it, and see that there were no men-of-war of the

enemy anchored there, and, continuing our courses, ran into
the anchorage of Fort de France and dropped our anchor at
about ten A. M.

Rear-Admiral Condé was still Governor, and I sent a lieutenant immediately to call on him and report our arrival.
He received me kindly, notwithstanding the little sharp-shoot-
ing that had passed between us in the way of official correspondence—and franked the ports of the island to me as
before. . . .

In an hour or two we had landed our prisoners; the ladies
and their husbands taking a very civil leave of us. In the course
of the afternoon our decks were crowded with curious French-
men, come off to look at the "pirate" ship of which they
had heard so much through Mr. Seward's interesting volumes
of "English Composition," called "State Papers," and the
villification and abuse of the Northern press. They were
evidently a little puzzled at finding in the *Alabama* a rather
stylish-looking ship of war with polite young officers to receive
them at the gangway and show them round the ship, instead of the disorderly privateer or pirate they had expected
to find. I could see some of these gentlemen eying me with
curiosity and with evident disappointment depicted in their
countenances, as my young officers would point me out to
them. They had come on board to see a Captain Kidd or
Blue Beard at the least, and had found only a common mortal
in no wise distinguished from the officers by whom he was
surrounded, except, perhaps, that his gray coat was a little
more faded, and his moustache a little more the color of his
coat.

The ship was surrounded with bumboats, laden with fruits
and other supplies for the sailors, and a brisk traffic was going on alongside and in the port gangway, in pipes, and
tobacco, orchata, and orange water; and, as we found as night
began to set in, in something a little stronger. We had no
marine guard on board the *Alabama*, and there was, consequently, no sentinel at the gangway in the daytime. We
were necessarily obliged to rely upon the master-at-arms and
the quartermasters, for examining all boats that came alongside, to see that no liquor was smuggled into the ship. These
petty officers were old sailors like the rest, and I have rarely
seen a sailor who could be relied upon for any purpose of
police where his brother sailor was concerned.

Whilst I was below a little after sunset, taking a cup of tea and enjoying some of the delicious fruit which Bartelli had provided for me, I heard some confusion of voices and a tramping of feet on the deck over my head; soon afterward the first lieutenant came into my cabin to tell me that there was considerable disorder in the ship. I repaired on deck immediately and saw at a glance that the crew was almost in a state of mutiny. It was evidently a drunken mutiny, however, and not very alarming. An officer had gone forward to quell some disturbance on the forecastle, when one of the sailors had thrown a belaying pin at him, and others had abused him and threatened him with personal violence. Some of the men, when directed to assist in seizing and confining their more disorderly comrades, had refused; and as I reached the deck there was a surly, sulky crowd of half-drunken sailors gathered near the foremast, using mutinous language and defying the authorities of the ship. I immediately ordered the first lieutenant to beat to quarters. The drum and fife were gotten up, and such was the effect of previous discipline upon the crew that the moment they heard the well-known beat and the shrill tones of the fife, they fell in mechanically at their guns —some of them so drunk that their efforts to appear sober were quite ludicrous.

This was what I had reckoned upon. At quarters, the officers always appeared armed as if they were going into battle. There were very few arms about the deck upon which the sailors could lay their hands—the cutlasses and pistols being kept locked up in the arm chests. Of course, I now had it all my own way—thirty armed officers being more than a match for 110 men armed with nothing but sheath knifes and belaying pins. I began now to quell the mutiny; or rather it was already quelled, and I began to bring Jack back to his senses. In company with my first lieutenant and aide-de-camp, I passed along the platoons of men as they stood at their guns, and stopping wherever I observed a drunken man, I ordered his comrades to arrest him. This was immediately done without demur in any instance, and the culprit was ironed. In this way I got as many as twenty disorderly fellows. These drunken men, the moment the attempt was made to arrest them, began to show fight and to be abusive in their language. They were, however, soon overpowered and rendered harmless. In this way I passed forward and aft two or three times, eying the

men as I passed to be certain I had gotten hold of all the
rioters.

When I had done this, I directed the mutineers to be taken
to the gangway, and calling two or three of the most active of
the quartermasters, I made them provide themselves with
draw buckets, and commencing with the most noisy and
drunken of the culprits, I ordered them to dash buckets of
water over them in quick succession. The punishment was
so evidently novel to the recipients that they were at first
disposed to deride it. With drunken gravity they would
laugh and swear by turns and tell the "bloody quartermasters" to "come on with their water, *they* were not afraid
of it." But I was quite sure of my remedy, for I had tried
it before; and as the drunken fellows would call for more
water in contempt and derision, I gratified them and caused
bucketsful to be dashed on them with such such rapidity that
pretty soon they found it difficult to catch their breath in the
intervals between the showers. The more they would struggle
and gasp for breath, the more rapidly the buckets would be
emptied upon them.

The effect was almost electric. The maudlin fellows, somewhat sobered by the repeated shocks of the cold water, began
now to swear less vociferously. In fact, they had no voice to
swear with, for it was as much as they could do to breathe.
They no longer "bloodied" the quartermasters, or called for
more water. Being reduced thus to silence, and still the water
descending upon them as rapidly as ever, with half-sobered
brain, and frames shivering with the cold, they would now
become seriously alarmed. Did the captain mean to drown
them? Was this the way he designed to punish them for
mutiny, instead of hanging them at the yardarm? They now
turned to me and begged me, for God's sake, to spare them.
If I would only let them go this time, I should never have
cause to complain of them again. I held off a little while, as
if inexorable to their prayers and entreaties, the better to impress upon them the lesson I was teaching them, and then
ordered them to be released. When their irons were taken
off, they were sober enough to go below to their hammocks
without another word and turn in like good boys! It took
me some time to get through with this operation, for I had the
delinquents—about a dozen of the most noisy—soused one
at a time. The officers and crew were all this while—some

two hours—standing at their guns, at quarters, and I could, now and then overhear quite an audible titter from some of the sober men as the drunken ones who were undergoing the shower bath would now defy my authority and now beg for mercy. When at last I had finished, I turned to my first lieutenant and told him to beat the retreat.

And this was the way I quelled my first and only mutiny on board the *Alabama*. It became a saying afterward among the sailors that "Old Beeswax was hell upon watering a fellow's grog."

Chapter Nine—*1862*

The Alabama at Martinique . . . Is blockaded by the enemy's steamer, San Jacinto . . . How she escaped the "old wagon" . . . The island of Blanquilla, the new rendezvous . . . Coaling ship . . . A Yankee skipper . . . How the officers and men amused themselves . . . The capture of the Parker Cooke, Union, and Ariel

I found . . . the *Agrippina;* she had been lying here eight days. Her master, an old Scotchman, who, like most old sailors, was fond of his grog, had been quite indiscreet in talking about his ship and her movements. Instead of pretending to have come in for water or repairs, or to hunt a market, or for something of the kind, he had frequently, when half seas-over in the coffee houses on shore, boasted of his connection with the *Alabama* and told his brother tars that that ship might be daily looked for. Eight days were a sufficient space of time for these conversations to be repeated in the neighboring islands; and as I knew that the enemy had several cruisers in the West Indies, I was only surprised that some one of them had not looked in upon the *Agrippina* before. It would not do for me to think of coaling in Mar-

141

tinique under the circumstances, and so I orderd my coal-
ship to get under way forthwith and proceed to a new
rendezvous—a small island on the Spanish Main. . . . I had
the satisfaction of seeing her get a good offing before nightfall
and knew she was safe.

It was well that I took this precaution, for on the very next
morning before I had turned out, an officer came below to inform me that an enemy's ship-of-war had appeared off the harbor! Dressing myself and going on deck, sure enough, there
was one of the enemy's large steamships lying close within
the mouth of the harbor with one of the brightest and largest
of "old flags" flying from her peak. She did not anchor lest
she should come under the twenty-four-hours' rule* but pretty
soon lowered a boat, and communicated with the authorities
on shore. It soon transpired that she was the famous *San
Jacinto*, a name which has become inseparably connected in
the American memory with one of the greatest humiliations
ever put upon the Great Republic. Wilkes, and Seward,
and the *San Jacinto* have achieved fame [in the Trent case].
They began by attempting to make a little war capital out of
John Bull and ended by singing the seven penitential
psalms; or at least as many of these psalms as could be
sung in *seven days, short meter being used*. I could not help
thinking as I looked at the old ship, of Mr. Seward's elaborate
despatch to Lord Russell . . . and of the screams of Miss
Slidell, as she had been gallantly charged by the American
marines, commanded for the occasion by an officer bearing the
proud old name of Fairfax and born in the state of Virginia!

We paid no sort of attention to the arrival of this old wagon
of a ship. She was too heavy for me to think of engaging, as
she threw more than two pounds of metal to my one—her
battery consisting of fourteen eleven-inch guns—and her crew
was more than twice as numerous as my own; but we had the
speed of her and could, of course, go to sea whenever we
pleased. I was glad, however, that I had gotten the *Agrippina*
safely out of her way as she might otherwise have been indefinitely blockaded. We remained quietly at our anchors
during the day; such of the officers visiting the shore as desired, and the stewards of the messes being all busy in laying

* By international law, the incoming enemy ship had to allow her
adversary a twenty-four-hour headstart if she anchored in a neutral port.

in a supply of fruits and other refreshments. We were in the meantime quite amused at the warlike preparations that were going on on board the *San Jacinto*. The captain of that ship, whose name, I believe, was Ronckendorff, made the most elaborate preparations for battle. We could see his men aloft, busily engaged in slinging yards, stoppering topsail sheets, getting up preventer braces, and making such other preparations, as the *Victory* or *Royal Sovereign* might have made on the eve of Trafalgar.

Poor Ronckendorff, what a disappointment awaited him! The *Alabama* was going to sea that very night. There was a Yankee merchant ship in the harbor, and just at nightfall a boat pulled out from her to the *San Jacinto* to post her, probably, as to the channels and outlets, and to put her in possession of the rumors afloat. . . .

The night set in dark and rainy. We ran up our boats, lighted our fires, and when the steam was ready, got under way, as we would have done on any ordinary occasion, except only that there were no lights permitted to be seen about the ship, and that the guns were loaded and cast loose, and the crew at quarters. In the afternoon, a French naval officer had come on board, kindly bringing me a chart of the harbor, from which it appeared that I could run out in almost any direction I might choose. I chose the most southern route, and giving my ship a full head of steam, we passed out without so much as getting a glimpse of the *San Jacinto!* The next news that we received from the States informed us that the *San Jacinto* was perfectly innocent of our escape until the next morning revealed to her our vacant place in the harbor. Her commander was even then incredulous and remained cruising off the harbor for a day or two longer, until he could satisfy himself that I had not hauled my ship up into some cunning nook or inlet and hid her away out of sight!

The next afternoon I had joined my coal ship, and we ran in to our anchorage in the little barren island of Blanquilla, off the coast of Venezuela, where we came to about nightfall. This was one of those little coral islands that skirt the South American coast, not yet fully adapted to the habitation of man. It was occasionally visited by a passing fisherman or turtler, and a few goat herds, from the mainland had come over to pasture some goats on the coarse grass. As we ran in to this anchorage, which I remembered well from having visited it once in a ship of war of the old service, I was surprised to see a Yankee whaling schooner at anchor. She was lying very close in with the beach, on which she had a tent pitched and some boilers in operation, trying out the oil from a whale which she had recently struck. The master of this little vessel, seeing us running down the island under the United States colors, came off in one of his boats to pilot us in and was apparently quite pleased to find himself on board one of his own gunboats. He told us all he had heard about the *Alabama* and went into ecstasies over our fine battery and the marvellous accounts of our speed, which some of the young men gave him, and declared that we were the very ship to "give the pirate Semmes fits."

A terrible collapse awaited him. When I had let go my anchor, I sent for him and told him who we were. That we were no less than the terrible *Alabama* herself. He stood aghast for a moment. An awful vision seemed to confront him. His little schooner, and his oil, and the various little ventures which he had on board with which to trade with the natives along the coast and turn that "honest penny," which has so many charms in the eyes of his countrymen, were all gone up the spout! And then he stood in the presence of the man whose ship he had characterized as a "pirate," and whom he had told to his face he was no better than a freebooter. But I played the magnanimous. I told the skipper not to be alarmed; that he was perfectly safe on board the *Alabama*, and that out of respect for Venezuela, within whose maritime jurisdiction we were, I should not even burn his ship. I should detain him, however, as a prisoner, for a few days to prevent his carrying news of me to the enemy until I was ready myself to depart. He gladly assented to these terms and was frequently afterward on board the ship during our stay.

We lay five days at the little island of Blanquilla, coaling ship, and getting ready for another cruise. We broke out our hold for the first time and cleansed and whitewashed it. We hoisted out our boats and rigged them for sailing; and in the afternoons, after the excessive heats had moderated a little, sailing and fishing parties were formed, and the officers had some very pleasant little picnics on shore. Fish were abundant, and on occasion of these picnics, a fine red-fish, weighing twenty pounds and more, would sometimes be found cut up and in the frying pan almost before it had ceased floundering. The crew were sent on shore on liberty, in quarter watches, taking their rifles and ammunition, and fish-spears, and fishing lines along with them. The water was as clear as crystal, and there being some beautiful bathing places along the beach, bathing became a favorite amusement. Although this coast abounds in sharks of large size, they are not found to be dangerous when there is a number of bathers enjoying the sport together. The shark is a great coward and rarely attacks a man unless it can surprise him.

My gig was a fine boat, fitted with a lug sail, and I used frequently to stretch off long distances from the land in her, enjoying her fine sailing qualities in the fresh sea breeze that would be blowing the greater part of the day. At other times I would coast the island along for miles, now putting into one little cove, and now into another, sometimes fishing, and at others hunting sea shells, and exploring the wonders of the coral banks. Pelican, gulls, plover, and sand snipe were abundant, and my boat's crew, when we would land and haul our boat up for a stroll, would sometimes make capital shots. Indeed, we generally returned on board laden with fish, game, and marine curiosities of various kinds—prominent among which would be specimens of the little coral insect and its curious manufactures. Miniature limestone trees, with their pointed branches, shrubs, fans, and a hundred other imitations of the flora of the upper world would be fished up from beneath the sparking waters, live their day of wonder, and when they had faded and lost their beauty, be thrown overboard again.

We found here flocks of the flamingo—a large bird of the crane species with long legs and bill for wading and feeding in the shallow lagoons which surround the island. Its plumage is of the most delicate pink, inclining to scarlet, and when the tall birds are drawn up in line upon a sand beach, where there is some mirage or refraction, they look not unlike a regiment of red-coated soldiers. They are quite shy, but we carried some of them on board, out of the rich plumage of which Bartelli made me some fans. Officers and men, both of whom had been long confined on board ship—it being now three months since the *Alabama* was commissioned—visibly improved in health whilst we lay in Blanquilla. The reader may recollect that we captured in the brig *Dunkirk*, a deserter from the *Sumter*. We had tried him by court-martial before reaching Martinique and sentenced him to serve out his term under certain penalties. At Martinique, we found him a chief spirit among the mutineers whose grog I had "watered" as described in the last chapter. Another court now sat upon his case, and in obedience to its sentence, the fellow was turned upon the beach at Blanquilla with bag and hammock. This worthy citizen of the Great Republic joined the Yankee whaling schooner and went into more congenial company and pursuits.

Having finished our coaling and made the other preparations necessary for sea, I dispatched my coal ship, which had still another supply of coal left, to another rendezvous—the Arcas Islands in the Gulf of Mexico, and gave the Yankee schooner leave to depart, telling the master to make a free sheet of it and not let me catch him on the high seas, as it might not be so well for him a second time. He took me at my word, had all the sail on his little craft in the twinkling of an eye, and I question whether he stopped this side of Nantucket.

My object in running into the Gulf of Mexico was to strike a blow at Banks' expedition, which was then fitting out for the invasion of Texas. This gentleman, who had been a prominent Massachusetts politician, but who had no sort of military talent, had risen to the surface with other scum, amid the bubbling and boiling of the Yankee caldron, and was appointed by "Honest Abe" to subjugate Texas. Banks had mounted a stud-horse on Boston Common on militia-review days before the war, and had had himself lithographed, stud-horse, cocked hat, feathers, and all, and these were credentials not to be despised. I had learned from captured Northern papers that he was fitting out at Boston and New York a large expedition to consist of not less than 30,000 men. A large proportion of this army was to consist of cavalry and light artillery. To transport such an army, a large number of transport ships would be required. The expedition was to rendezvous at Galveston, which the enemy had captured from us not a great while before.

As there were but twelve feet of water on the Galveston bar, very few of these transport ships would be able to enter the harbor; the great mass of them, numbering perhaps a hundred and more, would be obliged to anchor pell-mell in the open sea. Much disorder, and confusion would necessarily attend the landing of so many troops, encumbered by horses, artillery, baggage wagons, and stores. My design was to surprise this fleet by a night attack, and if possible destroy it, or at least greatly cripple it. The Northern press, in accordance with its usual habit, of blabbing everything, had informed me of the probable time of the sailing of the expedition, and I designed so to time my own movements, as to arrive simultaneously with the stud-horse and the major-general, or at least a day or two afterward.

It was to be presumed, of course, that some of the enemy's gunboats would accompany the expedition, but I hoped to be able to fall so unexpectedly upon their convoy, as to find them off their guard. There was no Confederate cruiser in the Gulf, and I learned from the enemy's own paper that the *Alabama* was *well on her way to the coast of Brazil and the East Indies*. The surprise would probably be complete in the dead of night, and when the said gunboats of the enemy would be sleeping in comparative security with but little, if any, steam in their boilers. Half an hour would suffice for any purpose of setting fire to the fleet, and it would take the gunboats half an hour to get up steam and their anchors to pursue me.

It was with this object in view that we were now getting under way from the island of Blanquilla. But the Banks' expedition would not arrive off Galveston, probably, before about the 10th of January, and as we were now only in the latter days of November, I had several weeks on my hands before it would become necessary for me to proceed to my new rendezvous. I resolved to devote this interval to the waylaying of a California treasure steamer, as a million or so of dollars in gold deposited in Europe would certainly aid me in my operations upon the sea. I could purchase several more *Alabamas* to develop the nautical enterprise of our people and assist me to scourge the enemy's commerce.

There were two routes by which the California steamers returned from Aspinwall [the eastern terminus of the railroad across the isthmus of Panama]—one by the east end of Cuba, and the other by the west end. I chose the former for my ambuscade, as being probably the most used. To reach my new cruising ground, I put my ship under sail and made a detour by the way of the islands of Puerto Rico and St. Domingo, passing through the Mona Passage, through which much of the West India commerce of the enemy passed, with the hope of picking up something by the way. We left our anchorage at Blanquilla on the 26th of November and made the island of Puerto Rico on the morning of the 29th. We coasted along the south side of this island with a gentle breeze and smooth sea, sufficiently near to enjoy its fine bold scenery, passing only a couple of sail during the day—one a large French steamer bound to the eastward, and the other an English bark. We showed them the United States colors. The bark saluted the "old flag" by striking her colors to it, but the "old flag" did not return the salute, as it was hoisted at the wrong peak. The Englishman must have thought his Yankee friend rather discourteous.

We entered the Mona Passage, lying between St. Domingo and Puerto Rico, after nightfall, but the moon was shining sufficiently bright to enable us to get hold of the small islands of Mona and Desecho, and thus grope our way in safety. The currents in this strait being somewhat uncertain, the navigation is treacherous when the weather is dark. Early on the next morning, we were off the Bay of Samana and were running with a flowing sheet along the coast of St. Domingo. I had approached the Mona Passage with much caution, fully expecting to find so important a throughfare guarded by the enemy, but there was nothing in the shape of a ship of war to be seen. The enemy was too busy blockading the Southern coasts to pay much attention to his commerce. In the course of the morning, we boarded a Spanish schooner from Boston, bound for the old city of St. Domingo, from which we received a batch of late newspapers giving us still further accounts of the preparation of the Banks' expedition, about which all New England seemed just then to be agog.

The great Massachusetts leader had been given *carte blanche*, and he was making the best possible use of it. He was fitting himself out very splendidly, but his great expedition resembled rather one of Cyrus' or Xerxes' than one of Xenophon's. The Boston papers dilated upon the splendid bands of music, the superb tents, the school-marms, and the relays of stud-horses that were to accompany the hero of Boston Common. But the best feature of the expedition was the activity and thrift which had suddenly sprung up in all the markets of New England, in consequence. The looms, spindles and the shoemakers' awls were in awful activity. In short, every man or boy who could whittle a stick, whittled it, and sold it to the Government. The whalemen in New Bedford, Nantucket, and Martha's Vineyard were in especial glee. They were selling all their whaling ships, which were too old, or too rotten for further service, to the Government for transports at enormous prices. Many a bluff old whaler that had rode out a gale under the lee of an iceberg at the Navigators' Islands or scraped her keel on Coromandel's coast forty years before, was patched and caulked and covered over with pitch and paint, and sold to an ignorant, if not corrupt, army quartermaster for as good as "bran new." No wonder the war was popular in New England. There was not only Negro in it, but there was money in it also.

Filling away from the Spanish schooner, which we requested to report us in St. Domingo as the United States steamer *Iroquois*, we continued our course down the island. It was Sunday, and the day was fine. The crew was dressed as usual for muster, and what with the ship in her gala dress of awnings and glitter of bright-work, the island, the sea, and the weather, a more beautiful picture could not well have been presented to the beholder. In the distance were the blue and hazy hills, so fraught with the memories of Columbus and the earlier Spanish explorers. Nearer to, was the old town of Isabella, the first ever built in the New World by civilized men, and nearer still was the bluff, steep, rock-bound coast, against which the most indigo of seas was breaking in the purest and whitest of foam. The sailors had thrown themselves upon the deck in groups, each group having its reader, who was reading aloud to attentive listeners the latest war-news as gleaned from the papers we had received from the Spanish schooner; and the officers, through whose hands the said newspapers had already passed, were smoking and chatting, now of Columbus, and now of the war. Presently the shrill cry of "Sail ho!" came ringing from aloft; and the scene on board the *Alabama* shifted almost as magically as it does in a theater. Every man sprang to his feet without waiting for an order; the newspapers were stuck away in cracks and crannies; the helm was shifted to bring the ship's head around to the proper point for chasing, and studding-sails and kites were given simultaneously to the wind.

When we began to raise the spars and sails of the chase above the sea from the deck, there was a general exclamation of "Yankee!" The tapering royal and sky-sail masts with the snowiest of canvas told the tale, as they had told it so often before. A run of a few hours more brought us up with the American bark *Parker Cooke* of and from Boston, bound to Aux Cayes on the south side of the island of St. Domingo. If the *Cooke* had been chartered and sent out for our especial benefit, the capture could not have been more opportune. The *Alabama's* commissariat was beginning to run a little low, and here was the *Cooke* provision-laden. We had found, by experience in the *Sumter*, that our Boston friends put up the very best of crackers and ship bread, and sent excellent butter, and cheese, salted beef, pork, and dried fruits to the West India markets; nor were we disappointed on the present occasion. Both ships were now hove to under short sail within convenient boating distance, and the rest of the day was consumed in transporting provisions from the prize. It was sunset before we concluded our labors, and at the twilight hour, when the sea breeze was dying away, and all nature was sinking to repose, we applied the torch to the *Cooke*. . . .

We began now to receive some returns of the effect of our late captures upon Northern commerce. The papers captured on board the *Cooke* were full of lamentations. Our pious brethren did not confine themselves to the forms set down by Jeremiah, however, but hissed their execrations through teeth grinding with rage. . . .

The *Parker Cooke* made a beautiful bonfire, lighting up the sea and land for leagues; and as the wind continued light, it was near midnight before we had run it below the horizon. Before morning we gave chase to another sail, but at daylight, by which time we were within a couple of miles of her, she showed us the Spanish colors. We chased and overhauled soon afterward a Dutch galliot, and later in the day, a Spanish bark. The land was still in sight on our port beam, and toward nightfall we passed Cape François.

Between midnight and dawn on this same night, we had quite an alarm. A large ship-of-war came suddenly upon us in the darkness! Like ourselves she was running down the coast, but she was under both steam and sail, having her studding-sails set on both sides, whereas the *Alabama* was entirely without steam, with her propeller triced up. If the stranger had been an enemy, we should have been almost entirely at her. mercy. The reader may imagine, therefore, how anxious I was for the next few minutes. She soon dispelled my fears, however, for she passed rapidly on, at no greater distance from us than a hundred yards, her lights lighting up the countenances of my men as they stood at their guns—for by this time I had gotten them to their quarters. . . . She did not take the least notice of us or swerve a hair's-breadth from her course. I knew, from this, she could not be an enemy, and told my first lieutenant, even before she had well passed us, that he might let his men leave their guns. She was probably a Spanish steam frigate on her way to the island of Cuba.

On the evening of the 2d of December, we passed the little island of Tortuga, so famous in the history of the buccaneers and pirates who once infested these waters, and on the next day found ourselves in the passage between St. Domingo and Cuba. There were many sails passing in different directions, all of which we overhauled, but they proved to be neutral. Here was another important thoroughfare of the enemy's commerce entirely unguarded. There was not only no ship-of-war of the enemy to be seen, but none of the neutrals that I had spoken had fallen in with any. We had, therefore, a clear sea before us for carrying out our design of waylaying a California steamer. In the afternoon, we stretched over to the east end of Cuba and took our station in watch and wait.

On the same night we chased and overhauled a French bark. The sea was smooth, and a bright moon shining. The chase paid no attention to our blank cartridge, though we were close on board of her, and stood a shot before she would come to the wind. As we threw this purposely between her masts and pretty close over the heads of her people, she came to the conclusion that it would not be safe to trifle longer and rounded to and backed her main yard. When asked by the boarding-officer why he did not heave to at the first signal, the master replied naively that he was a Frenchman and at war with nobody! Philosophical Frenchman!

We had accurate timetables of the arrivals and departures of the California steamers in the files of the New York papers that we had captured, and by these tables the homeward-bound steamer would not be due for a few days yet. We spent this interval in lying off and on the east end of Cuba under easy sail, chasing more or less during the day, but without success, all the vessels overhauled being neutrals, and closing in with Cape Maize during the night and holding on to its very brilliant light until morning. The weather was clear, and the moon near her full, so that I had almost as good a view of the passage by night as by day.

On the 5th of December, a prize ran into our arms without the necessity of a chase. It was a Baltimore schooner called the *Union*, old and of little value She had, besides, a neutral cargo properly documented for a small town called Port Maria on the north side of Jamaica. I transferred the prisoners of the *Cooke* to her and released her on ransom-bond. My original orders were not to capture Maryland vessels, but that good old state had long since ceased to occupy the category in which our Congress and the Executive had placed her. She was now ranged under the enemy's flag, and I could make no discrimination in her favor.

On the next day the California steamer was due, and a very bright lookout was kept; a number of the young officers volunteering their services for the occasion. In the transparent atmosphere of this delightful climate we could see to great distances. The west end of St. Domingo, about Cape Tiburon, was visible, though distant ninety miles. But not so much as a smoke was seen during the entire day, and the sun went down upon disappointed hopes. The next day was Sunday, and the holy stones had been busy over my head during all the morning watch, putting the decks in order for muster. I had turned out and dressed, and swept the entire horizon with my telescope without seeing anything to encourage me. The crew had breakfasted, and the word, "All hands clean yourselves, in white frocks and trousers for muster!" had been growled out by the boatswain and echoed by his mates. The decks were encumbered with clothes bags, and Jack was arraying himself as directed. I had gone down to my own breakfast and was enjoying one of Bartelli's cups of good coffee, hopeless for that day of my California steamer and my million dollars in gold. Suddenly the prolonged cry of "S-a-i-l h-o!" came ringing in a clear musical voice from aloft; the lookout having at length descried a steamer, and being anxious to impart the intelligence in as emphatic a manner as possible to the startled listeners on the deck below. The "Where-away?" of the officer of the deck, shouted through his trumpet, followed, and in a moment more came the rejoinder, "Broad on the port bow, sir!" "What does she look like?" again inquired the officer of the deck. "She is a large steamer, brig-rigged,

sir!" was the reply. An officer now came below to announce
to me what I had already heard.

Here was a steamer at last, but unfortunately she was not in
the right direction, being in the northwest instead of the
southeast—the latter being the direction in which the California steamer should appear. All was excitement now on
deck. The engineers and firemen were set at work in great
haste to get up their steam. The sailors were hurried with
their cleaning, and the bags stowed away. "All hands work
ship!" being called, the first lieutenant took the trumpet, and
furled the sails, making a "snug roll-up of it," so that they
might hold as little wind as possible, and lowered the propeller. In twenty minutes we were ready for the chase, with
every thing snug alow and aloft, and with the steam hissing
from the gauge cocks. The strange steamer came up very
rapidly, and we scrutinized her anxiously to see whether she
was a ship of war or a packet ship. She showed too much
hull out of water to be a ship of war, and yet we could not
be sure, as the enemy had commissioned a great many packet
steamers and put heavy armaments on board of them. When
she was within three or four miles of us, we showed her the
United States colors, and she responded in a few minutes by
hoisting the same. Like ourselves, she had her sails furled
and was carrying a very large "bone in her mouth" under
steam alone.

We could now see that she was fast, and from the absence
of guns at her sides, a packet ship. I now put my ship in
motion with a view to lay her across the stranger's path as
though I would speak her. But I missed doing this by about a
couple of ship's lengths, the stranger passing just ahead of me.
A beautiful spectacle presented itself as I passed under the
stern of the monster steamship. The weather was charming,
there being a bright, clear sky with only a few fleecy trade-
clouds passing. There was just enough of the balmiest and
gentlest of winds to ruffle without roughening the surface of
the sea. The islands of Cuba, St. Domingo, and Jamaica—
the two latter, in the blue and hazy distance, and the former
robed in the gorgeous green known only to the tropics—were
in sight. The great packet steamer had all her awnings set,
and under these awnings on the upper deck, was a crowd of
passengers, male and female. Mixed with the male passengers were several officers in uniform, and on the forward deck,

there were groups of soldiers to be seen. This crowd presented a charming picture, especially the ladies, most of whom were gayly dressed, with the streamers from their bonnets, their veils, and their waist ribbons flirting with the morning breeze. We were sufficiently close to see the expression of their countenances. Many of them were viewing us with opera glasses, evidently admiring the beautiful proportions, fine trim, and general comeliness of one of their own gunboats —for we were wearing still the United States flag.

As I passed the wake of the steamer, I wheeled in pursuit, fired a blank cartridge, and hauling down the Federal, threw the Confederate flag to the breeze. It was amusing to witness the panic which ensued. If that old buccaneer Blue Beard himself had appeared, the consternation could not have been greater. The ladies screamed—one of those delightful, dramatic screams, half fear, half acting, which can only ascend from female voices—and scampered off the deck in a trice; the men running after them and making quite as good, if not better time. The effect of my gun and change of flags on the steamer herself seemed to be scarcely less electric. She had no intention, whatever, of obeying my command to halt. On the contrary, I could see from the increased impetus with which she sprang forward, and the dense volumes of black smoke that now came rushing and whirling from her smokestack that she was making every possible effort to escape. She had gotten a little the start of me, as I was wheeling to pursue her, and might be now some three or four hundred yards distant. . . .

We had not stretched a mile, when it became quite evident that the stranger had the heels of me, and that if I would capture her, I must resort to force. I ordered my "persuader," as the sailors called my rifled bow-gun, to be cleared away, and sent orders to the officer to take aim at the fugitive's foremast, being careful to throw his shot high enough above the deck not to take life. When the gun was ready to be fired, I yawed the ship a little, though the effect of this was to lose ground, to enable the officer the better to take his aim. A flash, a curl of white smoke, and a flying off of large pieces of timber from the steamer's mast, were simultaneous occurrences. It was sufficient. The mast had not been cut quite away, but enough had been done to satisfy the master of the steamer that he was entirely within our power, and that prudence would be the better part of valor. In a moment after, we could see a perceptible diminution in the motion of the walking-beam, and pretty soon the great wheels of the steamer ceased to revolve, and she lay motionless on the water.

We slowed down our own engines and began to blow off steam at once, and ranging up alongside of the prize, sent a boat on board of her. It was thus we captured the steamer *Ariel*, instead of going to muster on Sunday, the 7th of December, 1862. But Fortune, after all, had played us a scurvy trick. The *Ariel* was indeed a California steamer, but instead of being a homeward-bound steamer with a million dollars in gold in her safe, I had captured an outward-bound steamer with five hundred women and children on board! This was an elephant I had not bargained for, and I was seriously embarrassed to know what to do with it. I could not take her into any neutral port even for landing the passengers, as this was forbidden . . . and I had no room for the passengers on board the *Alabama*. The most I could hope to do was to capture some less valuable prize within the next few days, turn the passengers of the *Ariel* on board of her, and destroy the steamer. Our capture, however, was not without useful results. The officers and soldiers mentioned as being on board of her were a battalion of marines going to the Pacific to supply the enemy's ships of war on that station. There were also some naval officers on board for the same purpose. These were all *paroled* and deprived of their arms. The rank and file numbered 140.

When my boarding-officer returned, he reported to me that there was a great state of alarm among the passengers on board. They had been reading the accounts which a malicious, and mendacious Northern press had been giving of us, and took us to be no better than the "plunderers," and "robbers" we had been represented to be. The women, in particular, he said, were, many of them, in hysterics, and apprehensive of the worst consequences. I had very little sympathy for the terrors of the males, but the tear of a woman has always unmanned me. And as I knew something of the weakness of the sex, as well as its fears, I resorted to the following stratagem to calm the dear creatures. I sent for my handsomest young lieutenant—and I had some very handsome young fellows on board the *Alabama*—and when he had come to me, I told him to go below, and array himself in his newest and handsomest uniform, buckle on the best sword there was in the wardroom, ask of Bartelli the loan of my brightest sword knot, and come up to me for his orders. Sailors are rapid dressers, and in a few minutes my lieutenant was again by my side, looking as bewitching as I could possibly desire. I gave him my own boat, a beautiful gig that had been newly painted, and which my coxswain, who was a bit of a sea dandy, had furnished with scarlet cushions and fancy yoke and steering ropes, and directed him to go on board the *Ariel* and coax the ladies out of their hysterics.

"Oh! I'll be sure to do that, sir," said he, with a charming air of coxcombry. "I never knew a fair creature who could resist me more than fifteen minutes." As he shoved off from the side in my beautiful little cockleshell of a boat with its fine-looking, lithe and active oarsmen bending with the strength of athletes to their ashen blades, I could but pause a moment myself in admiration of the picture.

A few strokes of his oars put him alongside of the steamer, and asking to be shown to the ladies' cabin, he entered the scene of dismay and confusion. So many were the signs of distress, and so numerous the wailers, that he was abashed for a moment, as he afterward told me, with all his assurance. But summoning courage, he spoke to them about as follows: "Ladies! The Captain of the *Alabama* has heard of your distress and sent me on board to calm your fears by assuring you that you have fallen into the hands of Southern gentlemen under whose protection you are entirely safe. We are by no means the ruffians and outlaws that we have been represented by your people, and you have nothing whatever to fear." The sobs ceased as he proceeded, but they eyed him askance for the first few minutes. As he advanced in their midst, however, they took a second and more favorable glance at him. A second glance begat a third more favorable still, and when he entered into conversation with some of the ladies nearest him—picking out the youngest and prettiest, as the rogue admitted—he found no reluctance on their part to answer him. In short, he was fast becoming a favorite. The ice being once broken, a perfect avalanche of loveliness soon surrounded him, the eyes of the fair creatures looking all the brighter for the tears that had recently dimmed them.

Presently a young lady, stepping up to him, took hold of one of the bright buttons that were glittering on the breast of his coat and asked him if he would not permit her to cut it off as a memento of her adventure with the *Alabama.* He assented. A pair of scissors was produced, and away went the button! This emboldened another lady to make the same request, and away went another button; and so the process went on, until when I got my handsome lieutenant back, he was like a plucked peacock—he had scarcely a button to his coat! There were no more Hebes drowned in tears on board the *Ariel.*

But what struck my young officer as very singular was the deportment of the male passengers. Some of these seemed to be overhauling their trunks in a great hurry, as though there were valuables in them which they were anxious to secrete. Their watches, too, had disappeared from some of their vest-pockets. "I verily believe," said he, as he was giving me an account of the manner in which he performed his mission, "that these fellows think we are no better than the Northern thieves who are burning dwelling houses and robbing our women and children in the South!"

I take pleasure in contrasting in these memoirs the conduct of my officers and crew, during the late war, in the uniform respect which they paid to the laws of war and the dictates of humanity, with that of some of the generals and colonels of the Federal Army who debased our common nature and disgraced the uniforms they wore by brutality and pilferings. There were 500 passengers on board the *Ariel.* It is fair to presume that each passenger had with him a purse of from three to five hundred dollars. Under the laws of war, all this money would have been good prize. But not one dollar of it was touched, or indeed so much as a passenger's baggage examined.

I carried out my intention of keeping the *Ariel* in company with me for two or three days, hoping that I might capture some less valuable ship into which to turn her passengers that I might destroy her. I was very anxious to destroy this ship as she belonged to a Mr. Vanderbilt of New York, an old steamboat captain who had amassed a large fortune in trade and was a bitter enemy of the South. Lucrative contracts during the war had greatly enhanced his gains, and he had ambitiously made a present of one of his steamers to the Federal Government, to be called after him, to pursue "rebel pirates."

Failing to overhaul another ship of the enemy in the few days that I had at my disposal, I released the *Ariel* on ransom bond and sent her and her large number of passengers on their way rejoicing. I found Captain Jones of the *Ariel* a clever and well-informed gentleman, and I believe he gave a very fair account of the capture of his ship when he reached New York. He pledged me that Vanderbilt's ransom bond, which he signed as his agent, would be regarded as a debt of honor. The bond is for sale, cheap, to any one desiring to redeem Mr. Vanderbilt's honor.

Chapter Ten—*1862*

The Alabama is disabled and stops to repair her machinery . . . Proceeds to her new rendezvous, the Arcas Islands, and thence to Galveston . . . Combat with the United States Steamer Hatteras

The *Alabama* was disabled for two or three days by an accident which occurred to her engine—the giving way of one of the valve castings. I was, in consequence, obliged to withdraw from the tracks of commerce and lie as perdue as possible until the damage could be repaired. For this purpose, I ran close in with the land, on the north side of the island of Jamaica, where, with the exception of an occasional fishing boat and a passing coasting sloop, nothing was to be seen. Mr. Freeman, my chief engineer, was a capital machinist, and a man of great fertility of resource, and he went to work at once to remedy the mishap. Nothing but the puffing of the bellows, the clinking of the hammer on the anvil, and the rasping of files was heard now for forty-eight hours. At the end of this time the engine was again in order for service. But we should have no occasion to use it for some days yet.

It was now the 12th of December, and it was time for us to begin to think of running into the Gulf of Mexico in pursuit of General Banks. Accordingly we put the ship under sail

and ran along down the island of Jamaica to the west end.
Hence we stretched over into the other track of the California steamers returning to the United States by the west
end of Cuba; intending to follow this track as far as Cape San
Antonio, hoping that we might stumble upon something by
the way. The California steamer was not now my principal object, however, but only an incident to my Mexican Gulf
scheme. I did not design to waste time upon her. Whilst
pursuing our way leisurely along this track, we experienced a
most singular series of bad weather. We took an old-fashioned norther, which lasted us three days and blew us well
down into the Gulf of Honduras. Here we became the sport
of a variety of currents—setting generally to the westward,
but sometimes in a contrary direction. We sighted some of
the islands lying parallel with the coast, but being anxious to
get forward did not touch at any of them. As we drew out of
the Gulf of Honduras, we again crossed the track of the California steamers, but fortune continued adverse, and none came
along. A delay of a week or two here might enable me to pick
up one of these treasure steamers, but this would interfere with
my designs against Banks, and I forbore.

On the 20th of December we made the Mexican province of
Yucatan, and just before nightfall got hold of Cape Catoche.
My landfall was a very happy one, though, owing to the bad
weather, I had had no observation for thirty-six hours.
I sounded soon after dark in twenty-eight fathoms of water,
and being quite sure of my position, ran into the Yucatan
passage by the lead, the night being too dark to permit us to
discern anything. The coast is clean, and the soundings
regular, and I felt my way around the Cape without the least
difficulty, finding myself the next morning in the Gulf of
Mexico, running off to the westward with a free wind. The
water was of a chalky whiteness, a little tinged with green,
resembling the water on the Bahama Banks, and we ran along
in a depth of twenty fathoms the entire day, scarcely varying
a foot. I had accomplished my object thus far with perfect
success. I had not sighted a sail since leaving the west end
of Jamaica which could report me, and had entered the Gulf
of Mexico by night, unseen of any human eye on the land
or the sea. On the day after entering the Gulf, we did pass a
solitary sail—a large steamer—steering in the direction of
Havana, but she was hull down and could make nothing of

us. She may have been an enemy, but was probably a French
ship of war or transport from Vera Cruz; the French expedition that culminated in the death of the unfortunate Maximilian having landed in Mexico about a year before, and
there being much passing of steamships between France and
Vera Cruz.

On the 22d of December, night overtaking us within about
twenty miles of the Arcas, we anchored in twenty fathoms of
water in the open sea. The Yucatan coast is like that of
West Florida and the Guianas. It is a continuous harbor, a
ship being able to hold on to her anchors in the heaviest gale.
Getting under way the next morning, we continued on our
course and pretty soon made a bark standing in the same
direction with ourselves. It was our old friend, the *Agrippina*,
with her bluff bows and stump top-gallant masts. She had
been all this time making her way hither from Blanquilla—a
period of nearly four weeks; the incorrigible old Scotch captain having stopped on his way to refresh his crew and do
a little private trading. However, he was in good time, and so,
letting him off with a gentle reprimand, we ran in to the
Arcas together and anchored at about five o'clock in the afternoon.

We remained at these little islands a week, coaling ship,
and refitting and repainting. We could not have been more
thoroughly out of the world if we had been in the midst of the
great African desert. A Robinson Crusoe here might have
had it all to himself; and to give color to the illusion, we
found on one of the islands a deserted hut, built of old boards
and pieces of wreck, with an iron pot or two, and some pieces
of sail cloth lying about. An old dugout, warped and cracked
by the sun, lay hauled up near the hut, and a turtle net in
pretty good repair was found stowed away in one corner of
Crusoe's abode. But what had become of the hermit who once
inhabited these desolate little coral islands, over which the
wild sea bird now flew and screamed in undivided dominion?
An humble grave, on the headboard of which had been rudely
carved with a knife, a name and a date, told the brief and
mournful story. A companion had probably laid the hermit
away and departed. A more fitting burial place for a sailor
could not well be conceived; for here the elements with which
he was wont to battle had full sweep, and his requiem was
sung without ceasing by the booming wave that shook and

rocked him in his winding sheet of sand when the storm raged.

The islands are three in number, lying in a triangle. They are surrounded by deep water, and it is probably not a great many years since the little stone mason of the sea, the coralline insect, first brought them to the surface, for the only vegetation as yet on any of them is a carpet of sea kale on the largest of them, and a stunted bush or two. In the basin in the center of the triangle, the *Alabama* is anchored, and so pellucid is the water that not only her anchor, which lies in seven fathoms, is visible from stock to fluke, but all the wonders of the coral world lie open to inspection; with the turtle groping about amid the sea fern, the little fishes feeding, or sporting, and madrepore and sponges lying about in profusion. Bartelli drew up from this submarine forest one of the largest of the latter, and having cured it in the sun and rendered it sweet by frequent ablution transferred it to my bathroom. The naturalist would have revelled at the Arcas in viewing the debris of sea shells, and coral, and the remains of stranded fish that lay strewn along the beach; and in watching the habits of the gannet, man-of-war bird, and a great variety of the sea gull, all of which were laying and incubating. As the keel of one of our boats would grate upon the sand, clouds of these birds would fly up and circle around our heads, screaming in their various and discordant notes at our intrusion. Beneath our feet, the whole surface of the islands was covered with eggs, or with young birds in various stages of growth. Here, as at Blanquilla, all our boats were hoisted out and rigged for sailing; and fishing and turtling parties were sent out to supply the crew, and in the evening sailing and swimming matches and target shooting took place. This was only the byplay, however, whilst the main work of the drama was going forward, viz., the coaling and preparation of the *Alabama* for her dash at the enemy.

Our upper deck had again become open and required recaulking; and some patching and refitting was necessary to be done to the sails. As we wanted our heels to be as clean as possible, we careened the ship, and gave her copper a good scrubbing below the waterline, where it had become a little foul. Having taken all the coal out of the *Agrippina*, we ballasted her with the coral rock which we found lying abundantly at our hands, watered her from the *Alabama*, and gave her sailing orders for Liverpool. She was to report to Captain Bulloch for another cargo of coal to be delivered at another rendezvous. . . . During the week that we lay at the Arcas, there had evidently been several gales of wind at work around us, though none of them had touched us. On two or three occasions, when the wind was quite light, and the sky clear overhead, a heavy sea was observed to be breaking on the northern shores of the islands. There is no doubt that on these occasions there were northers prevailing along the Mexican coast. I was led hence to infer that these terrible gales do not extend as a general rule a great distance seaward from that coast. We were very little more than a hundred miles from Vera Cruz, which is in the track of these terrible storms, and yet we had only felt the pulsations of them, as it were; the huge breakers on the Arcas beating time in a still atmosphere to the storm which was raging at Vera Cruz. It was seventeen days from the time we doubled Cape Catoche until we left the Arcas. During all this time, we were off the coast of Yucatan, the season was near mid-winter, and yet we had not had a norther. Along the Mexican coast from Tampico to Vera Cruz at this season of the year the usual interval between these gales is from three to five days.

The Banks' expedition was expected to rendezvous at Galveston on the 10th of January. On the 5th of that month we got under way from the Arcas, giving ourselves five days in which to make the distance under sail. Our secret was still perfectly safe, as only a single sail had passed us whilst we lay at anchor, and she at too great a distance to be able to report us. We had an abundant supply of coal on board, the ship was in excellent trim, and as the sailors used to say of her at this period, could be made to do everything but talk. My crew were well drilled, my powder was in good condition, and as to the rest, I trusted to luck, and to the "creek's not being too high." The weather continued fine throughout our run, and on the 11th at noon—having been delayed a day by a calm—we observed in latitude 28° 51′ 45″ and longitude 94° 55′, being just thirty miles from Galveston. I now laid my ship's head for the Galveston lighthouse, and stood in, intending to get a distant sight of the Banks' fleet before nightfall, and then haul off and await the approach of night before I ran in and made the assault.

I instructed the man at the masthead to keep a very bright

lookout and told him what to look out for, viz., an immense
fleet anchored off a lighthouse. The wind was light, and the
afternoon was pretty well spent before there was any sign from
the masthead. The lookout at length cried, "Land ho! Sail
ho!" in quick succession, and I already began to make sure of
my game. But the lookout, upon being questioned, said he did
not see any fleet of transports, but only five steamers which
looked like ships of war. Here was a damper! What could have
become of Banks and his great expedition, and what was this
squadron of steam ships-of-war doing here? Presently a shell,
thrown by one of the steamers, was seen to burst over the city.
"Ah, ha!" exclaimed I to the officer of the deck who was
standing by me, "there has been a change of program here.
The enemy would not be firing into his own people, and we
must have recaptured Galveston since our last advices." "So
it would seem," replied the officer. And so it turned out. In
the interval between our leaving the West Indies and arriving
off Galveston, this city had been retaken by General Magruder,
assisted by a gallant seaman of the merchant service, Captain
Leon Smith. Smith, with a couple of small river steamers
protected by cotton bags and having a number of sharp-
shooters on board, assaulted and captured, or drove to sea
the enemy's entire fleet, consisting of several heavily armed
steamships.

The recapture of this place from the enemy changed the
destination of the Banks' expedition. It rendezvoused at New
Orleans, whence General Banks afterward attempted the invasion of Texas by the valley of the Red River. He was here
met by General Dick Taylor, who, with a much inferior force,
demolished him, giving him such a scare that it was with difficulty Porter could stop him at Alexandria to assist him in the
defence of his fleet until he could extricate it from the shal-
lows of the river where it was aground. The hero of Boston
Common had not had such a scare since Stonewall Jackson
had chased him through Winchester, Virginia.

What was best to be done in this changed condition of
affairs? I certainly had not come all the way into the Gulf of
Mexico, to fight five ships of war, the least of which was
probably my equal. And yet, how could I very well run away
in the face of the promises I had given my crew? for I had
told them at the Arcas Islands that they were, if the fates
proved propitious, to have some sport off Galveston. Whilst

I was pondering the difficulty, the enemy himself happily came to my relief; for pretty soon the lookout again called from aloft, and said, "One of the steamers, sir, is coming out in chase of us." The *Alabama* had given chase pretty often, but this was the first time she had been chased. It was just the thing I wanted, however, for I at once conceived the design of drawing this single ship of the enemy far enough away from the remainder of her fleet to enable me to decide a battle with her before her consorts could come to her relief.

The *Alabama* was still under sail, though, of course, being so near the enemy, the water was warm in her boilers and in a condition to give us steam in ten minutes. To carry out my design of decoying the enemy, I now wore ship as though I were fleeing from his pursuit. This, no doubt, encouraged him, though, as it would seem, the captain of the pursuing ship pretty soon began to smell a rat. I now lowered my propeller, still holding on to my sails, however, and gave the ship a small head of steam to prevent the stranger from overhauling me too rapidly. We were still too close to the fleet to think of engaging him. I thus decoyed him on, little by little, now turning my propeller over slowly, and now stopping it altogether. In the meantime night set in before we could get a distinct view of our pursuer. She was evidently a large steamer, but we knew from her build and rig that she belonged neither to the class of old steam frigates, or that of the new sloops, and we were quite willing to try our strength with any of the other classes.

At length, when I judged that I had drawn the stranger out about twenty miles from his fleet, I furled my sails, beat to quarters, prepared my ship for action, and wheeled to meet him. The two ships now approached each other very rapidly. As we came within speaking distance, we simultaneously stopped our engines, the ships being about one hundred yards apart.

The enemy was the first to hail. "What ship is that?" cried he.

"This is her Britannic Majesty's steamer *Petrel*," we replied. We now hailed in turn and demanded to know who he was. The reply not coming to us very distinctly, we repeated our question, when we heard the words, "This is the United States ship———," the name of the ship being lost to us. But we had heard enough. All we wanted to know was

that the stranger was a United States ship and therefore our
enemy. A pause now ensued—a rather awkward pause.

Presently the stranger hailed again and said, "If you please,
I will send a boat on board of you." His object was, of course,
to verify or discredit the answer we had given him that we
were one of her Britannic Majesty's cruisers.

We replied, "Certainly, we shall be happy to receive your
boat;" and we heard a boatswain's mate call away a boat, and
could hear the creaking of the tackles as she was lowered into
the water.

Things were now come to a crisis, and it being useless to
delay our engagement with the enemy any longer, I turned to
my first lieutenant and said, "I suppose you are all ready for
action?"

"We are," he replied; "the men are eager to begin, and
are only waiting for the word."

I then said to him, "Tell the enemy who we are, for we
must not strike him in disguise, and when you have done so,
give him the broadside."

Kell now sang out, in his powerful, clarion voice, through
his trumpet, "This is the Confederate States steamer *Alabama!*" and turning to the crew, who were all standing at
their guns—the gunners with their sights on the enemy,
and lock strings in hand—gave the order, fire! Away went
the broadside in an instant, our little ship feeling perceptibly,
the recoil of her guns. The night was clear. There was no
moon, but sufficient starlight to enable the two ships to see
each other quite distinctly at the distance of half a mile or
more, and a state of the atmosphere highly favorable to the
conduct of sound. The wind besides, was blowing in the direction of the enemy's fleet. As a matter of course, our guns
awakened the echoes of the coast, far and near, announcing
very distinctly to the Federal Admiral—Bell, a Southern man
who had gone over to the enemy—that the ship which he had
sent out to chase the strange sail had a fight on her hands. He
immediately, as we afterward learned, got under way with
the *Brooklyn*, his flagship, and two others of his steamers,
and came out to the rescue.

Our broadside was returned instantly; the enemy, like ourselves, having been on his guard with his men standing at
their guns. The two ships, when the action commenced, had
swerved in such a way that they were now heading in the

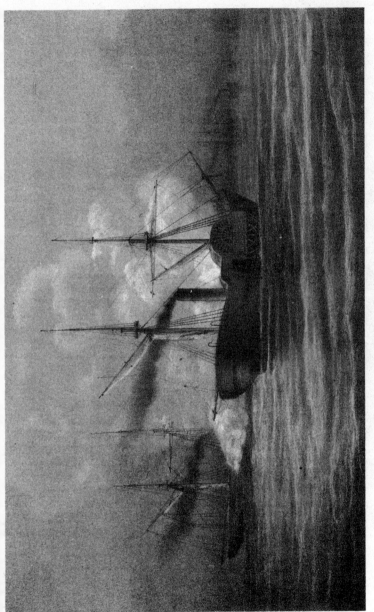

Combat between *The Alabama* and *The Hatteras*

A Yankee clipper trying to escape from *The Alabama*

same direction—the *Alabama* fighting her starboard-broadside, and her antagonist her port-broadside. Each ship, as she delivered her broadside, put herself under steam, and the action became a running fight in parallel lines, or nearly so, the ships now nearing and now separating a little from each other. My men handled their pieces with great spirit and commendable coolness, and the action was sharp and exciting while it lasted; which, however, was not very long, for in just *thirteen minutes* after firing the first gun, the enemy hoisted a light and fired an off-gun as a signal that he had been beaten.

We at once withheld our fire, and such a cheer went up from the brazen throats of my fellows as must have astonished even a Texan if he had heard it. We now steamed up quite close to the beaten steamer and asked her captain formally if he had surrendered. He replied that he had. I then inquired if he was in want of assistance, to which he responded promptly that he was, that his ship was sinking rapidly, and that he needed all our boats. There appeared to be much confusion on board the enemy's ship; officers and crew seemed to be apprehensive that we would permit them to drown, and several voices cried aloud to us for assistance at the same time. When the captain of the beaten ship came on board to surrender his sword to me, I learned that I had been engaged with the United States steamer *Hatteras*, Captain Blake. I will now let Captain Blake tell his own story. The following is his official report to the Secretary of the Federal Navy:

UNITED STATES CONSULATE

KINGSTON, JAMAICA, Jan. 21, 1863

SIR: It is my painful duty to inform the Department of the destruction of the United States steamer *Hatteras*, recently under my command, by the rebel steamer *Alabama* on the night of the 11th inst., off the coast of Texas. The circumstances of the disaster are as follows:

Upon the afternoon of the 11th inst., at half-past two o'clock, while at anchor in company with the fleet under Commodore Bell, off Galveston, Texas, I was ordered by signal from the United States flagship *Brooklyn* to chase a sail to the southward and eastward. I got under way immediately and steamed with all speed in the direction indicated. After some time the strange sail could be seen from the *Hatteras*, and was ascertained to be a steamer, which fact I communicated to the flagship by signal. I continued the chase and rapidly gained upon the suspicious vessel. Knowing the slow rate of speed of the *Hatteras*, I at once suspected that deception was being practised and hence ordered the ship to be cleared for action, with everything in readiness for a determined attack and a vigorous defence.

When within about four miles of the vessel, I observed that she had ceased to steam and was lying broadside and awaiting us. It was nearly seven o'clock and quite dark; but, notwithstanding the obscurity of the night, I felt assured, from the general character of the vessel and her manœuvres, that I should soon encounter the rebel steamer *Alabama*. Being able to work but four guns on the side of the *Hatteras*—two short 32-pounders, one 30-pounder rifled Parrott gun, and one 20-pounder rifled gun—I concluded to close with her that my guns might be effective, if necessary.

I came within easy speaking range—about seventy-five yards —and upon asking, "What steamer is that?" received the answer, "Her Britannic Majesty's ship Vixen." I replied that I would send a boat aboard, and immediately gave the order. In the meantime, the vessels were changing positions, the stranger endeavoring to gain a desirable position for a raking fire. Almost simultaneously with the piping away of the boat, the strange craft again replied, "We are the Confederate steamer *Alabama*," which was accompanied with a broadside. I, at the same moment, returned the fire. Being well aware of the many vulnerable points of the *Hatteras*, I hoped, by closing with the *Alabama* to be able to board her and thus rid the seas of the piratical craft. I steamed directly for the *Alabama*, but she was enabled by her great speed (and the foulness of the bottom of the *Hatteras*, and, consequently, her diminished speed) to thwart my attempt when I had gained a distance of but thirty yards from her. At this range, musket and pistol shots were exchanged. The firing continued with great vigor on both sides. At length a shell entered amidships in the hold, setting fire to it, and at the same instant—as I can hardly divide the time—a shell passed through the sick bay, exploding in an adjoining compartment, also producing fire. Another entered the cylinder, filling the engine-room and deck with steam, and depriving me of my power to manœuvre the vessel or to work the pumps upon which the reduction of the fire depended.

With the vessel on fire in two places, and beyond human power, a hopeless wreck upon the waters, with her walking beam shot away, and her engine rendered useless, I still main-

tained an active fire with the double hope of disabling the
Alabama and attracting the attention of the fleet off Galveston, which was only twenty-eight miles distant.

It was soon reported to me that the shells had entered the
Hatteras at the waterline, tearing off entire sheets of iron,
and that the water was rushing in, utterly defying every attempt to remedy the evil, and that she was rapidly sinking.
Learning the melancholy truth, and observing that the *Alabama* was on my port bow, entirely beyond the range of my
guns, doubtless preparing for a raking fire of the deck, I felt
I had no right to sacrifice uselessly and without any desirable
result the lives of all under my command.

To prevent the blowing up of the *Hatteras* from the fire
which was making much progress, I ordered the magazine to
be flooded, and afterward a lee gun was fired. The *Alabama*
then asked if assistance was desired, to which an affirmative
answer was given.

The *Hatteras* was then going down, and in order to save
the lives of my officers and men, I caused the armament on
the port side to be thrown overboard. Had I not done so, I am
confident the vessel would have gone down with many brave
hearts and valuable lives. After considerable delay, caused by
the report that a steamer was seen coming from Galveston,
the *Alabama* sent us assistance, and I have the pleasure of
informing the Department that every living being was conveyed safely from the *Hatteras* to the *Alabama*.

Two minutes after leaving the *Hatteras* she went down,
bow first, with her pennant at the masthead, with all her
muskets and stores of every description, the enemy not being
able, owing to her rapid sinking, to obtain a single weapon.

The battery upon the *Alabama* brought into action against
the *Hatteras* numbered seven guns, consisting of four long
32-pounders, one 100-pounder, one 68-pounder, and one
24-pounder rifled gun. The great superiority of the *Alabama*,
with her powerful battery and her machinery under the waterline, must be at once recognized by the Department, who are
familiar with the construction of the *Hatteras* and her total
unfitness for a conflict with a regular built vessel of war.

The distance between the *Hatteras* and the *Alabama* during
the action varied from twenty-five to one hundred yards.
Nearly fifty shots were fired from the *Hatteras*, and I presume
a greater number from the *Alabama*. . . .

To the men of the *Hatteras* I cannot give too much praise.
Their enthusiasm and bravery was of the highest order.

I enclose the report of Assistant Surgeon E. S. Matthews, by which you will observe that five men were wounded and two killed. The missing, it is hoped, reached the fleet at Galveston.

I shall communicate to the Department in a separate report the movements of myself and my command, from the time of our transfer to the *Alabama* until the departure of the earliest mail from this place to the United States.

I am, very respectfully, your obedient servant,

H. C. BLAKE
Lieutenant Commanding

Hon. GIDEON WELLES
Secretary of the Navy, Washington

Setting aside all the discourteous stuff and nonsense about "a *rebel* steamer" and a "piratical craft," of which Captain Blake, who had been bred in the old service, should have been ashamed, especially after enjoying the hospitalities of my cabin for a couple of weeks, the above is a pretty fair report of the engagement. I am a little puzzled, however, by the Captain's statement that he could use but four guns on a side. We certainly understood from all the officers and men of the *Hatteras* at the time that she carried eight guns; six in broadside and two pivots, just like the *Alabama*,—the only difference between the two ships being that the *Alabama's* pivot guns were the heaviest.

There is another remark in the report that is quite new to me. I am informed for the first time that Captain Blake desired to board me. I cannot, of course, know what his intentions were, but I saw no evidence of such an intention in the handling of his ship; and Captain Blake must himself have known that in the terribly demoralized condition of his crew, when they found that they had really fallen in with the *Alabama*, he could not have depended upon a single boarder. What Captain Blake means by saying that his ship went down with her pennant flying, I am at a loss, as every seaman must be, to understand. Did he not surrender his ship to me? And if so, what business had his pennant, any more than his ensign, to be flying? But this, I suppose, was a little claptrap, like his expressions "rebel" and "pirate," thrown in to suit the Yankee taste of the day. Indeed, nothing was more lamentable to me during the whole war than to observe how readily the officers of the old Navy, many of whom belonged to the gentle families of the land, and all of whom had been bred in a school of honor, took to the slang expressions of the day and fell pell-mell into the ranks of the vulgar and fanatical rabble that was hounding on the war.

The officers of the Confederate States Navy, to say the least, were as much entitled to be regarded as fighting for a principle as themselves, and one would have thought that there would have been a chivalrous rivalry between the two services as to which should show the other the most courtesy. This was the case, a thousand years ago, between the Christian and the Saracen. . . .

As soon as the action was over . . . I caused all lights to be extinguished on board my ship and shaped my course again for the passage of Yucatan. In the meantime, the enemy's boat, which had been lowered for the purpose of boarding me, pulled in vigorously for the shore as soon as it saw the action commence, and landed safely; and Admiral Bell with his three steamers passed on either side of the scene of action—the steamers having been scattered in the pursuit to cover as much space as possible and thus increase their chances of falling in with me. They did not find the *Alabama* or indeed anything else during the night, but as one of the steamers was returning to her anchorage off Galveston the next morning in the dejected mood of a baffled scout, she fell in with the sunken *Hatteras*, the tops of whose royal masts were just above water, and from the main of which, the pennant—the *night* pennant, for the action was fought at night—spoken of by Captain Blake, was observed to be flying. It told the only tale of the sunken ship which her consort had to take back to the Admiral. The missing boat turned up soon afterward, however, and the mystery was then solved. There was now as hurried a saddling of steeds for the pursuit as there had been in the chase of the young Lochinvar, and with as little effect, for by the time the steeds were given the spur, the *Alabama* was distant a hundred miles or more.

There was very little said by the enemy about this engagement between the *Alabama* and the *Hatteras*, as was usual with him when he met with a disaster; and what was said was all false. My own ship was represented to be a monster of speed and strength, and the *Hatteras*, on the other hand, to be a tug, or river steamer, or some such craft, with two or three small guns at the most. The facts are as follows: The *Hatteras* was a larger ship than the *Alabama* by one hundred tons. Her armament as reported to us by her own people was as follows: four 32-pounders; two Parrott 30-pounder rifles; one 20-pounder rifle; and one 12-pounder howitzer—making a total of eight guns. The armament of the *Alabama* was as follows: six 32-pounders; one 8-inch shell gun; one Blakeley rifle of 100 pounds—total, eight guns. There was, besides, a little toy rifle—a 9-pounder—on the quarter-deck of the *Alabama*, which had been captured from a merchant ship, and which, I believe, was fired once during the action. The crew of the *Hatteras* was 108 strong; that of the *Alabama* 110. There was thus a considerable disparity between the two ships in the weight of their pivot-guns, and the *Alabama* ought to have won the fight; and she did win it in *thirteen minutes*—taking care, too, though she sank her enemy at night, to see that none of his men were drowned—a fact which I shall have occasion to contrast with another sinking. The only casualty we had on board the *Alabama* was one man wounded. The damages to our hull were so slight that there was not a shot hole which it was necessary to plug to enable us to continue our cruise; nor was there a rope to be spliced. Blake behaved like a man of courage and made the best fight he could, ill supported as he was by the volunteer officers by whom he was surrounded, but he fell into disgrace with the Demos and had but little opportunity shown him during the remainder of the war to retrieve his disaster.

Chapter Eleven —*1863*

The Alabama proceeds to Jamaica and lands her prisoners . . . The captain visits the country . . . Intercourse with the English naval officers . . . Earl Russell's letter . . . Preparations for sea . . . A boat race by moonlight . . . Captain Blake complains of "Dixie" . . . How the matter is settled

The little byplay in the Gulf of Mexico related in the last chapter being over, I determined to make the best of my way to the island of Jamaica, there land my prisoners on *parole*, patch up the two or three shot holes the enemy had made above the water line, re-coal, and proceed on my eastern cruise against the enemy's commerce as originally contemplated. We had a long passage to Jamaica, as we took a succession of southerly gales that greatly retarded our speed. My first intention was to make the whole run under steam, but after struggling against these gales for three or four days, I found my fuel diminishing so rapidly that it became prudent to let the fires go down and put the ship under sail. This delay was very vexatious, as our little ship was greatly inconvenienced by the number of prisoners we had on board.

Friday, the 16th of January, is noted on my journal as follows: The gale continued all day, moderating toward night.

173

The sky is overcast with a dull canopy of leaden clouds, the sun barely showing himself to us for a moment at a time through an occasional rift during the entire day. Observing the water to be discolored, at one P. M. we sounded on the Yucatan Bank. The soundings on this bank being an excellent guide, I continued to run along the edge of it until eleven P. M., when we passed off it into the deep waters of the Yucatan Passage. We now put the ship under steam again, and aiding the steam by reefed trysails, we battled with an adverse sea and current during the rest of the night. We found the current setting into the passage to be as much as two and a half knots, which was greater than I had ever known it before.

I may take this occasion to remind the reader that the old theory of Dr. Franklin and others was that the Gulf Stream, which flows out of the Gulf of Mexico between the north coast of Cuba and the Florida Reefs and Keys, flows into the Gulf through the channel between the west end of Cuba and the coast of Yucatan, in which the *Alabama* now was. But the effectual disproof of this theory is that we know positively from the strength of the current and its volume, or cross section, in the two passages, that more than twice the quantity of water flows out of the Gulf of Mexico than flows into it through this passage. Upon Dr. Franklin's theory, the Gulf of Mexico in a very short time would become dry ground. Nor can the Mississippi River, which is the only stream worth noticing in this connection that flows into the Gulf of Mexico, come to his relief, as we have seen that that river only empties into the Gulf of Mexico about one three thousandth part as much water as the Gulf Stream takes out. We must resort, of necessity, to an under-current from the north, passing into the Gulf of Mexico under the Gulf Stream, rising to the surface when heated, and thus swelling the volume of the outflowing water. I refer my readers, curious in this matter, to the work of Captain Maury, entitled the *Physical Geography of the Sea*. It is full of profound philosophy on the subjects of which it treats, and is written in so pleasing a style, and is so strewn with flowers as to make the reader forget that he is traveling the thorny paths of science.

The 18th of January was Sunday, and we were obliged to intermit the usual Sunday muster on account of the bad weather, which continued without intermission—the wind still blowing a gale, and the passing clouds deluging us with rain. Two days afterward, viz., on the 20th, we made the west end of the island of Jamaica a little after midnight, and as we crawled under the lee of the coast, we broke for the first time the force of the wind with which we had been so long struggling. We had been thus nine days making the passage from Galveston to the west end of Jamaica and were the greater part of another day in coasting the island up to Port Royal. We had shown first one and then another neutral flag to several neutral ships that we had passed, but the enemy's flag was nowhere to be seen. Giving chase to a bark whilst we were still in the Gulf of Mexico, we were quite amazed, as we came up with her, to find that she was our old consort, the *Agrippina!* This bluff-bowed old Scotch ship had been all the time since she left us at the Arcas Islands—eight days— battling with adverse winds, and was still only a couple of hundred miles or so advanced on her voyage.

We made the Plum Point lighthouse at half-past four P. M., and were off the mouth of the harbor of Port Royal just as the evening began to deepen into twilight. We hoisted the French flag, and firing a gun, and making the usual signal for a pilot, one came promptly on board of us. Day was fading into night so fast that we had scarcely light enough left to enable us to grope our way through the tortuous and narrow channel, and it was quite dark when our anchor was let go. Of course, we did not permit the pilot to anchor us as a *Frenchman*, and when we told him that it was the *Alabama* he was taking in, he did not appear at all surprised but remarked very coolly, "I knew all the while that you were no Frenchman." I felt much relieved when at length I heard the plunge of the anchor into the water, followed by the rattling of the chain cable through the hawse hole. On the high seas, with the enemy all the time in full chase of me, constant vigilance was required to guard against surprise; and my battle with the elements was almost as constant as that with the enemy. When I reached the friendly shelter, therefore, of a neutral port belonging to such of the powers of the earth as were strong enough to prevent themselves from being kicked by the enemy, my overtaxed nervous system relaxed in a moment, and I enjoyed the luxury of a little gentlemanly idleness. Kell was of wonderful assistance to me in this respect. I always left the ship in his hands with the utmost confidence, and my confidence was never misplaced. He was an excellent disciplinarian, and being, besides, a thorough master of his profession, I had in him all that I could desire.

We were boarded by a lieutenant from the English flagship, immediately upon anchoring, and the news spread like wildfire through all Port Royal that the *Alabama* had arrived with the officers and crew of a Federal gunboat which she had sunk in battle on board as prisoners. Night as it was, we were soon swarmed with visitors come off to welcome us to the port and tender their congratulations. The next morning I called on Commodore Dunlap, who commended a squadron of Admiral Milne's fleet and was the commanding naval officer present. This was the first English port I had entered since the *Alabama* had been commissioned, and no question, whatever, as to the antecedents of my ship was raised. I had, in fact, brought in pretty substantial credentials that I was a ship of war—130 of the officers and men of one of the enemy's sunken ships. Great Britain had had the good sense not to listen to the frantic appeals either of Mr. Seward or Minister Adams, both of whom claimed that it was her duty to stultify herself and ignore the commission of my ship. Nor did Commodore Dunlap say anything to me of my destruction of British property or of the three ships of war which that adept in international law, the *Commercial Advertiser* of New York, had asserted Admiral Milne had sent after me. These questions, indeed, had all been authoritatively settled, I found, by Earl Russell, the British Foreign Secretary, by the following letter to the Liverpool Chamber of Commerce, which had applied to him for information. It is copied from the New York *World*:

SIR: I am directed by Earl Russell to reply to your letters of the 6th inst., respecting the destruction by the Confederate steamer *Alabama* of British property embarked in American vessels and burned by that steamer. Earl Russell desires me to state to you that British property on board a vessel belonging to one of the belligerents must be subject to all the risks and contingencies of war, so far as the capture of the vessel is concerned. The owners of any British property, not being contraband of war, on board a Federal vessel captured and destroyed by a Confederate vessel of war, may claim in a Confederate Prize Court compensation for the destruction of such property.

The *World* said lachrymosely of the above that "it was but one of a crowd of eloquent indications which constantly multiply upon us to prove that Earl Russell, like Mr. Gladstone, whatever his sympathies may be, really regards the 'nation of Jefferson Davis' as substantially created and looks upon recognition as simply a question of time."

I forwarded through Commodore Dunlap an official report of my arrival to the Governor of the island, with a request to be permitted to land my prisoners and put some slight repairs upon my ship; both of which requests were promptly granted. Governor Eyre was then in authority. He behaved with great spirit and firmness, afterward, in nipping in the bud a widespread Negro insurrection which had for its object the massacre of the whites and the plunder of their property. A few Negroes were killed by the troops, and I have been sorry to learn since that his Excellency has been much harassed in consequence by both English and American fanatics. The English squadron at anchor consisted of the *Jason*, the *Challenger*, and *Greyhound*. The most cordial relations were at once established between the officers of all these ships and those of the *Alabama*. Indeed, many of them were our old acquaintances.

An English friend having come on board to invite me to pass a few days with him in the mountains while my ship was being prepared for sea, I accepted his invitation, and turning over all the unfinished business of the ship to Kell, we pulled up to Kingston in my gig. Here I found my friend's carriage in waiting, and entering it, we were soon whirled out of the limits of the dusty city into the most charming of tropical scenery. Except landing occasionally for a few hours at a time at the desert little islands I had visited in the Caribbean Sea and the Gulf of Mexico, I had not had a holiday on shore since leaving the Mersey on my way to commission the *Alabama*, five months before. I needed a little rest and recreation to restore my wasted energies, and I found both with my excellent friend, Mr. Fyfe.

For the first ten miles we rode over a beautiful macadamized road, or rather avenue, lined with the gigantic cactus, growing frequently to the height of twenty and thirty feet, and several specimens of the palm; chief among which was the cocoanut tree, shooting its trunk with the straightness of an arrow to a great height and waving gracefully in the breeze its superb feather-like foliage. The way was lined with many picturesque country houses, each surrounded by its extensive and well-kept grounds on which were growing crops, chiefly of fruits and vegetables, but interspersed occasionally with a field of Indian corn or sugar cane. Hedgerows and shade trees adorned the front yards and protected the residences from the sun, giving them an air of seclusion, coolness, and quiet that was very inviting. We occasionally obtained glimpses of beautiful valleys, on the right hand, and on the left, in which fairy cottages were nestled. The scenery was continually changing as the road wound along, now skirting the base of abrupt hills, now running over a stream, and now plunging into the recesses of a wood with the trees arching overhead like the groined work of a cathedral.

At the end of our ten miles of carriage drive, we found ourselves at the foot of the mountains. Here we alighted at a large hostelry, which was a sort of combination of the inn, caravansary, and country store, and after some refreshment, mounted saddle horses which we found in waiting. The roads soon became mere bridle paths. As we ascended the slopes of the mountains, we changed rapidly the character of the vegetation; every hundred feet of elevation being equivalent to a change of a degree or more of latitude, and bringing us in the presence of new forest trees and new plants, until we dismounted on the lawn of my friend, the immediate surroundings of which were all English; the cedar, and other well-known trees and shrubs of the temperate latitudes supplanting the tropical vegetation we had left in the *tierra caliente* below us. The air, too, was so delightfully changed from the sultry heats of the coast that we found a fire lighted of the dry and fragrant branches of the cedar tree quite pleasant as the night set in.

The reader may imagine how magical the change was from the cramped quarters and other *desagremens* of a small ship to the ample halls and elegant leisure of an English home perched on the mountain side and overlooking a perfect wilderness of tropical vegetation. The sea was in plain sight to the eastward of us, and Kingston and Port Royal lay at our feet. With the aid of a fine telescope which my friend had mounted in his piazza, I could distinguish my own ship from the other vessels in the harbor, though they all appeared as diminutive as so many sea gulls nestling upon the water. I need not say how soundly I slept that night, far away from war's alarms, fanned by the gentlest of sea breezes, in the sweetest of sheets, and lullabied by the distant breaker as it stranded itself at regular intervals upon the beach.

I was awakened the next morning by the merry songs of a hundred birds that came appropriately blended with the perfume of the flowers that clustered around my windows; and I have seldom looked upon a more beautiful picture than when I threw back the blinds and caught a view of the landscape, rejoicing in the morning's sun with all its wealth of tropical fruits and flowers, and the sea—the glorious sea—glittering like a mirror in the distance. Nothing can be more charming than the interior of an English household when the ice has been broken and you have fairly gained admission into the interior of the temple. The successful entertainment of a guest is one of those artless arts of which the English gentleman above all others is master; and the art consists in putting the guest so entirely at ease as to make him feel at home in the first half hour. With a library, servants, and horses at your command, you are literally left to take care of yourself—meeting the family in the parlors and sitting rooms as much or as little as you please.

From Flamstead, which was the name of the country seat of my friend, we rode over to Bloxburg, the country seat of his brothers, where some ladies from the neighborhood did me the honor to make me a visit; and from Bloxburg we made several other agreeable visits to neighboring plantations. I was in an entirely new world—those mountains of Jamaica—and was charmed with everything I saw. All was nature; and nature presented herself in her most lovely aspect, whether we viewed the sky overhead, the sea at our feet, or the broken and picturesque country around us. Time flew rapidly, and what with delightful rides, and lunches, and evening parties, where music and the bright eyes of fair women beguiled the senses, I should have been in danger of forgetting the war and the *Alabama* if Kell had not sent me a courier on the third or fourth day, informing me that he was nearly ready for sea.

I descended at once from the empyrean in which I had been wandering, took a hasty leave of my friends, and in company with Mr. Fyfe, rode back to the coast. We took a new route

back and re-entered Kingston through a different suburb—
stopping to lunch with one of Mr. Fyfe's friends, an English
merchant, at his magnificent country house. But, alas! much
of the magnificence of the Kingston of former years is passing
away. I had known it in its palmiest days, having visited it
when a midshipman in the old service before the happy slave
had been converted into the wretched freedman. It was then
a busy mart of commerce, and the placid waters of its un-
rivaled harbor were alive with shipping bearing the flags of all
nations, come in quest of her great staples, sugar, coffee, cocoa,
gensing, &c. Now a general air of dilapidation and poverty
hangs over the scene. A straggling ship or two only are seen
in the harbor; the merchants have become shopkeepers, and
the sleek, well-fed Negro has become an idler and a vagrant
with scarce rags enough to hide his nakedness. My host, in
the few days I remained with him gave me much valuable
information concerning the Negro since his emancipation,
which I will not detain the reader to repeat. I may say in a
few words, however, that the substance of this information
was that there has been no increase either in numbers, intelligence, or morals among them; and that, too, under circumstances all of which were favorable to the Negro. He was the
pet of the government for years after his emancipation, and
English fanatics have devoted their lives to his regeneration,
but all without success. He is, today, with a few exceptions
about the towns, the same savage that he is in his native
Dahomey. An English parliament had declared that he was
the political equal of the white man—that is, of the colonial
white man, for England takes the best care that the imperial
legislature is never tainted by his presence—and I found him
a generation afterward far below his former level of slave.

I found my gig in waiting for me at the wharf in Kingston,
and taking leave of my friend with many thanks for his hospitality, I pulled on board of my ship about sunset. And here,
what a scene of confusion met me, and what reports Kell had
to make of how my fellows had been cutting up! [Clarence R.
Yong], the paymaster, had been drunk ever since he landed,
neglecting his duty and behaving in a most disreputable manner. He was hail fellow, well met with all the common sailors
and seemed to have an especial fancy for the sailors of the
enemy. Kell had suspended his functions; and had sent on
shore and had him brought off under arrest. He had become

partially sobered, and I at once ordered him to pack up his clothing and be off. He was landed, bag and baggage, in half an hour, and in due time he married a Negro wife, went over to England with her, swindled her out of all her property, and turned Yankee, going over to Minister Adams and becoming one of his right-hand men when there was any hard swearing wanted in the British courts against the Confederates.

This little matter disposed of, we turned our attention to the crew. They had had a run on shore, and Kell was just gathering them together again. The ship's cutters as well as the shore boats, were constantly coming alongside with small squads, all of them drunk, some in one stage of drunkenness, and some in another. Liquor was acting upon them like laughing gas; some were singing jolly, good-humored songs, whilst others were giving the war whoop and insisting on a fight. They were seized, ironed and passed below to the care of the master-at-arms as fast as they came on board.

A couple of them, not liking the appearance of things on board, jumped into a dugout alongside, and seizing the paddles from the Negroes, shoved off in great haste and put out for the shore. It was night, and there was a bright moon lighting up the bay. A cutter was manned as speedily as possible and sent in pursuit of the fugitives. Jack had grog and Moll ahead of him, and irons and a court-martial behind him, and he paddled like a good fellow. He had gotten a good start before the cutter was well under way, but still the cutter with her long sweeping oars was rather too much for the dugout, especially as there were five oars to two paddles. She gained and gained, coming nearer and nearer, when presently the officer of the cutter heard one of the sailors in the dugout say to the other, "I'll tell you what it is, Bill, there's too much cargo in this here damned craft, and I'm going to lighten ship a little," and at the same instant he saw the two men lay in their paddles, seize one of the Negroes, and pitch him head foremost overboard! They then seized their paddles again, and away darted the dugout with renewed speed.

Port Royal Bay is a large sheet of water and is . . . full of ravenous sharks. It would not do, of course, for the cutter to permit the Negro either to drown or to be eaten by the sharks, and so, as she came up with him, sputtering and floundering for his life, she was obliged to "back of all" and take him in. The sailor who grabbed at him first, missed him, and the boat shot ahead of him, which rendered it necessary for her to turn and pull back a short distance before she could rescue him. This done, he was flung into the bottom of the cutter, and the pursuit renewed. By this time the dugout had gotten even a better start than she had had at first, and the two fugitive sailors, encouraged by the prospect of escape, were paddling more vigorously than ever. Fast flew the dugout but faster flew the cutter. Both parties now had their blood up, and a more beautiful and exciting moonlight race has not often been seen. We had watched it from the *Alabama* until in the gloaming of the night it had passed out of sight. We had seen the first maneuver of the halting and pulling back of the cutter, but did not know what to make of it. The cutter began now to come up again with the chase. She had no musket on board, or in imitation of the *Alabama*, she might have hove the chase to with a blank cartridge or a ball. When she had gotten within a few yards of her a second time, in went the paddles again and overboard went the other Negro! and away went the dugout! A similar delay on the part of the cutter ensued as before, and a similar advantage was gained by the dugout.

But all things come to an end, and so did this race. The cutter finally captured the dugout, and brought back Tom Bowse and Bill Bower to their admiring shipmates on board the *Alabama*. This was the only violation of neutrality I was guilty of in Port Royal—chasing and capturing a neutral craft in neutral waters. My excuse was the same that Wilkes made —she had contraband on board. I do not know whether Commodore Dunlap ever heard of it; but if he had complained, I should have set off the rescuing of two of Her Majesty's colored subjects from drowning against the recapture of my own men. The fact is, the townspeople themselves were responsible for all these disorders. They had made heroes of all my fellows and plied them with an unconscionable number of drinks. Every seaport town has its sailor quarter, and this in the good old town of Kingston was a constant scene of revelry by day as well as by night during the stay of the *Alabama*'s liberty men on shore. There was no end to the "breakdowns" and "double-shuffles" which had been given in their honor by the beaux and belles of Water Street. Besides my own crew, there were always more or less English man-of-war sailors on shore on liberty from the different ships, and upwards of a hundred had been landed from the *Hatteras*.

It was quite remarkable that in these merrymakings and debaucheries the Confederate sailors and the Yankee sailors harmonized capitally together. They might frequently be seen arm and arm in the streets, or hob-nobbing together—the Confederate sailor generally paying the score, as the Yankee sailor's strong box had gone down with his ship, and his paymaster was rather short of cash. They sailed as amicably together up and down the contradance, and hailed each other to heave to, when it was time to "freshen the nip," as though the *Alabama* and *Hatteras* had never been yard-arm and yard-arm throwing broadsides into each other. In short, my men behaved capitally toward their late enemies. There was no unmanly exultation over their victory. The most that could be seen was an air of patronage very delicately put on, as though they would say, "Well, you know we whipped you, but then you did the best you could, and there's an end of it."

Among the amusing things that had occurred during my absence in the Jamaica mountains was a flare-up which Captain Blake, my prisoner, had had with the British Commodore.

The steamer *Greyhound* had a band of music on board, and as one of the young lieutenants was an old acquaintance of several of my officers whom he had met at Nassau, he ordered the band on the evening after our arrival and whilst Captain Blake was still on board the *Alabama*, to play "Dixie;" which, I may remark, by the way, had become a very popular air everywhere, as much on account of the air itself perhaps as because of its association with a weak and gallant people struggling for the right of self-government. Captain Blake chose to construe this little compliment to the *Alabama* as an insult to Yankeedom and made a formal protest to the British Commodore in behalf of himself and the "old flag." Commodore Dunlap must have smiled when he read Blake's epistle. He was certainly a man of humor, for he hit upon the following mode of settling the grave international dispute. He ordered the offending *Greyhound*, when she should get up her band on the following evening first to play "Dixie" and then "Yankee Doodle."

When the evening which was to salve the Yankee honor arrived, great was the expectation of everyone in the squadron. The band on board the *Jason*, flagship, led off by playing "God save the Queen," that glorious national anthem which electrifies the Englishman, as the Marseilles' hymn does the

Frenchman, the world over. The *Challenger's* band followed and played a fine opera air. The evening was still and fine, and the poops of all the ships were filled with officers. It then came the *Greyhound's* turn. She first played something unusually solemn, then "Dixie," with slowness, sweetness, and pathos, and when the chorus

> In Dixie's land, I'll take my stand,
> I'll live, and die in Dixie!

had died away on the soft evening air, such an infernal din of drums, and fifes, and cymbals, and wind instruments, each after its fashion, going it strong upon

> Yankee Doodle Dandy!

arose, as to defy all description! The effect was electric; the officers had to hold their sides to preserve their dignity, and—Captain Blake was avenged. There could be no protest made against this time-honored rogue's march. It was the favorite tune of the b'hoys, and there the matter had to end. I have never learned whether Mr. Seward ever called Lord Palmerston to an account about it in any one of his "Essays on English Composition."

Chapter Twelve—*1863*

Departure from Jamaica . . . Capture of the Golden Rule . . . Coasting the island of Hayti . . . Capture of the Chastelaine . . . The old city of St. Domingo and its reminiscences . . . The Dominican Convent and the palace of Diego Columbus . . . The capture of the Palmetto, the Olive Jane, and the Golden Eagle . . . How the roads are blazed out upon the sea . . . Captain Maury

On the 25th of January, 1863, or just five days after our arrival at Jamaica, we had completed all our preparations for sea, and at half-past eight P. M. steamed out of the harbor of Port Royal, bound to the coast of Brazil and thence to the Cape of Good Hope. We had made many friends during our short stay, and mutual regrets were expressed at departure. My gallant young officers had not been idle, whilst I had been visiting the mountains. Many little missives, put up in the tiniest and prettiest of envelopes, were discovered among the mail as our last mail bag was prepared for the shore, and as a good deal of damage may be done in five days, there were probably some heart beatings among the fair islanders as those P. P. Cs. were perused. There is no lover so susceptible, or so devoted, or whose heart is so capacious as that of the young seaman. His very life upon the sea is a poem, and his habitual absence from the sex prepares him to see loveliness in every female form.

Though it was night when we emerged from the harbor, and when we ought to have met with the blandest and gentlest of land breezes, laden with the perfume of shrub and flower, we passed at once into a heavy head sea with a stiff northeaster blowing. With yards pointed to the wind, and a laboring engine, we steamed along past Point Mayrant light, off which we discharged the *Ariel* some weeks before, and the morning's light found us in the passage between Jamaica and St. Domingo. The sun rose brightly, the wind moderated, and the day proved to be very fine.

My first duty after the usual morning's muster at quarters was to hold a court of general sessions for the discharge of my vagabonds, many of whom were still in irons and a beautiful-looking set of fellows they were when their irons were removed, and they were brought on deck for this purpose. They were now all sober, but the effects of their late debauches were visible upon the persons of all of them. Soiled clothing, blackened eyes, and broken noses, frowsy, uncombed hair, and matted and disordered beard, with reddened eyes that looked as if sleep had long been a stranger to them—these were the principal features. Poor Jack! how much he is to be pitied! Cut loose early from the gentle restraints of home and brought into contact with every description of social vice at an age when it is so difficult to resist temptation, what wonder is it that we find him a grownup child of nature subject to no other restraint than such as the discipline of his ship imposes upon him?

"When wine is in, wit is out," was the proverb I always acted upon on occasions similar to the present; that is to say, when the "wine" had any business to be "in." I expected, as a matter of course when I sent my sailors on shore on liberty that the result was to be a frolic, and I was always lenient to the mere concomitants of a frolic; but I never permitted them to abuse or maltreat the inhabitants or perpetrate any malicious mischief. But if they got drunk on board in violation of the discipline of the ship, or, in other words, if the wine had no business to be "in," I considered that the wit had no business to be "out." And so I listened to their penitential excuses one by one and restored them to duty, retaining one or two of the greatest culprits for trial by court-martial as an example to the rest. Having disposed of the other cases, I turned to Tom Bowse and Bill Bower, the heroes of the moonlight chase, and said to them, "And so you are a pretty set of fellows; you not only tried to desert your ship and flag, but you endeavored to commit murder in your attempt to escape!"

"Murder!" replied Bowse with a start of horror that I could see was entirely honest, "we never thought of such a thing, sir; them Jamaica niggers, they take to the water as natural as South Sea Islanders, and there's no such thing as drowning them, sir."

"That was it, your honor," now put in Bowse; "it was only a bit of a joke, you see, sir, played upon the officer of the cutter. We knew he'd stop to pick 'em up, and so give us the weathergauge of him."

"That may do very well for the murder," I now rejoined, "but what about the desertion?"

"Nary-a-bit of it, your honor," again replied Bowse; "we only meant to have another bit of a frolic and come back all in good time before the ship sailed."

"Just so," added Bower; "the fact is, your honor, we were hardly responsible for what we did that night, for we had a small drop aboard, and then the moon was so bright, and Moll Riggs she had sent us such a kind message!" The moonlight and Moll clinched the argument, and turning to the master-at-arms with an ill-suppressed smile, I directed him to turn the prisoners loose.

I had scarcely gotten through with this jail delivery before the cry of "Sail ho!" rang out upon the clear morning air from the masthead. There was no necessity to alter our course, for the sail was nearly ahead. In an hour more, a very pretty, newly-painted bark, with her sails flapping idly in the calm which was now prevailing, arose to view from the deck. She had the usual Yankee earmarks, tapering masts and cotton sails, and we felt sure of another prize. We showed her the United States colors as we approached, and a very bright "old flag" soon afterward ascended to her peak, drooping despondently for want of wind to blow it out. The cat did not torture the mouse long, for we soon changed flags, and gave the master of the doomed ship the same satisfaction that Jacob Faithful received, when he found his missing son's shirt

in the maw of the shark—the satisfaction of being put out
of doubt and knowing that his ship would be burned. The
prize proved upon being boarded to be the *Golden Rule* from
New York for Aspinwall. She belonged to the Atlantic and
Pacific Steamship Company and was filled with an assorted
cargo—having on board, among other things, masts, and a
complete set of rigging for the United States brig *Bainbridge*,
which had recently had everything swept by the board in a
gale at Aspinwall.

Judging from the bills of lading found on board, some
small portions of the cargo appeared to be neutral, but there
being no sworn evidence to vouch for the fact in the way of
Consular or other certificates, I applied the well-known rule of
prize law to the case, viz., that everything found on board an
enemy's ship is presumed to belong to the enemy until the
contrary is shown by proper evidence; and at about six P. M.
applied the torch. The islands of St. Domingo and Jamaica
were both sufficiently near for their inhabitants to witness the
splendid bonfire, which lighted up the heavens far and near
soon after dark. A looker-on upon that conflagration would
have seen a beautiful picture, for besides the burning ship,
there were the two islands mentioned, sleeping in the dreamy
moonlight on the calm bosom of a tropical sea, and the rakish-
looking "British Pirate" steaming in for the land with every
spar and line of cordage brought out in bold relief by the
bright flame—nay, with the very "pirates" themselves visible,
handling the boxes and bales of merchandise which they had
"robbed" from this innocent Yankee, whose countrymen at
home were engaged in the Christian occupation of burning
our houses and desolating our fields.

One of the pleasant recollections connected with the picture was that I had tied up for a while longer one of the
enemy's gun-brigs for want of an outfit. It must have been
some months before the *Bainbridge* put to sea. There was
another good act performed. Lots of patent medicines with
which the enemy was about inundating the South American
coast for the benefit of the livers of their fellow-democrats
were consigned to the flames. The reader had an opportunity
to observe when we captured the *Dunkirk* how zealously our
pious brethren of the North were looking out for the religion
and morals of the Portuguese *in a sly way*. He now sees what
a regard they have for the health of the atrabilious South

Americans. Both operations *paid*, of course, and whether it was a tract or a pill that was sold could make but little difference to the manufacturers of the merchandise.

We steamed along the coast at a distance of seven or eight miles the remainder of that night without further adventure; and the next morning dawned clear with a slight change of program as to weather. There were clouds hurrying past us, wetting our jackets now and then without interrupting the sunshine, and a stiff northeaster blowing. This was a head-wind, and we labored against it all day with diminished speed. At three P.M. we made the remarkable island, or rather mountain of rock, called in the beautiful Spanish, Alta Vela, or Tall Sail, from its resemblance to a ship under sail at a distance. It rises at a distance of ten or twelve miles from the main island of St. Domingo with almost perpendicular sides, to the height of several hundred feet, and affords a foothold for no living creature but the sea gull, the gannet, and other water fowl. Soon after nightfall, we boarded a Spanish brig from Montevideo, bound for Havana; and at eleven P.M., Alta Vela bearing north and being distant from us about five miles, we hove to with a shot, another sail that was running down the coast. She was a rakish-looking hermaphrodite brig, and in the bright moonlight looked Yankee. The report of our heavy gun, reverberated by a hundred echoes from Alta Vela, had a magical effect upon the little craft. Flying like a sea gull before a gale only a moment before, she became in an instant like the same sea gull with its wings folded and riding upon the wave without other motion than such as the wave gave it. Ranging within a convenient distance, we lowered and sent a boat on board of her. She proved to be American, as we had suspected. She was the *Chastelaine* of Boston, last from the island of Guadeloupe, whither she had been to deliver a cargo of staves, and was now on her way to Cienfuegos in the island of Cuba, in quest of sugar and rum for the Boston folks. We applied the torch to her, lighting up the sea-girt walls of Alta Vela with the unusual spectacle of a burning ship, and disturbing the slumber of the sea gulls and gannets for the balance of the night.

The next morning found us still steaming to the eastward along the Haytian coast. Having now the crews of two ships on board as prisoners, I hauled in closer to the coast with the intention of running into the old town of St. Domingo and landing them. We got sight of this old city early in the afternoon, and at about four P. M. ran in and anchored. The anchorage is an open roadstead formed by the *debouchement* of the picturesque little river Ozama, which seems to have burst through the rocky barrier of the coast to find its way to the sea. We found but two vessels anchored here—one of them being a New York brig recently put under English colors. She had a "bran-new" English ensign flying. Admiral Milne having failed to respond to the frantic cries of the New York *Commercial Advertiser* to protect the Yankee flag, the Yankee shipowners with many loathings and contortions were at last forced to gulp the English flag. There was no other way of coaxing England to protect them. Being in a neutral port, I had no opportunity, of course, of testing the verity of this cross of St. George, as the Yankees were fond of calling the hated emblem of England—hated, but hugged at the same time for the protection which it gave ship and cargo.

At the time of my visit Spain had repossessed herself of the eastern or Dominican end of the island of St. Domingo; and a Spanish naval commander now came on board to visit me. I had no difficulty in arranging with him for the landing of my prisoners. I sent them to the guardship, and he sent them thence to the shore. This done, and arrangements being made for some fresh provisions and other refreshments to be sent off to the crew in the morning, I landed for a stroll on this most classical of all American soil.

The old city of St. Domingo! How many recollections does it not call up! It was a large and flourishing city a hundred years before that pestiferous little craft called the *Mayflower* brought over the cockatrice's egg that hatched out the Puritan. It was mentioned whilst we were running down the north side of the island on our way to catch Mr. Vanderbilt's California steamer that the little town of Isabella on that side of the island was the first city founded in the New World; and that the new settlement was soon broken up and transferred to the city of St. Domingo. The latter city grew apace and flourished and was for many years the chief seat of the Spanish empire in the New World. It is today in its ruins the most interesting city in all the Americas. Columbus himself lived here and hither his remains were brought from Spain and reposed for many years until they were transferred

to Cuba with great pomp and ceremony. The names of
Las Casas, Diego Columbus, the son and successor of the
admiral, Oviedo, Hernando Cortez, and a host of others are
bound up in its history. The latter, the renowned conqueror
of Mexico, was for several years a notary in an adjoining
province.

We have not much time to spare, as the *Alabama* will be
on the wing again with the morning's light, but I cannot forbear pointing out two of the principal ruins of this famous
old city. One of them is the Dominican Convent, and the
other the *Palacio*, or residence of Diego Columbus. The old
city being named in honor of St. Dominic, great pains were
evidently bestowed upon the church and convent that were
to bear his name; and so substantially was the former built,
that it stands entire and is still used as a place of worship
after the lapse of three hundred and fifty years. The altars
are all standing, though faded and worm-eaten, and see! there
is a lamp still burning before the altar of the Holy Eucharist.
That lamp was lighted in the days of Columbus and has been
burning continuously ever since! Observe these marble slabs
over which we are walking. The entire floor is paved with
them. They are the tombstones of the dead that were distinguished in their day, but who have long since been forgotten.
Here is a date of 1532 on one of them. It is much defaced
and worn by the footsteps of the generations that have passed
over it, but we can see by the miter and crozier that have
been sculptured on it in *bas-relief* that the remains of a
bishop lie beneath. His name? We cannot make it out. The
record of a bishop carved upon the enduring marble and
placed upon the floor of his own cathedral has been lost.
What a sermon is here in this stone! Raise your eyes now
from the floor and cast them on the wall opposite. In that
niche, in the great cathedral wall, sang the choir of ancient
days. These vaulted roofs have resounded with music from
the lips of many generations of beauties that have faded like
the butterfly of the field, leaving no more trace of their names
and lineage than that little wanderer of an hour. There stands
the silent organ, whose last note was sounded a century or
more ago, with its gilding all tarnished, its stately carving
tumbled down and lying in debris at its feet, and the bat and
the spider building their nests in the cylinders that once
mimicked the thunder and sent thrills of devotion through

the hearts of the multitude. There are remains of frescoes on the walls, but the damp and the mildew in this humid climate have so effectually performed their office that the bright colors have disappeared and only a dim outline of their design is visible.

Let us step over from the cathedral to the conventual portion of the massive block. The walls are extensive and are standing in a sufficient state of preservation to enable us to trace out the ground plan and reconstruct in imagination the ancient edifice. Its design is that of a hollow square after the fashion prevalent in Spain. On all four sides of the square are arrayed the cells of the monks, the colonnades in front of which are still standing. In the center of the square, occupying the space, which, in a private house, would have been appropriated to a *jet d'eau* and flowers in vases, is an oblong hall connected at either end with the main building. This was the refectory of the ancient establishment. What scenes does not the very sight of this refectory present to the imagination? We see the table spread, with its naked board, humble service, and still more humble food; we hear the dinner signal sound; and we see long lines of bearded and hooded monks with crosses and beads pendent from their girdles, enter and seat themselves to partake of the wonted refreshment. We hear the subdued hum of many voices—the quiet joke and half-suppressed merriment. There, at the head of the board, sits the venerable abbot, whilst the chaplain reads his Latin text from his stand during the repast. Let now the years begin to roll by. We shall miss first one familiar face from the humble board and then another until finally they all disappear, being carried away one by one to their silent tombs! The abbots repose beneath those marble slabs in the cathedral that we so lately wandered over with lightened footfall and subdued breath; but the brothers are carried to the common burial ground of the order in the outskirts of the town. New generations enter, occupy the same seats, go through the same routine of convent life, and in turn disappear to give place to newer comers still; and thus is ever swollen the holocaust of the mighty dead! "What is man, O Lord! that thou shouldst be mindful of him?"

> The dead—the honored dead are here—
> For whom, behind the sable bier,
> Through many a long-forgotten year,

Forgotten crowds have come
With solemn step and falling tear,
Bearing their brethren home.

Beneath these boughs, athwart this grass,
I see a dark and moving mass,
Like Banquo's shades across the glass,
    By wizard hand displayed;
Stand back and let these hearses pass
    Along the trampled glade.

The Convent of St. Dominic, being situated in the southern part of the old city in the angle formed by the river Ozama, and the sea, observe what a delightful sea breeze meets us as we emerge from the ruined refectory. Let us pause a while to lift our hats from our heated brows and refresh ourselves while we listen to the unceasing roar of the surf as it beats against the rocky cliff below and throws its spray halfway to our feet. What a charming view we have of the sea as it lies in its blue expanse, dotted here and there with a sail; and of the coasts of the island east and west of us—those blackened, rock-bound shores that seem hoary with age, and so much in unison with the train of thought we have been pursuing.

There are but three crafts anchored in the roadstead, where formerly fleets used to lie. Of two of these we have already spoken. The third is the *Alabama*. There is a little current setting out of the river, and she lies in consequence broadside to the sea, which is setting in to the beach. She is rolling gently to this sea, displaying every now and then bright streaks of the copper on her bottom. She is full of men, and a strange flag is flying from her peak—not only strange to the dead generations of whom we have been speaking, but new even to our own times and history. It is the flag of a nation which has just risen above the horizon and is but repeating the history of the world. The oppressed has struggled against the oppressor since time began. The struggle is going on still. It will go on forever, for the nature of man will always be the same. The cockatrice's egg has been hatched, and swarms of the Puritan have come forth to overrun the fair fields of the South that they may possess them; just as the wild Germans overran the plains of Italy centuries before.

But away with such thoughts for the present! We came on

shore to get rid of them. They madden the brain and quicken the pulse. The little craft with the strange flag has borne her captain hither on a pilgrimage to the shrine of the great discoverer, whose history may be written in a single couplet:

A Castilla, y Leon
Nuevo Mundo, dio Colon.

On her way hither, her keel has crossed the very track of the three little vessels from Palos—two of them mere open caravels—that first ventured across the vast Atlantic; and now her commander is standing where the great admiral himself once stood—on the very theater of his early glory. And alas! for Spain on the theater of his shame, or rather of her shame, too; for there stands the fortress still in which are exhibited to the curious spectator the rings in the solid masonry of the wall to which Columbus was chained!

A short walk will take us to the ruins of the palace of Diego Columbus. We must ascend the river a few hundred yards. Here it is, a little below the port of the present day. When built it stood alone, and we may remember that the townspeople complained of it on this account—saying that it was intended as a fortress to keep them in subjection. It is now surrounded by the ruins of many houses. If you have read Oviedo's description of it, you are disappointed in its appearance, for that historian tells us that "no man in Spain had a house to compare with it." Its form is that of two quadrangles connected by a colonnade, but it by no means comes up to the modern idea of a palace. The roof has entirely disappeared, and the quadrangles are mere shells filled with the accumulating debris of centuries amid which large forest trees have taken root and are flourishing. It was built of solid and substantial blocks of stone, and in any other country but the tropics would have scarcely shown signs of age in three centuries. But here the fierce rays of a perpendicular sun, the torrents of rain in the wet season, and the occasional hurricanes and earthquakes that desolate and destroy everything in their path, soon beat down the stanchest buildings—the very blocks of granite being disintegrated by the alternate rain and sunshine, and crumbling away beneath their influence. It is situated on a rising ground, commanding a fine view of the sea and the surrounding country. It is surrounded by walls and battlements, but the most imposing feature about it must have been the approach to it from the city—the visitor passing through a wide avenue of shade trees, and gaining admission to it by a majestic flight of stone steps. The shade trees have disappeared, and the stone steps have been removed to be worked up into other buildings.

We have called this house the palace of Diego Columbus, but it must have been constructed either by his father, the admiral, or his uncle Bartholomew, the *Adelantado*, as we read that when Diego came out after his father's death to assume the viceroyalty, he found it ready built at his hand. Its blackened walls and dirt-filled salons now in the midst of a squalid purlieu of the modern city must have witnessed many a scene of revelry in its day, as Oviedo tells us, that when the young admiral was restored to the honors and command of his father, he brought out to his new government with him some of the most elegant young women of Spain as maids of honor to his own beautiful young wife—the marriage portions of all of whom he undertook to provide. And that in due time these young women were all happily bestowed upon gallant knights and wealthy planters.

There, now, reader, we have taken a stroll through the classical old city of St. Domingo—a piece of good fortune, which falls to the lot of very few. Its romantic history seems to have been forgotten; it has fallen into the hands of a mongrel race of blacks and whites, and is rarely visited for any other purpose than that of trade. The Negro and the mulatto in this oldest of American cities are thought rather more of than the white man, and the Yankee skipper finds in it a congenial mart, in which to vend his cheese and his codfish and distribute his tracts—political and moral—and put forth his patent medicines!

We did not get under way the next morning until eight o'clock, as the supplies from the butchers and fruiterers could not be gotten on board at an earlier hour. Bartelli came off from the market, loaded as usual, bringing with him a bunch of wild pigeons very similar to those found in our forests, and some excellent cigars. The flavor of the latter is not quite equal to those of the Havana, but they are mild and pleasant smokers. He brought off, also, a specimen of the Haytian paper money worth five cents on the dollar. Like the American greenback, it is the offshoot of revolution and political corruption.

As eight o'clock struck, turning out of the ship the motley crowd of Negroes and mulattoes who had come off to trade with the sailors, we tripped our anchor and turning the ship's head again to the eastward gave her the steam. The day was fine and the sea smooth, and we had a picturesque run along the Haytian coast for the rest of the day. The coast is generally clean, what few dangers there are being all visible. The only sails sighted were fishing boats and small coasters laden with farm produce, running down to St. Domingo for a market. At times a number of these were in sight, and the effect was very pleasing. The coasts of Hayti abound in fish, and as there is a succession of fruits all the year round, it is the paradise of the Negro. A canoe and a fishing line, or cast-net, and a few plantain and mango trees supply his table; and two or three times a year he cuts a mahogany log and floats it down the little mountain streams to the coast, where he sells it for paper money enough to buy him a few yards of cotton cloth or calico. Voila tout!

We entered the Mona Passage at half-past eight P.M. It was unguarded as before. During the night we let our steam go down to give the engineer an opportunity of screwing up the cylinder head. Under way again before daylight. The weather continued fine, and we began again to fall in with sails. They were all neutral, however. We spoke a Spanish schooner among the rest and gave her the longitude. As soon as we had well cleared the passage, we banked fires, and hoisting the propeller, put the ship under sail. On Sunday, February 1st, we had our first muster since leaving Jamaica. We had been out now a week, and in that time I had gotten my crew straightened up again. The rum had been pretty well worked out of them; most of the black rings around the eyes had disappeared, and beards had been trimmed, and heads combed. The court-martial, which had been trying the few culprits that had been retained for trial, had gotten through its labors and been dissolved, and Jack, as he answered to his name and walked around the capstan, was himself again in all the glory of white ducks, polished shoes, straw hats, and streaming ribbons. No more than two or three desertions had occurred out of the whole crew, and this was very gratifying.

The next day we had an alarm of fire on board. It was near

twelve o'clock. I happened to be standing on the horse-block at the time, observing the sun for latitude, when suddenly I heard a confusion of voices below, and simultaneously the officer of the deck with evident alarm depicted in his countenance came running to me and said, "The ship is on fire, sir!" This is an alarm that always startles the seaman. The fire bell in the night is sufficiently alarming to the landsman, but the cry of fire at sea imports a matter of life and death—especially in a ship of war, whose boats are always insufficient to carry off her crew, and whose magazine and shell rooms are filled with powder, and the loaded missiles of death. The fire bell on board a ship of war, whose crew is always organized as a fire company, points out the duty of every officer and man in such an emergency. The first thing to be done is to beat to quarters, and accordingly I gave this order to the officer; but before the drummer could brace his drum for the operation, it was announced that all danger had disappeared. When we had a little leisure to look into the facts, it appeared that the alarm had arisen from the carelessness of the captain of the hold, who, in violation of the orders of the ship, had taken a naked light below with him, into the spirit room to pump off the grog by. The candle had ignited some of the escaping gas, but the flame was suppressed almost immediately. The captain of the hold, who is a petty officer, paid the penalty of his disobedience by being dismissed from his office; and in half an hour the thing was forgotten.

Since leaving the Mona Passage, we had been steering about N. N. W., or as near north as the trade wind would permit us. We expected, as a matter of course, to meet with the usual calms as we came up with the Tropic of Cancer, but the northeast trade, instead of dying away as we had expected, hauled to the southeast and shot us across the calm belt with a fine breeze all the way. We carried this wind to the twenty-seventh parallel, when we took, with scarcely any intermission, a fresh northwester. This does not often happen. . . .

On the 3d of February, we made our first capture since leaving St. Domingo. It was the schooner *Palmetto*, bound from New York to St. John's in the island of Puerto Rico. We gave chase to her soon after breakfast and came up with her about half-past one P. M. It was a fair trial of heels with a fine breeze and a smooth sea; both vessels being on a wind; and it was beautiful to see how the *Alabama* performed her task, working up into the wind's eye and overhauling her enemy with the ease of a trained courser coming up with a saddle nag. There was no attempt to cover the cargo of the *Palmetto*. The enemy merchants seemed to have come to the conclusion that it was no longer of any use to prepare bogus certificates, and that they might as well let their cargoes run the chances of war without them. Upon examination of the papers of the schooner, it appeared that the cargo was shipped by the Spanish house of Harques & Maseras, domiciled and doing business in New York, to Vincent Brothers in San Juan, Puerto Rico on joint account; the shippers owning one third, and the consignee two thirds. The case came, therefore, under the rule applied in a former case, viz., that when partners reside, some in a belligerent and some in a neutral country, the property of all of them, which has any connection with the house in the belligerent country, is liable to confiscation (3 *Phillimore*, 605, and 1 *Robinson*, 1, 14, 19, Also, *The Susa, ib.* 255.) Getting on board from the *Palmetto* such articles of provisions—and she was chiefly provision-laden—as we needed, we applied the torch to her about sunset and filled away and made sail.

The next afternoon we sighted a sail on our weather bow, close hauled, like ourselves, and continued to gain upon her until night shut her out from view, when we discontinued the chase. We were satisfied from her appearance that she was neutral, or we should probably have expended a little steam upon her. At night the weather set in thick, and the wind blew so fresh from the northeast, that we took a single reef in the topsails. This bad weather continued for the next two or three days, reducing us part of the time to close reefs. A ship bound from the West Indies to the coast of Brazil is compelled to run up into the variables and make sufficient easting to enable her to weather Cape St. Roque. This is what the *Alabama* is now doing—working her way to the eastward on the parallel of about 30°. We observed on the 20th of February in latitude 28° 32'; the longitude being 45° 05'.

The next day, the weather being very fine with the wind light from the southward and eastward, a sail was descried from aloft, and soon afterward another, and another, until four were seen. We gave chase to the first sail announced; standing to the eastward in pursuit of her for an hour or two, but she being a long distance ahead and to windward, and the chase being likely in consequence to be long, and to draw us away from the other three sail besides, we abandoned it and gave chase to two of the latter. These were fine, tall ships, under a cloud of canvas, steering, one to the eastward, and the other to the westward. Being quite sure that they were Americans, and the wind falling light, we got up steam for the chase. Coming up with the eastward-bound ship, we hove her to, but not until we had thrown a couple of shot at her in succession—the latter whizzing over the master's head on the quarter-deck. She was evidently endeavoring to draw us after her as far to the eastward as possible to give her consort, with whom she had spoken, and who was running to the westward, an opportunity to escape. Throwing a boat crew hastily on board of her and directing the prize-master to follow us, we now wheeled in pursuit of the other fugitive. The latter was by this time fifteen miles distant—being hull down—and was running before the wind with studding sails alow and aloft. Fortunately for the *Alabama*, the wind was light, or the chase might have put darkness between us before we came up with her. As it was, it was three P. M. before we overhauled her, and we had run our other prize nearly out of sight. She was less obstinate than her consort, and shortened sail and hove to at the first gun, hoisting the United States colors at her peak. She proved to be the bark *Olive Jane* of New York from Bordeaux, bound to New York with an assorted cargo of French wines, brandies, canned meats, fruits, and other delicacies. There was no attempt to cover the cargo. There were a great many shippers. Some few of these had consigned their goods to their own order, but most of the consignments were to New York houses. It is possible that some of the consignments, to order, really belonged to French owners, but if so, I was relieved from the necessity of making the investigation by the carelessness of the owners themselves, who had taken no pains to protect their property by proper documentary evidence of its neutral character. In the absence of sworn proof the rule of law is imperative that all property found on board of an enemy's ship is presumed to belong to the enemy. I acted upon this presumption and set fire to the *Olive Jane*. What a splendid libation was here to old Neptune! I did not permit so much as a bottle of brandy or a basket of champagne to be brought on board the *Alabama*, though I doubt not the throats of some of my vagabonds, who had so recently cooled off from the big frolic they had had in Jamaica, were as dry as powder horns. There were the richest of olives and *patés de fois gras* going to tickle the palates of the New York shoddyites and other *nouveau-riche* plebeians destroyed in that terrible conflagration. I should have permitted Bartelli and the other stewards to have a short run among these delicacies but for the wine and the brandy. A Fouché could not have prevented the boats' crews from smuggling some of it on board, and then I might have had another Martinique grog-watering on my hands.

Amid the crackling of flames, the bursting of brandy casks, the shrivelling of sails as they were touched by the fire, and the tumbling of the lighter spars of the *Olive Jane* from aloft, we turned our head to the eastward again and rejoined our first prize, coming up with her just as the shades of evening were closing in. I had now a little leisure to look into her character. She, like the *Olive Jane*, had shown me the "old flag," and that, of course, had set at rest all doubts as to the nationality of the ship. There was as little doubt about the cargo. The ship was the *Golden Eagle*, and I had overhauled her near the termination of a long voyage. She had sailed from San Francisco in ballast for Howland's Island in the Pacific; a guano island of which some adventurous Yankees had taken possession. There she had taken in a cargo of guano for Cork and a market; the guano being owned by and consigned to the order of the American Guano Company. This ship had buffeted the gales of the frozen latitudes of Cape Horn, threaded her pathway among its icebergs, been parched with the heats of the tropic and drenched with the rains of the equator, to fall into the hands of her enemy only a few hundred miles from her port. But such is the fortune of war. It seemed a pity, too, to destroy so large a cargo of a fertilizer that would else have made fields stagger under a wealth of grain. But those fields would be the fields of the enemy; or if it did not fertilize his fields, its sale would pour a stream of gold into his coffers; and it was my business upon the high seas to cut off or dry up this stream of gold. The torch followed the examination of the papers. The reader may perhaps by this time have remarked how fond the Yankees had become of the qualifying adjective "golden" as a prefix to the names of their ships. I had burned the *Golden Rocket*, the *Golden Rule*, and the *Golden Eagle*.

We were now in latitude 30° and longitude 40°, and if the curious reader will refer to a map or chart of the North Atlantic Ocean, he will see that we are on the charmed crossing leading to the coast of Brazil. By "crossing" is meant the point at which the ship's course crosses a given parallel of latitude. We must not, for instance, cross the thirtieth parallel going southward until we have reached a certain meridian —say that of 40° W. If we do, the northeast trade-wind will pinch us and perhaps prevent us from weathering Cape St. Roque.

And when we reach the equator, there is another crossing recommended to the mariner as being most appropriate to his purpose. Thus it is that the roads upon the sea have been blazed out,—the blazes not being exactly cut upon the forest trees but upon parallels and meridians. The chief blazer of these roads is an American, of whom all Americans should be proud—Captain Maury, before mentioned in these pages. He has so effectually performed his task in his "Wind and Current Charts" that there is little left to be desired. The most unscientific and practical navigator may by the aid of these charts find the road he is in quest of. Maury has been in an eminent degree the benefactor of the very men who became most abusive of him when they found that he, like other Southern statesmen—for he is a statesman as well as sailor— was obliged to preserve his self-respect by spitting upon the "old flag." He has saved every Yankee ship, by shortening her route on every distant voyage she makes, thousands of dollars. The greedy shipowners pocket the dollars and abuse the philosopher.*

* Now let us make a calculation of the annual saving to the commerce of the United States effected by these charts and sailing directions. According to Mr. Maury, the average freight from the United States to Rio Janeiro, is 17.7 cents per ton per day; to Australia, 20 cents; to California, 20 cents. The mean of this is a little over 19 cents per ton per day; but to be within the mark, we will take it at 15 cents and include all the ports of South America, China, and the East Indies. The "Sailing Directions" have shortened the passage to California, thirty days; to Australia, twenty days; and to Rio Janeiro, ten days. The mean of this is twenty, but we will take it at fifteen

and also include the above named ports of South America, China, and the East Indies. We estimate the tonnage of the United States engaged in trade with these places at 1,000,000 tons per annum. With these data, we see that there has been effected a saving for each one of those tons of 15 cents per day for a period of fifteen days, which will give an aggregate of $2,250,000 saved per annum. This is on the outward voyage alone, and the tonnage trading with all other parts of the world is also left out of the calculation. Take these into consideration, and also the fact that there is a vast amount of foreign tonnage trading between those places and the United States, and it will be seen that the annual sum saved will swell to an enormous amount.—*Hunt's Merchants' Magazine,* May 1854.

Chapter Thirteen—*1863*

---

*The crossing of the thirtieth parallel . . . The toll gate
upon the sea . . . How the travelers pass along the
highway . . . Capture of the Washington; John A.
Parks; Bethiah Thayer; Punjaub; Morning Star; Kingfisher; Charles Hill; and Nora . . . Crosses the equator
. . . Capture of the Louisa Hatch . . . Arrival at
Fernando de Noronha*

Reaching the blazed road of which I spoke in the last
chapter, I shortened sail at the crossing mentioned, so that
I might waylay such of the passengers as chanced to be enemies. There were a great many ships passing both ways on
this road, some going to the Pacific or the Far East, and
others returning from those distant points; but they were
nearly all neutral. The American ships having, by this time
become thoroughly alarmed, especially since they learned that
neither English sealing wax nor Admiral Milne could save
them, had dodged the highways, as skulkers and thieves are
wont to do, and taken to the open fields and byways for
safety. On the day after the capture of the *Olive Jane* and
Golden Eagle, the weather being cloudy and rainy and the
wind light, four more sail were seen—all European bound.

At eight A. M. we showed the United States colors to one of them, which proved to be a French bark. It now became calm, and we were compelled to get up steam to overhaul the rest. They lay long distances apart, and we were several hours in passing from one to the other. They were all Englishmen with various histories and destinations, one of them— a fine frigate-built ship—being a Melbourne and Liverpool packet. We received a paper from her printed at the antipodes, but there was not much in it besides the proceedings of the Australian Parliament, news from the gold diggings, and the price of wool; in neither of which subjects were we much interested.

On the next day but a solitary passenger came over the road. It was late at night when she made her appearance— there being a bright moon and a brisk breeze. We made sail in chase, and the chase, taking the alarm, gave us a very pretty run for a few hours. We overhauled her, however at length, and fired the usual blank cartridge to heave her to. She was an hermaphrodite brig, and might be for aught we could see in the uncertain light, American. The gun had no effect. We waited a few minutes for a response, but none coming, we fired again—sending a shot whizzing, this time over the little craft. Still no response. We were now only a few hundred yards distant. What could the fellow mean? All was as silent on board the chase as death, and not a tack or sheet had been started. We ran now almost on board of her and hailing her, commanded her to heave to. Great confusion followed. We could hear voices speaking in a foreign tongue, and presently a disorderly array of sails whipping and flapping in the wind, and of yards swinging to and fro presented itself. At last the little craft managed to come to the wind and make a halt. She proved to be a Portuguese brig, and the crew had been so alarmed at being chased and fired at by night as to lose all presence of mind and become incapable of any action whatever until they were somewhat reassured by the near presence of our ship and the sound of our voices. She was bound from Pernambuco to Lisbon with a cargo of hides and sugar. It was, indeed, something like a ghost chase to see the *Alabama* coming in the dead night after the little craft with her seven-league boots on, and those awful trysails of hers spread out in the moonlight like so many winding sheets.

On the day after this adventure, a Dutch bark and an Eng-

lish brig came along; and on the same night we boarded the
English four-master, the *Sarah Sands*, from the East Indies for
Falmouth. At daylight the next morning, the lookout at the
mast-head began to cry sails until he reported as many as
seven in sight at one time. They were all European bound,
and were jogging along in company, following Maury's blazes,
like so many passengers on a highway. The *Alabama* stood
like a toll gate before them, and though we could not take toll
of them, as they were all neutral, we made each traveler show
us his passport as he came up. One obstinate fellow—a
Hamburger—refused to show us his colors until he was commanded to do so by a gun. I made it a practice to punish
these unmannerly fellows for their want of civility. On the
present occasion, the Hamburger was detained a considerable
time whilst I exercised at my leisure my belligerent right of
viséing his papers. When his traveling companions were
some miles ahead of him, I told the surly fellow to pick up
his hat and be off.

On the next day, being still in latitude 30° and longitude
40°, or at the crossing, an English and an American ship
came along. The Englishman saluted us civilly as he passed.
He was from the East Indies, laden with silks and wines. But
the American, seeing that we were under short sail—though
the weather was fine—resting by the wayside, as it were, and
remembering that there was a little unpleasantness between
the North and South, fought rather shy of us and endeavored
to get out of the way of possible harm. She was a fine, large
ship, and the moment she showed an intention not to pass
through the toll gate, we made sail in pursuit. She had heels,
but they were not quite as clean as the *Alabama's*, and we
came up with her in the course of two or three hours; she
having approached pretty close before she smelt the rat. She
was obstinate and compelled me to wet the people on her
poop by the spray of a shot before she would acknowledge
that she was beaten. The shower bath made a stir among the
bystanders; there was a running hither and thither, a letting
go of sheets and halliards, and pretty soon the main-yard
swung aback, and the stars and stripes were seen ascending
to the stranger's peak. When the boarding-officer brought the
master of the captured ship on board with his papers, she
proved to be the ship *Washington* of New York from the
Chincha Islands, bound to Antwerp with a cargo of guano,

laden on account of the Peruvian government and consigned
to its agent at Antwerp for sale. Being unable to destroy
the ship because of the neutral ownership of her cargo, I released her on ransom bond, sent my prisoners on board of her
to be landed and permitted her to depart. This capture was
made on the 27th of February. On the 28th we overhauled
two English ships from the East Indies, homeward bound,
and a French ship from Batavia for Nantes. The weather
continued very fine, and we had had a uniformly high barometer ever since we had reached the crossing.

The morning of the 1st of March dawned charmingly with
a very light breeze. The night had been rather dark, and we
had been lying to under topsails. In the darkness of the
night, an enemy's ship had approached us unawares. She had
been following the blazes without seeing the toll gate, and
the revelations made by the morning's light must have startled
her, for she found herself within half a mile of an exceedingly
saucy-looking gunboat lying in wait for somebody or something. It was nearly calm, and she could not help herself
if she would. On the other hand, the gunboat was delighted
to see a tall ship, whose masts tapered like a lady's fingers,
arrayed in the whitest of petticoats—to carry out our figure—
and which, from the course she was steering, was evidently just
out from Yankee land with that mail on board, which we
had been anxiously looking for, for several days past. We were
in the midst of the scrubbing and cleaning of the morning
watch, and to effect the capture, it was not even necessary to
lay aside a holy stone or a scrubbing-brush. A gun and a
Confederate flag were all that was required to bring the tall
ship to a halt and remove her doubts if she had had any.
She was the *John A. Parks* of Hallowell, Maine.

The cargo of the *Parks* consisted of white pine lumber
which she had taken on board at New York, and she was
bound to Montevideo or Buenos Ayres, as the consignee
might elect. There was an affidavit found among her papers,
made by one Snyder before a Mr. Edwards Pierrepont, who
appears to have been acting as British Consul, claiming that
the cargo was shipped on account of a London house. The
real facts of the case, however, as gathered from the correspondence and the testimony of the master, were that one Davidson, a lumber dealer in New York had chartered the ship and
shipped the lumber in the usual course of his business to the

parties in Montevideo; that he had paid most of the freight,
in advance and insured himself against the war risk, both
upon the cargo and the freight. The manner in which this
case was "put up" in the papers, was an improvement upon
some others I had examined. The New York merchants were
evidently becoming expert in the preparation of bogus certificates. It was no longer merely stated that the property belonged to neutral owners, but the owners themselves were
named. In short, the certificate found on board the *Parks*
was in due form, but unfortunately for the parties who contrived the clever little plot, the master forgot to throw overboard his letterbag, and among the letters found in that bag
was one written by Davidson giving instructions to the
consignees, in which the following expressions occur: "The
cargo of the *John A. Parks*, I shall have certified to by the
British Consul as the property of British subjects. You will
find it a very good cargo and should command the highest
prices." By the time that I had finished the examination of the
case, Bartelli announced breakfast, and I invited my Hallowell
friend to take a cup of coffee with me, telling him at the same
time that I should burn his ship. As well as I recollect, he
declined the coffee, but I am quite certain that the ship was
burned. The carpenter of the *Alabama* was thrown into ecstasies by this capture. All the other departments of the ship
had been kept well supplied, except his own. The paymaster,
who was also commissary, the boatswain, the sailmaker, had
all been "plundering" the enemy quite extensively, but no
boards had come along until now for the poor carpenter.
Here they were at last, however, and if I had not put some
restraint upon my zealous officer of the adze and chisel, I believe he would have converted the *Alabama* into a lumberman.

We received from the *Parks*, sure enough, the mail we had
been waiting for. There must have been a barrelful and more
of newspapers and periodicals going to the *Montevideans* and
Buenos Ayreans—many of them in the best of Spanish, and
all explaining the "great moral ideas" on which the Southern
people were being robbed of their property and having their
throats cut. We gleaned one gratifying piece of intelligence,
however, from these papers. "The Pirate *Florida*" had put to
sea from Mobile to assist the "British Pirate," in plundering
and burning the "innocent merchant ships of the United
States, pursuing their peaceful commerce," as Mr. Charles

Francis Adams so often and so *naively* expressed it to Earl Russell. Whilst the *Parks* was still burning, an English bark passed through the toll gate, the captain of which was prevailed upon to take the master of the burning ship, his wife, and two nephews to London. We were glad on the poor lady's account that she was so soon relieved from the discomforts of a small and crowded ship.

The next traveler that came along was the *Bethiah Thayer* of Rockland, Maine, last from the Chinca Islands with a cargo of guano for the Peruvian Government. The cargo being properly documented, I put the ship under ransom bond and permitted her to pass. It was Sunday; the *Bethiah* was dressed in a new suit of cotton canvas and looked quite demure and saintlike while her papers were being examined. I have no doubt if I had questioned her master that he would have been found to have voted for Breckinridge.*

I now resolved to fill away, stand down toward the equator, and hold myself stationary for a few days at the crossing of the famous great circle. I was far enough to the eastward to make a free wind of the northeast trade, and we jogged along under topsails, making sail only when it became necessary to chase. We lost our fine weather almost immediately upon leaving the crossing, and took a series of moderate gales—sometimes, however, reducing us to close reefs—which lasted us for a week or ten days, or until we began to approach the rains and calms of the equator. We met a number of sails on the road, and now and then chased one, but they all proved to be neutral. On the night of the 15th of March, at a few minutes before midnight, the weather being thick and murky, the lookout at the cat-head suddenly cried "Sail ho; close aboard;" and in a few minutes a large ship passed us on the opposite tack within speaking distance. We hailed, but she passed on like a goblin ship without giving us any reply. She had all sails set, there was no one stirring on board of her, and the only light that was visible was the one which twinkled in the binnacle. We wore ship with all expedition, shook the reefs out of the topsails, and made sail in pursuit. It took us some minutes to accomplish this, and by the time we were well under way, the stranger was nearly out of

* One of the three candidates who ran against Lincoln in the 1860 election. ED.

sight. Both ships were on a wind, however, and this was the *Alabama's* best point of sailing. Our nightglasses soon began to tell the usual tale. We were overhauling the chase; and at a quarter past three, or a little before dawn, we were near enough to heave her to with a gun. She proved to be the *Punjaub* of Boston from Calcutta for London. Her cargo consisted chiefly of jute and linseed and was properly certificated as English property. The goods were, besides, of foreign growth, and were going from one English port to another. I released her on ransom bond and sent on board of her the prisoners from the last ship burned.

Soon after daylight, we gave chase to another sail in the E. S. E., with which we came up about eight A. M. She was an English ship from the Mauritius for Cork. She confirmed our suspicion that the Yankee ships were avoiding as a general rule the beaten tracks, having spoken one of them on the line bound to the coast of Brazil, which had traveled as far east as the twenty-third meridian; or about four hundred miles out of her way. We were still standing to the southward, and on the 21st of March we were very near the sun, for while he was crossing the equator, we were in latitude 2° 47′ N.; our longitude being 26° W. On that day the weather is thus recorded in my journal: "Cloudy with squalls of rain, and the wind shifting, indicating that we have lost the trades. It is pleasant to hear the thunder roll for the first time in several months, sounding like the voice of an old friend; and the crew seem to enjoy a ducking from the heavy showers—rain having been a rare visitor of late." And on the next day, the following is the record: "Rains and calms all day; the officers and crew alike are paddling about the deck in bare feet and enjoying the pelting of the rain like young ducks. Three neutrals in company bound like ourselves across the line. They look at a distance with their drooping sails flapping idly in the calm as disconsolate as wet barnyard fowls at home on a rainy day."

On the 23d of March, the weather being still as described, and very little change having taken place in our position, we made two more captures; the first, the *Morning Star* of Boston from Calcutta for London, and the second the whaling schooner *Kingfisher* of Fairhaven, Massachusetts. The cargo of the *Morning Star* being in the same category as that of the *Punjaub*, we released her also on ransom bond. The *Kingfisher* we burned. This adventurous little whaler had a crew of twenty-three persons, all of whom were Portuguese except the master and mate, and one or two boat steerers. We set fire to her just at nightfall, and the conflagration presented a weird-like spectacle on the line amid the rumbling of thunder, the shifting, but ever black scenery of the nimbi, or rain clouds, and the pouring and dashing of torrents of rain. Sometimes the flames would cower beneath a drenching shower as though they had been subdued, but in a moment afterward, they would shoot up, mast-head high as brightly and ravenously as before. The oil in her hold kept her burning on the surface of the still sea until a late hour at night.

On the next day we boarded as usual a number of neutral ships of different nationalities, some going south, and some going north. We were at the crossing of the equator, blazed by Maury, and with the main topsail at the mast, were reviewing the commerce of the world. We were never out of sight of ships. They were passing by ones and twos and threes in constant succession, wreathed in rain and mist and presenting frequently the idea of a funeral procession. The honest traders were all there except the most honest of them all—the Yankees—and they were a little afraid of the police. Still we managed to catch a rogue now and then.

On the second day after burning the *Kingfisher*, we made two more captures. Later in the afternoon of that day we descried two large ships approaching us in company. They came along lovingly, arm-in-arm as though in the light airs and calms that were prevailing, they had been having a friendly chat, or one of the masters had been dining on board of the other. They were evidently American ships and had most likely been having a cosy talk about the war. The "sainted" Abraham's Emancipation Proclamation was the favorite topic of the day, as we had learned from the mail bags of the *Parks*, and perchance they had been discussing that; or perhaps the skippers were congratulating themselves upon having escaped the *Alabama*; they probably supposing her to be at the other toll gate still. Whatever may have been the subject of their discourse, they evidently pricked up their ears as soon as they saw the *Alabama* stripped like a gentleman who was taking it coolly with nothing but her topsails set, and lying across their path. They separated gradually; and quietly and by stealth a few more studding-sails were sent up aloft.

It was time now for the _Alabama_ to move. Her main yard was swung to the full, sailors might have been seen running up aloft like so many squirrels who thought they saw nuts ahead, and pretty soon, upon a given signal, the top-gallant sails and royals might have been seen fluttering in the breeze for a moment, and then extending themselves to their respective yard arms. A whistle or two from the boatswain and his mates, and the trysail sheets are drawn aft, and the _Alabama_ has on those seven-league boots which the reader has seen her draw on so often before. A stride or two, and the thing is done. First, the _Charles Hill_ of Boston shortens sail and runs up the "old flag," and then the _Nora_ of the same pious city follows her example. They were both laden with salt, and both from Liverpool. The _Hill_ was bound to Montevideo or Buenos Ayres, and there was no attempt to cover her cargo. The _Nora_ was bound to Calcutta under a charter party with one W. N. de Mattos. In the bill of lading, the cargo was consigned to order, and on the back of the instrument was the following indorsement: "I hereby certify, that the salt shipped on board the _Nora_ is the property of W. N. de Mattos of London, and that the said W. N. de Mattos is a British subject and was so at the time of the shipment." This certificate was signed by one H. E. Folk, and at the bottom of the certificate were the words, "R. C. Gardner, Mayor"—presumed to mean the Mayor of Liverpool.

Here was a more awkward attempt to cover a cargo than any of my Yankee friends of New York or Boston had ever made. There was very little doubt that the salt was English-owned, but the certificate did not amount even to an _ex parte_ affidavit, it not being sworn to. As a matter of course I was bound to presume the property to be enemy, it being found unprotected by any legal evidence in an enemy's ship. The _Hill_ and the _Nora_ were therefore both consigned to the flames after we had gotten on board from them such articles as we stood in need of. We received from the two ships between thirty and forty tons of coal, or about two days' steaming. It took us nearly all the following day to transport it in our small boats, and we did not set fire to the ships until five in the afternoon. We received, also, half a dozen recruits from them. I had now quite as many men as I wanted.

Among the papers of the *Hill* was found the following brief letter of instructions from her owner to her master. It is dated from the good city of Boston, and was written while the ship was lying at the other good city, Philadelphia. It is addressed to Captain F. Percival and goes on to say:

DEAR SIR: I have received your several letters from Philadelphia. As a rebel privateer has burned several American ships, it may be as well if you can have your bills of lading indorsed as English property and have your cargo certified to by the British Consul.

Such nice little missives as these, written from one city of "grand moral ideas" to another city, whose ideas were no less grand or moral, quietly instructing ship masters to commit perjury were of great assistance to me when in the classical words of the New York *Commercial Advertiser*, I had a "Yankee hash" to deal with.

On the 29th of March we crossed the equator. The event is thus recorded in my journal: "Crossed the equator at five P. M. in the midst of a dense rain squall, with lowering, black clouds, and the wind from the southwest. We were in chase of a sail at the time but lost her in the gloom. It rained all night with light airs and calms. We have experienced a southeasterly current setting at the rate of a knot and a half for the last twenty-four-hours." We made our crossing a little farther to the eastward than usual—26°—on purpose to counteract the Yankee dodge spoken of a little while back. We now encountered a variety of currents, some setting to the southeast as just mentioned, others to the east, others to the south, until finally we fell in with the great equatorial current setting to the westward.

The study of the phenomena of the currents is one of the most interesting that can engage the attention of the marine philosopher. We have already had occasion to explain the circulation of the atmosphere—how the wind "cometh and goeth," not at random but in obedience to certain well-defined natural laws. The circulation of the sea is no less regular than that of the atmosphere and has equally important offices to perform. If the sea were a stagnant mass of waters, some portions of the earth which now enjoy temperate climates and teem with millions of population in the enjoyment of an abundant fauna and flora, would be almost uninhabitable because of the extreme cold. Some portions of the sea would dry up and become beds of salt, and others again would, from the superabundance of precipitation, become fresh, or nearly so. In short, there would be a general disturbance of the harmonies of creation. To obviate this, and to put the sea in motion, various agencies have been set at work by the great Architect; chief among which is the unequal distribution of heat over the earth's surface. We have already called the sun the Father of the Winds; he is equally the father of the currents. The warm water of the equator is constantly flowing off to the poles, and the cold water of the poles flowing back as undercurrents to the equator. This flow is not directly north, or directly south, but by a variety of tortuous channels. The different depths of the ocean, the obstructions of islands, and continents, clouds and sunshine, and a great many other agencies combine to give this tortuosity and seeming irregularity to the currents.

Let us take an example. The *Alabama* has just experienced a southeast current in a locality where the current sets as a general rule to the westward. How are we to account for this? It may be due to a variety of causes, all working in harmony, however, with the general design. In the first place, it may be a counter-current going to fill the place left vacant by some other current; for, as a matter of course, when a given quantity of water flows away from a place, the same quantity must flow back to it. Or it may be a principal, and not an accessory current, set in motion, say by heat. Let us see how easily this may be accomplished. Suppose a dense canopy of clouds to overshadow some considerable space of the sea for a day, or it may be, for a few hours only. Whilst the rays of the sun are shut out from this space, they are pouring down their heat with tropical fervor, say to the south of this cloud bank. Under the cloud bank the water is cooling, beyond the bank it is being heated. Under the bank, evaporation has ceased almost altogether, beyond the bank it is going on at the rate of about an inch in twenty-four hours. Here are powerful agencies at work, changing both the temperature and specific gravity of the waters.

Waters to be at rest must have the same temperature and specific gravity. These waters therefore cannot remain at rest, and a current is the consequence. Tomorrow, perhaps, the process will be reversed, the cloud and the sunshine changing places, and the current flowing in a contrary direction. These are local disturbances of the system of oceanic circulation—little venous derangements, as it were, the great arterial system not being materially affected by them.

There are other exceedingly beautiful agencies at work on a smaller scale to disturb the oceanic equilibrium and set the waters in motion. It has puzzled philosophers to account for the saltness of the sea. Whatever may be its cause, it plays a very important part in giving vitality to its circulation. If sea water were fresh, evaporation would not produce any change in its specific gravity. One element of motion, therefore, would be wanted. But being salt, and the salts not being taken up by the thirsty air in the process of evaporation, every rain drop that is withdrawn from it helps to put the currents in motion.

But these are surface operations; let us dive beneath the surface and witness some of the wonders that are going on in the depths below. We have before shown the reader the coralline insect, that wonderful little stone mason of the sea, which, in the hands of Providence, is the architect of islands and continents. The sea water is the quarry from which this little toiler extracts his tiny blocks of masonry. If the water were fresh, it would not hold the materials in solution which he needs for his work. But being salt, it has just the materials which he needs.

But how does he affect the currents? the reader will ask. As follows: Every particle of solid matter that he extracts from the sea-water—and he must have limestone to build those islands and continents of which he is the architect—alters its specific gravity. The little globule of water, from which he has just taken the block of stone that would be scarcely visible under a powerful microscope, has become lighter than the surrounding globules and ascends to the surface. In obedience to the law which we have mentioned that as much water must flow back to a place as flows away from it, a globule of water from the surface now descends to take the place of that which has arisen; descends to the little stone mason that he may rob it in turn of the block of stone it contains. The globules of water thus become the hod carriers for these little stone masons, working away in countless myriads at the bottom of the sea.

But what becomes of this lighter globule of water which

has arisen to the surface, because it has been deprived of its solid matter? It must flow away somewhere in search of the salts it has lost, for if it remains stationary, in course of time the sea in its neighborhood will all be deprived of its salts, and there will be no more globules to descend to the little stone mason. But when the globules starts to flow off, a current is established.

When we were at the Azores breaking up the Yankee whaling station, we spoke of the currents in connection with the whales and other fishes; how, like reapers and gleaners, they bore to them the food which was prepared for them in other latitudes. The reader sees, now, how the currents build the coral bank. Every sea shell, as it secretes the solid matter for its edifice, helps on the movement set on foot by the coral insect.

On the 3d of April, we observed in latitude 2° 11′ S.; our longitude being 26° 02′. The weather was still thick and rainy, and we had fitful gusts of wind and calms by turns. During the morning watch, the dense clouds lifted for a while and showed us a fine, tall ship, steering like ourselves to the southward. We immediately made sail in chase. The wind was blowing quite fresh from the southwest at the time, and we gained very rapidly upon the stranger. At twelve o'clock the wind died away, and the heavy rains being renewed, she was entirely shut out from view. We continued the chase all day; now being sure of her, and now being baffled by the ever-shifting clouds and changing wind and weather. At length, at five P. M., it being no longer safe to trust to contingencies, as night would set in in another hour, I sent a whale-boat to board and halt her, although she was still two miles distant. The boarding was successfully accomplished, and just before dark we could see the stranger's head turned in our direction. We knew from this circumstance that she was a prize, and hoisting a light as night set in to guide the boarding-officer, in an hour or two more she was alongside of us.

The prize proved to be the *Louisa Hatch* of Rockland, Maine, from Cardiff with a cargo of the best Welsh coal for Point-de-Galle in the island of Ceylon. The bill of lading required the cargo to be delivered to the *Messageries Imperiales* steamship company, and there was a certificate on the back of the bill of lading to the effect that the coal belonged to that company, but the certificate was not sworn to by the subscriber. This was tantamount to no evidence at all, and I condemned both ship and cargo as prize of war. Here was quite a windfall—a thousand tons of coal near the coast of Brazil, where it was worth $17 per ton. But what was I to do with the prize? It would be an interminable job to attempt to supply myself from her by means of my boats, and hauling the two ships alongside of each other at sea was not to be thought of. I was bound to the island of Fernando de Noronha, that being the second rendezvous which I had assigned to my old Scotch collier, the *Agrippina*, and I resolved to take the *Hatch* in with me to abide contingencies. If the *Agrippina* should arrive in due time, I could burn the *Hatch*; if not, the *Hatch* would supply her place.

This being determined upon, I sent a prize crew on board the captured ship and directed the prize-master to keep company with me. We overhauled an English bark the next day, bound from Lisbon to Rio Janeiro, from which we received some late Portuguese newspapers of no particular interest; and on the day afterward, we chased what we took certainly to be a Yankee whaling schooner, but which we found upon coming up with her to be a Portuguese. The schooner was a capital imitation of the down East fore-and-after, but upon being boarded, she not only proved to be foreign built, but her master and crew were all Portuguese, nearly as black as Negroes, with a regular set of Portuguese papers. What added considerably to the cheat was that the little craft had heels, and I was some two or three hours in coming up with her.

The weather was so thick for the next two or three days that it was necessary to keep the prize very close to me to prevent losing sight of her. At night I showed her a light from my peak, and we jogged along within speaking distance of each other. Having had no observation for fixing the position of my ship during the prevalence of this thick weather, and the direction and velocity of the currents being somewhat uncertain, I was quite anxious lest I should drift past the island I was in quest of and fall upon some of the foul ground lying between it and the coast of Brazil. On the 9th of April, the sun showed himself for an hour or two near noon, and I got latitude and longitude and found that we were in the great equatorial current, as I had supposed, setting us about S.W. by W. at the rate of a knot and a half. I now got up steam, and taking the prize in tow, for it was nearly calm, with but a few cats' paws playing upon the water, made the best of my way toward Fernando de Noronha.

At daylight the next morning, we made the famous peak, some forty miles distant, and at half-past two P. M. we came to anchor in thirteen fathoms water. The prize, having been cast off as we ran in, anchored near us. The *Agrippina* had not arrived; nor did I ever see her afterward. Captain Bulloch had duly dispatched her, but the worthless old Scotch master made it a point not to find me, and having sold his coal in some port or other (I have forgotten where), returned to England with a cock-and-a-bull story to account for his failure. The fact is, the old fellow had become alarmed lest he should fall into the hands of the Yankees. It was fortunate that I had not burned the *Louisa Hatch*.

Frightened passengers watch approach of *The Alabama*
(by Winslow Homer)

Chapter Fourteen—*1863*

Fernando de Noronha . . . Its famous peak . . . Is a penal settlement of Brazil . . . A visit from the Governor's ambassadors . . . A visit to the Governor in return . . . The aristocracy of the island . . . Capture of the Lafayette and the Kate Cory . . . Burning of the two last ships with the Louisa Hatch . . . Prisoners sent to Pernambuco . . . The cloud ring and the rainy and dry seasons

Fernando De Noronha lies not a great way from Cape St. Roque in Brazil. It forms the western end of a chain of volcanic islands and deep-sea soundings that extend some distance along the equator. Earthquakes have been frequently experienced by ships when passing along this chain, and the charts point out a number of supposed dangers hereabout. Many of these dangers have no real existence, but still the prudent mariner gives them a wide berth when sailing past the localities assigned them. The island of Fernando de Noronha is evidently of volcanic origin. Its whole appearance indicates that it was thrown from the depths of the sea by nature, when in one of her most fearful paroxysms. Its abrupt and rugged sides of solid rock, rent and torn, and blackened by the torrents, rise almost perpendicularly from the waters to the height of several hundred feet.

Fighting in a circle

The famous peak before spoken of, and which the mariner at sea descries long before the body of the island becomes visible, is a queer freak of nature. It looks as though the giants had been playing at church steeples, and had upraised this immense shaft of granite to mark one of nature's cathedrals. The illusion is almost perfect. When "Land ho!" is first cried by the lookout at the mast-head, and the glass is applied in the given direction, the observer is startled at the resemblance. Nor is his surprise diminished as his ship approaches nearer, and the body of the island begins to make its appearance above the water; for there is the roof of the massive cathedral, to which the steeple belongs! The peak is a mass of solid granite, shot by the earthquake through the solid crust of the mountain, and is almost symmetrical enough to have been shaped by human hands. We lay nearly two weeks at Fernando de Noronha, and I was never tired of gazing upon this wonderful evidence of the power of volcanic forces.

The winds, the rains, and the sunshine have in the course of ages disintegrated enough of the surface of this rocky island to form a rich soil, which is covered with a profusion of tropical vegetation, including forest trees of considerable size; and a number of small farms with neat farmhouses, add to the picturesqueness of the scene. Fruits and vegetables, Indian corn, and sugar cane flourish in great perfection, and a few ponies and horned cattle have been introduced from the mainland. Swine, goats, and domestic fowls abound. Fernando de Noronha stands as a great signboard, on the principal commercial thoroughfare of the world. Almost all the ships that cross the line, from Europe and America, to the East Indies and Pacific Ocean, and *vice versa*, sight it for the purpose of taking a new departure from it. The dwellers on its lonely hills look out upon a constant stream of commerce, but they are like prisoners looking out from their prison windows upon a scene of which they are not a part. A ship rarely ever touches at the island. There is nothing to invite communication. It is too insignificant for traffic, and has no good harbor where a ship could repair damages or refit. It is, besides, a penal colony of Brazil, to which it belongs. It is under the government of an officer of the Brazilian Army, who has a battalion of troops under him, and hither are sent from Rio Janeiro and the other cities of the empire, all the noted criminals who are condemned to long terms of imprisonment. Very few of the prisoners are kept in close confinement. The island itself is prison enough, and there are no possible means of escape from it. The prisoners are therefore permitted to run at large, and mitigate the horrors of their lot by manual labor on the farms, or engage in the mechanic arts.

Our arrival was announced in due form to the Governor, and the paymaster had, at my suggestion, addressed him a letter on the subject of supplies. In the meantime, we hauled the *Louisa Hatch* alongside and commenced coaling. The next morning a couple of gentlemen visited me on the part of the Governor to arrange personally with the paymaster the matter of supplies, and to welcome me to the island. No objection was made to our bringing in the *Hatch*, or to our receiving coal from her. The state of my diplomatic relations with the Governor was thus so satisfactory that I invited his ambassadors into the cabin, and summoned Bartelli to provide champagne. A popping of corks and a mutual clinking of glasses ensued, and when we had resumed conversation and lighted cigars, one of the gentlemen diplomats informed me in the most easy and *san souciant* manner possible that he was one of the convicts of the island! He had been sentenced for six years, he said, but had nearly served his term out. He was a German and spoke very good English. Several of my officers were present, and there was, of course, a casting of glances from one to the other. But Bartelli, who was still standing a few paces in the rear, with a fresh bottle of uncorked champagne in his hand, seemed to be most shocked. My faithful steward felt the honors and dignity of my station much more than I did myself, and it was amusing to see the smile of derision and contempt with which he wheeled round and replaced the uncorked bottle in the champagne basket.

The next day, accompanied by my paymaster—by the way, I have forgotten to mention that I had appointed Dr. Galt, my esteemed surgeon, paymaster at the time I made a present of my former paymaster to Mr. Adams; and that I had promoted Dr. Llewellyn to be surgeon—I made a visit to the Governor at his palace. He had kindly sent horses for us to the beach, and we had a pleasant ride of about a mile before we reached his headquarters. It was about eleven A.M.,

when we alighted and were escorted by an aide-de-camp to
his presence. The Governor was a thin, spare man, rather
under the medium height, and of sprightly manners and conversation. His complexion, like that of most Brazilians, was
about that of a side of tanned sole leather. His rank was that
of a major in the Brazilian Army. He received us very cordially. We found him at breakfast with his family and some
guests, and he insisted that we should be seated at the break-
fast-table and partake of a second breakfast, though we endeavored to decline. The meal was quite substantial, consisting of a variety of roast meats as well as fruits and vegetables.

As soon as I could find a little time to look around me, I
discovered that her ladyship, the governess, was a very sprightly and not uncomely mulatto, and that her two little children,
who were brought to me with all due ceremony to be praised
and have their heads patted, had rather kinky, or, perhaps, I
should say curly, hair. But I was a man of the world and was
not at all dismayed by this discovery; especially when I
observed that my vis-a-vis—one of the guests—was a beautiful
blonde of sweet seventeen with a complexion like a lily, tinted
with the least bit of rose, and with eyes so melting and lovely
that they looked as though they might have belonged to one
of the houris of whom that old reprobate Mahomet used to
dream. To set off her charms still further, she was arrayed in
a robe of the purest white, with a wreath of flowers in her
flaxen hair. She was a German, and was seated next to her
father, a man of about sixty, who, as the Governor afterward
informed me, was one of his chief criminals.

The Governor, seeing me start a little as he gave me this
information, made haste to explain that his guest was not of
the *canaille*, or common class of rogues, but a gentleman who
in a moment of weakness had signed another gentleman's
name to a check for a considerable amount, which he had
been clever enough to have cashed.

"He is only a forger, then!" said I to the Governor.

"That is all," replied he; "he is a very clever old gentleman,
and, as you see, he has a very pretty daughter." There was
certainly no gainsaying the latter proposition.

The chaplain of the penal colony—which numbered
about one thousand convicts, the entire population of the
island being about two thousand—a portly and dignified
priest, was also at the breakfast table, and my paymaster and

myself spent a very pleasant half-hour around this social board, at which were represented so many of the types of mankind, and so different moral elements.

From the breakfast table, we retired to a withdrawing-room which was pretty well filled when we entered, showing that his Excellency had done me the honor to get some guests together to greet me. The paymaster and myself were personally presented to most of these distinguished gentlemen—some military men, some civilians. Among others, was present the ambassador of the day previous, who had given such a shock to Bartelli's nerves as to render him incapable of doing that which he loved above all other things to do—draw a champagne cork for the Captain's guests, whom he regarded after a certain fashion as his own. The Governor had evidently been select in his society, for most of these gentlemen were not only well dressed, but well-mannered, and some of them were even distinguished in appearance. They were mostly homicides and forgers, and seemed rather to pride themselves upon the distinction which they had attained in their *professions*. There was one young fellow present, upon whom all seemed to look with admiration. He was a dashing young German, who had evidently driven fast horses and kept the best of company. He wore an elaborately embroidered shirt-bosom on which glittered a diamond brooch of great brilliancy, and there were chains hung about his neck, and signet and other rings on his fingers. This fellow was such a master of the pen that he could cheat any man out of his signature after having seen him write but once. To give us an example of his skill, he sketched, whilst we were talking to him, the *Alabama* and her surroundings as they appeared from the window of the saloon in which we were sitting, so perfectly, with pen and ink as to create a murmur of applause among the bystanders. This charming young gentleman had "done" the Bank of Rio Janeiro out of a very large sum, which was the cause of his being the guest of the Governor.

Wine and cigars were brought in, and as we chatted and smoked with these fellows, the paymaster and I were highly amused—amused at our own situation and by the variety of characters by whom we were surrounded. The levée being at an end, the Governor ordered horses, and accompanied by an orderly, we rode over his dominions. It was in the midst of the rainy season, and the island was almost constantly wreathed in mists and rain, but as these rains continue for months, no one thinks of housing himself on account of them.

We passed within a stone's throw of the Peak and were more struck than ever with the grandeur of its proportions and the symmetry of its form. The island is broken and picturesque, as all volcanic countries are, and in the midst of the rains, it was one mass of rank vegetation, it being as much as the farmers could do to keep a few patches of cultivation free from the encroaching weeds and jungle. We had not been in the saddle more than twenty minutes, when a heavily laden, vaporous cloud swept over us and drenched us to the skin. But I found that this was not to interfere in the least with our ride. Its only effect was to induce the Governor to call a temporary halt at a Manioc factory in which he was interested, and whistle up a boy, who brought each of us a very small glass filled with the villanous *aguadiente* of the country. The Governor tossed his off at a single gulp, and not to be discourteous, we made wry faces and disposed of as much of ours as we could.

We passed through tangled forests, the trees of which were all new to us, and through dells and ravines in which the living and the decaying vegetation seemed to be struggling for the mastery, and emerged in a beautiful cocoanut plantation on the south end of the island, which lay only a few feet above the sea level. I was now at the end of the Governor's dominions—an hour's ride had brought me from the sea on one side of them, to the sea on the other, and there was nothing more to be seen. Other showers coming on, we entered a tiny country house of the Governor's and had some grapes, figs, and melons brought in to us by the major domo. The green cocoanut was brought to us among other delicacies to be eaten with spoons. We were quite amused at the manner in which these nuts were gathered. The major domo called a boy, and tying his legs together just above the ankles, so that the ankles were about six inches apart, set him down at the foot of a tree. These trees grow to a great height, are perfectly cylindrical, and have not an excrescence of any kind from root to top; and yet the boy, by the aid of the bandage described, wriggled himself to the top of one of the tallest with the agility of a squirrel.

There being at length a pause in the rains, the sun even peeping through an occasional rift in the ragged and watery clouds, we remounted and rode back. The tiny mountain paths had, many of them, by this time become rills and torrents, and our horses were frequently knee-deep in water. The paymaster and I pulled on board at five P. M., without having suffered any inconvenience either from the rains or the Governor's *aguadiente;* nor did our morals suffer materially by what we had seen and heard in the island of Fernando de Noronha. The next morning the Governor's wife sent me a fat turkey for dinner, accompanied by the most charming of bouquets. This was evidently my reward for patting the little curly heads of her children. My diplomacy from this time onward was all right. I did not hear a word from the Governor or any one in authority about neutral rights, or the violation of neutral jurisdictions. Brazil had, I knew, followed the lead of the European powers in excluding prizes from her ports, and I had fully expected to receive some remonstrance against my bringing in the *Louisa Hatch,* but Madame was too strong for the Governor, and, as the reader has seen, I received fat turkeys and bouquets instead of remonstrances. The anchorage being nothing but an open roadstead, we soon found it too rough to permit a ship to lie alongside of us and so were obliged to haul the *Hatch* off to her anchors and continue our coaling with boats. This was rather a tedious process, and it was not until the 15th of April, or five days after our arrival, that we were coaled.

We had not once thought of a prize since we came in. Our whole attention had been given to coaling ship, refitting for another cruise, refreshing the crew, and attending to the ladies at the Government House. But the ubiquitous Yankee would turn up in spite of us. Just as we had gotten our last boatload of coal on board, two ships appeared off the harbor and were seen to heave to and lower boats. We soon made them out to be whalers, and knew them to be American, though they had not as yet hoisted any colors. The boats pulled in apace and soon entered the harbor. They contained the masters of the two whalers, who had come in to barter a little whale oil for supplies. The *Alabama* was lying without any colors hoisted, as was her wont while she remained at this island, and, of course, the *Louisa Hatch,* her prize, had none set. The boats pulled in quite unsuspiciously, and observing that the *Hatch* was an American-built ship, went alongside of her. The prize-master, who was taking it easily in his shirt-sleeves, and so had no uniform on which could betray him, went to the gangway and threw them a rope. The two masters declined to come on board as they were in a hurry, they said, but remained some time in conversation—the prize-master, who was an Englishman, endeavoring to play Yankee, the best he could. He repeatedly invited them to come on board, but they declined. They wanted to know what steamer "that was," pointing to the *Alabama*. They were told that it was a Brazilian packet steamer come over to the colony to bring some convicts.

"What are you doing here," they now inquired.

"We sprang a pretty bad leak in a late gale and have come in to see if we can repair damages."

Presently there was a simultaneous start on the part of both the boat's crews, and the words "starn, all!" being bawled rather than spoken, both boats backed out in double quick and put off with the most vigorous strokes of their oars for the shore, like men who were pulling for their lives. The prize-master, a little astonished at this sudden movement, looked around him to see what could have caused it. The cause was soon apparent. A small Confederate flag—a boat's ensign— had been thrown by the coxswain of one of the boats on the spanker-boom to dry, and while the conversation was going on, a puff of wind had blown out the folds and disclosed the little telltale to the gaze of the astonished whalers. It was not precisely a Gorgon's head; they did not turn to stone, but perhaps there was some of the tallest pulling done that day at Fernando de Noronha that was ever done by a Yankee boat's crew.

In the meantime, the "Brazilian packet steamer" having gotten up steam, was moving quietly out of the harbor to look after the ships outside. They were still lying to, and fortunately for me, they were four or five miles off; outside the charmed marine league. There was an outlying shoal or two in the direction in which they were, and this was the reason probably why they had not ventured nearer. It did not take us long to come up with them. We fired the usual gun as we approached, and as there was no occasion for *ruse*, we showed them our own flag. They saw in a moment that their fate was sealed and did not attempt to stir, but hoisted the United States colors and patiently waited to be taken possession of. The first we came up with was the bark *Lafayette* of New

Bedford. There were no papers to be examined—the mate, in the absence of the captain, having thrown them overboard as we approached—and we gave her a short shrift. She was burning brightly in less than an hour We now ranged up alongside of the other, which proved to be the hermaphrodite brig *Kate Cory* of Westport. Instead of burning the *Cory*, I took her in tow and stood back to the anchorage with her, it being my intention to convert her into a cartel and dispatch her to the United States with my prisoners, who were now quite as numerous as my crew, there being 110 of them. By seven P. M., we had again anchored in our old berth; the burning ship outside lighting us into the roadstead and throwing a bright glare over much of the island A number of ships that passed Fernando de Noronha that night must have been astonished at this illumination of the lonely mile post. The sea was smooth, and the ship was still burning the next morning, though by this time she had drifted so far that there was nothing visible except a column of smoke. I afterward changed my determination of converting the *Cory* into a cartel. A small Brazilian schooner having come into the anchorage, offered to take all my prisoners to Pernambuco, if I would provision them and give her besides a few barrels of pork and flour for her trouble. This I at once consented to do, and the Governor having no objection, the arrangement was forthwith made. I was thus enabled to burn the *Cory*, and to put the enemy to the expense of sending his released prisoners to the United States. I burned the *Louisa Hatch* along with the *Cory*, having no farther use for her; taking the pains to send them both beyond the marine league that I might pay due respect to the jurisdiction of Brazil.

And now we were ready for sea again, though I remained a few days longer at my anchors, hoping that the *Agrippina* might arrive. She was past due, but I had not yet given up all hope of her.

We were now getting well along into the latter part of April, and a great change was taking place in the weather. It had been raining ever since we reached the vicinity of the equator. The rains were now becoming less frequent from day to day, and we had the showers agreeably alternated with sunshine. The rainy season was passing away, and the dry season was about to set in. I watched this phenomenon with great interest—all the more narrowly because I had nothing to do but look out for the weather and the *Agrippina;* except to attend to the refreshment and recreation of my crew, and send Bartelli on shore occasionally with messages to the ladies at the Government House. The reader . . . has watched the trade winds as he has crossed the tropics, and has fanned himself and panted for breath when we have been working our tedious way through the calm belts. He has seen how this system of trade winds and calm belts wanders up and down the earth from north to south, and south to north, drawn hither and thither by the sun. But we have had no conversation as yet about the Equatorial Cloud Ring. He has been for the last three weeks under this very Cloud Ring but has probably failed to remark it. He has only seen that the floodgates of the heavens have been raised, and witnessed the descending torrents and the roll of the thunder and the play of the lightning without stopping to ask himself the reason.

Let us pause a moment and look into this beautiful phenomenon of the Equatorial Cloud Ring before we flit away to other seas and are absorbed by new phenomena. The northeast and southeast trade winds, meeting near the equator, produce the Cloud Ring. Let us suppose the *Alabama* back at the crossing of the 30th parallel, where we established the toll gate. She had, whilst there, a high barometer. Starting thence on her way to the equator, as soon as she enters the northeast trade, she finds that her barometer settles a little—perhaps a tenth of an inch on an average. We had whilst passing through this region a series of half gales and bad weather; but this was an exceptional state of the atmospheric phenomena. The normal condition of the weather is that of a clear sky with passing trade clouds, white and fleecy, and with moderate breezes. If the reader has watched his barometer narrowly, he has observed a very remarkable phenomenon, which is not known to prevail outside of the trade-wind belts —an atmospheric tide. The atmosphere ebbs and flows as regularly as the sea. This atmospheric tide is due no doubt to the same cause that produces the aqueous tides—the attraction of the moon. It occurs twice in twenty-four hours just like the aqueous tides, and there is no other cause to which we can attribute it.

The needle has a like semi-diurnal—indeed, hourly variation—showing the normal, electrical condition of the atmosphere. The atmospherical tidal wave, as it ebbs and flows, seems to carry the needle backward and forward with it. The average barometer being but a very little under thirty, there is an agreeable elasticity in the atmosphere, and officers and crew are generally in fine spirits. The sailors enjoy their evening dances and story tellings, and when the night watches are set, sleep with impunity about the decks—guarded, however, by those woollen garments of which I spoke when describing our routine life. But observe what a change will take place as we approach the equator. We are approaching not only the calm belt, which has been before described, but the Cloud Ring, for the latter is the concomitant of the former. The winds die away, the muttering of thunder is heard, and a pall of black clouds, along which dart frequent streaks of lightning, is seen hanging on the verge of the horizon ahead of the ship. As she advances, fanned along by puffs of wind from various quarters, she loses sight of the sun altogether and enters beneath the belt of clouds, where she is at once deluged with rain. She is at once in the equatorial calm belt and under the Equatorial Cloud Ring.

The northeast and southeast trade winds, as they came sweeping along charged to saturation with the vapors which they have licked up from a torrid sea, have ascended as they met, and when they have reached the proper dew point, or point of the wet-bulb of the thermometer, precipitation has commenced. The barometer falls another tenth of an inch or so, all elasticity departs from the atmosphere, and officers and crew lose their cheerfulness. They feel all the lassitude and weariness of men in a perpetual vapor bath. The sailor no longer mounts the ratlines as if he had cork in his heels, but climbs up sluggishly and slothfully, devoid of his usual pride to be foremost. In other words, though not absolutely sick, he is under the weather. The rays of the sun being perpetually excluded, the thermometer stands lower under the Cloud Ring than on either side of it. At least this is the normal condition. Sometimes, however, the most oppressive heats occur. They are local and of short duration. These local heats are occasioned as follows: When a cooler stratum of the upper air sweeps down nearer the earth than usual, bringing with it the dew point, condensation takes place so near the surface that the rain drops have not time to cool, at the same time that an immense quantity of latent heat has been liberated in the act of condensation. At other times, when the dew point is far removed from the earth, the latent heat is not only thrown off at a greater distance from us, but the rain drops cool in their descent and greatly reduce the temperature.

The Cloud Ring is being perpetually formed and is perpetually passing away. Fresh volumes of air, charged as described, are constantly rushing in from the north and from the south and as constantly ascending, parting with a portion of their water, and continuing their journey to the poles in obedience to the laws providing for the equal distribution of rain to the two hemispheres, before explained. The Cloud Ring encircles the entire earth, and if it could be viewed by an eye at a distance from our planet, would appear like a well-defined black mark drawn around an artificial globe. Its width is considerable, being from three to six degrees.

It remains to speak of the offices which this remarkable ring performs. It is an important cogwheel in the great atmospherical machine, for the distribution of water over the earth; but, besides its functions in the general system, it has local duties to perform. These are the hovering by turns over certain portions of the earth, giving them an alternation of rain and sunshine. In short, it causes the rainy and dry seasons in certain parallels, north and south, within the limits assigned to it. The ancients were of the opinion that the equatorial regions of the earth were a continuous burning desert, devoid of vegetation, and of course uninhabitable; and perhaps this opinion would not be very far wrong, but for the arrangement of which I am about to speak. The Cloud Ring is a part of the system of calm belts and trade winds. It overhangs the equatorial calm belt, and it travels north and south with it. It travels over as much as twenty degrees of latitude—from about 5° S. to 15° N., carrying rain to the regions over which it hovers and letting in the sunshine upon those regions it has left. If the reader will inspect a map, he will find that it extends as far into our hemisphere as the island of Martinique in the West Indies. Fernando de Noronha, where we are now lying in the *Alabama*, is near its southern limit, being in the latitude of about 4° S. The rainy season was still prevailing when we arrived at this island on the 10th of April; and it had begun to pass away while we still lay there—the rain and the sunshine playing at April showers. The preceding diagram will explain how the Cloud Ring travels:

Figure 1 represents the island of Fernando de Noronha still under the Cloud Ring. It is early in April, and only about three weeks have elapsed since the sun crossed the equator on his way back to the northern hemisphere. When he was in the southern hemisphere, he had drawn the ring so far south as to cover the island. His rays had been shut out from it, and it was constantly raining. The little island would have been drowned out if this state of things had continued; but it was not so ordered by the great Architect.

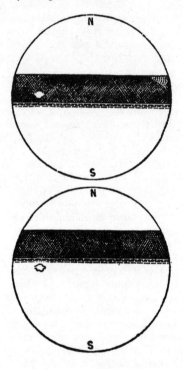

Suppose now a month to elapse. It is early in May, and behold! the sun has traveled sufficiently far north to draw the Cloud Ring from over the island and leave it in sunshine as represented in figure 2. Thus the island is neither parched by perpetual heat nor drowned by perpetual rains, but its climate is delightfully tempered by an alternation of each, and it has become a fit abode for men and animals.

As we have seen in a former chapter, a benign Providence has set the trade winds in motion that they might become the water carriers of the earth, ordering them for this purpose to cross the equator, each into the hemisphere of the other. We now see that he has woven with those same winds, a shield impenetrable to the sun's rays, which he holds in his hand, first over one parched region of the earth and then over another—the shield dropping "fatness" all the while!

Chapter Fifteen—*1863*

The Alabama leaves Fernando de Noronha for a cruise on the coast of Brazil . . . Enters the great highway and begins to overhaul the travelers . . . Capture of the whaler Nye; of the Dorcas Prince; of the Union Jack; of the Sea Lark . . . A reverend consul taken prisoner . . . The Alabama goes into Bahia . . . What occurred there . . . Arrival of the Georgia . . . The Alabama proceeds to sea again . . . Captures the following ships: the Gildersleeve; the Justina; the Jabez Snow; the Amazonian, and the Talisman

The 22d of April having arrived, we gave up all further hopes of the *Agrippina* and went to sea. As we passed out of the roadstead, we cut adrift the four whale-boats we had brought in from the captured whalers rather than destroy them. They would be valuable to the islanders, who had treated us kindly, and it was amusing to see the struggle which took place for the possession of them. The good people seemed to have some anticipation of what was to take place, and all the boatmen of the island had assembled to contest the prizes in every description of craft that would float, from the dugout to the tidy cutter. The boatmen stripped themselves like athletes for the fray, and as whale boat after boat was cut adrift, there was a pulling and splashing, a paddling and a screaming that defy all description; the victors waving their hats and shouting their victory and their good-bye to us in the same breath.

We steamed due east from the island some forty miles, when we let our steam go down, raised the propeller, and put the ship under sail. The *Alabama* with full coal-bunkers and a refreshed crew was again in pursuit of the enemy's commerce. I had at last accomplished my cherished design—which had been frustrated in the *Sumter*—of a cruise on the coast of Brazil. In my stanch and fleet little ship, I was in a condition to defy both winds and currents. On the day after leaving Fernando de Noronha, I observed in latitude 5° 45′ S. and had thus run entirely from under the Cloud Ring. We were met by a bright sky and the first gentle breathings of the southeast trade. This change in the weather had an electric effect upon my people. Cheerfulness returned to their countenances and elasticity to their step. It took us some time to dry and ventilate the ship, the rigging being filled for a day or two with wet pea-jackets and mattresses, and decks strewed with moldy boots and shoes.

Before we had been twenty-four hours at sea, the usual bugle note was sounded from the mast head, and the *Alabama* had pricked up her ears in chase. It was another unfortunate whaler. The fates seemed to have a grudge against these New England fishermen and would persist in throwing them in my way, although I was not on a whaling ground. This was the sixteenth I had captured—a greater number than had been captured from the English by Commodore David Porter in his famous cruise in the Pacific in the frigate *Essex* during the war of 1812. The prize proved to the the bark Nye of New Bedford. This bluff old whaler was returning home from a cruise of thirty-one months in the far-off Pacific, during which her crew had become almost as much Sandwich Islanders as Americans in appearance, with their garments so saturated with oil that they would have been quite valuable to the soap boiler. She had sent home one or two cargoes of oil and had now on board 425 barrels more. It seemed a pity to break in upon the *menage* of these old salts, who had weathered so many gales and chased the whale through so many latitudes, but there was no alternative. The New England wolf was still howling for Southern blood, and the least return we could make for the howl was to spill a little "*ile*." Everything about the Nye being greased to saturation, she made a splendid conflagration.

The next day the wind freshened, and we might now be said to be in the well-pronounced southeast trades. Indeed, it blew so fresh at nightfall that we took the single reefs in the topsails. We were jogging along leisurely on the great Brazilian highway, waiting for the passengers rather than hunting them up. Presently another came along—a fine, taut ship that represented the boxes and bales of merchandise rather than harpoons and whale oil. We gave chase under the enemy's colors, but the chase was coy and shy and refused to show colors in return until she was commanded to do so by a gun. The stars and stripes, which now fluttered to the breeze, sufficiently explained her reluctance. Upon being boarded she proved to be the *Dorcas Prince* of New York, bound for Shanghai. Her cargo consisted chiefly of coal. She had been forty-four days out, an unusually long passage, and what was quite wonderful for an American ship, she had no documents on board from the college, either of the political or religious propaganda, and only three or four old newspapers. When we learned she was from New York, we had been in hopes of capturing a mail. We burned her as soon as we could transfer her crew, there being no claim of neutral cargo found among her papers. Her master had his wife on board, which resulted, as usual, in sending one of my young lieutenants into the "country."

Reducing sail again, we jogged along as before, but for the next few days we overhauled nothing but neutrals. A St. John's, New Brunswick, ship, brought us the mail we had expected to receive by the *Dorcas Prince*, but it contained nothing of interest. On the 3d of May, the weather being fine, though interrupted occasionally by a rain squall, we gave chase about eleven A. M. to a clipper ship with square yards, white canvas, and long mast heads—and the reader must be enough of an expert by this time to know what these mean. In an hour and a half of fine sailing we came near enough to the chase to make her show the Federal colors and heave to. She proved to be the *Union Jack* of Boston, bound for Shanghai. Whilst we had been pursuing the *Union Jack*, another "suspicious" sail hove in sight, and as soon as we could throw a prize-crew on board the former, we started off in pursuit of the latter. This second sail proved also to be a prize, being the *Sea Lark* of New York, bound for San Francisco. Here were two prizes in as many hours.

There was no attempt to cover the cargo of the *Sea Lark*, and the only attempt that was made in the case of the *Union Jack*, was made by one Allen Hay, who was anxious to save five cases of crackers and ten barrels of butter from capture. In this case, a Mr. Thomas W. Lillie made oath before the British Consul in New York that the said articles were shipped "for and on account of subjects of her Britannic Majesty." The reader has seen me burn several other ships with similar certificates, the reasons for which burnings were assigned at the time. I will not stop therefore to discuss this. In due time both ships were consigned to the flames. I was sorry to find three more women and two small children on board of the *Union Jack*. That ship was, in fact, about to expatriate herself for several years after the fashion of many of the Yankee ships in the Chinese coasting trade, and the master was taking his family out to domicile it somewhere in China. There were several male passengers also on board this ship, among them an ex-New England parson, the Rev. Franklin Wright, who was going out as consul to Foo Chow. The Rev. Mr. Wright had been editor of a religious paper for some years in one of the New England villages, and probably owed his promotion to the good services he had rendered in hurrying on the war. He had Puritan written all over his lugubrious countenance, and looked so solemn that one wondered how he came to exchange the clergyman's garb for the garb of Belial. But so it was; Franklin was actually going out to India in quest of the dollars. We deprived him of his consular seal and commission, though we did not molest his private papers, and of sundry very pretty consular flags that had been carefully prepared for him by Mr. Seward, *fils*, at the State Department in Washington. I am pained to see by that "little bill" of Mr. Seward, *père*, against the British Government for "depredations of the *Alabama*," before referred to, that the Rev. Mr. Wright puts his damages down at $10,015. I had no idea that a New England parson carried so much plunder about with him.

We received large mails from these two last ships and had

our "moral ideas" considerably expanded for the next few days by the perusal of Yankee newspapers. We found among other interesting items a vivid synopsis of the war news in a speech of Governor Wright of Indiana, who, if I mistake not, had been chargé to Berlin, where he had been in the habit of holding conventicles and prayer meetings. The Governor is addressing a meeting of the "truly loil" at Philadelphia, and among other things, said:

The stars and stripes now wave over half the slave grounds. I believe in less than thirty days we will open the Mississippi and take Charleston. [Loud applause.] Leave Virginia alone, that can't sprout a black-eyed pea. [Laughter.] Scripture teaches us that no people can live long where there is no grass. The question then is only, whether they can live thirty or sixty days.

Thus, amid the laughter and jeers of an unwashed rabble did an ex-Governor, and ex-U. S. Minister, gloat over the prospect of *starving* an entire people, women and children included. Did we need other incitement on board the *Alabama* to apply a well-lighted torch to the enemy's ships?

There were copious extracts from the English papers found in this mail, and I trust the reader will excuse me while I give a portion of a speech made to his constituents by a member of the British Parliament, who was also a member of the Cabinet. The speaker is Mr. Milner Gibson, President of the Board of Trade. A great war, which covered a continent with the fire and smoke of battle, was raging between a people, who were the near kinsmen of the speaker. Battles were being fought daily that dwarfed all the battles that had gone before them. Feats of brilliant courage were being performed on both sides that should have made the blood of the speaker course more rapidly through his veins and stir to their depths the feelings of humanity and brotherhood. Under such circumstances, what think you, reader, was the subject of Mr. Gibson's discourse? It was bacon and eggs! Listen:

Now . . . these large importations of foreign wheat and flour and other provisions into this country must to some extent have tended to mitigate the distress and have enabled many to provide for the wants of others out of their own surplus means. But supposing that the Government of this country had been induced, as they were urged frequently, to involve themselves in interference in the affairs of the United States; supposing, by some rash and precipitate recognition of those who are conducting hostilities against the United States —called the Confederate States of America—we had brought ourselves into collision with the United States, where would have been this flour, and ham, and bacon, and eggs? I suppose, if we had been compelled to take up arms against the United States by any unfortunate policy, blockading would have been resorted to, and we should have been obliged to establish a blockade of the coast of America for the very purpose of keeping out of this country all this wheat, flour, and eggs which have gone to mitigate the distress of the cotton industry in the present alarming state of affairs. We have from the commencement carried out the doctrine of non-intervention. We have endeavored to preserve a strict neutrality between the two contending parties. It was impossible to avoid recognizing the belligerent rights of the South at the outset of the contest, because it was a contest of such magnitude, and the insurgents, as they were called, were so numerous and so powerful that it would have been impossible to recognize them in any other capacity but as persons entitled to bear arms; and if we had not done so, and if their armed vessels found on the seas were treated as pirates, it must be obvious to every one that this would have been an unparalleled course of action. We were compelled to recognize the belligerent rights of the South, but there has been no desire on the part of the Government to favor either the one side or the other. My earnest desire is to preserve strict neutrality; and, whatever may be my individual feelings—for we must have our sympathies on the one side or the other—whatever may be my feelings as a member of Parliament and the executive administration, I believe it to be for the interest of England that this neutrality should be observed.

Poor old John Bull! What a descent have we here from the Plantagenets to Mr. Milner Gibson? From Cœur de Leon, striking for the right, to Mr. Milner Gibson, of the Board of Trade, advising his countrymen to smother all their more noble and generous impulses that they might continue to fry cheap bacon and eggs!

We had been working our way for the last few days toward Bahia in Brazil, and being now pretty well crowded with prisoners, having no less than the crews of four captured ships on board, I resolved to run in and land them. We anchored about five P. M., on the 11th of May. Bahia is the second city in size and commercial importance in the Brazilian empire. We found a large number of ships at anchor in the harbor, but no Yankees among them. The only man-of-war present was a Portuguese. We were struck with the spaciousness of the bay and the beauty of the city as we approached. The latter crowns a crescent-shaped eminence, and its white houses peep cosily from beneath forest trees of the richest and greenest foliage. The business part of the city lies at the foot of the crescent near the water's edge. It, too, looks picturesque with its quays, and shipping, and tugs, and wherries. But, as is the case with most Portuguese towns—for the Brazilians are only a better class of Portuguese—the illusion of beauty is dispelled as soon as you enter its narrow and crooked streets and get sight of its swarthy population, the chief features of which are sombreros and garlic. We were boarded by the health officer just at dark and admitted to pratique.

The next morning, the weather set in gloomy and rainy. The requisite permission having been obtained, we landed our prisoners, there being upward of a hundred of them. Parson Wright here took the back track, I believe. Whether, after stating his grievances at the State Department in Washington, he renewed his commission and proceeded in some more fortunate Yankee ship to Foo Chow, or went back to his religious paper and his exhortations against the Southern heathen, I have never learned. The reverend gentleman forgot his Christian charity and did not come to say good-bye when he landed, though we had treated him with all due consideration.

I had now another little diplomatic matter on my hands. I had scarcely risen from the breakfast table on the morning after my arrival, when an aide-de-camp of the Governor, or rather President of the Department, came off to see me on official business. He brought on board with him a copy of the *Diario de Bahia*, a newspaper very respectable for its size and typography, containing an article which I was requested to read and answer in writing. This I promised to do, and the messenger departed. I found upon glancing over the article, which filled a couple of columns, that it was a Yankee production done into very good Portuguese—the joint work probably of the Yankee Consul at Pernambuco, where the article had originated—for it had been copied into the Bahia paper—and the President of that province. It was written after the style of a proclamation, was signed by the President, and strangely enough addressed to myself—supposed to be still at Fernando de Noronha with the *Alabama*. After charging me with sundry violations of the neutrality of Brazil, it ordered me to depart the island within twenty-four hours.

Instead of sending a ship of war to examine into the facts and enforce his order if necessary, the President had been satisfied to send this paper bullet after me. It reminded me very much of the stink pots which the Chinese are in the habit of throwing at their enemies, and I could not restrain a smile as I called upon Bartelli to produce my writing materials. The aide-de-camp who had brought me the paper had brought off a message along with it from the President to the effect that he desired I would hold no communication with the shore until I had answered the article, which was tantamount to informing me that he was somewhat in doubt whether he would permit me to communicate at all or not. I really wanted nothing—though I afterward took in a few boat loads of coal merely to show the President that I was disposed to be civil—and this consideration, along with the fact that I had the heaviest guns in the harbor, induced me to be rather careless, I am afraid, in the choice of phraseology as I penned my despatch. I simply charged that the whole proclamation was a budget of lies and claimed that I had been insulted by the Government of Brazil by the lies having been put into an official shape by it without first communicating with me.

The Brazilians are a very polite people and my reply was "perfectly satisfactory." Jack went on shore and had his frolic, and the *Alabama* remained a week in the port, enjoying the hospitalities of the numerous English and other foreign residents. Among other entertainments, we had a splendid ball given us by Mr. Ogilvie, a British merchant, at which much of the foreign and native beauty was present. Mr. Ogilvie's tasteful residence overlooked the bay from the top of the crescent I have described; his grounds, redolent of the perfumes of tropical flowers, were brilliantly illuminated, and a fine band of music charmed not only the revellers but the numerous ships in the Bay. Several Brazilian dignitaries and foreign consuls were present. I took all my young gentlemen on shore with me who could be spared from the ship, and they did their devoirs as only gallant knights can and carried on board with them in the "wee sma'" hours of the morning, several tiny kid gloves and scarfs as mementos to accompany them on their cruises—every villain of them swearing to return at some future day. So it is always with the sailor. As before remarked, his very life is a poem, and his heart is capacious enough to take in the whole sex.

On the morning after this brilliant entertainment, an officer came below to inform me that a strange steamer of war had entered during the night, which as yet had shown no colors. I directed our own colors to be shown to the stranger—for the regular hour of hoisting them had not yet arrived—and the reader may judge of our delight when we saw the Confederate States flag thrown to the breeze in reply by the new-comer. It was the *Georgia*, Commander Lewis F. Maury, on a cruise like ourselves against the enemy's commerce. She had come in to meet her coal ship, the *Castor*, which had been ordered to rendezvous here. We had now other troubles with the authorities. The President, seeing another Confederate steamer arrive, became nervous lest he should be compromised in some way and be called to account by the Emperor. The little gadfly of a Yankee consul was, besides, constantly buzzing around him. He declined to permit the *Georgia* to receive coal from her transport, though he was forced to admit that the transport had the right to land it, and that when landed the *Georgia* might receive it on board like any other coal. Still it must be landed. The gadfly had buzzed in his ear that there was a "cat in the meal tub;" the *Castor* having, as he alleged, some guns and ammunition covered up in her coal! His Excellency then wanted to see my commission— the gadfly having buzzed "pirate! pirate!" To add to the complication, news now came in that the *Florida* also had arrived at Pernambuco! Diablo! what was to be done? An aide-de-camp now came off with a letter from his Excellency telling me that I had already tarried too long in the port of Bahia, and that he desired me to be off. I wrote him word that I was not ready and sent another batch of liberty men on shore. Presently another missive came. His Excellency had learned from the gadfly that I had enlisted one of my late prisoners after setting him on shore, which, as he said, was a grave breach of the laws of nations. I replied that I had not only not enlisted one of my late prisoners after setting him on shore, but that, my crew being full, I had refused to enlist a good many of my late prisoners who had applied to me before being set on shore, which was the literal fact. I mention these occurrences to show what a troublesome little insect I found the gadfly in Brazil.

We had a few days of very pleasant intercourse with the *Georgia.* Maury had been my shipmate in the old service, and two of my old *Sumter* lieutenants, Chapman and Evans, were serving on board of her. In company with her officers, we made a railroad excursion into the interior upon the invitation of the English company which owned the road. A splendid collation was prepared in one of the cars, decorated and furnished for the occasion, and a variety of choice wines broke down the barrier between strangers and drew men of the same blood closer together.

At length, when I was entirely ready for sea, I delighted the President one evening by sending him word that I should go to sea the next morning. The *Georgia* was nearly through coaling and would follow me in a day or two. The poor President of the province of Bahia! The Yankees treated him afterward as they do everybody else with whom they have to do. They first endeavored to use him and then kicked him. The *Florida* coming into Bahia a few months afterward . . . a Federal ship of war violated the neutrality of the port by seizing her and carrying her off; and the Yankee nation, rather than make the amends which all the world decided it was bound to make, by delivering back the captured ship to Brazil, ordered her to be sunk by *accident* in Hampton Roads! The trick was eminently Yankee, and I presume could not possibly have been practised in any other civilized nation of the earth.

Whilst the *Alabama* is heaving up her anchor, I deem it proper to say a word or two, about emigration to Brazil; a subject which has been a good deal canvassed by our people. Brazil is an immense Empire and has almost all the known climates and soils of the world. Nature has bestowed upon her her choicest gifts, and there is perhaps no more delightful country to reside in than Brazil. But men live for society as well as for climate and soil. The effete Portuguese race has been ingrafted upon a stupid, stolid, Indian stock in that country. The freed Negro is, besides, the equal of the white man, and as there seems to be no repugnance on the part of the white race—so called—to mix with the black race and with the Indian, amalgamation will go on in that country until a mongrel set of curs will cover the whole land. This might be a suitable field enough for the New England school-ma'am and carpetbagger, but no Southern gentleman should think of mixing his blood or casting his lot with such a race of people.

Sail ho! was shouted from the mast head of the *Alabama* on the afternoon of the 25th of May, a few days after she had put to sea from Bahia. We had regained the track of commerce and were again looking out for our friends. We immediately gave chase and had scarcely gotten the canvas on the ship before the lookout announced a second sail in the same direction. The wind was fresh, there was a heavy sea on, and the *Alabama* darted forward, making her eleven and twelve knots. As we began to raise the fugitives above the horizon from the deck, it was plain to see that they were both American. We overhauled them rapidly, making them show their colors and heaving them to with the accustomed guns. By the time we had gotten up with them, the sun had set, and it was blowing half a gale of wind. Our boats had a rough job before them, but they undertook it with a will. The first ship boarded was the *Gilderslieve*, and the second the *Justina*. The former was a New York ship, last from London with a cargo of coal purporting to be shipped for the service of the Peninsular, and Oriental Steam Navigation Company, but there was no certificate of neutral ownership on board. Ship and cargo were therefore condemned. The *Justina* was a Baltimore ship with some neutral property not amounting to a full cargo on board. I converted her into a cartel, and throwing the prisoners from the *Gilderslieve* on board of her, released her on ransom bond. I then burned the *Gilderslieve*. The sea was so rough and the boating so difficult that it was eleven P. M. before the torch could be applied to the doomed ship. We lay to during the remainder of the night under reefed topsails.

The next day the weather moderated somewhat, though the wind still continued fresh from about S. S. E. At about half-past eight P. M., the night being quite light, we gave chase to an exceedingly rakish-looking ship whose canvas showed white under the rays of the moon and which was carrying a press of sail. We, too, crowded sail and for a long time it was doubtful which ship was the faster. The *Alabama* seemed to have found her match at last. Our pride was aroused, and we put our best foot foremost. We saw all the sheets snugly home, the sails well hoisted, and properly trimmed, and put the most skilful seamen at the wheel. Little by little we began to crawl upon the chase, but hour after hour passed and still we were almost as far astern as ever. Midnight came, and the watch was relieved, and still the fugitive was beyond our grasp. Four A. M. arrived, and the old watch came back on deck again only to wonder that the chase still continued. At last the day dawned and still the ship with the square yards and white canvas was four or five miles ahead of us. We had been all night in chase of a single ship—a thing which had never happened to us before. When daylight appeared, I went below and turned in, handing the chase over to the first lieutenant. At half-past seven—my usual time for rising—I heard the report of a gun and pretty soon afterward an officer came below to say that the chase proved to be a Dutchman! I must have looked a little sour at the breakfast table that morning as Bartelli was evidently a little nervous and fidgety.

Forty-eight hours after this night chase, we had another, though with better success, as a prize rewarded me for my loss of rest. The chase commenced about two A. M., and it was half-past seven A. M., before we were near enough to heave the fugitive to with a gun. She proved to be the *Jabez Snow* of Buckport, Maine, last from Cardiff with a cargo of coal for Montevideo. On the back of the bill of lading was the following certificate: "We certify that the cargo of coals per *Jabez Snow*, for which this is the bill of lading, is the *bona fide* property of Messrs. Wilson, Helt, Lane & Co., and that the same are British subjects and merchants, and also that the coals are for their own use." This certificate was signed by "John Powell & Sons," but unfortunately for the owners of the coals was not sworn to, and was therefore of no more validity as evidence than the bill of lading itself. Having gotten on board from the prize a quantity of provisions and cordage, of both of which we were in need, we consigned her to the flames. We found on board this ship from the sober State of Maine, a woman who passed under the *sobriquet* of "chamber-maid." These shameless Yankee skippers make a common practice of converting their ships into brothels and taking their mistresses to sea with them. For decency's sake, I was obliged to turn the junior lieutenant out of his stateroom for her accommodation.

There were some letters found on board the *Snow* not intended for our eyes inasmuch as they informed us of the damage we were doing the Yankee commerce. Here is one of them from the owner to the master. It is dated Boston, November 25th, 1862. "We hope you may arrive safely and in good season, but we think you will find business rather flat at Liverpool, as American ships especially are under a cloud, owing to dangers from pirates, more politely styled privateers, which our kind friends in England are so willing should slip out of their ports to prey on our commerce." Our torches always grew brighter as we read such effusions of joint stupidity and malice.

Here is another wail from Buckport, Maine, under date of January 16th, 1863. It instructs the master as to the best mode of employing his ship. "In the first place, it will not do to come this way with the ship; as New York business for ships is flat enough—a large fleet in that port, and nothing for them to do that will pay expenses, and more arriving daily."

And another from the same place. "I hope you will be as prudent and economical as possible in managing your ship matters, as your owners want all the money they can get hold of to aid in putting down this terrible rebellion of ours. The progress our war is making, I shall leave for you to gather from the papers, for it makes me sick to think of it, much more to talk about it." No doubt—the ships were being laid up, and no freights were coming in. We knew very well on board the *Alabama*, the use to which all the "money the ship-owners could get hold of" was being put. It was to purchase "gold bonds" at half price, and push on the war. Hence our diligence in scouring the seas and applying the torch. Whenever we heard a Yankee howl go up over a burned ship, we knew that there were fewer dollars left with which to hire the *canaille* of Europe to throttle liberty on the American continent.

We captured the *Jabez Snow* on the 29th of May. On the 2d of June, being in latitude 15° 01' and longitude 34° 56' at half-past three A. M., or just before daylight, we passed a large ship on the opposite tack. We were under topsails only, standing leisurely across the great highway. We immediately wore ship and gave chase, crowding all sail. When day dawned, the fugitive was some six or seven miles ahead of us, and as the chase was likely to be long, I fired a gun and hoisted the Confederate colors to intimate to the stranger that I would like him to be polite and save me the trouble of catching him by heaving to. Pretty soon, I fired a second gun—blank cartridge—with the same intent. But the stranger had faith in his heels, and instead of heaving to, threw out a few more kites to the balmy morning breeze. But it was of no use. Both ships were on a wind, and the *Alabama* could in consequence use her monster trysails. My large double glasses—themselves captured from a Yankee ship, the captain of which had probably bought them to look out for the "pirate"—soon told the tale. We were gaining, but not very rapidly. Still anxious to save time, when we had approached within about four miles of the stranger, we cleared away our pivot rifle and let him have a bolt. We did not quite reach him, but these rifle bolts make such an ugly whizzing and hissing and humming as they pass along that their commands are not often disobeyed. The stranger clewed up and backed his main yard and hoisted the Federal colors. We were alongside of him about half-past eleven A. M.—the chase having lasted eight hours.

The prize proved to be the bark *Amazonian* of Boston, from New York with an assorted cargo for Montevideo. There was an attempt to cover two of the consignments of this ship in favor of French citizens, but the "hash" being evidently Yankee, the certificates were disregarded. The prisoners and such "plunder" as we desired, being brought on board the *Alabama*, the ship was consigned to the flames. The following letter from a merchant in New York to his correspondent in Buenos Ayres was found among a very large commercial and literary mail—the literature being from the college of the Republican Propaganda—on board the *Amazonian*. "When you ship in American vessels, it would be well to have the British consul's certificate of English property attached to bill of lading and invoice, as in the event of falling in with the numerous privateers, it would save both cargo and vessel in all probability. An American ship recently fallen in with, was released by the *Alabama* on account of British consul's certificate showing greater part of cargo to be English property.

If you ship in a neutral vessel, we save five per cent. war insurance."

On the day after capturing the *Amazonian*, we boarded an English brig, and I made an arrangement with the master to take my prisoners—forty-one in number—to Rio Janeiro, whither he was bound. The consideration was twice as many provisions as the prisoners could consume, and a chronometer. The master had been afraid of offending Earl Russell until the chronometer was named to him, when his scruples were at once removed. Virtuous Briton! thou wert near akin to the Yankee.

On the following night, a little before daylight, whilst we were lying to with the main-topsail to the mast, a large, tall ship suddenly loomed up in close proximity to us and as suddenly passed away into the gloom, gliding past us like a ghost. We filled away and made chase on the instant and being still within gun shot fired a blank cartridge. The chase at once hove to, and we ranged up just as day was breaking alongside of the clipper ship *Talisman* from New York with an assorted cargo for Shanghai. There was no claim of neutral cargo among her papers, and as soon as we could remove the crew and some necessary articles, we consigned her also to that torch which Yankee malice had kept burning so brightly in our hands.

The rebellion of the Taepings was still going on in China, and we found a nice little speculation in connection with it embarked on board the *Talisman*. The speculators had put on board four very pretty rifled 12-pounder brass guns, and steam boilers and machinery for a gunboat; the design being to build and equip one of this class of vessels in the East and take part in the Chinese war. I am afraid I spoiled a good thing. With a Yankee Mandarin on board, and a good supply of opium and tracts, what a smashing business this little cruiser might have done? We took a couple of these brass pieces on board the *Alabama*, and in due time sent them afloat after the Yankee commerce.

The next vessel that we overhauled was a "converted" ship —that is, a Yankee turned into an Englishman. I desired very much to burn her but was prevented by the regularity of her papers and the circumstances surrounding her. She was a Maine-built ship, but had evidently been *bona fide* transferred, as her master and crew were all Englishmen, and she was then on a voyage from London to Calcutta. She received on board from us a couple of the passengers—an Irishman and his wife—captured on board of the *Talisman*, who were anxious to go to Calcutta. For the next two or three days we had a series of blows amounting almost to gales of wind. We had arrived off the Abrolhos Shoals—a sort of Brazilian Cape Hatteras for bad weather. On the 9th and 10th of June we were reduced to close reefs; and, which was remarkable, we had a high barometer all the time. We had for some days experienced a northerly current. The whole coast of Brazil is coral-bound and it is for this reason very dangerous. The coral shoals rise abruptly from great depths and are sometimes found in very small patches with deep water all around them. Many of these patches have been missed by the surveyor and are not laid down on any charts in consequence. Hence it behooves the prudent mariner to give the banks that fringe the coasts of Brazil a pretty wide berth.

Chapter Sixteen—*1863*

*The Alabama continues her cruise on the coast of
Brazil . . . American ships under English colors . . .
The enemy's carrying trade in neutral bottoms . . .
The capture of the Conrad . . . She is commissioned
as a Confederate States Cruiser . . . The highways of
the sea, and the tactics of the Federal Secretary of
the Navy . . . The phenomenon of the winds in the
Southern Hemisphere . . . Arrival at Saldanha Bay on
the coast of Africa*

W e captured our last ship off the Abrolhos, as related in
the last chapter. We have since worked our way as far
south as latitude 22° 38′, and it is the middle of June—
equivalent in the southern hemisphere to the middle of December in the northern. Hence the blows and other bad
weather we are beginning to meet with. On the 16th of June,
we overhauled two more American ships under English colors.
One of these was the *Azzapadi* of Port Louis in the Mauritius.
She was formerly the *Joseph Hale* and was built at Portland,
Maine. Having put into Port Louis in distress, she had been
sold for the benefit of "whom it might concern" and purchased by English parties two years before. The other was

the *Queen of Beauty*, formerly the *Challenger*. Under her new colors and nationality, she was now running as a packet between London and Melbourne, Australia. These were both *bona fide* transfers and were evidence of the straits to which Yankee commerce was being put. Many more ships disappeared from under the "flaunting lie" by sale than by capture, their owners not being able to employ them.

The day after we overhauled these ships, we boarded a Bremen bark from Buenos Ayres for New York with hides and tallow on Yankee account. The correspondents of the New York merchants were taking the advice of the latter and shipping in neutral bottoms to avoid paying the premium on the war risk.

On the 20th of June, we observed in latitude 25° 48′ and found the weather so cool as to compel us to put on our thick coats. On that day we made another capture. It was the *Conrad* of Philadelphia from Buenos Ayres for New York with part of a cargo of wool. There were certificates found on board claiming the property as British, but as there were abundant circumstances in the *res gestæ* pointing to American ownership, I disregarded the certificates and condemned both ship and cargo as good prize. The *Conrad* being a tidy little bark of about three hundred and fifty tons with good sailing qualities, I resolved to commission her as a cruiser. Three or four officers and ten or a dozen men would be sufficient crew for her, and this small number I could spare from the *Alabama* without putting myself to material inconvenience. Never, perhaps, was a ship of war fitted out so promptly before. The *Conrad* was a commissioned ship with armament, crew, and provisions on board, flying her pennant, and with sailing orders signed, sealed, and delivered before sunset on the day of her capture. I sent Acting-Lieutenant [John] Low on board to command her and gave him Midshipman George T. Sinclair as his first lieutenant; and promoted a couple of active and intelligent young seamen as master's mates to serve with Mr. Sinclair as watch officers. Her armament consisted of the two 12-pounder brass rifled guns which we had captured from the Yankee mandarin who was going out on board the *Talisman* to join the Taepings; twenty rifles, and half a dozen revolvers. I called the new cruiser the *Tuscaloosa*, after the pretty little town of that name on the Black Warrior River in the state of Alabama. It was meet that a child of the *Alabama* should be named after one of the towns of the state. The baptismal ceremony was not very elaborate. When all was ready—it being now about five P. M.—at a concerted signal the *Tuscaloosa* ran up the Confederate colors, and the crew of the *Alabama* leaped into the rigging, and taking off their hats, gave three hearty cheers! The cheers were answered by the small crew of the newly commissioned ship, and the ceremony was over. Captain Low had now only to fill away and make sail on his cruise. Our first meeting was to be at the Cape of Good Hope. My bantling was thus born upon the high seas in the South Atlantic Ocean, and no power could gainsay the legitimacy of its birth. As the reader will see, England was afterward compelled to acknowledge it, though an ill-informed Cabinet minister—the Duke of Newcastle—at first objected to it.

On the same evening that we parted with the *Tuscaloosa* we boarded the English bark, *Mary Kendall* from Cardiff for Point de Galle, but which having met with heavy weather and sprung a leak, was putting back to Rio Janeiro for repairs. At the request of her master I sent my surgeon on board to visit a seaman who had been badly injured by a fall. As we were within a few days' sail of Rio, I prevailed upon the master of this ship to receive my prisoners on board to be landed. There were thirty-one of them, and among the rest, a woman from the *Conrad* who claimed to be a passenger.

The time had now arrived for me to stretch over to the Cape of Good Hope. I had been three months near the equator and on the coast of Brazil, and it was about time that some of Mr. Welles' ships of war, in pursuance of the tactics of that slow old gentleman, should be making their appearance on the coast in pursuit of me. I was more than ever astonished at the culpable neglect or want of sagacity of the head of the Federal Navy Department when I arrived on the coast of Brazil and found no Federal ship of war there. Ever since I had left the island of Jamaica early in January, I had been working my way gradually to my present cruising ground. My ship had been constantly reported, and any one of his clerks could have plotted my track from these reports so as to show him past all peradventure where I was bound. But even independently of any positive evidence, he might have been sure that sooner or later I would make my way to that great thoroughfare.

As has been frequently remarked in the course of these

pages, the sea has its highways and byways as well as the land. Every seaman now knows where these highways are, and when he is about to make a voyage, can plot his track in advance. None of these highways are better defined, or perhaps so well defined, as the great public road that leads along the coast of Brazil. All the commerce of Europe and America bound to the Far East or the Far West takes this road. The reader has seen a constant stream of ships passing the toll gate we established at the crossing of the thirtieth parallel, north, all bound in this direction. And he has seen how this stream sweeps along by the island of Fernando de Noronha on its way to the great highway on the coast of Brazil. The road thus far is wide—the ships having a large discretion. But when the road has crossed the equator and struck into the region of the southeast trades, its limits become much circumscribed. It is as much as a ship can do now to stretch by the coast of Brazil without tacking. The southeast trades push her so close down upon the coast that it is touch and go with her. The road, in consequence, becomes very narrow. The more narrow the road, the more the stream of ships is condensed. A cruiser, under easy sail, stretching backward and forward across this road, must necessarily get sight of nearly everything that passes. If Mr. Welles had stationed a heavier and faster ship than the *Alabama*—and he had a number of both heavier and faster ships—at the crossing of the 30th parallel; another at or near the equator a little to the eastward of Fernando de Noronha, and a third off Bahia, he must have driven me off or greatly crippled me in my movements. A few more ships in the other chief highways, and his commerce would have been pretty well protected. But the old gentleman does not seem once to have thought of so simple a policy as stationing a ship anywhere.

The reader who has followed the *Alabama* in her career thus far, has seen how many vital points he left unguarded. His plan seemed to be, first to wait until he heard of the *Alabama* being somewhere, and then to send off a number of cruisers post-haste in pursuit of her as though he expected her to stand still and wait for her pursuers! This method of his left the game entirely in my own hands. My safety depended upon a simple calculation of times and distances. For instance, when I arrived off the coast of Brazil, I would take up my pencil and make some such an estimate as this: I discharged my prisoners from the first ship captured on such a day. It will take these prisoners a certain number of days to reach a given port. It will take a certain other number of days for the news of the capture to travel thence to Washington. And it will take a certain other number still for a ship of war of the enemy to reach the coast of Brazil. Just before this aggregate of days elapses, I haul aft my trysail sheets and stretch over to the Cape of Good Hope. I find no enemy's ship of war awaiting me here. I go to work on the stream of commerce doubling the Cape. And by the time, I think, that the ships which have arrived on the coast of Brazil in pursuit of me, have heard of my being at the Cape and started in fresh chase; I quietly stretch back to the coast of Brazil and go to work as before. *Voila tout!* The reader will have occasion to remark by the time we get through with our cruises, how well this system worked for me; as he will have observed that I did not fall in with a single enemy's cruiser at sea at any time during my whole career!

We had some days since crossed the tropic of Capricorn and entered the "variables" of the southern hemisphere; and having reached the forks of the great Brazilian highway, that is to say, the point at which the stream of commerce separates into two principal branches, one passing around Cape Horn, and the other around the Cape of Good Hope, we had taken the left-hand fork. We had not proceeded far on this road, however, before we found upon examination of our bread room, that the weevil, that pestilent little destroyer of bread-stuffs in southern climates, had rendered almost our entire supply of bread useless! It was impossible to proceed on a voyage of such length as that to the Cape of Good Hope in such a dilemma, and I put back for Rio Janeiro to obtain a fresh supply; *unless I could capture it by the way.* We were now in latitude 28° 01′ and longitude 28° 29′, or about 825 miles from Rio; some little distance to travel to a baker's shop. We were saved this journey, however, by a Yankee ship which came very considerately to our relief.

For the next few days, the weather was boisterous and unpleasant—wind generally from the northwest with a south-easterly current. Ships were frequently in sight, but they all proved to be neutral. On the 30th of June, the weather moderated and became fine for a few days. On the 1st of July, after overhauling as many as eleven neutral ships, we gave chase at eleven P. M. to a twelfth sail looming up on the horizon. She looked American, and had heels, and the chase continued all night. As the day dawned, a fine, tall ship, with taper spars and white canvas, was only a few miles ahead of us. A blank cartridge brought the United States colors to her peak, but still she kept on. She was as yet three miles distant and probably had some hope of escape. At all events, her captain had pluck and held on to his canvas until the last moment. It was not until we had approached him near enough to send a shot whizzing across his bow that he consented to clew up and heave to. She proved to be the *Anna F. Schmidt* of Maine from Boston for San Francisco with a valuable cargo of assorted merchandise; much of it consisting of ready-made clothing, hats, boots, and shoes. Here was a haul for the paymaster! But unfortunately for Jack, the coats were too fine, and the tails too long. The trousers and undergarments were all right, however, and of these we got a large supply on board. The *Schmidt* had on board, too, the very article of bread, and in the proper quantity, that we were in want of. We received on board from her thirty days' supply, put up in the nicest kind of airtight casks. Crockery, chinaware, glass, lamps, clocks, sewing machines, patent medicines, clothespins, and the latest invention for killing bed bugs, completed her cargo. No Englishman or Frenchman could possibly own such a cargo, and there was, consequently, no attempt among the papers to protect it. It took us nearly the entire day to do the requisite amount of "robbing" on board the *Schmidt*, and the torch was not applied to her until near nightfall. We then wheeled about and took the fork of the road again for the Cape of Good Hope.

Whilst we were yet busy with the prize, another American ship passed us, but she proved upon being boarded to have been sold by her patriotic Yankee owners to an Englishman and was now profitably engaged in assisting the other ships of John Bull in taking away from the enemy his carrying trade. I examined the papers and surroundings of all these ships, with great care, being anxious, if possible, to find a peg on which I might hang a doubt large enough to enable me to burn them. But thus far all the transfers had been *bona fide*. In the present instance, the papers were evidently genuine, and there was a Scotch master and English crew on board. At about nine P.M. on the same evening, the *Schmidt* being in flames and the *Alabama* in the act of making sail from her, a large, taut ship with exceedingly square yards, passed us at rapid speed under a cloud of canvas from rail to truck, and from her course seemed to be bound either to Europe or the United States. She had paid no attention to the burning ship but flew past it as though she were anxious to get out of harm's way as soon as possible. I conceived thence the idea that she must be one of the enemy's large clipper-ships from round the Horn and immediately gave chase, adding in my eagerness to seize so valuable a prize, steam to sail. It was blowing half a gale of wind, but the phantom ship, for such she looked by moonlight, was carrying her royals and top-gallant studding-sails. This confirmed my suspicion, for surely, I thought, no ship would risk carrying away her spars under such a press of sail unless she were endeavoring to escape from an enemy. By the time we were well under way in pursuit the stranger was about three miles ahead of us. I fired a gun to command him to halt. In a moment or two, to my astonishment, the sound of a gun from the stranger came booming back over the waters in response. I now felt quite sure that I had gotten hold of a New York and California clipper ship. She had fired a gun to make me believe, probably, that she was a ship of war, and thus induce me to desist from the pursuit. But a ship of war would not carry such a press of sail or appear to be in such a hurry to get out of the way—unless, indeed, she were an enemy's ship of inferior force; and the size of the fugitive in the present instance forbade such a supposition. So I sent orders below to the engineer to stir up his fires and put the *Alabama* at the top of her speed. My crew had all become so much excited by the chase, some of the sailors thinking we had scared up the Flying Dutchman, who was known to cruise in these seas, and others expecting a fight, that the watch had forgotten to go below to their hammocks. About midnight we overhauled the stranger near enough to speak her. She loomed up terribly large as we approached. She was painted black with a white streak around her waist, man-of-war fashion, and we could count with the aid of our night glasses, five guns of a side frowning through her ports. "What ship is that?" now thundered my first lieutenant through his trumpet.

"This is her Britannic Majesty's ship, *Diomede!*" came back in reply very quietly. "What ship is that?" now asked the *Diomede*.

"This is the Confederate States steamer *Alabama*."

"I suspected as much," said the officer, "when I saw you making sail by the light of the burning ship." A little friendly chat now ensued, when we sheared off and permitted her Britannic Majesty's frigate to proceed without insisting upon an examination of her papers, and the sailors slunk below, one by one, to their hammocks, disappointed that they had neither caught the Flying Dutchman, a California clipper, or a fight.

The next day and for several days, the weather proved fine. We were running to the eastward on the average parallel of about 30°, with the wind from N.N.E. to the N.W. Saturday, July 4th, 1863, is thus recorded in my journal: "This is 'Independence day' in the 'old concern;' a holiday, which I feel half inclined to throw overboard, because it was established in such bad company, and because we have to fight the battle of independence over again against a greater tyranny than before. Still, old feelings are strong, and it will not hurt Jack to give him an extra glass of grog."

The morning of the 6th proved cloudy and squally, and we had some showers of rain, though the barometer kept steadily up. At thirty minutes past midnight, an officer came below to inform me that there was a large sail in sight not a great way off. I sent word to the officer of the deck to chase and repaired on deck pretty soon myself. In about three hours we had approached the chase sufficiently near to heave her to with a shot, she having previously disregarded two blank cartridges. She proved to be another prize, the ship *Express*, of Boston from Callao for Antwerp with a cargo of guano from the Chincha Islands. This cargo probably belonged to the Peruvian Government, for the guano of the Chincha Islands is a government monopoly, but our Peruvian friends had been unfortunate in their attempts to cover it. It had been shipped by Messrs. Sescau, Valdeavellano & Co., and consigned to J. Sescau & Co. at Antwerp. On the back of the bill of lading was the following indorsement:—"Nous soussigné, Chargé d'Affaires et Consul General de France à Lima, certifions que la chargement de mille soixante deuze tonneaux, de register, de Huano, specifié au présent connaissement, est propriéte neutre. Fait à Lima, le 27 Janvier, 1863." This certificate was no better than so much waste paper for two reasons. First, it was not sworn to, and secondly, it simply averred the property to be neutral without stating who the owners were. I was sorry to burn so much property belonging in all probability to Peru, but I could make no distinction between that government and an individual. I had the right to burn the enemy's ship, and if a neutral government chose to put its property on board of her, it was its duty to document it according to the laws of war or abide the consequences of the neglect. The certificate would not have secured individual property, and I could not permit it to screen that of a government which was presumed to know the law better than an individual. As the case stood, I was bound to presume that the property, being in an enemy's bottom, was enemy's. The torch followed this decision.

The *Express* had had a long and boisterous passage around Cape Horn and gave signs of being much weatherbeaten—some of her spars and sails were gone, and her sides were defaced with iron rust. The master had his wife on board, a gentle Englishwoman, with her servant maid, or rather humble companion, and it seemed quite hard that these two females, after having braved the dangers of Cape Horn, should be carried off to brave other dangers at the Cape of Good Hope.

We were now in mid-winter, July 15th, when the storms run riot over these two prominent headlands of our globe. We were fast changing our skies as we proceeded southward. Many of the northern constellations had been buried beneath the horizon to rise no more until we should recross the equator, and other new and brilliant ones had risen in their places. We had not seen the familiar North Star for months. The Southern Cross had arisen to attract our gaze to the opposite pole instead. The mysterious Magellan clouds hovered over the same pole by day, and caused the mariner to dream of far-off worlds. They were even visible on very bright nights. The reader will perhaps remember the meteorological phenomena which we met with in the Gulf Stream—how regularly the winds went around the compass from left to right, or with the course of the sun, obeying the laws of storms. Similar phenomena are occurring to us now. The winds are still going round with the sun, but they no longer go from left to right, but from right to left; for this is now the motion of the sun. Instead of watching the winds haul from northeast to east; from east to southeast; from southeast to south, as we were wont to do in the northern hemisphere, we now watch them haul from northeast to north; from north to northwest; and from northwest to west. And when we get on shore, in the gardens and vineyards at the Cape of Good Hope, we shall see the tendrils of the vine, and the creeping plants, twining around their respective supports in the opposite direction, from left to right, instead of from right to left as . . . in the writer's garden in Alabama.

After capturing the *Express*, we passed into one of the byways of the sea. The fork of the road which we had been hitherto pursuing, now bore off to the southeast—the India-bound ships running well to the southward of the Cape. We turned out of the road to the left and drew in nearer to the coast of Africa. With the exception of an occasional African trader or a chance whaler, we were entirely out of the track of commerce. In the space of seven or eight hundred miles, we sighted but a single ship.

As we drew down toward the Cape, that singular bird, the Cape pigeon, came to visit us. It is of about the size of a small sea gull and not unlike it in appearance. Like the petrel, it is a storm bird and seems to delight in the commotion of the elements. It is quite gentle, wheeling around the ship and uttering from time to time its cheerful scream, or rather whistle. A peculiarity of this bird is that it is entirely unknown in the northern hemisphere; from which it would appear that like the "right" whale, it is incapable of enduring the tropical heats. It would probably be death to it to attempt to cross the equator.

On the 28th of July, we observed in latitude 33° 46′ and longitude 17° 31′, and the next day at about nine A. M. we made Daffen Island with its remarkable breaker, lying a short distance to the northward of the Cape of Good Hope. Instead of running into Cape Town, I deemed it more prudent to go first to Saldanha Bay and reconnoitre. There might be enemy's ships of war off the Cape, and if so I desired to get news of them before they should hear of my being in these seas. As we were running in for the bay, we overhauled a small coasting schooner, the master of which volunteered to take us in to the anchorage; and early in the afternoon, we came to in five and three quarter fathoms of water in a cosy

little nook of the bay sheltered from all winds. There was
no Yankee man-of-war at the Cape, nor had there been any
there for some months! Mr. Welles was asleep, the coast was
all clear, and I could renew my "depredations" upon the
enemy's commerce whenever I pleased.

There is no finer sheet of land-locked water in the world
than Saldanha Bay. Its anchorage is bold and clean and
spacious enough to accommodate the largest fleets. It is within
a few hours' sail of the Cape, which is the halfway mile-post
between the extreme east and the extreme west, and yet
commerce with a strange caprice has established its relay-
house at Cape Town, whose anchorage is open to all the winter gales, from which a ship is in constant danger of being
wrecked. We did not find so much as a coaster at anchor in
this splendid harbor. The country around was wild and picturesque in appearance; the substratum being of solid rock,
and nature having played some strange freaks when chaos was
being reduced to order. Rocky precipices and palisades meet
the beholder at every turn, and immense boulders of granite
lie scattered on the coast and over the hills as if giants had
been amusing themselves at a game of marbles. A few farmhouses are in sight from the ship, surrounded by patches of
cultivation, but all the rest of the landscape is a semi-barren
waste of straggling rocks and coarse grass. The country im-
proves, however, a short distance back from the coast, and
the grazing becomes fine. Beef cattle are numerous and of
fair size, and the sheep flourishes in great perfection—wool
being one of the staple products of the colony. The cereals
are also produced, and as every one knows, the Cape has long
been famous for its delicate wines.

My first care was to send the paymaster on shore to contract for supplying the crew with fresh provisions during our
stay, and my next to inform the Governor at the Cape of my
arrival. As I turned into my cot that night with a still ship,
in a land-locked harbor, with no strange sails or storms to disturb my repose, I felt like a weary traveler who had laid
down for the time a heavy burden. The morning after our
arrival—the 30th of July—was bright and beautiful, and I
landed early to get sights for my chronometers. It was the
first time I had ever set foot on the continent of Africa, and I
looked forth from the eminence on which I stood upon a wild,
desolate, and yet picturesque scene. The ocean was slumber-

ing in the distance, huge rocky precipices were around me, the newly risen sun was scattering the mists from the hills, and the only signs of life save the *Alabama* at my feet, and the ox-team of a Boer which was creeping along the beach, were the screams of the sea fowl as they whirled around me and from time to time made plunges into the still waters in quest of their prey. A profusion of wild flowers bloomed in little parterres among the rocks, and among others, I plucked the geranium in several varieties. This was evidently its native home.

Returning on board at the usual breakfast hour, I found that Bartelli had made excellent use of his time. There was a hut or two on the beach to which a market boat had been sent from the ship to bring off the fresh beef and vegetables for the crew, which the paymaster had contracted for on the previous evening. Bartelli had accompanied it, and the result was a venison steak cut fresh from a spring bok that a hunter had just brought in, simmering in his chafing dish. There were some fine pan fish on the table, too; for my first lieutenant, ever mindful of the comfort of his people, had sent a party on shore with the seine, which had had fine success, and reported the bay full of fish. Jack, after having been nearly three months on a diet of salted beef and pork, was once more in clover, and my young officers were greatly excited by the reports that came off to them from the shore of the variety and abundance of game, in the neighborhood. Besides the curlew, snipe, and plover that were to be found on the beach and in the salt marshes adjacent, the quail, pheasant, deer in several varieties, and even the ostrich, the lion, and the tiger* awaited them if they should think proper to go a little distance inland. The small islands in the bay abounded in rabbits, which might be chased and knocked on the head with sticks. Hunting parties were soon organized, and there was a great cleaning and burnishing of fowling pieces and adjusting and filling of powder flasks and shot pouches going on.

But all was not to be pleasure; there was duty to be thought of as well. The *Alabama* required considerable overhauling after her late cruise, both in her machinery and hull and rigging. Among other things, it was quite necessary that she should be recaulked inside and out and repainted. There were working parties organized, therefore, as well as hunting

---

* Semmes is mistaken. The tiger is an Asiatic, not an African, beast. Ed.

and fishing parties. We soon found, too, that we had the duties of hospitality to attend to. The fame of the "British Pirate" had preceded her. Every ship which had touched at the Cape had had more or less to say of the *Alabama*. Mr. Seward and Mr. Adams, Lord Russell and the London *Times* had made her famous, and the people manifested great curiosity to see her. We were in a measure, too, among our own kinsmen. The Cape of Good Hope had been a Dutch colony and was now inhabited by a mixed population of Dutch and English. The African had met the usual fate of the savage when he comes in contact with civilized man. He had been thrust aside and was only to be seen as a straggler and stranger in his native land.

From far and near the country people flocked in to see us in every description of vehicle from the tidy spring wagon, with its pair of sleek ponies, to the ox-cart. The vehicles, containing mostly women and children, were preceded or followed by men on horseback by twos and threes, and sometimes by the dozen. The men brought along with them their shotguns and rifles, thus converting their journey into a hunting party, as well as one of curiosity. Those from a distance came provided with tents and camp equipage. Almost every one had some present of game or curiosity to offer as he came on board. One would bring me a wild peacock for dinner, which he had shot on the wayside; another a brace of pheasants; others ostrich eggs fresh from the nest, plumes of ostrich-feathers, spikes from the head of the spring bok three and four feet in length, &c. We showed them around the ship—the young Boers lifting our hundred-pound rifle shot and looking over the sights of our guns, and the young women looking at the moustaches of my young officers.

The Saldanha settlement is almost exclusively Dutch, notwithstanding it has been fifty years and more in possession of the English. Dutch is the language universally spoken; all the newspapers are published in that melodious tongue, and the "young idea" is being taught to "shoot" in it. One young man among our visitors, though he was twenty-three years of age and lived within twenty miles of the sea, told me he had never been on board a ship before. He became very much excited and went into ecstasies at everything he saw, particularly at the size and weight of the guns, which seemed to transcend all his philosophy—the largest gun which he had hitherto seen being his own rifle with which he was in the habit of bringing down the ostrich or the tiger. The climate seemed to be well suited to these descendants of the Hollanders. The men were athletic and well-proportioned, and the young women chubby and blooming with the blended tints of the lily and the rose—the rose rather preponderating. The beauty of these lasses—and some of them were quite pretty—was due entirely to mother Nature, as their large and somewhat rough hands and awkward courtesies showed that they were rather more familiar with milking the cows and churning the butter than with the airs and graces of the salon.

We remained a week in Saldanha Bay during the whole of which we had exceedingly fine weather; the wind generally prevailing from the southeast, and the sky being clear with now and then a film of gray clouds. This was quite remarkable for the first days of August—this month being equivalent, at the stormy Cape to the month of February in the northern hemisphere. The natives told us that so gentle a winter had not been known for years before. The temperature was delightful. Although we were in the latitude of about 34°—say the equivalent latitude to that of southwestern Virginia—we did not feel the want of fires. Indeed, the grasses were green, and vegetation seemed to have been scarcely suspended. The graziers had no need to feed their cattle.

A schooner came in while we lay here, bringing us some letters from merchants at Cape Town welcoming us to the colony, and offering to supply us with coal or whatever else we might need. I had left orders both at Fernando de Noronha and Bahia for the *Agrippina*, if she should arrive at either of those places after my departure, to make the best of her way to Saldanha Bay and await me there. She should have preceded me several weeks. She was not here—the old Scotchman, as before remarked, having played me false.

When Kell had put his ship in order, he took a little recreation himself and in company with one or two of his messmates went off into the interior on an ostrich hunt. Horses and dogs, and hunters awaited them at the country seat of the gentleman who had invited them to partake of this peculiarly African sport. They had a grand hunt and put up several fine birds, at which some of the party—Kell among the number, got shots—but they did not bring any plumes on board; at least of their own capturing. The devilish birds, as big as horses and running twice as fast, as some of the young officers described them, refused to heave to, they said, though they had sent sundry whistlers around their heads in the shape of buckshot.

A sad accident occurred to one of our young hunters before we left the bay. One afternoon, just at sunset, I was shocked to receive the intelligence that one of the cutters had returned alongside with a dead officer in it. Third Assistant Engineer Cummings was the unfortunate officer. He had been hunting with a party of his messmates. They had all returned with well-filled game bags to the boat at sunset, and Cummings was in the act of stepping into her when the cock of his gun striking against the gunwale, a whole load of buckshot passed through his chest in the region of the heart, and he fell dead in an instant upon the sands. The body was lifted tenderly into the boat and taken on board, and prepared by careful and affectionate hands for interment on the morrow. This young gentleman had been very popular with both officers and crew, and his sudden death cast a gloom over the ship. All amusements were suspended, and men walked about with softened footfall as though fearing to disturb the slumbers of the dead. Arrangements were made for interring him in the graveyard of a neighboring farmer, and the next morning the colors of the ship were half-masted, and all the boats—each with its colors also at halfmast—formed in line, and as many of the officers and crew as could be spared from duty followed the deceased to his last resting place. There were six boats in the procession, and as they pulled in for the shore with the well-known funeral stroke and drooping flags, the spectacle was one to sadden the heart. A young life had been suddenly cut short in a far distant land. A subscription was taken up to place a proper tomb over his remains, and the curious visitor to Saldanha Bay may read on a simple but enduring marble slab this mournful little episode in the history of the cruise of the *Alabama*.

Chapter Seventeen—*1863*

The connecting thread of the history of the war taken up . . . A brief review of the events of the twelve months during which the Alabama has been commissioned . . . Alabama arrives at Cape Town . . . Capture of the Sea Bridge . . . Excitement thereupon . . . Correspondence between the American Consul and the Governor on the subject of the capture

The *Alabama* has been commissioned now one year. In accordance with my plan of connecting my cruises with a thread—a mere thread—of the history of the war, it will be necessary to retrace our steps and take up that thread at the point at which it was broken—August, 1862. At that date the splendid army of McClellan had been overwhelmed with defeat and driven in disorder from before Richmond, and the fortunes of the Confederacy had greatly brightened in consequence. Lee followed up this movement with the invasion of Maryland not for the purpose of fighting battles but to free the people of that Southern State from the military despotism which had been fastened upon them by the enemy, and enable them, if they thought proper, to join their fortunes with those of the Confederacy. But he penetrated only that portion of the state in which the people had always been but lukewarm Southerners, and an indifferent, if not cold, reception awaited him. The result might have been different if he could have made his way into the city of Baltimore and the more Southern parts of the state. There the enemy was as cordially detested as in any part of the Confederacy. The Federal Government had by this time gotten firm military possession of the state through the treason of Governor Bradford, Mayor Swann and others, and nothing short of driving out the enemy from the city of Baltimore and occupying it by our troops, could enable the people of that true and patriotic city to move in defence of their liberties and save their state from the desecration that awaited her.

Harper's Ferry was captured by a portion of Lee's forces; the battle of Sharpsburg was fought (17th September, 1862) without decisive results, and Lee recrossed his army into Virginia.

In the West, Corinth was evacuated by General Beauregard, who was threatened with being flanked by an enemy of superior force.

Memphis was captured soon afterward by a Federal fleet, which dispersed the few Confederate gunboats that offered it a feeble resistance.

The fall of Fort Pillow and Memphis opened the way for the enemy as far down the Mississippi as Vicksburg. Here Farragut's and Porter's fleets—the former from below, the latter from above—united in a joint attack upon the place, but Van Dorn beat them off.

The Confederates made an attempt to dislodge the enemy from Baton Rouge, the capital of Louisiana, about forty miles below the mouth of the Red River, but failed. The expedition was to be a joint naval and military one, but the naval portion of it failed by an unfortunate accident. Breckinridge, with less than 3000 men, fought a gallant action against a superior force and drove the enemy into the town, but for want of the naval assistance promised could not dislodge him. We now occupied Port Hudson below Baton Rouge, and the enemy evacuated Baton Rouge in consequence. We thus held the Mississippi River between Port Hudson and Vicksburg, a distance of more than 200 miles.

General Bragg now made a campaign into Kentucky, which state he occupied for several weeks but was obliged finally to evacuate, by overwhelming forces of the enemy. During this campaign, the battles of Richmond and Perryville were fought. Bragg gathered immense supplies during his march, killed, wounded, or captured 25,000 of the enemy's troops and returned with a well-clothed, well-equipped, more numerous, and better disciplined army than he had at the beginning of the campaign. The effect of this campaign was to relieve North Alabama and Middle Tennessee of the presence of the enemy for some months.

In September, 1862, Van Dorn attacked Rosencrans at Corinth, but was obliged to withdraw after a gallant and bloody fight. He retreated in good order.

After Lee's retreat into Virginia from his march into Maryland, McClellan remained inactive for some time, and the Northern people becoming dissatisfied, clamored for a change of commanders. Burnside was appointed to supersede him—a man in every way unfit for the command of a large army. With an army of 150,000 men, this man of straw crossed the Rappahannock and attacked Lee at Fredericksburg in obedience to the howl of the Northern Demos, of "On to Richmond!" A perfect slaughter of his troops ensued. As far as can be learned, this man did not cross the river at all himself but sent his troops to assault works in front which none but a madman would have thought of attempting—especially with a river in his rear. It is only necessary to state the result. Federal loss in killed, 1152; wounded, 7000. Confederate loss in killed and wounded, 1800. During a storm of wind and rain, the beaten army regained the shelter of its camps on the opposite side of the river. Burnside was now thrown overboard by the Northern Demos as McClellan had been before him.

As the old year died and the new year came in, the battle of Murfreesborough in Middle Tennessee was fought between Bragg and Rosencrans, which was bloody on both sides and indecisive. Bragg retired from Murfreesborough but was not molested by the enemy during his retreat. The year 1862 may be said, upon the whole, to have resulted brilliantly for the Confederate arms. We had fought drawn battles and had made some retrograde movements, but on the other hand we had gained splendid victories, made triumphant marches into the enemy's territory, and even threatened his capital. The nations of the earth were looking upon us with admiration, and we had every reason to feel encouraged.

One of the first events of the year 1863 was the dispersion of the enemy's blockading fleet off Charleston by Commodore Ingraham with two small iron-clads, the *Chicora* and the *Palmetto State*. This gallant South Carolinian, in his flagship, the *Palmetto State*, first attacked the *Mercedita*, Captain Stellwagen. Having run into this vessel and fired one or two shots at her, she cried for quarter and surrendered, believing herself to be in a sinking condition. In a few minutes, the *Mercedita* sent a boat alongside the *Chicora* with her first lieutenant, who by authority of his captain, surrendered the ship and assented to the *paroling* of the officers and crew. The two little ironclads then went in pursuit of the enemy's other ships and succeeded in getting a shot at one or two of them, but they were all too fast for them, and betaking themselves to their heels, soon put themselves out of harm's way. In a short time there was not a blockader to be seen!

Judge of the surprise of Commodore Ingraham, when upon his return, he found that his prize, the *Mercedita*, which he had left at anchor under *parole*, had cleared out. Captain Stellwagen and every officer and man on board the *Mercedita*, had solemnly promised *on honor*—for this is the nature of a parole —that they would do no act of war until exchanged. From the moment they made that promise, they were *hors de combat*. They were prisoners at large on board the ship which they had surrendered to the enemy. And yet, when that enemy turned his back—relying upon the *parole* which they had given him—they got up their anchor and steamed off to Port Royal and reported to their Admiral—Dupont! Did Dupont send her back to Ingraham? No. He reported the facts to Mr. Secretary Welles. And what did Mr. Secretary Welles do? He kept possession of the ship at the sacrifice of the honor of the Department over which he presided. And what think you was the excuse? It is a curiosity. Admiral Dupont reported the case thus to Mr. Welles: "Unable to use his [Stellwagen's] guns, and being at the mercy of the enemy which was lying alongside on his starboard quarter, all further resistance was deemed hopeless by Captain Stellwagen, and he surrendered. The crew and officers were paroled *though nothing was said about the ship*; the executive officer, Lieutenant-Commander Abbot, having gone on board the enemy's ship and made the arrangements." Mr. Welles, thus prompted by Admiral Dupont, adopted the exceedingly brilliant idea that as *nothing* had been said about the ship—that is, as the ship had not been paroled, she might like every other unparoled prisoner, walk off with herself and make her escape! But to say nothing of the odd idea of paroling a ship, these honorable casuists overlooked the small circumstance that the ship could not make her escape without the assistance of the paroled officers; and it was an act of war for paroled officers to get under way and carry off from her anchors a prize-ship of the enemy. It was a theft and breach of honor besides.

A few days after Ingraham's raid, Galveston was recaptured by the Confederates, as already described when speaking of the victory of the *Alabama* over the *Hatteras.*

Sherman made an attempt upon Vicksburg and failed. Admiral Dupont, with a large and well appointed fleet of ironclads, attacked Charleston and was beaten back—one of his ships being sunk and others seriously damaged. On the Potomac, Hooker had been sent by the many-headed monster to relieve Burnside, which was but substitution of one dunderhead for another. But Hooker had the *sobriquet* of "fighting Joe," and this tickled the monster. "With the most splendid army on the planet," as characterized by the hyperbolous Joe himself, he crossed the Rappahannock on *his way to Richmond.* Lee had no more than about one third of Hooker's force with which to oppose him. Three battles ensued— at the Wilderness, Chancellorsville, and Salem Church, which resulted in the defeat and rout of "fighting Joe" and his rapid retreat to the north bank of the Rappahannock. But these victories cost us the life of Stonewall Jackson, the Cœur de Lion of the Southern Confederacy. His body has been given to the worms, but his exploits equal, if they do not excel, those of Napoleon in his first Italian campaign, and will fire the youth of America as long as our language lives and history continues to be read.

A third attempt was made upon Vicksburg; this time by General Grant with a large army that insured success. With this army and a fleet of gunboats, he laid siege to Pemberton. On the 4th of July Pemberton surrendered. This was a terrible blow to us. It not only lost us an army but cut the Confederacy in two by giving the enemy the command of the Mississippi River. Port Hudson followed. As a partial setoff to these disasters, General Dick Taylor captured Brasher City, a very important base which the enemy had established for operations in Louisiana and Texas. Nearly five million dollars' worth of stores fell into Taylor's hands.

After the defeat of Hooker, Lee determined upon another move across the enemy's border. Hooker followed, keeping himself between Lee and Washington, supposing the latter to be the object of Lee's movement. But Lee moved by the Shenandoah Valley upon Gettysburg in Pennsylvania. Hooker now resigned the command for which he found himself unfitted, and Meade was sent to relieve him. The latter marched forthwith upon Gettysburg, cautiously disposing his troops meanwhile so as to cover both Baltimore and Washington. The greatest battle of the war was fought here during the first three days of July. Both parties were whipped, and on the 4th of July, when Pemberton was surrendering Vicksburg to Grant, Lee was preparing to withdraw from Gettysburg for the purpose of recrossing the Potomac. If the battle had been fought in Virginia, Meade would have been preparing in like manner to cross the same river but to a different side. Lee withdrew without serious molestation, Meade being too badly crippled to do more than follow him at a limping gait. The disproportion of numbers in this battle was greatly in favor of Meade, and he had, besides, the advantage of acting on the defensive in an intrenched position.

Vicksburg and Gettysburg mark an era in the war. The Confederates from this time began to show signs of weakness. In consequence of the great disparity of numbers, we had been compelled at an early day in the war to draw upon our whole fighting population. The Northern hive was still swarming and apparently as numerous as ever. All Europe was, besides, open to the North as a recruiting station, and we have seen in the course of these pages how unscrupulously and fraudulently the Federal agents availed themselves of this advantage. We were being hard pressed, too, for material, for the enemy was maintaining a rigid blockade of our ports, and was, besides, with a barbarity unknown in civilized war, laying waste our plantations and cornfields. We need no better evidence of the shock which had been given to public confidence in the South by those two disasters than the simple fact that our currency depreciated almost immediately a thousand per cent.! Later in the summer another attempt was made upon Charleston, which was repulsed as the others had been. Dupont, after his failure, had been thrown overboard, and Admiral Foote ordered to succeed him; but Foote dying before he could assume command, Dahlgren was substituted. This gentleman had from a very early period in his career directed his attention to ordnance and turned to account the experiments of Colonel [Henri-Joseph] Paixans with shell guns and shell firing. He had much improved upon the old-fashioned naval ordnance in vogue before the advent of steamships, and for these labors of his in the foundries and workshops, he had been made an Admiral. He was now sent to aid General Gilmore, an engineer of some reputation, to carry out the favorite Boston idea of razing Charleston to the ground as the original hotbed of secession. They made a lodgment on Morris Island, but failed, as Dupont had done, against the other works.

We have thus strung, as it were, upon our thread of the war, the more important military events that occurred during the first year of the cruise of the *Alabama*. We will now return to that ship. We left her at Saldanha Bay near the Cape of Good Hope.

On the morning of the 5th of August, the weather being fine and the wind light from the south, we got under way for Table Bay. As we were steaming along the coast, we fell in with our consort, the *Tuscaloosa*, on her way to join us at Saldanha Bay in accordance with her instructions. She had been delayed by light winds and calms. She reported the capture of the enemy's ship *Santee* from the East Indies laden with rice on British account and bound for Falmouth, England. She had released her on ransom bond. The *Tuscaloosa* being in want of supplies, I directed her to proceed to Simon Town in Simon's Bay, to the eastward of the Cape, and there refit and provide herself with whatever might be necessary. A little after midday as we were hauling in for Cape Town, "Sail ho!" was cried from aloft; and when we had raised the sail from the deck, we could see quite distinctly that the jaunty, newly painted craft with the taper spars and white canvas was an American bark, bound like ourselves into Table Bay. As before remarked, the wind was light, and the bark was not making much headway. This was fortunate, for if there had been a brisk breeze blowing, she must have run within the charmed marine league before we could have overhauled her.

Hoisting the English colors, we gave the *Alabama* all steam in chase and came near enough to heave the stranger to when she was still five or six miles from the land. She proved to be the *Sea Bride* of Boston from New York and bound with an assorted cargo of provisions and notions on a trading voyage along the eastern coast of Africa. I threw a prize crew on board of her, and as I could not take her into port with me, I directed the officer to stand off and on until further orders—repairing to Saldanha Bay by the 15th of the month in case he should be blown off by a gale. The capture of this ship caused great excitement at Cape Town, it having been made within full view of the whole population. The editor of a daily newspaper published at the Cape—the *Argus*—witnessed it, and we will let him describe it. The following is an extract from that paper of the date of the 6th of August, 1863:

Yesterday, at almost noon, a steamer from the northward was made down from the signal post on Lion's Hill. The Governor had on the previous day received a letter from Captain Semmes, informing his Excellency that the gallant captain had put his ship into Saldanha Bay for repairs. This letter had been made public in the morning and had caused no little excitement. Cape Town, that has been more than dull—that has been dismal for months, thinking and talking of nothing but bankruptcies—bankruptcies fraudulent, and bankruptcies unavoidable—was now all astir, full of life and motion. The stoop of the Commercial Exchange was crowded with merchants, knots of citizens were collected at the corner of every street; business was almost, if not entirely suspended.

All that could be gleaned, in addition to the information of Captain Semmes' letter to the Governor, a copy of which was sent to the United States Consul immediately it was received, was that the schooner *Atlas* had just returned from Malagas Island, where she had been with water and vegetables for men collecting guano there. Captain Boyce, the master of the *Atlas*, reported that he had himself actually seen the *Alabama*; a boat from the steamer had boarded his vessel, and he had been on board of her. His report of Captain Semmes corroborated that given by everyone else. He said the Captain was most courteous and gentlemanly. He asked Captain Boyce to land thirty prisoners for him in Table Bay, with which request Captain Boyce was unable to comply. Captain Semmes said that the *Florida* was also a short distance off the Cape, and that the *Alabama*, when she had completed her repairs and was cleaned and painted, would pay Table Bay a visit. He expected to be there, he said, very nearly as soon as the *Atlas*. Shortly after the *Atlas* arrived, a boat brought up some of the prisoners from Saldanha Bay, and among them one of the crew of the *Alabama*, who said he had left the ship. All these waited on the United States Consul, but were unable to give much information beyond what we had already received.

The news that the *Alabama* was coming into Table Bay and would probably arrive about four o'clock this afternoon added to the excitement. About noon, a steamer from the northwest was made down by the signal-man on the hill. Could this be the *Alabama*? or was it the *Hydaspes* from India, or the *Lady Jocelyn* from England? All three were now hourly expected, and the city was in doubt. Just after one, it was made down 'Confederate steamer *Alabama* from the northwest, and Federal bark from the southeast.' Here was to be a capture by the celebrated Confederate craft close to the entrance of Table Bay. The inhabitants rushed off to get a sight. Crowds of people ran up the Lion's Hill and to the Kloof Road. All the cabs were chartered—every one of them; there was no cavilling about fares; the cabs were taken and no questions asked, but orders were given to drive as hard as possible.

"The bark coming in from the southeast, and, as the signal-man made down, five miles off; the steamer coming in from the northwest, eight miles off, led us to think that the Kloof Road was the best place for a full view. To that place we directed our Jehu to drive furiously. We did the first mile in a short time; but the Kloof-hill for the next two and a half miles is uphill work. The horse jibbed, so we pushed on on foot as fast as possible and left the cab to come on. When we reached the summit, we could only make out a steamer on the horizon from eighteen to twenty miles off. This could not be the *Alabama*, unless she was making off to sea again. There was no bark. As soon as our cab reached the crown of the hill, we set off at a breakneck pace down the hill, on past the Round-house, till we came near Brighton, and as we reached the corner, there lay the *Alabama* within fifty yards of the unfortunate Yankee. As the Yankee came around from the southeast and about five miles from the Bay, the steamer came down upon her. The Yankee was evidently taken by surprise. The *Alabama* fired a gun and brought her to.

When first we got sight of the *Alabama*, it was difficult to make out what she was doing; the bark's head had been put about, and the *Alabama* lay off quite immovable, as if she were taking a sight of the 'varmint.' The weather was beautifully calm and clear, and the sea was as smooth and transparent as a sheet of glass. The bark was making her way slowly from the steamer with every bit of her canvas spread. The *Alabama*, with her steam off, appeared to be letting the bark get clear off. What could this mean? No one understood. It must be the *Alabama*. 'There,' said the spectators, 'is the Confederate flag at her peak; it must be a Federal bark, too, for there are the stars and stripes of the States flying at her main.' What could the *Alabama* mean lying there—

> As idly as a painted ship
> Upon a painted ocean.

What it meant was soon seen. Like a cat, watching and playing with a victimized mouse, Captain Semmes permitted his prize to draw off a few yards, and then he up steam again and pounced upon her. She first sailed round the Yankee from stem to stern, and stern to stem again. The way that fine, saucy, rakish craft was handled was worth riding a hundred miles to see. She went round the bark like a toy, making a complete circle and leaving an even margin of water between herself and her prize of not more than twenty yards. From the hill it appeared as if there was no water at all between the two vessels. This done, she sent a boat with a prize crew off, took possession in the name of the Confederate States, and sent the bark off to sea.

The *Alabama* then made for the port. We came round the Kloof to visit Captain Semmes on board. As we came, we found the heights overlooking Table Bay covered with people; the road to Green Point lined with cabs. The windows of the villas at the bottom of the hill were all thrown up, and ladies waved their handkerchiefs, and one and all joined in the general enthusiasm; over the quarries, along the Malay burying ground, the Gallows Hill, and the beach, there were masses of people—nothing but a sea of heads as far as the eye could reach. Along Strand Street and Alderley Street, the roofs of all the houses from which Table Bay is overlooked, were made available as standing places for the people who could not get boats to go off to her. The central, the north, the south, and the coaling jetties were all crowded. At the central jetty it was almost impossible to force one's way through to get a boat. However, all in good time, we did get a boat and went off in the midst of dingies, cargo boats, gigs, and wherries, all as full as they could hold. Nearly all the city was upon the bay; the rowing clubs in uniform with favored members of their respective clubs on board. The crews feathered their oars in double-quick time, and their pulling, our 'stroke' declared, was a 'caution, and no mistake.' On getting alongside the *Alabama*, we found about a dozen boats before us, and we had not been on board five minutes before she was surrounded by nearly every boat in Table Bay, and as boat after boat arrived, three hearty cheers were given for Captain Semmes and his gallant privateer. This, upon the part of a neutral people, is, perchance, wrong; but we are not arguing a case—we are recording facts. They did cheer, and cheer with a will, too. It was not, perhaps, taking the view of either side, Federal or Confederate, but in admiration of the skill, pluck, and daring of the *Alabama*, her captain, and her crew, who afford a general theme of admiration for the world all over.

Visitors were received by the officers of the ship most courteously and without distinction, and the officers conversed freely and unreservedly of their exploits. There was nothing like brag in their manner of answering questions put to them. They are as fine and gentlemanly a set of fellows as ever we saw; most of them young men. The ship has been so frequently described that most people know what she is like as we do who have seen her. We should have known her to be the *Alabama* if we had boarded her in the midst of the ocean with no one to introduce us to each other. Her guns alone are worth going off to see, and everything about her speaks highly of the seamanship and discipline of her commander and his officers. She had a very large crew, fine, lithe-looking fellows, the very picture of English man-of-war's men.

The editor of the *Argus* has not overdrawn the picture when he says, that nearly all Cape Town was afloat on the evening of the arrival of the *Alabama*. The deck of the ship was so crowded that it was almost impossible to stir in any direction. Nor was this simply a vulgar crowd come off to satisfy mere curiosity. It seemed to be a generous outpouring of the better classes. Gentlemen and ladies of distinction pressed into my cabin to tender me a cordial greeting. Whatever may have been the cause, their imaginations and their hearts seemed both to have been touched. I could not but be gratified at such a demonstration on the part of an entire people. The inhabitants of the Cape colony seemed to resemble our own people in their excitability and in the warmth with which they expressed their feelings, more than the phlegmatic English people of whom they are a part. This resemblance became still more apparent when I had the leisure to notice the tone, and temper of their press, the marshalling of political parties, and the speeches of their public men. The colony, with its own Legislature charged with the care of its own local concern, was almost a republic. It enjoyed all the freedom of a republic without its evils. The check upon the franchise, and the appointment of the Executive by the Crown, so tempered the republican elements that license was checked without liberty being restrained.

Bartelli, my faithful steward, was in his element during the continuance of this great levée on board the *Alabama*. He had dressed himself with scrupulous care, and posting himself at my cabin door with the air of a chamberlain to a king, he refused admission to all comers until they had first presented him with a card and been duly announced. Pressing some of the wardroom boys into his service, he served refreshments to his numerous guests in a style that did my *menage* infinite credit. Fair women brought bouquets with them which they presented with a charming grace, and my cabin was soon garlanded with flowers. Some of these were *immortelles* peculiar to the Cape of Good Hope, and for months afterward they retained their places around the large mirror that adorned the after-part of my cabin, with their colors almost as bright as ever. During my entire stay my table was loaded with flowers, the most luscious grapes, and other fruits sent off to me every morning by the ladies of the Cape, sometimes with, and sometimes without, a name. Something has been said before about the capacity of the heart of a sailor. My own was carried by storm on the present occasion. I simply surrendered at discretion, and whilst Kell was explaining the virtues of his guns to his male visitors and answering the many questions that were put to him about our cruises and captures, I found it as much as I could do to write autographs and answer the pretty little perfumed billets that came off to me. Dear ladies of the Cape of Good Hope! these scenes are still fresh in my memory, and I make you but a feeble return for all your kindness in endeavoring to impress them upon these pages that they may endure yet a little while. I have always found the instincts of women to be right, and I felt more gratified at this spontaneous outpouring of the sympathies of the sex for our cause than if all the male creatures of the earth had approved it in cold and formal words.

I found, at the Cape of Good Hope, the stereotyped American consult * ; half diplomat, half demagogue. Here is a letter which the ignorant fellow wrote to the Governor whilst I was still as Saldanha Bay:

SIR: From reliable information received by me, and which you are also doubtless in possession of, a war steamer called the *Alabama* is now in Saldanha Bay, being painted, discharging prisoners of war, &c. The vessel in question was built in England to prey upon the commerce of the United States and escaped therefrom while on her trial trip, forfeiting bonds of £20,000 (!) which the British Government exacted under the Foreign Enlistment Act. Now, as your Government has a treaty of amity and commerce with the United States, and has not recognized the persons in revolt against the United States as a government at all, the vessel alluded to should be at once seized and sent to England, whence she clandestinely escaped. Assuming that the British Government was sincere in exacting the bonds, you have doubtless been instructed to send her home to England where she belongs. But if, from some oversight, you have not received such instructions, and you decline the responsibility of making the seizure, I would most respectfully protest against the vessel remaining in any port of the Colony another day. She has been at Saldanha Bay four days already, and a week previously on the coast, and has forfeited all right to remain an hour longer by this breach of neutrality. Painting a ship [especially with Yankee paint] does not come under the head of necessary repairs, and is no proof that she is unseaworthy; and to allow her to vist other ports after she has set the Queen's proclamation of Neutrality at defiance, would not be regarded as in accordance with the spirit and purpose of that document.

This letter, in its loose statement of facts, and in its lucid exposition of the laws of nations, would have done credit to Mr. Seward himself, the head of the department to which this ambitious little consul belonged. Instead of a week, the *Alabama* had been less than a day on the coast before she ran into Saldanha Bay; and, if she had chosen, she might have cruised on the coast during the rest of the war in entire conformity with the Queen's Proclamation and the laws of nations. But

---

* The consul's name was Walter Graham. ED.

the richest part of the letter is that wherein the consul tells the Governor that inasmuch as the Confederate States had not been acknowledged as a nation, they had no right to commission a ship of war! It is astonishing how dull the Federal officials generally were on this point. The consul knew that Great Britain had acknowledged us to be in possession of belligerent rights, and that the only rights I was pretending to exercise in the *Alabama* were those of a belligerent. But the consul was not to blame. He was only a consul and could not be supposed to know better. Mr. Seward's dispatches on the subject of the *Alabama* had so muddled the brains of his subordinates that they could never make head or tail of the subject.

The following was the reply of the Governor through the Colonial Secretary:

I am directed by the Governor to acknowledge the receipt of your letter of yesterday's date relative to the *Alabama*. His Excellency has no instructions, neither has he any authority to seize or detain that vessel; and he desires me to acquaint you that he has received a letter from the Commander dated the 1st instant, stating that repairs were in progress, and as soon as they were completed he intended to go to sea. He further announces his intention of respecting the neutrality of the British Government. The course which Captain Semmes here proposes to take, is, in the Governor's opinion, in conformity with the instructions he has himself received relative to ships of war and privateers belonging to the United States, and the States calling themselves the Confederate States of America, visiting British ports. The reports received from Saldanha Bay induce the Governor to believe, that the vessel will leave that harbor as soon as her repairs are completed; but he will immediately, on receiving intelligence to the contrary, take the necessary steps for enforcing the observance of the rules laid down by her Majesty's Government.

Another correspondence now sprang up between the consul and the Governor in relation to the capture of the *Sea Bride*. The consul wrote to the Governor, as follows:

The Confederate steamer *Alabama* has just captured an American bark off Green Point, or about four miles from the nearest land—Robben Island. I witnessed the capture with my own eyes, as did hundreds of others at the same time. This occurrence at the entrance of Table Bay, and clearly in British waters, is an insult to England and a grievous injury to a friendly power, the United States."

This remark about the honor of England will remind the reader of the article I quoted some pages back, from the New York *Commercial Advertiser* to the same effect. How wonderfully alive these fellows were to English honor when Yankee ships were in danger! But as the consul admits upon the testimony of his "own eyes" that the capture was made four miles from the nearest land, the reader will perhaps be curious to see how he brings it within British waters. The marine league is the limit of jurisdiction, and the writers on international law say that that limit was probably adopted because a cannon shot could not be thrown farther than three miles from the shore. It may have been the cannon shot which suggested the league, but it was the league, and not the cannon shot, which was the limit. Now the consul argued that the Yankees had invented some big guns, which would throw a shot a long way beyond the league—ergo, the Yankee guns had changed the Laws of Nations.

But the consul wrote his letter in too great a hurry. He had not yet seen the master of the captured ship. This clever Yankee, backed by several of his crew equally clever, made a much better case for him; for they swore in a batch of affidavits before the consul himself, and in spite of the consul's own eyes, that the ship had been captured within *two miles and a half* of Robben Island! Imprudent consul, to have thus gone off half cocked! This discovery of new testimony was communicated to the Governor as follows: "I beg now to enclose for your Excellency's perusal the affidavit of Captain Charles F. White of the *Sea Bride*, protesting against the capture of the said bark in British waters. The bearings taken by him at the time of capture conclusively show that she was in neutral waters, being about two and a half miles from Robben Island. This statement is doubtless more satisfactory than the testimony of persons who measured the distance by the eye." Doubtless, if the bearings had been correct; but unfortunately for Captain White, there were too many other witnesses who were under no temptation to falsify the truth. A fine ship, and a lucrative trading voyage along the eastern coast of Africa were to be the reward of his testimony; the simple telling of the truth the reward of the other witnesses.

The usual consequences followed. The interested witness perjured himself and was disbelieved. I remained entirely neutral in the matter, volunteered no testimony, and only responded to such questions as were asked me—not under oath—by the authorities. The following was the case made in rebuttal of this "Yankee hash":

STATEMENT OF JOSEPH HOPSON

Joseph Hopson, keeper of the Green Point Lighthouse, states:

I was on the lookout on Wednesday afternoon when the *Alabama* and *Sea Bride* were coming in. When I first saw them, the steamer was coming round the northwest of Robben Island, and the bark bore from her about five miles W. N. W. The bark was coming in under all sail with a good breeze, and she took nothing in when the gun was fired. I believe two guns were fired, but the gun I mean was the last, and the steamer then crossed the stern of the bark and hauled up to her on the starboard side. He steamed ahead gently, and shortly afterward I saw the bark put round with her head to the westward, and a boat put off from the steamer and boarded her. Both vessels were then good five miles off the mainland, and quite five, if not six, from the northwest point of Robben Island.

STATEMENT OF W. S. FIELD, COLLECTOR OF THE CUSTOMS

I was present at the old lighthouse on Green Point on Wednesday afternoon at two P. M., and saw the *Alabama* capture the American bark *Sea Bride*, and I agree with the above statement as far as the position of the vessels and their distance from shore are concerned. I may also remark that I called the attention of Colonel Bisset and the lighthouse keeper, Hopson, to the distance of the vessels at the time of the capture, as it was probable we should be called upon to give our evidence respecting the affair, and we took a note of the time it occurred.

STATEMENT OF JOHN ROE

I was, yesterday, the 5th day of August, 1863, returning from a whale chase in Hunt's Bay, when I first saw the bark

Sea Bride standing from the westward, on to the land. I came on to Table Bay and when off Camp's Bay, I saw the smoke of the *Alabama* some distance from the westward of Robben Island. When I reached the Green Point lighthouse, the steamer was standing up toward the bark, which was about five miles and a half to the westward of Green Point, and about four and a half from the western point of Robben Island. This was their position—being near each other—when the gun was fired.

STATEMENT OF THE SIGNAL MAN AT THE LION'S RUMP
TELEGRAPH STATION

On Wednesday last, the 5th day of August, 1863, I sighted the bark *Sea Bride* about seven o'clock in the morning, about fifteen or twenty miles off the land, standing into Table Bay from the southwest. There was a light breeze blowing from the northwest, which continued until midday. About midday I sighted the *Alabama*, screw-steamer, standing from due north toward Table Bay, intending, as it appeared to me, to take the passage between Robben Island and the Blueberg Beach. She was then between fifteen and eighteen miles off the land. After sighting the steamer, I hoisted the demand for the bark, when she hoisted the American flag, which I reported to the port office, the bark being then about eight miles off the land from Irville Point. No sooner had the bark hoisted the American flag than the steamer turned sharp round in the direction of, and toward the bark. The steamer appeared at that time to be about twelve miles off the land from Irville Point, and about four or five miles outside of Robben Island, and about seven miles from the bark. The steamer then came up to and alongside of the bark when the latter was good four miles off the land, at or near the old lighthouse, and five miles off the island. The steamer, after firing a gun, stopped the farther progress of the bark, several boats were sent to her, and after that the bark stood out to sea again, and the *Alabama* steamed into Table Bay.

At the time of the capture, her Majesty's steamship *Valorous* was lying in Table Bay, and the Governor, in addition to the above testimony, charged Captain Forsyth, her commander, also to investigate the subject and report to him. The following is Captain Forsyth's report:

HER MAJESTY'S SHIP VALOROUS, August 6, 1863

In compliance with the request conveyed to me by your Excellency, I have the honor to report that I have obtained from Captain Semmes a statement of the position of the Confederate States steamer *Alabama* and the American bark *Sea Bride* when the latter was captured yesterday afternoon. Captain Semmes asserts that at the time of his capturing the *Sea Bride*, Green Point lighthouse bore from *Alabama*, southeast about six or six and a half miles. [The Yankee master said that it bore south by east.] This statement is borne out by the evidence of Captain Wilson, Port Captain of Table Bay, who has assured me that at the time of the *Sea Bride* being captured, he was off Green Point in the port boat, and that only the top of the *Alabama*'s hull was visible. I am of opinion if Captain Wilson could only see that portion of the hull of the *Alabama*, she must have been about the distance from shore which is stated by Captain Semmes, and I have, therefore, come to the conclusion that the bark *Sea Bride* was beyond the limits assigned when she was captured by the *Alabama*.

The Governor, after having thus patiently investigated the case, directed his Secretary to inform the consul of the result in the following letter:

With reference to the correspondence that has passed relative to the capture by the Confederate States steamer *Alabama* of the bark *Sea Bride*, I am directed by the Governor to acquaint you that on the best information he has been enabled to procure, he has come to the conclusion that the capture cannot be held to be illegal or in violation of the neutrality of the British Government by reason of the distance from the land at which it took place."

The consul was foiled; but he was a man of courage, and resolved to strike another blow for the *Sea Bride*. He next charged that the prize-master had brought her within the marine league *after her capture*. He made this charge upon the strength of another affidavit—that ready resource of the enemy when in difficulty. Enclosing this affidavit to the Governor, he wrote as follows:

From the affidavit of the first officer, it appears that the alleged prize was brought within one mile and a half of Green

Point lighthouse yesterday at one o'clock A. M. Now, as the vessel was at the time in charge of a prize-crew, it was a violation of neutrality, as much as if the capture had been made at the same distance from the land.

And he required that the ship should be seized.

Without stopping to inquire into the truth of the fact stated, the Governor directed his Secretary to reply, that—

His Excellency is not prepared to admit that the fact of a vessel having been brought by the prize-crew within one and a half mile of the Green Point lighthouse "was a violation of the neutrality, as much as if the capture had taken place at the same distance from the land," although both the belligerents are prohibited from bringing their prizes into British ports. The Governor does not feel warranted in taking steps for the removal of the prize-crew from the *Sea Bride*.

Chapter Eighteen—*1863*

A Gale at Cape Town . . . The Alabama gets under way for Simon's Town . . . Capture of the Martha Wenzell . . . The Tuscaloosa; her status as ship of war considered . . . The Tuscaloosa proceeds to sea . . . The Alabama follows her . . . They, with the Sea Bride, rendezvous at Angra Pequena

H aving brushed away Mr. Seward's gadfly as described in the last chapter, we may turn our attention again to the *Alabama*. On the 7th of August, we took one of the gales so common at the Cape in the winter season. Dense banks of black clouds hove up in the northwest, soon overspreading the whole heavens, and the wind came out whistling from that quarter. The reader must bear in mind that when he crossed into the southern hemisphere he reversed the points of the compass so far as wind and weather are concerned, and that the northwester at the Cape of Good Hope answers to our southeaster on the American coast—bringing with it thick, rainy weather. There was a number of ships in the harbor, and the gale drove in upon them without the least protection. These ships, forewarned by the usual signs, had all struck their upper masts, sent down their yards, and let go second anchors, and veered to long scopes. We did the same in the *Alabama*.

It was a sublime spectacle to look abroad upon the bay in the height of the gale. The elements seemed to be literally at war, a low scud rushing to the shore and climbing as if pursued by demons up and over the Lion's Rump and Table Mountain. Huge waves were rolling in upon the struggling shipping, trying its ground tackle to its utmost tension; the jetties and landings were covered with spray; and Cape Town, though only a mile off, looked like a specter town as viewed through the spray and driving scud. And what added much to the interest of the scene was the daring and skill of the watermen. These men, in substantial launches under close-reefed sails, and with spare anchors and cables on board for the use of any ships that might be in distress for want of sufficient ground tackle, were darting hither and thither like so many spirits of the storm. They seemed to be sporting with the dashing and blinding waves and the fury of the gale in very wantonness as though they would defy the elements. The ships at anchor were all fortunate enough to hold on; but a luckless Bremen brig outside, which had ventured too near the land, was wrecked during the night on Green Point. Fortunately no lives were lost.

The gale lasted about twenty-four hours; and when it had sufficiently abated, we communicated with the shore and got off such supplies as we needed; it being my intention to run round to Simon's Town on the opposite side of the Cape, where there is shelter from these gales, for the purpose of completing my repairs. On the 9th, the weather had again become fine. The wind had gone round to southeast, the fair weather quarter, and the Devil had spread his table cloth on Table Mountain. Every one has heard of this famous table cloth at the Cape of Good Hope. It is a fleecy, white cloud which hangs perpetually over Table Mountain during fine weather. The southeast winds, as they climb the steep ascent, bring with them more or less moisture. This moisture is sufficiently cooled as it passes over the "table"—a level space on the top of the mountain—to become condensed into a white vapor, very similar to that which escapes from a steam pipe. When the wind shifts, and the storm begins to gather, the table cloth disappears.

At nine o'clock on this morning we got under way and

steamed out of the harbor on our way to Simon's Town. The
day was charmingly fine. The atmosphere was soft and transparent, and the sun bright, bringing out all the beauties of the
bold promontories and the deep-water bays that indent the
coast. We were now really doubling the Cape of Good Hope.
As we approached the famous headland with its lighthouse
perched several hundred feet above the bold and blackened
rocks, our imaginations busy with the past, endeavoring to de-
pict the frail Portuguese bark which had first dared its stormy
waters, the cry of "Sail ho!" resounded most musically from
the mast-head. Imagination took flight at once at the sound
of this practical cry. It recalled us from our dream of John
of Portugal to one Abraham Lincoln and his surroundings.
Here was not the poetical bark of four centuries ago that had
at last found its way to those Indies which Columbus so
long sought for in vain, but a Yankee ship laden with rice;
for an hour's steaming brought us alongside of the *Martha
Wenzell* of Boston from Akyab for Falmouth, England.
The *Wenzell* had better luck than the *Sea Bride*, for she had
clearly entered the mouth of False Bay, and though seven or
eight miles yet from the land, was within a line drawn from
point to point of the Bay. Being thus within British jurisdiction, I astonished the master by releasing instead of burning his ship. He looked so dumfounded when I announced
to him this decision that if I had been a Yankee, he would no
doubt have suspected me of some Yankee trick. He gathered
his slow ideas together by degrees, however, and was profuse
in his thanks. I told him he had none to give me, for I was
only too sorry not to be able to burn him.

We now hauled in for the coast, and taking a pilot as we
approached the harbor, anchored at two P. M. in Simon's Bay.
This is the naval station of the colony, and we found here the
frigate *Narcissus* wearing the flag of Rear Admiral Sir Baldwin Walker, the commander-in-chief of the British naval
forces at the Cape. We were visited immediately upon anchoring by a lieutenant from the flagship. The *Tuscaloosa* had
preceded me a few days, and we found her still here, not having quite completed her preparations for sea. The gadfly, I
found, had been buzzing around her too, but her difficulties
were all ended. As the correspondence is short, I will give it
to the reader. The Federal consul wrote to the Governor, as
follows:

An armed vessel named the *Tuscaloosa*, claiming to act under the authority of the so-called Confederate States, entered Simon's Bay, on Saturday, the 8th instant. That vessel was formerly owned by citizens of the United States, and while engaged in lawful commerce [as if lawful commerce was not a subject of capture, during war] was captured as a prize by the *Alabama*. She was subsequently fitted out with arms by the *Alabama* to prey upon the commerce of the United States, and now, without having been condemned as a prize by any Admiralty Court of any recognized government, she is permitted to enter a neutral port in violation of the Queen's Proclamation with her original cargo on board. Against this proceeding, I, hereby, most emphatically protest, and I claim that the vessel ought to be given up to her lawful owners.

It is quite true that the *Tuscaloosa* had not been condemned by a prize court of the Confederacy, but it was equally true that the Sovereign Power of the Confederacy, acting through its authorized agent, had commissioned her as a ship of war, which was the most solemn condemnation of the prize that the Sovereign could give. It was equally true that no nation has the right to inquire into the *antecedents* of the ships war of another nation. But these were points beyond the comprehension of the gadfly. The following was the answer of the Governor. The Colonial Secretary writes:

I am directed by the Governor to acknowledge the receipt of your letter of this date and to acquaint you that it was not until late last evening that his Excellency received from the Naval Commander-in-Chief information that the condition of the *Tuscaloosa* was such as, as his Excellency is advised, to entitle her to be regarded as a vessel of war. The Governor is not aware, nor do you refer him to the provisions of the International Law by which captured vessels, as soon as they enter our neutral ports revert to their original owners and are forfeited by their captors. But his Excellency believes that the claims of contending parties to vessels captured can only be determined, in the first instance, by the courts of the captor's country.

We remained five days at Simon's Town. We did not need coal, but we had some caulking of the bends and replacing of copper about the waterline to do, and some slight repairs to put upon our engine. Whilst these preparations for sea were going on, we had some very pleasant intercourse with the officers of the station and the citizens on shore. Besides the *Narcissus*, flagship, there were one or two other British ships of war at anchor. There were some officers stationed at the navy yard, and there was a Chinese gunboat, the *Kwan-Tung*, with an English commander and crew, which had put into the harbor on her way to the East. Simon's Town was thus quite gay. The Governor, Sir Philip Wodehouse, also came over from Cape Town during our stay. Lunches on board the different ships, excursions on board the *Kwan-Tung*, and dinner parties were the order of the day. As I have before remarked, the English naval officers discarded all the ridiculous nonsense about our not being "recognized" and extended to us official as well as private civilities.

The Admiral was kind enough to give me a dinner party, at which the Governor and his lady, and the principal officers of his squadron were present. I found the ladies of the Admiral's family exceedingly agreeable. They were living in a picturesque cottage near the sea shore, and solaced themselves for their temporary banishment from dear old England by making their home as English as possible. They had surrounded themselves by fine lawns and shrubbery and flowers, and Mrs. Walker and one of the bewitching young ladies were kind enough to show me over their extensive and well-cultivated garden in which they took much interest. Horseback riding, picnics to the country, and balls on board the ships were the principal amusements of the young people. Whilst my officers and myself were thus relaxing ourselves, my sailors were also making the most of their time. Kell had told them off by quarter watches and sent them on liberty. Each batch was mustered and inspected as it was sent on shore, and pretty soon we had the old Jamaica scenes over again. Most of them went over to Cape Town in the stage-coach that was running between the two places and put that lively commercial town "in stays." The sailor quarter was a continuous scene of revelry for several days. The townspeople humored and spoiled them. They all overstayed their time, and we only got them back by twos and threes. It was of no use to muster and inspect them now. The tidy new suits in which they had gone on shore were torn and draggled, and old-drunks were upon nearly all of them.

The *Tuscaloosa* went to sea at daylight on the 14th, and we followed her in the *Alabama* the next day. The former was to proceed to Saldanha Bay and thence take the *Sea Bride* with her to one of the uninhabited harbors some distance to the northward, and the *Alabama* was to follow her thither after a cruise of a few days off the Cape. The object of these movements will be explained in due time. I now threw myself into that perpetual stream of commerce that comes setting around the Cape of Good Hope from the East Indies. From daylight until dark, ships are constantly in sight from the lighthouse on the Cape. The [sea] road is about twenty miles wide—no more. We kept our station in this road, day in and day out for ten days, during which we chased and overhauled a great number of ships, but there was not a Yankee among them! It was winter time, we were off the stormy Cape, and we had the weather suited to the season and the locality. Storms and fogs and calms followed in succession—the storm being the normal meteorological condition. As we would be lying to in this track under reefed sails in a dark and stormy night, our very hair would sometimes be made to stand on end by the apparition of a huge ship rushing past us at lightning speed before the howling gale at no more than a few ships' lengths from us. A collision would have crushed us as if we had been an egg shell.

At length, when I supposed the *Tuscaloosa* and the *Sea Bride* had reached their destination, I filled away and followed them. As we were making this passage it was reported to me that our fresh-water condenser had given out. Here was a predicament! The water was condensed once a week, and we had no more than about one week's supply on hand. The joints of the piping had worked loose, and the machine had become nearly useless. It was now still more necessary to make a harbor where we might get access to water and see what could be done in the way of repairs. We worked our way along the African coast somewhat tediously, frequently encountering head winds and adverse currents. On the morning of the 28th of August, we sighted the land after having been delayed by a dense fog for twenty-four hours, and in the course of the afternoon we ran into the Bay of Angra Pequeña and anchored. This was our point of rendezvous. I found the *Tuscaloosa* and the *Sea Bride* both at anchor. I had at last found a port into which I could take a prize! I was now, in short, among the Hottentots; no civilized nation claiming jurisdiction over the waters in which I was anchored.

When at Cape Town, an English merchant had visited me and made overtures for the purchase of the *Sea Bride* and her cargo. He was willing to run the risk of non-condemnation by a prize-court, and I could put him in possession of the prize, he said, at some inlet on the coast of Africa without the jurisdiction of any civilized power. I made the sale to him. He was to repair to the given rendezvous in his own vessel, and I found him here, according to his agreement, with the stipulated price—about one third the value of the ship and cargo—in good English sovereigns, which, upon being counted, were turned over to the paymaster for the military chest. The purchaser was then put in possesion of the prize. I had made an arrangement with other parties for the sale of the wool still remaining on board the *Tuscaloosa*. This wool was. to be landed at Angra Pequeña, also, the purchaser agreeing to ship it to Europe and credit the Confederate States with two thirds of the proceeds. The reader will see how easy it would have been for me to make available many of my prizes in this way, but the great objection to the scheme was the loss of time which it involved, and the risks I ran of not getting back my prize-crews. If I had undertaken, whenever I captured a prize, to follow her to some out-of-the-way port and spend some days there in negotiating for her sale and getting back my prize-crew, I should not have accomplished half the work I did. The great object now was to destroy as speedily as possible the enemy's commerce, and to this I devoted all my energies. I did not, therefore, repeat the experiment of the *Sea Bride*.

I could not have chosen a better spot for my present purpose. At Angra Pequeña I was entirely out of the world. It was not visited at all, except by some straggling coaster in quest of shelter in bad weather. There was, indeed, no other inducement to visit it. It was in a desert part of Africa. The region was rainless, and there was not so much as a shrub or even a blade of grass to be seen. The harbor was rock-bound, and for miles inland the country was a waste of burning sand. The harbor did not even afford fresh water, and we were obliged to supply ourselves from the vessel of my English

friend until our condenser could be repaired. The whole
country was a waste in which there was no life visible away
from the coast. On the coast itself, there were the usual sea
birds—the gannet and the sea gull—and fish in abundance.
We hauled the seine and caught a fine mess for the crews of
all the ships. Three or four naked, emaciated Hottentots, having seen the ships from a distance, had made their way to the
harbor and came begging us for food. They remained during
our stay and had their emptiness filled. Some thirty or forty
miles from the coast, they said, vegetation began to appear,
and there were villages and cattle.

I ordered Lieutenant Low, the commander of the *Tuscaloosa*, as soon as he should land his cargo, to ballast his ship
with the rock which abounded on every hand and proceed on
a cruise to the coast of Brazil. Sufficient time had now elapsed,
I thought, for the ships of war of the enemy, which had been
sent to that coast in pursuit of me to be coming in the direction of the Cape of Good Hope. Lieutenant Low would,
therefore, in all probability have a clear field before him.
Having nothing further to detain me in the *Alabama*, I got
under way, on my return to Simon's Town, intending to fill
up with coal and proceed thence to the East Indies in compliance with the suggestion of Mr. Secretary Mallory. The *Tuscaloosa*, after cruising the requisite time on the coast of Brazil,
was to return to the Cape to meet me on my own return from
the East Indies.

When I reached the highway off the Cape again, I held myself there for several days, cruising off and on, and sighting
the land occasionally to see if perchance I could pick up an
American ship. But we had no better success than before.
The wary masters of these ships, if there were any passing,
gave the Cape a wide berth and sought their way home by
the most unfrequented paths, illustrating the old adage that
"the farthest way round is the shortest way home." Impa-
tient of further delay without results, on Wednesday, the 16th
of September, I got up steam and ran into Simon's Bay. I
learned upon anchoring that the United States steamer *Vanderbilt*, late the flagship of Admiral Wilkes and now under
the command of Captain Baldwin, had left the anchorage
only the Friday before and gone herself to cruise off the Cape
in the hope of falling in with the *Alabama*. She had taken her
station, as it would appear, a little to the eastward of me off

Cape Agulhas and Point Danger. On the day the *Vanderbilt* went to sea, viz., Friday, the 11th of September, it happened that the *Alabama* was a little further off the land than usual, which accounts for the two ships missing each other. The following is the record on my journal, for that day: "Weather very fine, wind light from the southwest. At half-past six, showed the English colors to an English bark after a short chase." On the following Sunday, we were in plain sight of Table Mountain. The two ships were thus cruising almost in sight of each other's smoke.

The *Vanderbilt* visited both Cape Town and Simon's Town, and lay several days at each. I did not object that she had been painting ship and should have been sent to sea earlier. The more time Baldwin spent in port the better I liked it. Indeed, it always puzzled me that the gadflies should insist upon my being sent to sea so promptly when nearly every day that the *Alabama* was at sea cost them a ship.

I had scarcely come to anchor before Captain Bickford, of the *Narcissus* came on board of me on the part of the Admiral to have an "explanation." The gadfly had continued its buzzing, I found, during my late absence from the Cape. A short distance to the northward of the Cape of Good Hope in the direction of Angra Pequeña, there is an island called Ichaboe, a dependency of the Cape Colony. It had been represented to the Admiral by the consul that the transactions which had been related as taking place at Angra Pequeña, had taken place at this island in violation of British neutrality. In what the evidence consisted I did not learn, but the consul in his distress and extremity had probably had recourse to some more Yankee affidavits. It was this charge which Captain Bickford had come on board to ask an explanation of. The following letter from Sir Baldwin Walker to the Secretary of the Admiralty in London will show how easily I brushed off the gadfly for the second time:

With reference to my letters, dated respectively the 19th and 31st ult., relative to the Confederate States ship-of-war *Alabama* and the prizes captured by her, I beg to enclose for their lordships' information, the copy of a statement forwarded to me by the Collector of Customs at Cape Town, wherein it is represented, that the *Tuscaloosa* and *Sea Bride* had visited Ichaboe, which is a dependency of this colony. Since the receipt of the above-mentioned document, the *Alabama* arrived at this anchorage, (the 16th instant,) and when Captain Semmes waited on me, I acquainted him with the report, requesting he would inform me if it was true. I was glad to learn from him that it was not so. He frankly explained that the prize *Sea Bride*, in the first place, had put into Saldanha Bay through stress of weather, and on being joined there by the *Tuscaloosa*, both vessels proceeded to Angra Pequeña on the west coast of Africa, where he subsequently joined them in the *Alabama*, and there sold the *Sea Bride* and her cargo to an English subject who resides at Cape Town. The *Tuscaloosa* had landed some wool at Angra Pequeña and received ballast, but he states, is still in commission as a tender. It will, therefore, be seen, how erroneous is the accompanying report. I have no reason to doubt Captain Semmes' explanation; and he seems to be fully alive to the instructions of her Majesty's Government, and appears to be most anxious not to commit any breach of neutrality. The *Alabama* has returned to this port for coal, some provisions, and to repair her condensing apparatus. From conversation with Captain Semmes, I find he has been off this Cape for the last five days, and as the *Vanderbilt* left this on the night of the 11th inst., it is surprising they did not meet each other.

The *Vanderbilt*, I found, had exhausted the supply of coal at Simon's Town, having taken in as much as eight or nine hundred tons. Commodore Vanderbilt, as he is called, had certainly presented a mammoth coal consumer to the Federal Government, if nothing else. I was obliged, in consequence, to order coal for the *Alabama* around from Cape Town. And as the operation of coaling and making the necessary repairs would detain me several days, and as I was, besides, bound on a long voyage, I yielded to the petitions of my crew and permitted them to go on liberty again. The officers of the station were as courteous to us as before, and I renewed my very pleasant intercourse with the Admiral's family. The owner of the famous Constantia vineyard, lying between Simon's Town and Cape Town, sent me a pressing invitation to come and spend a few days with him, but I was too busy to accept his hospitality. He afterward sent me a cask of his world-renowned wine. This cask of wine, after making the voyage to India, was offered as a libation to the god of war. It went down in the *Alabama* off Cherbourg. We had another very pleasant dinner at the Admiral's—the guests being composed this time exclusively of naval officers. After our return to the drawing room, the ladies made their appearance and gave us some delightful music. These were some of the oases in the desert of my life upon the ocean.

In the course of five or six days, by the exercise of great diligence we were again ready for sea. But unfortunately all my crew were not yet on board. My rascals had behaved worse than usual on this last visit to Cape Town. Some of them had been jugged by the authorities for offences against the peace, and others had yielded to the seductions of the ever vigilant Federal consul and been quartered upon his bounty. The consul had made a haul. They would be capital fellows for "affidavits" against the *Alabama*. I need not say that they were of the cosmopolitan sailor class, none of them being citizens of the Southern States. I offered large rewards for the apprehension and delivery to me of these fellows; but the police were afraid to act—probably forbidden by their superiors in deference to their supposed duty under the neutrality laws. That was a very one-sided neutrality, however, which permitted the Federal consul to convert his quarters into a hostile camp for the seduction of my sailors and denied me access to the police for redress. My agent at Cape Town, having made every exertion in his power to secure the return of as many of my men as possible, finally telegraphed me on the evening of the 24th of September that it was useless to wait any longer. As many as fourteen had deserted; enough to cripple my crew, and that, too, with an enemy's ship of superior force on the coast.

What was to be done? Luckily there was a remedy at hand. A sailor-landlord, one of those Shylocks who coin Jack's flesh and blood into gold, hearing of the distress of the *Alabama*, came off to tell me that all his boarders, eleven in number, had volunteered to supply the place of my deserters. This seemed like a fair exchange. It was but swapping horses, as the "sainted Abraham" would have said if he had been in my place—only I was giving a little "boot"—fourteen well-fed, well-clothed fellows, for eleven ragged, whiskey-filled vagabonds. It was a swap in another sense, too, as, ten to one all these eleven fellows were deserters from other ships that had touched at this relay house of the sea. There was only one little difficulty in the way of my shipping these men. There was my good friend, her Majesty the Queen—I must not be ungallant to her and violate her neutrality laws. What monstrous sophists we are when interest prompts us? I reasoned out this case to my entire satisfaction. I said to myself, my sailors have gone on shore in her Majesty's dominions and refuse to come back to me. When I apply to her Majesty's police, they tell me that so sacred is the soil of England no man must be coerced to do what he doesn't want to do. Good! I reply that a ship of war is a part of the territory to which she belongs, and that if some of the subjects of the Queen should think proper to come into my territory and refuse to go back, I may surely apply the same principle and refuse to compel them.

When I had come to this conclusion, I turned to the landlord, and said: "And so you have some *gentlemen* boarding at your house who desire to take passage with me?" The landlord smiled and nodded assent. I continued: "You know I cannot ship any seamen in her Majesty's ports, but I see no reason why I should not take passengers to sea with me if they desire to go."

"Certainly, your honor—they can work their passage, you know."

"I'll suppose you'll charge something for bringing these gentlemen on board?"

"Some'at, your honor."

Here the landlord pulled out a greasy memorandum and began to read: "Bill Bunting, board and lodging, ten shillings—drinks, one pound ten. Tom Bowline, board and lodging, six shillings—Tom only *landed* yesterday from a Dutch ship—drinks, twelve shillings."

"Hold!" said I; "never mind the board and lodging and drinks—go to the paymaster,"—and turning to Kell, I told him to give the paymaster the necessary instructions—"and he will pay you your fares for bringing the passengers on board." The "passengers" were already alongside, and being sent down to the surgeon, were examined and passed as sound and able-bodied men.

It was now nine o'clock at night. It had been blowing a gale of wind all day from the southeast; but it was a fair-weather gale, if I may use the solecism; the sky being clear and the barometer high. These are notable peculiarities of the southeast gales at the Cape of Good Hope. The sky is always clear, and the gale begins and ends with a high barometer. I was very anxious to get to sea. A report had come in only a day or two before that the *Vanderbilt* was still cruising off Cape Agulhas, and I was apprehensive that she might get news of me and blockade me. This might detain me several days, or until I could get a dark night—and the moon was now near her full—in which to run the blockade. I need not remark that the *Vanderbilt* had greatly the speed of me and threw twice my weight of metal. The wind having partially lulled, we got up steam, and at about half-past eleven we moved out from our anchors. The lull had only been temporary, for we had scarcely cleared the little islands that give a partial protection to the harbor from these southeast winds, when the gale came whistling and howling as before. The wind and sea were both nearly ahead, and the *Alabama* was now put upon her metal, under steam, as she had been so often before under sail. False Bay is an immense sheet of water of a horseshoe shape, and we had to steam some twenty miles before we could weather the Cape of Good Hope under our lee. We drove her against this heavy gale at the rate of five knots.

This struggle of the little ship with the elements was a thing to be remembered. The moon was near her full, shedding a flood of light upon the scene. The Bay was whitened with foam as the waters were lashed into fury by the storm. Around the curve of the horseshoe arose broken, bald, rocky mountains, on the crests of which were piled fleecy white clouds blinking in the moonlight like banks of snow. These clouds were perfectly motionless. It appeared as if the Devil had spread a great many tablecloths around False Bay that night; or, rather, a more appropriate figure would be that he had touched the mountains with the stillness of death and wreathed them with winding sheets. The scene was wild and weird beyond description. It was a picture for the eye of a poet or painter to dwell upon. Nor was the imagination less touched when from time to time the revolving light upon the grim old Cape—that Cape which had so long divided the Eastern from the Western world—threw its full blaze upon the deck of the struggling ship. Overhead the sky was perfectly clear, there being not so much as a speck of a cloud to be seen—and this in the midst of a howling gale of wind! At three A. M. we cleared the Cape, and keeping the ship off a few points, gave her the trysails with the bonnets off. She bounded over the seas like a staghound unleashed. I had been up all night and now went below to snatch some brief repose before the toils of another day should begin.

Chapter Nineteen—*1863*

The Alabama on the Indian Ocean . . . The passengers
questioned and contracted with . . . The Agulhas
Current . . . The "Brave West Winds" . . . A theory
. . . The islands of St. Peter and St. Paul . . . The
Tropic of Capricorn . . . The Southeast Trades and
the monsoons . . . The Alabama arrives off the Strait
of Sunda and burns one of the ships of the enemy . . .
Runs in and anchors under the island of Sumatra

W hen Bartelli awakened me at the usual hour of seven bells
—half-past seven A. M.—on the morning after the events
described in the last chapter, the *Alabama* was well launched
upon the Indian Ocean. She had run the Cape of Good Hope
out of sight and was still hieing off before the gale, though
this had moderated considerably as she had run off the coast.
We were now about to make a long voyage, tedious to the
unphilosophical mariner, but full of interest to one who has
an eye open to the wonders and beauties of nature. My first
duty upon going on deck was to put the ship under sail and
let the steam go down; and my second to have an interview
with the "passengers" who had come on board overnight.
We were now on the high seas and might with all due re-

spect to Queen Victoria put them under contract. If the reader recollects Falstaff's description of his ragged battalion, he will have a pretty good idea of the *personnel* I had before me. These subjects of the Queen stood in all they possessed. None of them had brought any baggage on board with them. Ragged blue and red flannel shirts, tarred trousers, and a mixture of felt hats and Scotch caps composed their wardrobe. Their persons had passed muster of the surgeon, it is true, but it was plain that it would require a deal of washing and scrubbing and wholesome feeding, and a long abstinence from drinks, to render them fit for use. Upon questioning them, I found that each had his cock-and-a-bull story to tell, of how he was left by this ship or by that without any fault of his own, and how he had been tricked by his landlord. I turned them over to the first lieutenant and paymaster and they were soon incorporated with the crew. I hold that her Majesty owes me some "boot," for the swap I made with her on that remarkable moonlight night when I left the Cape. At all events, I never heard that she complained of it.

I was grieved to find that our most serious loss among the deserters was our Irish fiddler. This fellow had been remarkably diligent in his vocation and had fiddled the crew over half the world. It was a pity to lose him now that we were going over the other. half. When the evenings' amusements began, Michael Mahoney's vacant camp stool cast a gloom over the ship. There was no one who could make his violin talk like himself, and it was a long time before his place was supplied. Poor Michael! we felt convinced he had not been untrue to us—it was only a "dhrop" too much of the "crayture" he had taken.

For the first few days after leaving the Cape, we ran off due south, it being my intention to seek the fortieth parallel of south latitude and run my easting down on that parallel. As icebergs have been known to make their appearance near the Cape in the spring of the year, I ordered the temperature of the air and water to be taken every hour during the night to aid me in detecting their presence. We did not discover any icebergs, but the thermometer helped to reveal to me some of the secrets of the deep in this part of the ocean. Much to my surprise, I found myself in a sort of Gulf Stream; the temperature of the water being from three to five degrees higher than that of the air. My celestial observations for fixing the position of the ship informed me at the same time that I was experiencing a southeasterly current; the current bending more and more toward the east as I proceeded south, until in the parrallel of 40° it ran due east. The rate of this current was from thirty to fifty miles per day. This was undoubtedly a branch of the great Agulhas Current.

If the reader will inspect a map he will find that the North Indian Ocean is bounded wholly by tropical countries—Hindostan, Beloochistan, and Arabia to the Red Sea, and across that sea by Azan and Zanguebar. The waters in this great bight of the ocean are intensely heated by the fervor of an Indian and African sun and flow off in quest of cooler regions through the Mozambique Channel. Passing thence over the Agulhas Bank, which lies a short distance to the eastward of the Cape of Good Hope, they reach that Cape, as the Agulhas Current. Here it divides into two main prongs or branches; one prong pursuing a westerly course and joining in with the great equatorial current, which we encountered off Fernando de Noronha, and the other bending sharply to the southeast and forming the Gulf Stream of the South Indian Ocean in which the *Alabama* is at present. What it is that gives this latter prong its sudden deflection to the southward is not well understood. Probably it is influenced to some extent by the southerly current, running at the rate of about a knot along the west coast of Africa and debouching at the Cape of Good Hope. Here it strikes the Agulhas current at right angles, and hence possibly the deflection of a part of that current.

But if there be a current constantly setting from the Cape of Good Hope to the southeast, how is it that the iceberg finds its way to the neighborhood of the Cape from the south polar regions? There is but one way to account for it. There must be a counter undercurrent. These bergs, setting deep in the water, are forced by this counter-current against the surface current. This phenomenon has frequently been witnessed in the Arctic seas. Captain Duncan, of the English whaler *Dundee*, in describing one of his voyages to Davis' Strait, thus speaks of a similar drift of icebergs: "It was awful to behold the immense icebergs working their way to the northeast from us, and not one drop of water to be seen; they were working themselves right through the middle of the ice." Here was an under current of such force as to carry a mountain of ice ripping and crashing through a field of solid ice. Lieutenant De Haven, who made a voyage in search of Sir John Franklin, describes a similar phenomenon as follows: "The iceberg . . . came up very near to the stern of our ship; the intermediate space between the berg and the vessel was filled with heavy masses of ice, which, though they had been previously broken by the immense weight of the berg, were again formed into a compact body by its pressure. The berg was drifting at the rate of about four knots, and by its force on the mass of ice was pushing the ship before it, as it appeared, to inevitable destruction." And again, on the next day, he writes: "The iceberg still in sight but drifting away fast to the northeast." Here was another undercurrent driving a monster iceberg through a field of broken ice at the rate of four knots!

When we had traveled in the *Alabama* some distance to the eastward on the 39th and 40th parallels, the current made another curve—this time to the northeast. If the reader will again refer to a map, he will find that the Agulhas Current, as it came along through the Mozambique Channel and by the Cape of Good Hope, was a southwesterly current. It being now a northeasterly current, he observes that it is running back whence it came in an ellipse! We have seen that the Gulf Stream of the North Atlantic performs a circuit around the coasts of the United States, Newfoundland, the British Islands, the coasts of Spain and Portugal, the African coast, and so on, into the equatorial current and thence back again to the Gulf of Mexico. From my observation of currents in various parts of the world my impression is that the circle or ellipse is their normal law. There are, of course, offshoots from one circle or ellipse to another, and thus a general intermingling of the waters of the earth is going on— but the normal rule for the guidance of the water, as of the wind, is the curve.

As we approached the 40th parallel to latitude my attention was again forcibly drawn to the phenomena of the winds. The Brave West Winds—as the sailors call them—those remarkable polar tradewinds, now began to prevail with wonderful regularity. On the 30th of September, we observed in latitude 39° 12′ and longitude 31° 59′. The following is the entry on my journal for that day: "Rough weather with the wind fresh

from the N. N. W. with passing rain squalls. Sea turbulent.
Barometer 29.47; thermometer, air 55°; water 58°; distance
run in the last twenty-four hours, 221 miles. Weather looking
better at noon. The water has resumed its usual deepsea hue.
[We had been running over an extensive tract of soundings,
the water being of that pea-green tint indicating a depth
of from sixty to seventy-five fathoms.] In high southern
latitudes in the Indian Ocean, the storm fiend seems to hold
high carnival all the year round. He is constantly racing round
the globe from west to east, howling over the waste of waters
in his mad career. Like Sisyphus, his labors are never ended.
He not only does not rest himself, but he allows old Ocean
none, constantly lashing him into rage. He scatters the icebergs hither and thither to the great terror of the mariner,
and converts the moisture of the clouds into the blinding
snowflake or the pelting hail. As we are driven on dark nights
before these furious winds, we have only to imitate the
Cape Horn navigator—'tie all fast, and let her rip,' iceberg
or no iceberg. When a ship is running at a speed of twelve
or fourteen knots in such thick weather that the lookout at
the cat-head can scarcely see his own nose, neither sharp
eyes nor water thermometers are of much use."

These winds continued to blow from day to day, hurrying
us forward with great speed. There being a clear sweep of
the sea for several thousand miles, unobstructed by continent
or island, the waves rose into long, sweeping swells, much
more huge and majestic than one meets with in any other
ocean. As our little craft, scudding before a gale, would be
overtaken by one of these monster billows, she would be
caught up by its crest like a cock boat and darted half way
down the declivity that lay before her at a speed that would
cause the sailor to hold his breath. Any swerve to the right
or the left that would cause the ship to broach to, or come
broadside to the wind and sea, would have been fatal. These
brave west winds, though thus fraught with danger, are a
great boon to commerce. The reader has seen how the currents in this part of the ocean travel in an ellipse. We have
here an ellipse of the winds. The *Alabama* is hurrying to the
Far East before a continuous, or almost continuous northwest
gale. If she were a few hundred miles to the northward of
her present position, she might be hurrying, though not quite
with equal speed, before the southeast trades to the Far

West. We have thus two parallel winds blowing all the year round in opposite directions, and only a few hundred miles apart.

Storms are now admitted by all seamen to be gyratory, as we have seen. When I was cruising in the Gulf Stream, I ventured to enlarge this theory and suggested that rotation was the normal condition of all extra-tropical winds on the ocean where there was nothing to obstruct them—of the moderate wind, as well as of the gale. I had a striking confirmation of this theory in the brave west winds. These winds went regularly around the compass in uniform periods; the periods occupying about three days. We would take them at about N. N. W., and in the course of the period they would go entirely around the compass and come back to the same point; there being an interval of calm of a few hours. The following diagram will illustrate this rotary motion.

Let Figure 1 represent a circular wind—the wind gyrating

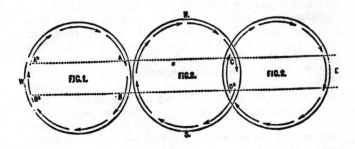

in the direction of the arrows and the circle traveling at the same time along the dotted lines from west to east. If the northern segment of this circular wind passes over the ship, the upper dotted line from A to A² will represent her position during its passage. At A, where the ship first takes the wind, she will have it from about northwest; and at A², where she is about to lose it, she will have it from about southwest. The ship is supposed to remain stationary whilst the circle is passing over her. Now this is precisely the manner in which we found all these winds to haul in the *Alabama*. We would have the wind from the northwest to the southwest, hauling gradually from one point to the other and blowing freshly for the greater part of three days. It would then become light and in the course of a few hours go round to the south, to the southeast, to the east, and then settle in the northwest as before.

Figure 2 represents two of these circular winds—and there is a constant series of them—one following the other so closely as to overlap it. Now, if the reader will cast his eye upon the letter C near the upper dotted line in the overlapped space, he will observe why it is that there is always a short interval of calm before the northwest wind sets in the second time. The wind within that space is blowing, or rather should blow, according to the theory, two opposite ways at once—from the N. N. W. and the S. S. E. The consequence is, necessarily, a calm. It is thus seen that the theory that these brave west winds are a series of circular winds harmonizes entirely with the facts observed by us. The lower dotted line is merely intended to show in what direction the wind would haul if the southern segment instead of the northern passed over the ship. In that case the ship would take the wind from about N. N. E., as at B, and lose it at southeast, as at B². In the region of the brave west winds it would seem that the northern segment always passes over that belt of the ocean. The received theory of these south polar winds is not such as I have assumed. Former writers have not supposed them to be circular winds at all. They suppose them to pass over the southeast trade winds as an upper current, and when they have reached the proper parallel, to descend, become surface-winds, and blow home as straight winds to the pole. But I found a difficulty in reconciling this theory with the periodical veering of the wind entirely around the compass. If these were straight winds blowing contrary to the trades, why should they not blow steadily like the trades? But if we drop the straight-wind theory and take up the circular hypothesis, all the phenomena observed by us will be conformity with the latter. The periodical hauling of the wind will be accounted for, and if we suppose that the northern half of the circle invariably passes over the ship in the passage-parallels, we shall see how it is that the wind is blowing nearly all the time from the westward. To account for the fact that the northern half of the circle invariably passes over these parallels, we have only to suppose the circle to be of sufficient diameter to extend to or near the pole.

Here is the figure. It extends from the parallel of 40° to the pole; it is therefore fifty degrees or three thousand miles in diameter. Halfway from its northern to its southern edge would be the 65th parallel. Along this parallel, represented by the dotted line which passes through the centre of the circle, the vortex V, or calm spot, would travel. There should be calms, therefore, about the 65th parallel. In the southern half of the circle, or that portion of it between the vortex and the pole, easterly winds should prevail. Navigators between the parallels of 65° and 75° speak of calms as the normal meteorological condition. All nature seems frozen to death,

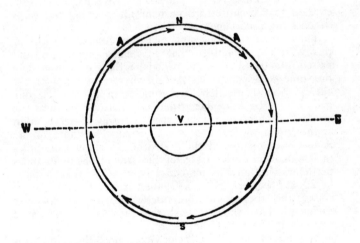

the winds included. Unfortunately, we have no reliable data for the parallels beyond and do not know, therefore, whether easterly winds are the prevalent winds or not. It is probable, as we approached the pole that we should find another calm. The winds, (see the arrows) as they come hurrying along the circle from its northern segment bring with them an impetus *toward* the east derived from the diurnal motion of the earth on its axis. As these winds approach the pole, this velocity increases in consequence of the diminishing diameter of the parallels. To illustrate: if a particle of air on the equator, having a velocity eastward of fifteen miles per hour—and this is the rate of the revolution of the earth on its axis— should be suddenly transported to a point distant five miles from the pole, it would have sufficient velocity to carry it entirely around the pole in one hour. Here we have two forces acting in opposition to each other—the impetus of the wind *toward* the east given to it by the diurnal motion of the earth, and an impetus *from* the east given to it by whatever causes are hurrying it around the circle. These two forces necessarily neutralize each other, and a calm is the consequence. It is in this calm region near the poles that the winds probably ascend to take their flight back to the equator in obedience to that beautiful arrangement for watering the earth which I described some pages back.

There remains but one other fact to be reconciled with our theory. It has been seen that consecutive circles of wind passed over the *Alabama* in periods of three days each. Did this time correspond with the known rate of travel of the circles? Almost precisely. Referring again to the last diagram, it will be remembered that the *Alabama* was near the northern edge of the circle. Let A A represent her position at the beginning and end of each wind. The chord of the segment, represented by the dotted line, is about 1500 miles in length. The circles travel at the rate of about 20 miles per hour. Multiply the number of hours—72—in three days, by 20, and we shall have 1440 miles. It is not pretended, of course, that these figures are strictly accurate, but they are sufficiently so to show, at least, that there is no discordance between the fact and the theory.

Soon after leaving the Cape of Good Hope, the storm birds began to gather around us in considerable numbers—the Cape pigeon, the albatross, and occasionally the tiny petrel, so abundant in the North Atlantic. These birds seemed to be quite companionable, falling in company with the ship and traveling with her for miles at a time. On the occasion of one of the short calms described, we caught an albatross with hook and line, which measured ten feet across the wings. The monster bird was very fat, and it was quite a lift to get it inboard. Though very active on the wing and rising with great facility from the water in which it sometimes alights, it lay quite helpless when placed upon the deck. It did not seem to be much alarmed at the strangeness of its position, but looked at us with the quiet dignity and wisdom of an owl, as though it would interrogate us as to what we were doing in its dominions. These birds live in the midst of the great Indian Ocean, thousands of miles away from any land—only making periodical visits to some of the desert islands; or, it may be, to the Antarctic Continent, to incubate and rear their young.

I have described at some length the nature of the great circles of wind which form the normal meteorological condition of the region of ocean through which we were passing. This normal condition was sometimes interfered with by the passage of cyclones of smaller diameter—a circle within a circle; both circles, however, obeying the same laws. We took one of these cyclones on the 5th of October. I do not design to repeat here the description of a cyclone and only refer to that which we now encountered for the purpose of showing that the *Alabama* ran a race with it and was not very badly beaten. This race is thus described in my journal: "Morning dull, cloudy, and cool. The wind hauled last night to north and is blowing a fresh breeze at noon. Barometer, 30.14. Thermometer, air 54°, water 60°. Current during the last twenty-four hours, thirty miles east. The weather continued to thicken in the afternoon, and the wind to increase, with a falling barometer indicating the approach of a gale. At nine P. M., the squalls becoming heavy, we furled the top-gallant sails and foresail, close-reefed the topsails, and took the bonnets off the trysails. Under this reduced sail we continued to scud the ship all night—the barometer still falling, the wind increasing, and a heavy sea getting up. We had entered the northeastern edge of a cyclone. The next morning the wind was still north by west, having hauled only a single point in twelve hours; showing that we had been running, neck and neck with the gale.

If the reader will recollect that in these circular gales the change of the wind is due to the passage of the circle over the ship, he will have no difficulty in conceiving that if the ship travels as fast as the circle and in the same direction, the wind will not change at all. Now, as the wind had changed but a single point in twelve hours, it is evident that the *Alabama* had been traveling nearly as fast as the circular gale. The race continued all the next day—the wind not varying half a point, and the barometer settling by scarcely perceptible degrees. Toward night, however, the barometer began to settle quite rapidly, and the wind increased and began to haul to the westward. The gale had acquired accelerated speed, and was now evidently passing ahead of us quite rapidly; for by half-past four A. M. the wind was at west, having hauled nearly a quadrant in twelve hours. At this point we had the lowest barometer, 29.65. The center of the storm was then just abreast of us, bearing about south and distant perhaps a hundred miles. At five A. M., or in half an hour afterward, the wind shifted suddenly from W. to W. S. W., showing that the vortex had passed us and that the *Alabama* was at last beaten! The wind being still somewhat fresher than I desired, I hove the ship to on the port tack to allow the gale to draw farther ahead of me. After lying to three hours, the barometer continuing to rise and the wind to moderate, we filled away and shaking out some of the reefs continued on our course.

On the 12th of October, we passed the remarkable islets of St. Peter and St. Paul, sort of halfway mile posts between the cape of Good Hope and the Strait of Sunda. These islets are the tops of rocky mountains shooting up from great depths in the sea. They are in the midst of a dreary waste of waters, having no other land within a thousand miles and more of them. They are composed of solid granite without vegetation, and inhabited only by the wild birds of the ocean. I cannot imagine a more fitting station for a meteorologist. He would be in the midst of constant tempests and might study the laws of his science without interruption from neighboring isle or continent. There being an indifferent anchorage under the lee of St. Paul, we scanned the island narrowly with our glasses, as we passed, not knowing but we might find some adventurous Yankee whaler or seal catcher trying out blubber or knocking a seal on the head. These islands are frequently sighted by India-bound ships, and it was my intention to cruise a few days in their vicinity, but the bad weather hurried me on.

We took another gale on the night after leaving them, and had some damage done to our head rail and one of our quarter-boats. The scene was a sublime one to look upon. The seas—those long swells before described—were literally running mountains high, the wind was howling with more than usual fury, and a dense snow storm was pelting us from the blackest and most angry-looking of clouds. I was now in longitude 83° E., and bore away more to the northward. Although the thermometer had not settled below 50°, we felt the cold quite piercingly—our clothing being constantly saturated with moisture. On the 14th of October, we had the first tolerably fine day we had experienced for the last two weeks, and we availed ourselves of it to uncover the hatches and ventilate the ship, getting up from below and airing the damp bedding and mildewed clothing. The constant straining of the ship in the numerous gales she had encountered had opened the seams in her bends, and all our staterooms were leaking more or less, keeping our beds and clothing damp. On the next day, another gale overtook us, in which we lay to ten hours to permit it, as we had done the gale we ran the race with, to pass ahead of us.

And thus it was that we ran down our easting in the region of the brave west winds with every variety of bad weather of the description of which the reader must by this time, be pretty well tired. On the 17th of October, I was nearly *antipodal* with my home in Alabama. By the way, has the reader ever remarked that land is scarcely ever antipodal with land? Let him take a globe, and he will be struck with the fact that land and water have been almost invariably arranged opposite to each other. May not this arrangement have something to do with the currents and the water carriers, the winds?

On the morning of the 21st of October at about five o'clock, we crossed the tropic of Capricorn on the 100th meridian of east longitude. We still held on to our west winds, though they had now become light. We took the trade wind from about S. S. E. almost immediately after crossing the tropic. We thus had the good fortune, a second time, to cross the tropic without finding a calm-belt; the two counter-winds blowing almost side by side with each other. We had been twenty-four days and three quarters from the Cape of Good Hope, and in that time had run under sail alone— occasionally lying to in bad weather—4410 miles; the average run per day being 178 miles. We had brought easterly current with us, too, all the way. It had set us twenty miles to the northeast on the day we reached the tropic. In all this lengthened run, we had sighted only two or three sails. One of these was a steamer which we overhauled and boarded, but which proved to be English. For nineteen days we did not see a sail; and still we were on the great highway to India. There must have been numerous travelers on this highway before and behind us, but each was bowling along at a rapid and nearly equal pace before the brave west winds, enveloped in his own circle and shut out from the view of his neighbor by the mantle of black rain clouds in which he was wrapped. Our mysterious friends, the Cape pigeons, disappeared as we approached the tropics.

We now ran rapidly through the southeast trades with fine weather until we reached the 12th parallel of south latitude, when we passed suddenly into the monsoon region. The monsoons were undergoing a change. The east monsoon was dying out, and the west monsoon was about to take its place. The struggle between the outgoing and the incoming wind would occupy several weeks, and during all this time I might expect sudden shifts and squalls of wind and rain with densely overcast skies and much thunder and lightning. My intention was to make for the Strait of Sunda, that well-known passage into and out of the China Seas between the islands of Java and Sumatra, cruise off it some days, and then run into the China Seas. On the evening of the 26th we spoke an English bark just out of the Strait, which informed us that the United States steamer *Wyoming* was cruising in the Strait in company with a three-masted schooner, which she had fitted up as a tender, and that she anchored nearly every evening under the island of Krakatoa. Two days afterward, we boarded a Dutch ship from Batavia to Amsterdam which informed us that a boat from the *Wyoming* had boarded her off the town of Anger in the Strait. There seemed, therefore, to be little doubt that if we attempted the Strait, we should find an enemy barring our passage.

As we drew near the Strait, we began to fall in with ships in considerable numbers. On the 31st of October, no less than six were cried from aloft at the same time, all standing to the southwest, showing that they were just out of the famous passage. The wind being light and baffling, we got up steam and chased and boarded four of them—three English and one Dutch. By this time the others were out of sight—

reported by those we had overhauled to be neutral—and the night was setting in dark and rainy. The Dutch ship, like the last one we had boarded, was from Batavia, and corroborated the report of the presence of the *Wyoming* in these waters. She had left her at Batavia which is a short distance only from the Strait of Sunda. The weather had now become exceedingly oppressive. Notwithstanding the almost constant rains, the heat was intense. On the morning of the 6th of November, we boarded an English ship from Foo Chow for London, which informed us that an American ship called the *Winged Racer* had come out of the Strait in company with her. In the afternoon, two ships having been cried from aloft, we got up steam and chased, hoping that one of them might prove to be the American ship reported. They were both English; but whilst we were chasing these two English ships, a third ship hove in sight, farther to windward, to which we gave chase in turn.

This last ship was to be our first prize in East Indian waters. A gun brought the welcome stars and stripes to her peak, and upon being boarded she proved to be the bark *Amanda* of Boston from Manilla bound to Queenstown for orders. The *Amanda* was a fine, rakish-looking ship and had a cargo of hemp, and sugar. She was under charter party to proceed first to Queenstown and thence to the United States for a market if it should be deemed advisable. On the face of each of the three bills of lading found among her papers was the following certificate from the British Consul at Manilla:—"I hereby certify that Messrs. Ker & Co., the shippers of the merchandise specified in this bill of lading are British subjects established in Manilla, and that according to invoices produced, the said merchandise is shipped by order and for account of Messrs. Holliday, Fox & Co., British subjects, of London in Great Britain." As nobody swore to anything before the consul, his certificate was valueless to protect the property, and the ship and cargo were both condemned. The night set in very dark and squally whilst we were yet alongside of this ship. We got on board from her some articles of provisions, and some sails and cordage to replace the wear and tear of the late gales we had passed through, and made a brilliant bonfire of her at about ten P. M. The conflagration lighted up the sea for many miles around and threw its grim and ominous glare to the very mouth of the Strait.

The next day we ran in and anchored under Flat Point on the north side of the Strait in seventeen fathoms water about a mile from the coast of Sumatra. My object was to procure some fruits and vegetables for my crew who had been now a long time on salt diet.

Chapter Twenty—*1863*

The Alabama passes through the Strait of Sunda, seeing nothing of the Wyoming . . . Burns the Winged Racer just inside the Strait . . . The Malay boatmen and their alarm . . . The Alabama makes for the Gaspar Strait and burns the Contest after an exciting chase . . . Passes through the Carimata Passage . . . Discharges her prisoners into an English ship . . . Miniature sea serpents . . . The currents . . . Pulo Condore . . . Arrival at Singapore

Soon after anchoring, we had a false alarm. It was reported that a bark some distance off had suddenly taken in all sail and turned her head in our direction as though she were a steamer coming in chase. Orders were given to get up steam to be ready for any emergency, but countermanded in a few minutes, when upon a partial lifting of the rain clouds, it was ascertained that the strange sail was a merchant ship and had only taken in her top-gallant sails to a squall and clewed down her topsails to reef. She was indeed coming in our direction but it was only to take shelter for the night. She was a Dutch bark from Batavia for the west coast of Sumatra.

The next morning we got under way at an early hour to

pass through the Strait of Sunda into the China Sea. We hove up our anchor in the midst of a heavy rain squall, but the weather cleared as the day advanced, and a fresh and favorable wind soon sprang up. We ran along by Keyser Island, and at half-past ten lowered the propeller and put the ship under steam. Under both steam and sail we made rapid headway. We passed between the high and picturesque islands of Beezee and Soubooko, the channel being only about a mile in width. Groves of cocoanut trees grew near the beach on the former island, among which were some straw-thatched huts. From these huts, the natives, entirely naked except for a breech cloth around the loins, flocked out in great numbers to see the ship pass. Ships do not often take this narrow channel, and the spectacle was no doubt novel to them. They made no demonstration but gazed at us in silence as we flew rapidly past them. We ran through the Strait proper of Sunda between one and two o'clock in the afternoon, passing to the westward of the island called Thwart-the-Way and close to the Stroom Rock, lying with its blackened and jagged surface but a few feet above the water. This course carried us in full view of the little town and garrison of Anjer, but we saw nothing of the *Wyoming*. We found the Strait of Sunda as unguarded by the enemy as we found the other highways of commerce along which we had passed.

Just where the Strait debouches into the China Sea we descried in the midst of a rain squall, to which we were both obliged to clew up our top-gallant sails, a tall clipper ship, evidently American. She loomed up through the passing shower like a frigate. We at once gave chase and in a very few minutes hove the stranger to with a gun. It was the *Winged Racer*, which our English friend told us had passed out of the Strait some days before in his company. She had lingered behind for some reason and as a consequence had fallen into the power of her enemy with no friendly gun from the *Wyoming* to protect her. The *Winged Racer* was a perfect beauty —one of those New York ships of superb model with taut, graceful masts and square yards known as clippers. She was from Manilla, bound for New York with a cargo consisting chiefly of sugar, hides, and jute. There was no claim of neutral property, and condemnation followed the capture as a matter of course. We anchored her near North Island and came to, ourselves, for the convenience of "robbing" her. She had

sundry provisions on board—particularly sugar and coffee—
of which we stood in need. She had, besides, a large supply
of Manilla tobacco, and my sailors' pipes were beginning to
want replenishing. It took us a greater part of the night—for
night had set in by the time the two ships were well anchored
—to transport to the *Alabama* such things as were needed. In
the meantime the master of the captured ship, who had his
family on borad, requested me to permit him and his crew
to depart in his own boats. The portion of the Javan sea in
which we were anchored was a mere lake, the waters being
shallow and studded every few miles with islands. He pro-
posed to make his way to Batavia and report to his consul
for further assistance. I granted his request, made him a
present of all his boats, and told him to pack into them as
much plunder as he chose. About one o'clock he was ready,
and his little fleet of boats departed. The prisoners from the
Amanda took passage with him.

Whilst these things were going on a number of Malay
bumboatmen had collected around us with their stores of
fruits, and vegetables, and live stock. These boatmen, like
the Chinese, live on the water and make a business of supplying ships that pass through the Strait. The stewards of the
different messes had all been busy trading with them, and
there was a great squalling of chickens and squealing of pigs
going on. An amusing scene was now to occur. The boatmen
had no suspicion that the *Alabama* had captured the *Winged
Racer* and was about to destroy her. They were lying on their
oars, or holding on to lines from the two ships with the most
perfect *insouciance*. Presently a flame leaped up on board the
Winged Racer and in a few minutes enveloped her. Terror at
once took possession of the Malay boatmen, and such a cutting
of lines, and shouting, and vigorous pulling were perhaps never
before witnessed in the Strait of Sunda. These boats had informed us that the *Wyoming* was at Anger only two days
before when they left.

It was now about two o'clock A. M., and the *Alabama*
getting up her anchor, steamed out into the China Sea by the
light of the burning ship. We had thus lighted a bonfire at
either end of the renowned old Strait of Sunda. After having
thus advertised our presence in this passage it was useless to
remain in it longer. Ships approaching it would take the alarm
and seek some other outlet into the Indian Ocean. Most of

the ships coming down the China Sea with a view of passing
out at the Strait of Sunda come through the Gaspar Strait. I
resolved now to steam in the direction of this latter strait
and forestall such as might happen to be on their way. By
daylight we had steamed the coast of Sumatra and Java out of
sight and soon afterward we made the little island called the
North Watcher, looking, as its name implied, like a lone
sentinel posted on the wayside. We had lost the beautiful blue
waters of the Indian Ocean with its almost unfathomable
depths and entered upon a sea whose waters were of a whitish
green with an average depth of no more than about twenty
fathoms. Finding that I should be up with Gaspar Strait some-
time during the night if I continued under steam, and prefer-
ring to delay my arrival until daylight the next morning, I let
my steam go down and put my ship under sail to take it more
leisurely.

We were about to lift the propeller out of the water when
the cry of "Sail ho!" came from the vigilant lookout at the
mast head. We at once discontinued the operation, not knowing but we might have occasion to use steam. As the stranger
was standing in our direction, we soon raised her from the
deck, and as my glass developed first one and then another of
her features, it was evident that here was another clipper
ship at hand. She had the well-known tall, raking masts,
square yards, and white canvas. She was on a wind with
everything set from courses to skysails, and was plowing her
way through the gently ruffled sea with the rapidity and
the grace of the swan. We made her a point or two on our
lee bow, and not to excite her suspicion we kept away for
her so gradually, that she could scarcely perceive the alteration
in our course. We hoisted at the same time the United
States colors. When we were within about four miles of
the chase, she responded by showing us the same colors.
Feeling now quite sure of her, we fired a gun, hauled down
the enemy's flag, and threw our own to the breeze. (We were
now wearing that splendid white [Confederate] flag, with its
cross and stars, which was so great an improvement upon the
old one.) So far from obeying the command of our gun, the
gallant ship kept off a point or two—probably her best point
of sailing—gave herself top-gallant and topmast studding-sails
and away she went!

I had been a little premature in my eagerness to clutch so

beautiful a prize. She was not as yet under my guns, and it was soon evident that she would give me trouble before I could overhaul her. The breeze was tolerably fresh but not stiff. We made sail at once in chase. Our steam had been permitted to go down, and as yet we had not much more than enough to turn over the propeller. The chase was evidently gaining on us. It was some fifteen or twenty minutes before the engineer had a head of steam on. We now gave the ship all steam and trimmed the sails to the best possible advantage. Still the fugitive ship retained her distance from us, if she did not increase it. It was the first time the *Alabama* had appeared dull. She was under both sail and steam, and yet here was a ship threatening to run away from her. She must surely be out of trim. I tried, therefore, the effect of getting my crew aft on the quarter-deck and shifting aft some of the forward guns. This helped us visibly, and the ship sprang forward with increased speed. We were now at least holding our own, but it was impossible to say as yet whether we were gaining an inch. If the breeze had freshened, the chase would have run away from us beyond all question. I watched the signs of the weather anxiously. It was between nine and ten o'clock A. M. Fortunately, as the sun gained power and drove away the mists of the morning, the breeze began to decline! Now came the triumph of steam. When we had come within long range, I threw the spray over the quarter-deck of the chase with a rifle shot from my bow-chaser. Still she kept on, and it was not until all hope was evidently lost that the proud clipper ship, which had been beaten rather by the failure of the wind, than the speed of the *Alabama*, shortened sail and hove to.

When the captain was brought on board, I congratulated him on the skilful handling of his ship and expressed my admiration of her fine qualities. He told me that she was one of the most famous clipper ships out of New York. She was the *Contest* from Yokohama, Japan, bound to New York. She was light and in fine sailing trim, having only a partial cargo on board. There being no attempt to cover the cargo, consisting mostly of light Japanese goods, lackerware, and curiosities, I condemned both ship and cargo. I was sorry to be obliged to burn this beautiful ship and regretted much that I had not an armament for her that I might commission her as a cruiser. Both ships now anchored in the open sea with no land visible, in fourteen fathoms of water, whilst the crew was being removed from the prize, and the necessary preparations were all completed, and the torch applied. We hove up our anchor and made sail by the light of the burning ship. Having now burned a ship off Gaspar Strait, I turned my ship's head to the eastward with the intention of taking the Carimata Strait.

My coal was running so short by this time that I was obliged to dispense with the use of steam except on emergencies and work my way from point to point wholly under sail. Fortune favored me however, for I passed through the Carimata Strait in the short space of five days against the northwest monsoon, which was a head wind. Ships have been known to be thirty days making this passage. I generally anchored at night on account of the currents and the exceeding difficulty of the navigation—shoals besetting the navigator on every hand in this shallow sea. We began now to fall in with some of the curiosities of the China Sea. Salt-water serpents made their appearance, playing around the ship, and cutting up their antics. These snakes are from three to five feet long, and when ships anchor at night, have been known to crawl up the cables and make their way on deck through the hawse-holes, greatly to the annoyance of the sailors who chance to be sleeping on deck. They are not known to be poisonous.* Never having been in the China seas before, I was quite amused at the gambols of these miniature sea serpents. Seeing an old sailor stopping up the hawse-holes with swabs one evening after we had anchored, I asked him what he was about.

"I'm stopping out the snakes, y'r honor," he replied.

"What," said I, "do they come on deck?"

"Oh! Yes, y'r honor; when I was in the ship *Flying Cloud,* we killed forty of them on deck in one morning watch."

Naked Malays frequently paddled off to us when we anchored near their villages, with fowls, and eggs, and fruits, and vegetables, which they desired to exchange for rice and ship bread. In frail piraguas, these amphibious bipeds will make long voyages from island to island. They seem to be a sort of wandering Arabs of the sea, and as a rule are a great set of villains, not hesitating to take a hand at piracy when

* They are poisonous. Ed.

opportunity offers. So intricate are some of the archipelagos which they inhabit that it is next to impossible to track them to their hiding places. These nomads, upon whom no civilization seems to make any impression, will probably long remain the pests of the China seas in spite of the steamship.

Emerging from the Carimata passage, we stood over to the west end of the island of Souriton, where we anchored at four P. M. on the 18th of November. Here we lay several days, and for the convenience of overhauling passing ships without the necessity of getting under way, we hoisted out and rigged our launch, a fine cutter-built boat, and provisioning and watering her for a couple of days at a time, sent her out cruising; directing her, however, to keep herself within sight of the ship. A number of sails were overhauled, but they all proved to be neutral—mostly English and Dutch. I was much struck with the progress the Dutch were making in these seas. Holland, having sunk to a fourth or fifth rate power in Europe, is building up quite an empire in the East. The island of Java is a little kingdom in itself, and the Boers, with the aid of the natives, whom they seem to govern with great success, are fast bringing its fertile lands into cultivation. Batavia, Sourabia, and other towns are rising rapidly into importance. The Dutch are overrunning the fine island of Sumatra, too. They have established military stations over the greater part of it, and are gradually bringing the native chiefs under subjection. They occupy the spice islands and are extending their dominion thence to the northward. In short, Great Britain must look to her laurels in the China seas if she would not divide them with Holland.

In the meantime, the inquiry naturally presents itself, Where is the Yankee that he is permitting all this rich harvest of colonization and trade in the East to pass away from him? It was at one time thought that he would contest the palm of enterprise with England herself, but this dream has long since been dispelled. Even before the war, his trade began to dwindle. During the war it went down to zero, and since the war it has not revived. Is he too busy with his internal dissensions and politics? Is the miserable faction which has ruled the country for the last seven years determined to destroy all its prosperity, foreign as well as domestic?

While lying at Souriton, we boarded the British ship Avalanche, two days from Singapore with newspapers from Amer-

ica just forty days old! Here was a proof of the British
enterprise of which we have just been speaking. The Atlantic,
the Mediterranean, the Red Sea, the Indian Ocean, and a
part of the China Sea are traversed by British steam and sail,
and the *Alabama* shakes out the folds of a newspaper from the
land of her enemy at an out-of-the-way island in the China
Sea, just forty days old! The *Avalanche* kindly consenting, we
sent by her our prisoners to Batavia. We now got under way
and stood over to the west coast of Borneo, where we cruised
for a few days, working our way gradually to the northward; it
being my intention as soon as I should take the northwest
monsoon, which prevails at this season in the China Sea to
the northward of the equator, to stretch over to the coast of
Cochin China and hold myself for a short time in the track
of the ships coming down from Canton and Shanghai. I was
greatly tempted as I passed Sarawak, in the island of Borneo,
to run in and visit my friend Rajah Brooke, whose career in
the East has been so remarkable a one. Cruising in these seas
years ago, when he was a young man, in his own yacht, a
jaunty little armed schooner of about 200 tons, he happened
in at Sarawak. The natives, taking a fancy to him and his
tiny man-of-war, insisted upon electing him their Rajah or
Governor. He assented, got a foothold in the island, grew in
favor, increased his dominions, and was, at the period of our
visit to the coast, one of the most powerful Rajahs in Borneo.
Since my return from the China seas, the Rajah has died, full
of years and full of honors, bequeathing his government to
a blood relation. It would be difficult for even a Yankee to
beat that!

Upon reaching this coast, we struck a remarkable northerly
current. It ran at the rate of two knots, its general set
being about northeast. The weather falling calm, we were
several days within its influence. When it had drifted us as
far to the northward as I desired to go, I was obliged to let
go a kedge in fifty fathoms water to prevent further drift. The
current now swept by us at so rapid a rate that we were
compelled to lash two deep sea leads together, each weighing
forty-five pounds to keep our drift-lead on the bottom. Here
was another of those elliptical currents spoken of a few pages
back. If the reader will look at a map of the China Sea, he
will observe that the northeast monsoon, as it comes sweeping
down that sea in the winter months, blows parallel with the

coasts of China and Cochin China. This wind drives a current before it to the southwest. This current, as it strikes the peninsula of Malacca, is deflected to the eastward toward the coast of Sumatra. Impinging upon this coast, it is again deflected and driven off in the direction of the island of Borneo. This island in turn gives it a northern direction, and the consequence is that the southwesterly current which came sweeping down the western side of the China Sea, is now going up on the eastern side of the same sea as a northeasterly current. We lay five days at our kedge during a calm that lasted all that time. The monsoons were changing; the west monsoon was setting in in the East Indian archipelago, and the northeastern monsoon in the China Sea. Hence the calms, and rains, and sudden gusts of wind, now from one quarter and now from another, which we had experienced. At the end of these five days of calm, we took the northeast monsoon, from about N. N. E., and getting up our kedge, we made our way over to the coast of Cochin China in accordance with the intention already expressed.

There is no navigation, perhaps, in the world so trying to the vigilance and nerves of the mariner as that of the China seas. It is a coral sea and filled with dangers in almost every direction, especially in its eastern portion from the Philippine Islands down to the Strait of Sunda. The industrious little stone mason, which we have before so often referred to, has laid the foundation of a new empire at the bottom of the China Sea and is fast making his way to the surface. He has already dotted the sea with ten thousand islands in its eastern portion, and is silently and mysteriously piling up his tiny blocks of stone one upon another in the central and western portions. He is working very irregularly, having large gangs of hands employed here, and very few there, and is running up his structures in very fantastic shapes, some in solid blocks with even surfaces, some as pyramids, and some as cones. The tops of the pyramids and cones are sometimes as sharp as needles and pierce a ship's bottom as readily as a needle would a lady's finger. It is impossible to survey such a sea with accuracy. A surveying vessel might drop a lead on almost every square foot of bottom and yet miss some of these mere needle points. A ship, with the best of modern charts, may be threading this labyrinth, as she thinks, quite securely, and suddenly find herself impaled upon one of these dangers.

To add to the perplexity of the navigator, days sometimes elapse, especially when the monsoons are changing, during which it is impossible to get an observation for fixing the position of his ship; and during these days of incessant darkness and drenching rains, he is hurried about by currents, he knows not whither. And then, perhaps, the typhoon comes along—that terrible cyclone of the China seas—at the very moment it may be, when he is by reason of the causes mentioned uncertain of his position, and compels him to scud his ship at hazard among shoals and breakers! I lost many nights of rest when in these seas and felt much relieved when the time came for me to turn my back upon them. The wind freshened as we drew out from the coast of Borneo, and by the time we had reached the track of the westward-bound ships, we found the monsoon blowing a whole topsail-breeze. We struck, at the same time, the southwesterly current described, and what with the wind and the current, we found it as much as we could do to hold our own and prevent ourselves from being drifted to leeward. It soon became apparent that it would be useless to attempt operations here unless assisted by steam. Every chase would probably carry us miles to leeward, whence it would be impossible under sail alone to regain our position. Still, we held ourselves a day or two in the track in accordance with my previous determination, overhauling several ships, none of which, however, proved to be enemy.

At the end of this short cruise, we made sail for the island of Condore, or, as it is called on the charts of the China Sea, Pulo Condore, the word "pulo" being the Chinese term for island. My intention was to run into this small island, which has a snug harbor sheltered from the monsoon, do some necessary repairs with my own mechanics, refit and repaint, and then run down to Singapore and fill up with coal. My future course would be guided by contingencies. We made Pulo Condore early in the afternoon of the second of December and passing to the northward of the White Rock, bore up and ran along the western side of the island until nightfall, when we anchored under the lee of a small rocky island near the mouth of the harbor. The scenery was bold, picturesque, and impressive. All was novelty; the shallow sea, the whistling monsoon, and the little islands rising so abruptly from the sea that a goat could scarcely clamber up their sides. The richest vegetation covered these islands from sea level to their summits. Occasionally a break or gap in the mountain—for Pulo Condore rises to the height of a mountain—disclosed charming ravines opening out into luxuriant plains, where were grazing the wild cattle of the country—the bison, or small-humped buffalo of the East.

At daylight the next morning, upon looking into the harbor with our glasses, we were surprised to see a small vessel at anchor wearing the French flag; and pretty soon afterward we were boarded by a French boat; Pulo Condore—lying off the coast of Cochin China—having recently become a French colony. The island had been taken possession of by France two years before. The vessel was a ship of war keeping watch and ward over the lonely waters. This was a surprise. I had expected to find the island in the hands of the Malay nomads who infest these seas, and to have converted it into Confederate territory, as I had done Angra Pequeña, on the west coast of Africa—at least during my stay. And so when I had invited the French officer, who was himself the commander of the little craft, into my cabin, I remarked to him, "You have spoiled a pet project of mine."

"How so?" said he.

I then explained to him how, in imitation of my friend Brooke, I had intended to play Rajah for a few weeks in Pulo Condore. He laughed heartily and said, "Sera tout le même chose, Monsieur. Vous portez plus de cannons que moi, et vous serez Rajah, pendant votre séjour." I did carry a few more guns than my French friend, for his little man-of-war was only a craft of the country of less than a hundred tons of burden, armed with one small carronade. His crew consisted of about twenty men.

I found him as good as his word with reference to my playing Rajah, for he did not so much as mention to me once any rule limiting the stay of belligerents in French waters. We now got under way and stood in to the anchorage, the French officer kindly consenting to show me the way in; though there was but little need as the harbor was quite free from obstructions, except such as were plainly visible. The water in this cosy little harbor was as smooth as a mill pond, notwithstanding occasional gusts of the monsoon swept down the mountain sides. There were mountains on two sides of us, both to the north and south. The harbor was, in fact, formed by two

mountainous islands, both passing under the name of Condore; there being only a boat passage separating them on the
east.

This was our first real resting place since leaving the Cape
of Good Hope, and both officers and men enjoyed the relaxation. The island was full of game, the bay full of fish, and
the bathing very fine. We felt quite secure, too, against the
approach of an enemy. The only enemy's steamer in these
seas was the *Wyoming*, for which we regarded ourselves as
quite a match. We had, besides, taken the precaution upon
anchoring to lay out a spring by which we could in the
course of a few minutes present our broadside to the narrow entrance of the harbor and thus rake anything that
might attempt the passage. The Governor of the island now
came on board to visit us. He had his headquarters at a small
Malay village on the east coast, where, by the aid of a sergeant's guard, he ruled his subjects with despotic sway. He
brought me on board a present of a pig and generously offered
to share with me a potato patch near the ship. What more
could a monarch do? This was an exceedingly clever young
Frenchman—Monsieur Bizot—he was an ensign in the French
Navy, about twenty-two years of age and a graduate of the
French naval school. The commander of his flagship—the
small country craft already described—was a midshipman.
These two young men had entire control of the government of
the island, civil and military.

Kell having set his mechanics at work in the various departments to effect the necessary repairs on the ship, I relaxed the
reins of discipline as much as possible that by boat sailing,
fishing, and hunting excursions, my people might recruit from
the ill effects of their long confinement on shipboard and the
storms and bad weather they had experienced. The northeast monsoon having now fairly set in, the weather had become
fine. The heat was very great, it is true, but it was much tempered by the winds. During the two weeks that we remained
in the island, almost every part of it was explored by my adventurous hunters—even the very mountain tops—and marvellous were the reports of their adventures which they brought
on board. Some small specimens of deer were found; the
bison—the bull of which is very savage, not hesitating to assault the hunter under favorable circumstances—abounded on
the small savannas; monkeys traveled about in troops; parrots

and other birds of beautiful plumage wheeled over our heads in flocks—in short, the whole island seemed teeming with life. The natives told us that there were many large and some poisonous serpents in the jungles, but fortunately none of my people were injured by them.

We found here the famous vampire of the East. Several specimens were shot and brought on board. Some of these monster bats measure from five to six feet from tip to tip of wing. The head resembles that of a wolf. It has long and sharp incisor-teeth and tusks and would be a dangerous animal to attack an unarmed man. The reptile tribe flourishes in perfection. A lizard, measuring five feet ten inches in length, was brought on board by one of the hunters. Nature runs riot in every direction, and the vegetable world is as curious as the animal. The engineer coming on board one day from one of his excursions, pulled out his cigar case and offered me a very tempting Havana cigar. Imagine my surprise when I found it a piece of wood! It had been plucked fresh from the tree. The size, shape, and color—a rich brown—were all perfect. It was not a capsule or a seed pod, but a solid piece of wood, with the ordinary woody fiber, and full of sap. I put it away carefully among my curiosities, but after a few days it shrivelled and lost its beauty.

The apes did not appear to be afraid of the gun—probably because they were not accustomed to be shot at. They would cluster around a hunting party and grin and chatter like so many old Negroes one sometimes sees on the coast of Africa. One of the midshipmen having shot one, described the death of the old gentleman to me and said that he felt almost as if he had killed his old "uncle" on his father's plantation. The wounded creature—whatever it may be, man or animal— threw its arms over the wound and moaned as plaintively and intelligibly as if it had been gifted with the power of speech and were upbraiding its slayer. During our stay I made the acquaintance—through my opera glass—of several of these lampoons upon human nature. A gang of apes, old and young, came down to the beach regularly every morning, to look at the ship. The old men and women would seat themselves in rows and gaze at us sometimes for an hour without changing their places or attitudes—seeming to be absorbed in wonder. I became quite familiar with some of their countenances. The young people did not appear to be so strongly impressed.

They would walk about the beach in twos and threes—making love, most likely and settling future family arrangements. The children, meanwhile, would be romping around the old people, screaming and barking in very delight. If a boat approached them, the old people would give a peculiar whistle, when the younger members of the trible would betake themselves at once to the cover of the adjoining jungle.

A hunting party, landing here one morning, shot one of these old apes. The rest scampered off and were seen no more that day. The next morning, upon turning my opera glass upon the beach, I saw the monkeys as usual, but they were broken into squads and moving about in some disorder instead of being seated as usual. I could plainly see some of them at work. Some appeared to be digging in the sand, and others to be bringing twigs and leaves of trees and such of the debris of the forest as they could gather conveniently. It was my usual hour for landing to get sights for my chronometers. As the boat approached, the whole party disappeared. I had the curiosity to walk to the spot to see what these semi-human beings had been doing. They had been burying their dead comrade and had not quite finished covering up the body when they had been disturbed! The deceased seemed to have been popular, for a large concourse had come to attend his funeral. The natives told us that this burial of the monkeys was a common practice. They believe in monkey doctors, too, for they told us that when they have come upon sick monkeys in the woods, they have frequently found some demure old fellows looking very wise, with their fingers on their noses sitting at their bedsides. The ladies may be curious to know from the same good authority how the monkeys of Pulo Condore treat their women. As among the Salt Lake saints, polygamy prevails, and there are sometimes as many as a dozen females "sealed" to one old patriarch—especially if he be broad across the shoulders and have sharp teeth. The young lady monkeys are required to form matrimonial connections during the third or fourth season of their belledom; that is to say, the parent monkeys will permit their daughters to sally out and return home as often as they please after they have "come out," until three or four moons have elapsed. After that time they are expected to betake themselves to their own separate trees for lodging.

I was frequently startled whilst we lay at Pulo Condore

at hearing what appeared to be the whistle of a locomotive—rather shrill, it may be, but very much resembling it. It proceeded from an enormous locust.

Pulo Condore lies in the route of the French mail steamer, between Singapore and Saigon, the latter the capital of the French possessions in Cochin China, and the Governor receiving a large mail while we were here, was kind enough to send us some late papers from Paris and Havre. Every two or three days, too, he sent us fresh beef, fowls, and fruits. On the Sunday evening after our arrival, he and his paymaster repeated their visit to us and brought in the same boat with themselves, a bullock—a fine fat bison! In a country comparatively wild, and where supplies were so difficult to be obtained, these presents were greatly enhanced in value. Poor Monsieur Bizot! we all regretted to learn upon our return to Europe that this promising young officer, so full of talent, life, energy, and hope had fallen a victim to a malarial fever.

Kell performed quite a feat at Pulo Condore in the way of ship carpentry. Our copper having fallen off some distance below the waterline, he constructed a coffer or caisson that fitted the side of the ship so nicely when sunk to the required depth that he had only to pump it out with our fire engine and suction hose to enable his mechanics to descend into a dry box and effect the necessary repairs. We found our ship so much out of order that it required two weeks to get her ready for sea. At the end of this time we took an affectionate leave of our French friends, and getting under way under sail, we again threw ourselves into the monsoon and southwest current and turned our head in the direction of Singapore. We crossed the Gulf of Siam under easy sail that we might have the benefit of any chance capture that might present itself. There was a number of vessels hurrying on before the brisk monsoon, but no Yankee among them. The Yankee flag had already become a stranger in the China Sea. On the evening of the 19th of December we ran in and anchored under Pulo Aor in twenty fathoms of water within half a mile of the village on the southwest end of the island. The island is high and broken—its forests being composed almost entirely of the cocoanut—and is inhabited by the same class of Malay nomads already described. Their houses were picturesquely scattered among the trees, and several large boats were hauled up near them on the beach, ready for any enterprise that might offer in their line. The head man came off to visit me, and some piraguas with fowls and fruits came alongside to trade with the sailors.

These islanders appeared to be a merry set of fellows, for during nearly the whole night we could hear the sound of tom-toms and other musical instruments, as though they were engaged in the mysteries of the dance. Some very pretty specimens of young women, naked to the middle, came off in their light piraguas, handling the paddle equally with the men and appearing quite as much at home on the water. The next day being Sunday, and the weather not being very propitious for our run to Singapore, it being thick and murky, we remained over at our anchors at this island, mustering the crew and inspecting the ship as usual. After muster, some of the officers visited the shore and were hospitably received by the natives. They saw no evidences of the cultivation of the soil or of any other kind of labor. Nature supplied the inhabitants spontaneously with a regular succession of fruits all the year round, and as for clothing, they needed none so near the equator. The sea gave them fish; and the domestic fowl, which seemed to take care of itself, and the goat which browsed without care also on the mountainside secured them against the caprice of the elements. Their *physique* was well developed, and life seemed to be with them a continual holiday. Who shall say that the civilized man is a greater philosopher than the savage of the China seas?

On the next morning at a very early hour—just as the cocks on shore were crowing for early daylight—we hove up our anchor, and giving the ship both steam and sail, shaped our course for Singapore. Soon after getting under way, we fell in company with an English steamer running also in our direction. The navigation, as one approaches the Strait of Malacca on which Singapore is situated, is very difficult, there being some ugly shoals by the wayside; and the weather coming on thick, and heavy rains setting in, we were obliged to anchor in the mouth of the Strait for several hours. The weather now lifting and the clouds breaking away, we got under way again, and taking a Malay pilot soon afterward, we ran into Singapore and anchored at about five P. M. The harbor was filled with shipping, but there was no United States ship of war among the number. The *Wyoming* was at Anger in the Strait of Sunda only two days before we burned the *Winged*

Racer. She must have heard of that event soon after its occurrence and also of our burning the *Contest* near Gaspar Strait. The English ship *Avalanche* had, besides, carried news to Batavia that we were off Sorouton, still higher up the China Sea. The *Wyoming*, if she had any intention of seeking a fight with us, was thus entirely deceived by our movements. These indicated that we were bound to Canton and Shanghai, and thither, probably, she had gone. She must have passed within sight of Pulo Condore while we were scraping down our masts, tarring our rigging, and watching the funeral of the dead monkey described; and about the time she was ready to run into Hongkong in the upper part of the China Sea, we had run into Singapore and anchored in the lower part.

Chapter Twenty-One—*1863*

The Alabama at Singapore . . . Panic among the enemy's shipping in the China Seas . . . The multitude flock to see the Alabama . . . A curious rumor concerning her . . . The author rides to the country and spends a night . . . The Chinese in possession of all the business of the place . . . The Alabama leaves Singapore . . . Capture of the Martaban, alias Texan Star . . . The Alabama touches at Malacca . . . Capture of the Highlander and Sonora . . . The Alabama once more in the Indian Ocean

It turned out as I had conjectured. The *Wyoming* had been at Singapore on the 1st of December. She had gone thence to the Rhio Strait where a Dutch settlement had given her a ball which she had reciprocated. Whilst these Yankee and Dutch rejoicings were going on, the *Alabama* was crossing the China Sea from Borneo to Pulo Condore. All traces of the *Wyoming* had since been lost. She had doubtless filled with coal at Rhio and gone northward. We had thus a clear sea before us.

A very gratifying spectacle met our eyes at Singapore.

There were twenty-two American ships there—large India-men—almost all of which were dismantled and laid up! The burning of our first ship in these seas, the *Amanda* off the Strait of Sunda, had sent a thrill of terror through all the Yankee shipping, far and near, and it had hastened to port to get out of harm's way. We had recent news here from all parts of the China seas by vessels passing constantly through the Strait of Malacca and touching at Singapore for orders or refreshments. There were two American ships laid up in Bankok in Siam; one or two at Canton; two or three at Shanghai; one at the Phillippine Islands; and one or two more in Japanese waters. These, besides the twenty-two ships laid up in Singapore, comprised all of the enemy's once numerous Chinese fleet! No ship could get a freight, and the commerce of the enemy was as dead for the time being as if every ship belonging to him had been destroyed. We had here the key to the mystery that the *Alabama* had encountered no American ship in the China Sea since she had burned the *Contest.* The birds had all taken to cover, and there was no such thing as flushing them. This state of things decided my future course. I had at first thought of running up the China Sea as far as Shanghai, but if there were no more than half a dozen of the enemy's ships to be found in that part of the sea, and these had all fled to neutral ports for protection, *cui bono?* It would be far better to return to the western hemisphere where the enemy still had some commerce left. Indeed, my best chance of picking up these very ships that were now anchored under my guns in Singapore and disconsolate for want of something to do, would be to waylay them on their homeward voyages. They would not venture out in a close sea like that of China so long as I remained in it. After I should have departed, and they had recovered somewhat from their panic, they might pick up partial cargoes at reduced rates and once more spread their wings for flight.

I had another powerful motive influencing me. My ship was getting very much out of repair. The hard usage to which she had been subjected since she had been commissioned had very much impaired her strength, and so constantly had she been under way that the attrition of the water had worn the copper on her bottom so thin that it was daily loosening and dropping off in sheets. Her speed had in consequence been much diminished. The fire in her furnaces, like that of

the fire-worshipping Persian, had never been permitted to go
out except for a few hours at rare intervals to enable the engineer to clink his bars and remove the incrustations of salt
from the bottoms of his boilers. This constant action of fire
and salt had nearly destroyed them. I resolved, therefore, to
turn my ship's head westward from Singapore, run up into the
Bay of Bengal along the coast of Hindostan to Bombay,
through the Seychelle Islands to the mouth of the Red Sea,
thence to the Comoro Islands; from these latter to the Strait
of Madagascar, and from the latter Strait to the Cape of Good
Hope—thus varying my route back to the Cape.

We were received with great cordiality by the people of
Singapore, and, as at the Cape of Good Hope, much curiosity
was manifested to see the ship. After she had hauled alongside of the coaling wharf, crowds gathered to look curiously
upon her and compare her appearance with what they had
read of her. These crowds were themselves a curiosity to
look upon, formed, as they were, of all the nations of the
earth from the remote East and the remote West. Singapore
being a free port and a great center of trade, there is always
a large fleet of shipping anchored in its waters, and its streets
and other marts of commerce are constantly thronged with a
promiscuous multitude. The canal—there being one leading
to the rear of the town—is filled with country boats from the
surrounding coasts laden with the products of the different
countries from which they come. There is the pepper boat
from Sumatra, and the coaster of larger size laden with tin
ore; the spice boats from the spice islands; boats with tin ore,
hides, and mats from Borneo; boats from Siam with gums,
hides, and cotton; boats from different parts of the Malay
Peninsula with canes, guttapercha, and India rubber. In the
bay are ships from all parts of the East—from China with
silks and teas; from Japan with lackerware, raw silk, and
curious manufactures of iron, steel, and paper; from the Phillippine Islands with sugar, hides, tobacco, and spices. Inter-
mixed with these are the European and American ships with
the products of their various countries. As a consequence, all
the races and all the religions of the world were represented
in the throngs that crowded the coaling jetty to look upon
the *Alabama* wearing the new flag of a new nation, mysterious
for its very distance from them. We were to their Eastern
eyes a curious people of the antipodes.

The physical aspect of the throng was no less curious than its moral. There was the Malay, the Chinese, the Japanese, the Siamese, the Hindoo, the Persian, the wild Tartar, the Bornese, the Sumatran, the Javanese, and even the New Zealander —all dressed, or undressed in the garb of their respective tribes and countries. Some of the most notable objects among the crowd, were jet-black Africans with the amplest of petticoat trousers gathered at the knee, sandalled feet, and turbaned heads—the more shining the jet of the complexion, the whiter the turban. The crowd, so far from diminishing, increased daily, so that it was at times difficult to pass into and out of the ship; and it was some time before we could learn what had excited all this curiosity among those simple inhabitants of the isles and continents. Some of these wonder-mongers actually believed that we kept chained in the hold of the *Alabama* several Negro giants—they had heard something about the Negro and slavery having something to do with the war—whom we armed with immense weapons and let loose in time of battle, as they were wont to do their elephants! They waited patiently for hours under their paper umbrellas, hoping to catch a sight of these monsters.

Singapore, which was a fishing village half a century ago, contains a hundred thousand inhabitants, and under the free-port system has become a great center of trade. It concentrates nearly all the trade of the southern portion of the China Sea. There are no duties on exports or imports; and the only tonnage due paid by the shipping is three cents per ton, register, as a lighthouse tax. The currency is dollars and cents; Spanish, Mexican, Peruvian, and Bolivian dollars are current. Great Britain, with an infinite forecaste, not only girdles the seas with her ships but the land with her trading stations. In her colonization and commerce consists her power. Lop off these, and she would become as insignificant as Holland. And so beneficent is her rule that she binds her colonies to her with hooks of steel. A senseless party in that country has advocated the liberation of all her colonies. No policy could be more suicidal. Colonization is as much of a necessity for Great Britain as it was for the Grecian States and for Rome when they became overcrowded with population. Probably, in order of nature, colonies, as they reach maturity, may be expected to go off to themselves, but for each colony which thus puts on the *toga virilis*, Great Britain should establish another if she would preserve her empire and her importance with nations of the earth.

The most notable feature about Singapore is its Chinese population. I consider these people in many respects the most wonderful people of the earth. They are essentially a people of the arts and of trade, and in the changing aspect of the world must become much more important than they have hitherto been. It is little more than half a century since Napoleon twitted the English people with being a nation of shopkeepers. So rapid have been the changes since that other nations besides Great Britain are beginning to covet the designation as one of honor. Even military France, the very country which bestowed the epithet in scorn, is herself becoming a nation of mechanics and shopkeepers. Industrial Congresses and Palaces of Industry attract more attention in that once martial country than military reviews and the marching and countermarching of troops on the Campus Martius. An Emperor of France has bestowed the cordon of the Legion of Honor on a Yankee pianomaker! These are some of the signs of the times in which we live. And they are signs which the wise statesman will not ignore. A nation chooses wisely and well which prefers the pursuits of peace to those of war; and that nation is to be envied, which is better constituted by the nature of its people for peaceful than for warlike pursuits. This is eminently the case with the Chinese. Nature has kindly cast them in a mold gentle and pacific. They are human, and have, therefore, had their wars, but compared with the western nations, their wars have been few. The Taeping rebellion of our day, which has lasted so long, had its origin in the brigandage of an idle and leprous soldiery who sought to live at ease at the expense of the honest producer.

It is only lately that we have been able to obtain an interior view of these people. A few years back, and China was a sealed book to us. Our merchants were confined to certain "factories" outside of the walls of Canton, and we were permitted to trade at no other points. But since we have gotten a glimpse of these wonderful people, we have been astonished at the extraordinary productiveness and vitality of Chinese commerce. We have been amazed whilst we have looked upon the wonderful stir and hum and bustle of so immense a hive of human beings, all living and prospering by the mechanic arts and commerce. The Chinaman is born to industry as naturally as the Negro is to sloth. He is the cheapest producer on the face of the earth because his habits are simple and frugal. The proof of this is that no Western nation can sell its goods in the Chinese market. We are all compelled to purchase whatever we want from them for cash. When we can work cheaper than the Chinese, we may hope to exchange our manufactured goods with them, but not until then.

Singapore is a miniature Canton, and the visitor, as he passes through its streets, has an excellent opportunity of comparing the industry of the Chinese with that of other nations. As a free port, Singapore is open to immigration from all parts of the earth, on equal terms. There are no jealous laws, guilds, or monopolies to shackle the limbs or dampen the energy or enterprise of anyone. Free competition is the presiding genius of the place. The climate is healthy—the English call it the Madeira of the East—and the European artisan can labor in it as well as the East Indian or the Chinese. All nations flock hither to trade. Now what is the result? Almost all the business of every description is in the hands of the Chinese. Large Chinese houses monopolize the trade, and the Chinese artisan and day laborer have driven out all others. Ninety thousand of the one hundred thousand of the population are Chinese.

Now that the exclusiveness of China has been broken in upon, and emigration permitted, what a destiny awaits such a people in the workshops ·and fields of the Western world! Already they are filling up the states on the Pacific Coast, and silently but surely possessing themselves of all the avenues of industry in those states, thrusting aside the more expensive European and American laborers. They will cross the Rocky Mountains and effect in course of time a similar revolution in the Western and Southern States. In the latter states their success will be most triumphant; for in these States, where the Negro is the chief laboror, the competition will be between frugality, forecast, and industry on the one hand, and wastefulness, indifference to the future, and laziness on the other. The Negro must, of necessity, disappear in such a conflict. Cheap labor must and will drive out dear labor. This law is as inexorable as any other of Nature's laws. This is the probable fate which the Puritan has prepared for his friend the Negro on the American continent. Our system of slavery might have saved his race from destruction—nothing else can.

The Governor of Singapore was a colonel in the British

army. He had a small garrison of troops—no more, I believe, than a couple of companies—to police this large population. I sent an officer as usual to call on him and acquaint him with my wants and intention as to time of stay. Mr. Beaver of the firm of Cumming, Beaver & Co., a clever English merchant, came on board and offered to facilitate us all in his power in the way of procuring supplies. I accepted his kind offer and put him in communication with the paymaster, and the next day rode out, and dined, and spent a night with him at his country seat. He lived in luxurious style, as do most European merchants in the East. The drive out took us through the principal streets of the city, which I found to be laid out and built with great taste—the edifices having a semi-English, semi-Oriental air. The houses of the better classes were surrounded by lawns and flower gardens, and cool verandahs invited to repose. Mr. Beaver's grounds were extensive and well kept, scarcely so much as a stray leaf being visible on his well-mown lawns. His household—the lady was absent in England—was a pattern of neatness and comfort. His bathrooms, bedrooms, library, and billiard room—all showed signs of superintendence and care, there being an air of cleanliness and neatness throughout which one rarely ever sees in a bachelor establishment. His servants were all Chinese and males. Chi-hi, and Hu-chin, and the rest of them, plowed his fields, mowed his hay, stabled his horses, cooked his dinners, waited on his guests, washed his linen, made his beds, and marked his game of billiards; and all at a ridiculously low rate of hire. If there had been a baby to be nursed, it would have been all the same.

On my return to the city next day, I lunched by invitation at the officers' mess. English porter, ale, and cheese, cold meats, and a variety of wines were on the table. An English officer carries his habits all over the world with him without stopping to consider climates. No wonder that so many of them return from the East with disordered hepatic arrangements.

When I returned to the ship in the evening, I found that Kell and Galt had made such good use of their time that everything was on board, and we should be ready for sea on the morrow. Our coaling had occupied us but ten hours—so admirable are the arrangements of the P. and O. Steamship Company, at whose wharf we had coaled. A pilot was engaged, and all the preparations made for an early start. There was nothing more to be done except to arrange a little settlement between the Queen and myself similar to the one which had taken place at the Cape of Good Hope. As we were obliged to lie alongside of the wharf for the convenience of coaling, it had been found impossible in the great press and throng of the people who were still anxious to get a sight of my black giants to prevent the sailors from having grog smuggled to them. When an old salt once gets a taste of the forbidden nectar, he is gone—he has no more power of resistance than a child. The consequence on the present occasion was that a number of my fellows left on a frolic. We tracked most of them up during the night and arrested them—without asking any aid of the police this time—and brought them on board. One of the boozy fellows dived under the wharf and played mud turtle for some time, but we finally fished him out. When we came to call the roll, there were half a dozen still missing. A number of applications had been made to us by sailors who wanted to enlist, but we had hitherto resisted them all. We were full and desired no more. Now, however, the case was altered, and the applications being renewed after the deserters had run off—for sailors are a sort of Freemasons and soon learn what is going on among their craft—we permitted half a dozen picked fellows to come on board to be shipped as soon as we should get out into the Strait.

The next morning, bright and early, the *Alabama* was under way, steaming through the Strait of Malacca. At half-past eleven A. M., "Sail ho!" was cried from the mast, and about one P. M. we came up with an exceedingly American-looking ship, which, upon being hove to by a gun, hoisted the English colors. Lowering a boat, I sent Master's Mate Fullam, one of the most intelligent of my boarding-officers, and who was himself an Englishman, on board to examine her papers. These were all in due form—were undoubtedly genuine and had been signed by the proper custom-house officers. The register purported that the stranger was the British ship *Martaban* belonging to parties in Maulmain, a rice port in India. Manifest and clearance corresponded with the register; the ship being laden with rice, and having cleared for Singapore—of which port she was within a few hours' sail. Thus far, all seemed regular and honest enough, but the ship was American—having been formerly known as the *Texan Star*—and her transfer to British owners, if made at all, had been made within the last ten days, after the arrival of the *Alabama* in these seas had become known at Maulmain. Mr. Fullam, regarding these circumstances as at least suspicious, requested the master of the ship to go on board the *Alabama* with him, that I might have an opportunity of inspecting his papers in person. This the master declined to do. I could not, of course, compel an English master to come on board of me, and so I was obliged to go on board of him—and I may state, by the way, that this was the only ship I ever boarded personally during all my cruises.

I could not but admire the beautiful "*bran new*" English flag as I pulled on board, but every line of the ship was American—her long, graceful hull with flaring bow and rounded stern, taut masts with sky-sail poles, and square yards for spreading the largest possible quantity of canvas. Passing up the side, I stepped upon deck. Here everything was, if possible, still more American, even to the black, greasy cook, who, with his uncovered woolly head, naked breast, and uprolled sleeves in the broiling sun, was peeling his Irish potatoes for his codfish. I have before remarked upon the national features of ships. These features are as well marked in the interior organism as in the exterior. The master received me at the gangway, and, after I had paused to take a glance at things on deck, I proceeded with him into his cabin, where his papers were to be examined. His mates were standing about the companionway, anxious, of course, to know the fate of their ship. If I had had any doubts before, the unmistakable persons of these men would have removed them. In the person of the master, the long, lean, angular-featured, hidebound, weather-tanned Yankee skipper stood before me. Puritan, *May Flower*, Plymouth Rock, were all written upon the well-known features. No amount of English custom-house paper or sealing wax could by any possibility convert him into that rotund, florid, jocund Briton who personates the English shipmaster. His speech was even more national—taking New England to be the Yankee *nation* —than his person; and when he opened his mouth, a mere novice might have sworn that he was from the State of Maine—there, or thereabouts. When he told me that I "hadn't ought to" burn his ship, he pronounced the shibboleth which condemned her to the flames.

The shrift was a short one. When the papers were produced, I found among them no bill of sale or other evidence of the transfer of the property—the register of an English ship, as every seaman knows, not being such evidence. His crew list, which had been very neatly prepared, was a mute but powerful witness against him. It was written throughout, signatures and all, in the same hand—the signatures all being like as two peas. After glancing at the papers and making these mental observations as I went along, I asked the master a few questions. As well as I recollect, he was from Hallowell, Maine. His ship had been two years in the East Indies, trading from port to port; and had only been transferred within a few days. The freshly painted assumed name on her stern was scarcely dry. The master had sat with comparative composure during this examination and questioning, evidently relying with great confidence upon his English flag and papers; but when I turned to him and told him that I should burn his ship, he sprang from his chair and said with excited manner and voice, "You dare not do it, sir; that flag"—suiting the action to the word and pointing with his long, bony finger up the companionway to the flag flying from his peak—"won't stand it!"

"Keep cool, captain," I replied, "the weather is warm, and as for the flag, I shall not ask it whether it will stand it or not—the flag that *ought* to be at your peak will have to stand it, though."

In half an hour, or as soon as the crew could pack their duds and be transferred to the *Alabama*, the *Texan Star*—alias the *Martaban*—was in flames; the beautiful new English ensign being marked with the day and latitude and longitude of the capture, and stowed away carefully by the old signal quartermaster in the bag containing his Yankee flags.

The cargo was *bona fide* English property, and if the owner of it, instead of combining with master of the ship to perpetrate a fraud upon my belligerent rights, had contented himself with putting it on board under the American flag properly documented as British property, he might have saved it, and along with it, the ship; as in that case I should have been obliged to bond her. But when I had stripped off the disguise, and the ship stood forth as American, unfortunately for the owner of the cargo, no document could be presented to show that it was English; for the very attempt to document it would have exposed the fraud. Unfortunate Englishman! He had lost sight of the copy he had been used to transcribe at school, "Honesty is the best policy."

It was still early in the afternoon when we resumed our course and gave the ship steam. After a few hours had elapsed, and Captain Pike—for this was the name of the master of the captured ship—had realized that his ship was no more, I sent for him, into my cabin, and directing my clerk to produce writing materials, we proceeded to take his formal deposition; preliminary to which, my clerk administered to him the usual oath. I felt pretty sure now of getting at the truth, for I had resorted to a little arrangement for this purpose quite common in the courts of law—I had *released* the interest of the witness. As soon, therefore, as the witness was put upon the stand, I said to him: "Now, captain, when you and I had that little conversation in your cabin, you had hopes of saving your ship, and, moreover, what you said to me was not under oath. You were, perhaps, only practising a pardonable *ruse de guerre*. But now the case is altered. Your ship being destroyed, you have no longer any possible interest in misstating the truth. You are, besides, under oath. Be frank; was, or was not, the transfer of your ship a *bona-fide* transaction?"

After a moment's reflection he replied: "I will be frank with you, captain. It was not a *bona-fide* transaction. I was alarmed when I heard of your arrival in the East Indies, and I resorted to a sham sale in the hope of saving my ship." Upon this answer being recorded, the court adjourned.

At a late hour in the night, the moon shining quite brightly, we ran in past some islands and anchored off the little town of Malacca—formerly a Portuguese settlement, but now like Singapore in the possession of the English. My object was to land my prisoners, and at early dawn we dispatched them for the shore with a note to the military commander asking the requisite permission. It was Christmas Day, and as the sun rose, we could see many signs of festive preparation on shore. The little town with its white houses peeping out of a wilderness of green was a pretty picture as it was lighted up by the rays of the rising sun. Back of the town, on an isolated hill, stood the lighthouse, whose friendly beacon had guided us into our anchorage overnight, and near by was the barrack, from whose flagstaff floated, besides the proud old flag of our fatherland, a number of gay streamers. Our ship in the offing and our boats in the harbor created quite a stir in this quiet Malay-English town; and forthwith a couple of boats filled with officers and citizens—ladies included—came off to visit us. It was still very early, and the excitement of the morning's row and the novelty of the presence of the *Alabama* seemed greatly to excite our new friends. The males grasped our hands as though they had been our brothers, and the ladies smiled their sweetest smiles —and no one knows how sweet these can be, better than the sailor who has been a long time upon salt water looking upon nothing but whiskers and mustachios. They were very pressing that we should remain a day and partake of their Christmas dinner with them. But we excused ourselves, telling them that war knows no holidays. They left us after a short visit, and at half-past nine A. M., our boats having returned, we were again under steam. Bartelli was seen lugging a basket-full of fine Malacca oranges into the cabin soon after the return of our boats—a gift from some of our lady friends who had visited us. . . .

After a good day's run—during which we overhauled an English bark from Singapore for Madras—we anchored at nightfall near Parceelar Hill in twenty-five fathoms of water. The only Christmas kept by the *Alabama* was the usual splicing of the main-brace by the crew. We were under way again the next morning at six o'clock; the weather was clear with a few passing clouds, and the lookout had not been long at the mast-head before he cried "Sail ho!" twice in quick suggestion. Upon being questioned, he reported two large ships at anchor that looked "sort o' Yankee." We soon began to raise these ships from the deck, and when we got a good view of them through our powerful glasses, we were of the same opinion with the lookout. They were evidently Yankee. As they were at anchor and helpless—waiting for a fair wind with which to run out of the Strait—we had nothing to gain by a concealment of our character and showed them at once the Confederate flag. That flag—beautiful though it was—must have been a terrible wet blanket upon the schemes of these two Yankee skippers. It struck them dumb, for they refused to show me any bunting in return. I captured them both with the "flaunting lie" stowed away snugly in their cabins. They were monster ships, both of them, being eleven or twelve hundred tons burden. In their innocence—supposing the *Alabama* had gone up the China Sea—they had ventured, whilst lying at Singapore, to take charter parties for cargoes of rice to be laden at Akyab for Europe; and were now on their way to Akyab in ballast. They had left Singapore several days before our arrival there and had been delayed by head winds.

Both were Massachusetts ships—one the *Sonora* of Newburyport, and the other, the *Highlander* of Boston. The master of one of these ships, when he was brought on board, came up to me good humoredly on the quarter-deck, and offering me his hand, which I accepted, said: "Well, Captain Semmes, I have been expecting every day for the last three years to fall in with you, and here I am at last!"

I told him I was glad he had found me after so long a search.

"Search!" said he; "it is some such search as the Devil may be supposed to make after holy water. The fact is," continued he, "I have had constant visions of the *Alabama* by night and by day; she has been chasing me in my sleep and riding me like a nightmare, and now that it is all over, I feel quite relieved."

I permitted the masters and crews of both these ships to hoist out and provision their own boats and depart in them for Singapore. The ships when overhauled were lying just inside of the lightship at the western entrance of the Strait of Malacca, and it was only pleasant lake or river sailing to Singapore. Having fired the ships, we steamed out past the lightship and were once more in the Indian Ocean. We found on board one of the prizes a copy of the Singapore *Times* of the 9th of December, 1863, from which I give the following extract. At the date of the paper, we were at Pulo Condore, and the Yankee ships were still flocking into Singapore:

From our today's shipping list it will be seen that there are no fewer than seventeen American merchantmen at present in our harbor, and that they include some of the largest ships at present riding there. Their gross tonnage may be roughly set down at 12,000 tons. Some of these have been lying here now for upward of three months, and most of them for at least half that period. And all this, at a time when there is no dullness in the freight market; but, on the contrary, an active demand for tonnage to all parts of the world. It is, indeed, to us, a home picture—the only one we trust to have for many years to come—of the widespread evils of war in these modern days. But it is a picture quite unique in its nature; for the nation to which these seventeen fine ships belong has a navy perhaps second only to that of Great Britain, and the enemy with which she has to cope is but a schism from herself, possessed of no port that is not blockaded, and owning not more than five or six vessels on the high seas; and yet there is no apathy and nothing to blame on the part of the United States Navy. The tactics with which the Federals have to combat are without precedent, and the means to enable them successfully to do so have not yet been devised.

Chapter Twenty-Two—*1864*

The Alabama crosses the Bay of Bengal . . . The Pilgrims to Mecca and the Black Giants . . . Burning of the Emma Jane . . . The Town of Anjenga and the Hindoos . . . The great deserts of Central Asia and the cotton crop of Hindostan . . . The Alabama crosses the Arabian Sea . . . The animalculæ of the sea . . . The Comoro Islands . . . Johanna and its Arab population . . . The Yankee whalers at Johanna . . . The Alabama passes through the Mozambique Channel and arrives at the Cape of Good Hope

On the afternoon after leaving the Strait of Malacca we overhauled another American ship under neutral colors—the Bremen ship *Ottone*. The transfer had been made at Bremen in the previous May; the papers were genuine, and the master and crew all Dutchmen, there being no Yankee on board. The change of property, in this case, having every appearance of being *bona fide*, I permitted the ship to pass on her voyage, which was to Rangoon for rice. For the next few days we coasted the island of Sumatra—taking a final leave of the north end of that island on the last day of the year 1863. A court martial had been in session several days, settling ac-

342

counts with the runaways at Singapore whom we had arrested and brought back. Having sentenced the prisoners and gotten through with its labors, it was dissolved on this last day of the old year that we might turn over a new leaf.

Clearing the Sumatra coast, we stretched across to the Bay of Bengal toward Ceylon, overhauling a number of neutral ships by the way. Among others, we boarded a large English ship which had a novel lot of passengers on board. She was from Singapore bound for Jiddah on the Red Sea, and was filled with the faithful followers of Mohammed on a pilgrimage to Mecca—Jiddah being the nearest seaport to that renowned shrine. My boarding-officer was greeted with great cordiality by these devotees, who exchanged salaams with him in the most reverential manner and entered into conversation with him. They wanted to know, they said, about those black giants we had on board the *Alabama*, and whether we fed them on live Yankees, as they had heard. The boarding-officer, who was a bit of a wag, told them that we had made the experiment, but that the Yankee skippers were so lean and tough that the giants refused to eat them. Whereupon there was a general grunt and as near an approach to a smile as a Mohammedan ever makes. They then said that they "had heard that we were in favor of a plurality of wives." They had heard of Brigham Young and Salt Lake. The officer said, "Yes, we had a few; three or four dozen apiece." They now insisted upon his smoking with them and plied him with other questions, to which they received equally satisfactory answers; and when he got up to depart, they crowded around him at the gangway and salaamed him over the side more reverentially than ever. I have no doubt that when these passengers arrived at Mecca and discussed learnedly the American war, half the pilgrims at that revered shrine became good Confederates.

Having doubled the island of Ceylon and hauled up on the coast of Malabar, we captured on the 14th of January the *Emma Jane* of Bath, Maine, from Bombay bound to Amherst. Having removed from her such articles of provisions as we required and transferred her crew to the *Alabama*, we burned her. She was in ballast, seeking a cargo, and there was, therefore, no claim of neutral property. The master had his wife on board. Being not a great distance from the land, we ran in for the purpose of discharging our prisoners; and descried the Ghaut Mountains the next day. Coasting along a short distance to the eastward, we made the small Hindoo-Portuguese town of Anjenga, where we came to anchor at about four p. m. The town lies on the open coast, having a roadstead but no harbor. We ran in and anchored without a pilot. We were soon surrounded by native boats—large canoes capable of carrying considerable burdens—filled with Portuguese and Hindoos, and a mixture of both. Though the dominion of Portugal on the Malabar coast has long since departed, there are many mementos of that once enterprising people still to be found. Her churches and fortifications are still standing, the blood of her people is still left—in most cases mixed—and her language, somewhat corrupted, is still spoken. There was no Englishman at Anjenga—the resident magistrate being a Portuguese. He sent his son off to visit us and make arrangements for landing our prisoners. Later in the afternoon, I sent a lieutenant to call on him. The boat being delayed until some time in the night, and a firing of musketry being heard, I feared that my lieutenant had gotten into some difficulty with 'the natives, and dispatched Kell with an armed boat to his assistance. It proved to be a false alarm. It was a feast day, the magistrate had gone to church—which caused the delay of the officer—and the firing was a *feu de joie*.

The next morning we sent the prisoners on shore. They were to proceed by inland navigation—parallel with the coast through a series of lagoons and canals—to Cochin, a seaport town about sixty miles distant, where they would find Englishmen and English shipping. I was to provision them, and the Resident Magistrate would send them forward free of expense. The prisoners landed in presence of half the town, who had flocked down to the beach to see the sight. As our boats approached the shore on which there was quite a surf breaking, a number of native boats came out to receive and land the prisoners. These boats were managed with great dexterity and passed in and out through the roaring surf without the least accident. This matter of business accomplished, the natives came off to visit us in considerable numbers, both men and women. They were a fine, well-formed, rather athletic people, nearly as black as the Negro, but with straight hair and prominent features. Very few of them wore any other dress than a cloth about the loins. They were sprightly and chatty and ran about the decks as pleased as children, inspecting the guns and other novelties. Some of the young women had very regular and pleasing features. The best description I can give of them is to request the reader to imagine some belle of his acquaintance to be divested of those garments which would be useless to her in Anjenga—latitude 8° —and instead of charming him with the lily and the rose, to be shining in lustrous jet.

Having received on board some fresh provisions for the crew and gotten rid of our lady and gentlemen visitors, we got under way and stood out to sea and were still in sight of the Ghaut Mountains when the sun went down. These mountains will be lost to our view tomorrow; but before they disappear, I have a word to say concerning them and the fertile country of Hindostan in which they are situated; for nature elaborates here one of her most beautiful and useful of meteorological problems. British India is the most formidable competitor of the Confederate States for the production of cotton for the supply of the spindles and looms of the world. The problem to which I wish to call the reader's attention may be stated thus: *The great deserts of Central Africa produce the cotton crop of Hindostan.* I have before had frequent occasion to speak of the monsoons of the East—those periodical winds that blow for one half of the year from one point of the compass, and then change and blow the other half of the year from the opposite point. It is these monsoons that work out the problem we have in hand; and it is the great deserts alluded to that produce the monsoons.

On the succeeding page will be found a diagram which will assist us in the conception of this beautiful operation of nature. It consists of an outline sketch of so much of Asia and the Indian Ocean as are material to our purpose. The great deserts, the Himalayas, and the Ghauts are marked on the sketch. Let the dotted line at the bottom of the sketch represent the equator and the arrows the direction of the winds. Hindostan being in the northern tropic, the northeast monsoon or trade wind, represented by the arrow A, would prevail there all the year round but for the local causes of which I am about to speak. This wind, coming from a high northern latitude, passes almost entirely over *land* before it reaches Hindostan. It is, therefore, a dry wind. It is rendered even more dry by its passage over the Himalaya range of mountains, which wring from it what little moisture it may have

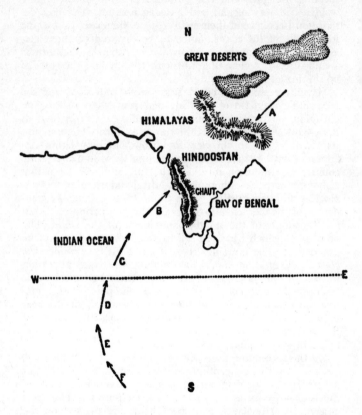

evaporated from the lakes and rivers over which it has passed. When it reaches the extensive plains between the Himalayas and Ghauts, which are the great cotton region of Hindostan, it has not a drop of water with which to nourish vegetation; and if it were to prevail all the year round, those plains would speedily become parched and waste deserts.

Let us see now how this catastrophe is avoided. When the sun is in the southern hemisphere, that is, during the winter season, the northeast monsoon prevails in Hindostan. When he is in the northern hemisphere, the southwest monsoon, which is the rainy monsoon, or crop monsoon, prevails. This change of monsoons is produced as follows: Soon after the sun crosses the equator into the northern hemisphere, he begins to pour down his fierce rays upon Hindostan, and passing farther and farther to the north in the latter part of April or the beginning of May, he is nearly perpendicularly over the great deserts marked in the sketch. These deserts are interminable wastes of sand in which there is not so much as a blade of grass to be found. They absorb heat very rapidly and in a short time become like so many fiery furnaces. The air above them rarefies and ascends, a comparative vacuum of great extent is formed, and a great change begins now to take place in the atmospheric phenomena. This vacuum being in the rear of the narrow A, or the northeast monsoon blowing over Hindostan, first slackens the force of this wind—drawing it back. It becomes weaker and weaker as the furnaces become hotter and hotter. Calms ensue, and after a long struggle the wind is finally turned back, and the southwest monsoon has set in.

If the reader will cast his eye on the series of arrows, B, C, D, E, and F, he will see how this gradual change is effected. I say gradual, for it is not effected *per saltum*, but occupies several weeks. The arrow F represents the southeast trade wind blowing toward the equator. As this wind nears the equator, it begins to feel the influence of the deserts spoken of. The calm which I have described as beginning at the arrow A is gradually extended to the equator. As the southeast wind approaches that great circle, it finds nothing to oppose its passage. Pretty soon it not only finds nothing to oppose its passage, but something to invite it over, for the calm begins now to give place to an indraft toward the great deserts. The southeast wind, thus encouraged, changes its course, first to the north and then to the northeast, and blows stronger and stronger as the season advances and the heat accumulates over the deserts; until at last the southeast trade wind of the southern hemisphere has become the southwest monsoon of the northern hemisphere! This monsoon prevails from about the 1st of May to the 1st of November, when the sun has again passed into the southern hemisphere and withdrawn his heat from the great deserts. The normal condition of things being thus restored, the vanquished northeast trade wind regains its courage, and chasing back the southwest monsoon, resumes its sway.

If the reader will again cast his eye upon the sketch, he will see that the southwest winds which are now blowing over Hindostan, instead of being dry winds must be heavily laden with moisture. They have had a clean sweep from the tropic of Capricorn with no land intervening between them and the coast of Hindostan. They have followed the sun in his course, and under the influence of his perpendicular rays have lapped up the waters like a thirsty wolf. The evaporation in these seas is enormous. It has been stated on the authority of the Secretary of the Geographical Society of Bombay that it has been found in the Bay of Bengal to exceed an inch daily. From having too little water during the winter months in Hindostan, we are now in the summer months in danger of having too much. The young cotton crop will be drowned out. What is to prevent it? Here we have another beautiful provision at hand. The reader has observed the Ghaut Mountains stretching along parallel with the west coast of Hindostan. These mountains protect the plains from inundation. They have, therefore, equally important functions to perform with the deserts. The southwest monsoon blows square across these mountains. As the heavily laden wind begins to ascend the first slopes, it commences to deposit its moisture. Incessant rains set in, and immense quantities of water fall before the winds have passed the mountains. The precipitation has been known to be as great as twelve or thirteen inches in a single day! The winds, thus deprived of their excess of water, are now in a proper condition to fertilize, without drowning the immense plains that lie between the Ghauts and the Himalayas—which is the cotton region of India. It is thus that the *great deserts of Central Asia produce the cotton crop of Hindostan.* To the ignorant Tartar who ventures across the margins of these deserts, all seems dreary, desolate, and deathlike, and he is at a loss to conceive for what purpose they were created. Clothe these deserts with verdure, and intersperse them with rivers and mountains, and forthwith the fertile plains of Hindostan would become a great desert, and its two hundred millions of inhabitants perish.

We captured on board the last prize a batch of Bombay newspapers—large dailies edited with ability and filled with news from all parts of the world. It is the press more than anything else that indicates the growth and prosperity of a country. One only needed to look at the long columns of these immense dailies filled with advertisements to realize the fact that Bombay was a beehive containing its three hundred thousand inhabitants. We were, indeed, in the midst of a great empire, of which, in the western world, we read, it is true, but of which we have no just conception until we visit it. The British Empire in India, stretching from the Persian Gulf to the Strait of Malacca, is a creation which does honor to our race and language. I had coasted nearly its whole extent, and everywhere I found evidences of contentment, thrift, and prosperity. A constant stream of British shipping was passing to and fro, developing its immense commerce and pouring its untold millions into the British exchequer. Powerful and swift steamships bring the home mails to three or four prominent points along the coast, as Aden, Ceylon, Singapore, Hong Kong, and from these points other steamers spread it broadcast over the empire. Railroads are pushed in every direction, there being as many as three thousand miles in operation, and the navigation of the coast districts of Hindostan has been carried by means of a series of lagoons and canals from Cape Comorin, hundreds of miles to the northward. These railroads and canals have opened up new fields of industry, and have been of especial service in developing that pet idea of England, the production of cotton.

Up to the breaking out of our war, the cultivation of this valuable staple in India was a mere experiment. It is now an assured success. Those great fields lying between the Ghauts and the Himalayas of which we have been speaking, are being brought into connection with the seaboard by lines of easy and cheap transportation. They have been found equal to our Southern plantations in the production of the article, and labor is a hundred per cent cheaper at least than with us. Here are all the elements of cheap production. Our Yankee brethren have talked a good deal of what they conquered in the war, and have been quarrelling ever since over the fruits of their victory. Here is one of their conquests which no one can doubt—the transfer of the cotton supply of the world from these Southern States to British India. The time is not far distant when Yankee spindles and looms will be spinning and weaving India cotton for the supply of their own people.

The moral conquest of India by the British people is even more remarkable and more admirable than its physical conquest. Since their last Indian war, the whole country, from one end of it to the other, has settled down in the most profound peace. Nor is this the peace of despotism, for in comparison with the extent of territory and the two hundred millions of people to be governed, the number of troops is ridiculously small. The conquest is one of arts and civilization, and not of arms. The railroads, the canal, the ship, the printing press, and above all, a paternal and beneficent government, have worked out the wonderful problem of the submission of teeming millions to the few. It is the conquest of race and of intellect. The docile Hindoo, not devoid of letters himself, has realized the fact that a superior people has come to settle in his country to still domestic broils, strip former despots of their ill-gotten and much-abused power, and to rule him with humanity and justice. The torch of civilization has shone in dark places, dispelled many prejudices, and brought to light and broken up many hideous practices. Schools and colleges have sprung up everywhere, and the natural taste of the native population for letters has been cultivated. In the very newspapers which we are reviewing are to be found long dissertations and criticisms by Hindoo scholars on various matters of morals, science, and literature.

A government whose foundations are thus laid will be durable. In Australia, New Zealand, and other colonies, where the white population in the course of a few years will greatly preponderate over the native, mere adolescence will bring about independence. But India will never become adolescent in this sense. She will remain indefinitely a prosperous ward in chancery—the guardian and the ward living amicably together, and each sharing the prosperity of the other.

On the day after leaving the Malabar coast, we spoke a Portuguese bark from Rio Janeiro bound to Goa, a short distance to the northward of us. This was the only Portuguese we met in these seas, of which they were, at one period of their history entire masters. Vasco de Gama had made the seas classic by his adventures, and his countrymen following in his track had studded the coast with towns, of which Goa was one of the most ancient and important. As between the Hindoo and the Portuguese, the latter would probably long have maintained his ascendency, but there came along that superior race

—that white race which has never submitted to any admixture of its blood—of which we have just been speaking, and nature, with her unvarying laws, had done the rest. the Portuguese gave place to the Englishman as naturally as the African, and afterward the Hindoo, had given place to the Portuguese.

Passing through the chain of islands which extends parallel with the Malabar coast for some distance, we stretched across the Arabian Sea in the direction of the east coast of Africa. We were now in the height of the season of the northeast monsoon, which was a fair wind for us, and the weather was as delightful as I have ever experienced it in any part of the globe—not even excepting our own Gulf of Mexico and coasts of Alabama and Florida in the summer season. For twelve successive days we did not have occasion to lower a studding sail day or night! We had a constant series of clear skies and gentle breezes. The nights were serene and transparent, and the sunsets were magnificent beyond description. The trade wind is *par excellence* the wind of beautiful sunsets. Bright, gauzy clouds float along lazily before it, and sometimes the most charming cumuli are piled up on the western horizon while the sun is going down. Stately cathedrals with their domes and spires complete may be traced by the eye of fancy, and the most gorgeous of golden, violet, orange, purple, green, and other hues light up now a colonnade, now a dome, and now a spire of the aërial edifice. And then came on the twilight with its gray and purple blended, and with the twilight the sounds of merriment on board the *Alabama*—for we had found a successor for Michael Mahoney, the Irish fiddler, and the usual evening dances were being held. We had been now some time at sea since leaving Singapore; the jail had been delivered, the proper punishments administered, and Jack, having forgotten both his offences and their punishment, had again become a good boy and was as full of fun as ever.

We had some fine fishing while passing through the Arabian Sea. The dolphin came around us in schools, and a number of them were struck with the grains and caught with lines —the bait being a piece of red flannel rag. And some of the seamen resorted to an ingenious device for entrapping the flying fish by night. A net being spread with outriggers, under the bow of the ship, and a light being held just above it, the fish, as they would rise in coveys—being flushed from time to time by the noise of the ship through the water—would rush at the light, and striking against the bow of the ship, tumble into the net beneath. Bartelli on several mornings spread my breakfast table with them.

On the 29th of January, we observed in latitude 2° 43' north and longitude 51° east; and on the following evening passed through a remarkable patch of the sea. At about eight P. M., there being no moon, but the sky being clear and the stars shining brightly, we suddenly passed from the deep blue water in which we had been sailing into a patch of water so white that it startled me, so much did it appear like a shoal. To look over the ship's side, one would have sworn that she was in no more than five or six fathoms of water. The officer of the deck became evidently alarmed and reported the fact to me, though I myself had observed it. There was no shoal laid down within several hundred miles of our position on the chart, and yet here was so manifestly one that I shortened sail—we were running seven or eight knots at the time, with a fresh breeze—hove the ship to and got a cast of the deep-sea lead. The line ran out and out, until a hundred fathoms had been taken by the lead, and still we found no bottom. We now checked the line, and hauling in the lead, made sail again. My fears thus quieted, I observed the phenomenon more at leisure. The patch was extensive. We were several hours in running through it. Around the horizon there was a subdued glare or flush, as though there were a distant illumination going on, whilst overhead there was a lurid, dark sky in which the stars paled. The whole face of nature seemed changed, and with but little stretch of the imagination, the *Alabama* might have been conceived to be a phantom ship lighted up by the sickly and unearthly glare of a phantom sea and gliding on under the pale stars one knew not whither.

Upon drawing a bucket of this water, it appeared to be full of minute luminous particles; the particles being instinct with life and darting and playing about in every direction; but upon a deck lantern being brought and held over the bucket, the little animals would all disappear and nothing but a bucket full of *grayish* water would be left. Here was an area of twenty miles square in which Nature, who delights in life, was holding one of her starlight revels with her myriads upon myriads of living creatures, each rejoicing in the life given it by its Creator and dying almost as soon as born. The sun would rise on the morrow over a sea as blue as usual with only some motes in the pellucid waters glinting back his rays; and this twenty miles square of life would be no longer distinguishable from the surrounding waters.

We crossed the equator on the 30th of January. The winds had now become light, and frequent calms ensued, though the bright weather continued. On the 9th of February we made the Comoro Islands that lie not a great way from the coast of Africa, and getting up steam, ran in and anchored at Johanna. This island is the most frequented of the group; ships bound to and from the East Indies by the way of the Mozambique Channel, frequently stopping here for refreshments. All these islands are volcanic in origin. They are of small extent, rise abruptly out of the sea with deep water around them and are mountainous. They are not claimed by any European nation; nor do any of the chiefs on the neighboring coast of Africa attempt to exercise jurisdiction over them. They are inhabited by a mixed race of Arabs, Africans, and East Indians, and each has its separate government, which is always a government of force, and is frequently overthrown by revolutions. Johanna, at the time we visited it, was under the rule of an Arab who styled himself the Sultan Abdallah. From the circumstance that English ships frequently stop here, most of the inhabitants who live on the seacoast speak a little English, and we were surprised when we anchored to find ourselves quite well known. The name of our ship was familiar to the dusky inhabitants and they were evidently much delighted at our arrival. The Sultan did not come on board —he was busy, he said, putting up a sugar mill—but he sent his Minister of Foreign Affairs and Commander-in-Chief of his army to see me; and with these, Galt, my paymaster, had no difficulty in contracting for the regular supply of bullocks and vegetables to be sent off to us during our stay.

I had come in solely for the purpose of refreshing my crew, and for this purpose we remained a week. During this time we became quite friendly with the Johannese—receiving frequent visits from them and visiting them at their houses in return. We were quite surprised at the intelligence and civilization which characterized them. They nearly all read and write, and the better classes set up some pretensions to literature. They are Mohammedans in faith, and I found some of their priests who were fond of visiting me, sprightly, well informed,

and liberal men, acknowledging both Moses and Christ to
have been prophets, and entertaining a respect for the Christian religion, doubtless the result of their intercourse with the
English.

I visited the houses of some of my friends with the hope of
getting a glimpse at their domestic life, but was disappointed.
They received me with all cordiality and respect, but the
females of their families were carefully kept out of sight. A
female slave would fan me and hand me my coffee and sher-
bet, but that was all. Their slavery appeared to be of a miti-
gated form, the slaves being on easy and even familiar terms
with their masters. The houris who fanned me could have
been bought for twenty dollars each. The price of a slave
fresh from the coast is not more than half that sum.

I gave my sailors a run on shore, but this sort of liberty
was awful hard work for Jack. There was no such thing
as a glass of grog to be found in the whole town, and as for a
fiddle, and Sal for a partner—all of which would have been a
matter of course in *civilized* countries—there were no such
luxuries to be thought of. They found it a difficult matter to
get through with the day and were all down at the beach long
before sunset—the hour appointed for their coming off—
waiting for the approach of the welcome boat. I told Kell to
let them go on shore as often as they pleased, but no one made
a second application.

On the 15th of February, having received on board a supply of half a dozen live bullocks and some fruits and vegetables, we got under way and again turned our head to the southwest. The winds were light, but we were much assisted by
the currents, for we were now approaching the Mozambique
Channel, and the southwest current of which I spoke when
we left the Cape of Good Hope for our run before the brave
west winds to the eastward was hurrying us forward, sometimes at the rate of forty or fifty miles a day. As we progressed, the wind freshened, and by the time we had entered
the narrowest part of the channel between Madagascar and the
African coast, which lies in about 15° south latitude, we lost
the fine weather and clear skies, which we had brought all the
way across the Arabian Sea. We now took several gales of
wind. Rain squalls were of frequent occurrence. As we approached the southwest end of Madagascar, which lies just
without the Tropic of Capricorn, we encountered one of the

most sublime storms of thunder and lightning I ever witnessed. It occurred at night. Black rain clouds mustered from every quarter of the compass, and the heavens were soon so densely and darkly overcast that it was impossible to see across the ship's deck. Sometimes the most terrific squalls of wind accompany these storms, and we furled most of the sails and awaited in silence the *denouement*. The thunder rolled and crashed as if the skies were falling in pieces; and the lightning—sheet lightning, streaked lightning, forked lightning—kept the firmament almost constantly ablaze. And the rain! I thought I had seen it rain before, but for an hour Madagascar beat the Ghaut Mountains. It came down almost literally by the bucketfull. Almost a continual stream of lightning ran down our conductors and hissed as it leaped into the sea. There was not much wind, but all the other meteorological elements were there in perfection. Madagascar is perhaps above all other countries the bantling and the plaything of the storm, and thunder and lightning. Its plains, heated to nearly furnace heat by a tropical sun, its ranges of lofty mountains, the currents that sweep along its coasts, and its proximity to equatorial Africa, all point it out as being in a region fertile of meteorological phenomena. Cyclones of small diameter are of frequent occurrence in the Mozambique Channel. They travel usually from southeast to northwest, or straight across the channel. We took one of these short gales, which lasted us the greater part of a day.

Leaving the channel and pursuing our way toward the Cape of Good Hope, we sounded on the Agulhas Bank on the 7th of March—our latitude being 35° 10′ and longitude 24° 08′. This bank is sometimes the scene of terrible conflicts of the elements in the winter season. Stout ships are literally swamped here by the huge, wall-like seas; and the frames of others so much shaken and loosened in every knee and joint as to render them unseaworthy. The cause of these terrible, short, racking seas, is the meeting of the winds and currents. Whilst the awful, wintry gale is howling from the west and northwest, the Mozambique or Agulhas Current, as it is now called, is setting in its teeth sometimes at the rate of two or three knots. A struggle ensues between the billows lashed into fury by the winds and the angry current which is opposing them. The ground swell contributes to the turmoil of the elements, and the stoutest mariner sometimes stands appalled at the

spectacle of seas with nearly perpendicular walls battering
his ship like so many battering rams, and threatening her
with instant destruction. Hence the name of the stormy cape,
applied to the Cape of Good Hope.

Arriving on our old cruising ground off the pitch of the
Cape, we held ourselves here a few days, overhauling the various ships that passed. But American commerce, which had
fled this beaten track before we left for the East Indies, had
not returned to it. The few ships of the enemy that passed
still gave the Cape a wide berth and winged their flight homeward over the byways, instead of the highways of the ocean.
We found the coast clear again of the enemy's cruisers. That
huge old coal box, the *Vanderbilt*, having thought it useless
to pursue us farther, had turned back and was now probably
doing a more profitable business by picking up blockade-
runners on the American coast. This operation paid—the
captain might grow rich upon it. Chasing the *Alabama* did
not. Finding that it was useless for us to cruise longer off the
Cape; we ran into Cape Town and came to anchor at half-past
four on the afternoon of the 20th of March. We had gone to
sea from Simon's Town on our way to the East Indies on the
24th of the preceding September; our cruise had thus lasted
within a day or two of six months.

Chapter Twenty-Three—*1864*

The Alabama again in Cape Town . . . The seizure of the Tuscaloosa . . . Final action of the Home Government and release of the Tuscaloosa

After our long absence·in the East Indies we felt like returning home when we ran into Table Bay. Familiar faces greeted us, and the same welcome was extended to us as upon our first visit. An unpleasant surprise awaited me, however, in the course the British Government had recently pursued in regard to my tender, the *Tuscaloosa*. The reader will recollect that I had dispatched this vessel from Angra Pequeña back to the coast of Brazil to make a cruise on that coast. Having made her cruise, she returned to Simon's Town in the latter part of December in want of repairs and supplies. Much to the astonishment of her commander, she was seized a few days afterward by Admiral Sir Baldwin Walker under orders from the Home Government. Since I had left the Cape, a correspondence had ensued between the Governor, Sir Philip Wodehouse, and the Secretary for the Colonies, the Duke of Newcastle; the latter disapproving of the conduct of the former in the matter of the reception of the *Tuscaloosa*. It was insisted by the Duke that inasmuch as the *Tuscaloosa* was an uncondemned prize she was not entitled to be regarded as a

357

ship of war; but that on the contrary, having been brought into British waters in violation of the Queen's orders of neutrality, she should have been detained and handed over to her original owners. Under these instructions the *Tuscaloosa* was seized upon her return to the Cape. . . .

Governor Wodehouse was from the first very clearly of the opinion that the *Tuscaloosa* was entitled to be considered and treated as a ship of war, and in his correspondence with the Duke of Newcastle, he maintained this opinion with great force and clearness. He was, besides, fortified by the opinion of the Attorney General of the Colony.

The seizure of the *Tuscaloosa* made some stir among the politicians in England. The subject was brought to the notice of the House of Commons and information asked for. The Cabinet took it up and were obliged to reverse the decision of the Duke of Newcastle. On the 4th of March, 1864, the Duke wrote to Governor Wodehouse as follows: "I have received your despatches of the 11th and 19th of January, reporting the circumstances connected with the seizure of the Confederate prize-vessel *Tuscaloosa* under the joint authority of the naval commander-in-chief and yourself. I have to instruct you to restore the *Tuscaloosa* to the lieutenant of the Confederate States who lately commanded her, or if he should have left the Cape, then to retain her until she can be handed over to some person who may have authority from Captain Semmes of the *Alabama*, or from the Government of the Confederate States, to receive her."

The London *Times* of the 8th of March, 1864, in reporting the proceedings of the House of Commons for the preceding day, contained the following paragraph:

The *Tuscaloosa*.   Mr. Peacocke asked on what grounds the *Tuscaloosa* had been seized at the Cape of Good Hope. Lord Palmerston said that it was in conformity with the instructions received that the authorities at the Cape of Good Hope had seized this vessel, but on representations that had been made to the Government and on full consideration of the case, it had been determined that there had been no proper ground for the seizure of the vessel, and its release had been ordered.

The order to restore the *Tuscaloosa* did not reach the Cape until after both Lieutenant Low and myself had left, and the war drew so speedily to a close that possession of her was never resumed. At the close of the war, she fell, along with other Confederate property, into the hands of the Federals. Besides embalming the beautiful name *Tuscaloosa* in history, this prize-ship settled the law point I had been so long contesting with Mr. Seward and Mr. Adams, to wit: that "one nation cannot inquire into the antecedents of the ships of war of another nation;" and consequently that when the *Alabama* escaped from British waters and was commissioned, neither the United States nor Great Britain could object to her *status* as a ship of war.

Chapter Twenty-Four—*1864*

*The Alabama at the Cape of Good Hope . . . Leaves
on her return to Europe . . . Capture of the Rockingham and of the Tycoon . . . Crosses the equator into
the Northern Hemisphere and arrives and anchors at
Cherbourg on the 11th of June, 1864 . . . The combat
between the Alabama and the Kearsarge*

We entered Table Bay on the 20th of March, and on the
next day we had the usual equinoctial gale. The wind was
from the southeast and blew very heavily for twenty-four
hours. We let go a second anchor and veered to ninety fathoms on the riding-chain. The usual phenomena accompanied
this southeast gale, viz., a clear sky and a high barometer.
The Devil kept his tablecloth spread on the top of the
mountain during the whole of the gale, and it was wonderful
to watch the unvarying size and shape of this fleecy cloud,
every particle of which was being changed from moment to
moment. Some boats visited us, notwithstanding the gale, and
brought us off some of the delightful grapes and figs of the
Cape. We were in the midst of the fruit season. Our old
friend, Mr. William Anderson, of the firm of Anderson, Saxon
& Co., who had acted as our agent on the occasion of our

former visit so much to our satisfaction, also came off to arrange for further supplies. There was no occasion any longer for him to draw upon our public chest, the proceeds of the merchandise shipped by him to Europe on our account being sufficient to pay all bills.

The gale having moderated the next day, lighters came alongside, and we began coaling and receiving such supplies of provisions as we needed. Visitors again thronged on board, and the energies and address of Bartelli were freshly taxed. For a phlegmatic, impassible people, the English are, perhaps, the greatest sightseekers in the world; and the Cape of Good Hope, being a relay station on the principal highway of travel, is always filled with newcomers. Military and naval officers, governors, judges, superintendents of boards of trade, attorney generals, all on their way to their missions in the Far East, came to see the *Alabama*. Though we were sometimes incommoded by the crowd in the midst of our coaling and provisioning ship, scraping masts and tarring down rigging, we received everybody politely and answered patiently their curious questions. When we were here last we had had occasion to notice an American bark called the *Urania*, a trader between Boston and the Cape, which took every opportunity to display a very large and very bright "old flag" during our stay. The *Urania* had made a voyage to Boston and back during our absence, and now came in tricked out so finely in her "bran-new" English flag that we hardly knew her!

In three days we were ready for sea. On the morning of the 25th, we got up steam and moved out of Table Bay for the last time, amidst lusty cheers and the waving of handkerchiefs from the fleet of boats by which we were surrounded. As we were going out, it so happened that a Yankee steamer was coming in. The *Quang Tung*, a fast steamer recently built for the China trade and now on her way to the Flowery Land, not dreaming that the *Alabama* was at the Cape, had made Table Mountain that morning and now come steaming into the harbor. Both ships being within the marine league, we could not touch her, which was a sore trial, for the *Quang Tung* was a beauty and passed so close under our guns that the Confederate and United States flags nearly touched each other, the crews of the two ships looking on in silence. Half an hour more, and the capture of the *Sea Bride* would have been repeated to the gratification of our many friends at the Cape.

Reaching the offing, we permitted our fires to go down and put the ship, as usual, under sail. My intention now was to make the best of my way to England or France for the purpose of docking and thoroughly overhauling and repairing my ship in accordance with my previously expressed design.

I had been so much occupied with business and visitors at the Cape that I had not even had time to read the newspapers. But my friends had brought me off a bountiful supply for sea, and I now had a little leisure to look at them. The news was not encouraging. Our people were being harder and harder pressed by the enemy, and post after post within our territory was being occupied by him. The signs of weakness on our part, which I mentioned as becoming for the first time painfully apparent after the battle of Gettysburg and the surrender of Vicksburg, were multiplying. The blockade of the coast, by reason of the constantly increasing fleets of the enemy, was becoming more and more stringent. Our finances were rapidly deteriorating, and a general demoralization, in consequence, seemed to be spreading among our people. From the whole review of the situation, I was very apprehensive that the cruises of the *Alabama* were drawing to a close. As for ourselves, we were doing the best we could with our limited means, to harass and cripple the enemy's commerce, that important sinew of war; but the enemy seemed resolved to let his commerce go rather than forego his purpose of subjugating us; rendering it up a willing sacrifice on the profane altar of his fanaticism and the devilish passions which had been engendered by the war. Probably, if the alternative had been presented to him in the beginning of the war, "Will you lose your commerce or permit the Southern States to go free?" he would have chosen the latter. But he seemed in the earlier stages of the war to have had no thought of losing his commerce; and when it became apparent that this misfortune would befall him, he was too deeply engaged in the contest to heed it.

Among the speeches that met my eye in the English papers, was another from my friend, Mr. Milner Gibson, President of the Board of Trade—him of the "ham and eggs," whom I quoted some chapters back. Mr. Gibson had risen above ham and eggs this time and was talking about English and American shipping. As President of the Board of Trade he was good authority, and I was glad to learn from him the extent to which, in conjunction with other Confederate cruisers, I had damaged the enemy's commerce. His speech was delivered at Ashton-under-Lyne, on the 20th of January, 1864, and among other things he said:

The number of British ships entering in and clearing out with cargoes in the United Kingdom has increased in the present year to an amount of something like fourteen million of tons and upward, against seven million tons of foreign shipping; thus showing that with a great increase altogether, British shipping has kept gradually in advance of foreign shipping in the trade with the United Kingdom. But it would not be fair to take credit for this improvement in shipping as due to any policy in this country. I am afraid that some of it is due to the transference of the carrying trade from American ships to British ships. And why this transference from American ships to British ships? No doubt, partially in consequence of the war that prevails in America, there may not be the same power in manning and fitting out merchant vessels. But I am afraid there is something more than that. There is the fear among the American merchant shipping of attacks by certain armed vessels that are careering over the ocean and that are burning and destroying all United States merchant ships that they find upon the high seas. The fear, therefore, of destruction of these cruisers has caused a large transfer of American carrying to British ships. Now the decrease in the employment of American shipping is very great in the trade between England and the United States. It is something like 46 or 47 per cent. I mention these facts to show you that it is right that the attention of this great commercial nation should be seriously turned to those laws which govern the action of belligerents upon the high seas—(hear! hear!)—for if some two or three armed steamers, which a country with no pretension to a navy can easily send upon the ocean armed with one or two guns, can almost clear the seas of the merchant shipping of a particular nation, what might happen to this country with her extensive commerce over the seas if she went to war with some nation that availed herself of the use of similar descriptions of vessels. (Hear! hear!)

Though the subject was done up in a new form, it was still "ham and eggs"—British interests—as the reader sees. Mr. Milner Gibson was not overstating the damage we had done the enemy. He was unfriendly to us and therefore inclined to

understate it. According to his statistics, we had destroyed, or
driven for protection under the English flag, in round numbers, one half of the enemy's ships engaged in the English
trade. We did even greater damage to the enemy's trade with
other powers. We broke up almost entirely his trade with
Brazil and the other South American States, greatly crippled
his Pacific trade, and as for his East India trade, it is only
necessary to refer the reader to the spectacle presented at
Singapore to show him what had become of that.

I threw my ship, now, into the fairway leading from the
Cape of Good Hope to the equatorial crossing east of our old
trysting place, Fernando de Noronha; shortening sail from
time to time and seesawing across the highway to give any
Yankee ships that might be traveling it the opportunity to
come up with me. I held myself in check a day or two in the
vicinity of St. Helena, experiencing all the vicissitudes of
weather so feelingly complained of by the Great Captive on
that barren rock. Leaving St. Helena, we jogged along leisurely
under topsails, the stream of commerce flowing past us, but
there being no Yankee ships in the stream.

> Howl, ye ships of Tarshish,
> For your strength is laid waste.

On the 22d of April, having reached the track of the
homeward-bound Pacific ships of the enemy, we descried an
unlucky Yankee to whom we immediately gave chase. The
chase continued the whole night, the moon shining brightly,
the breeze being gentle, and the sea smooth. The Yankee
worked like a good fellow to get away, piling clouds of canvas
upon his ship, and handling her with the usual skill, but it
was of no use. When the day dawned we were within a couple
of miles of him. It was the old spectacle of the panting,
breathless fawn, and the inexorable stag-hound. A gun brought
his colors to the peak and his main-yard to the mast. The prize
proved to be the ship *Rockingham* from Callao, bound to
Cork for orders. Her cargo consisted of guano from the
Chincha Islands, and there was an attempt to protect it. It
was shipped by the Guano Consignment Company of Great
Britain. Among the papers was a certificate of which the
following is the purport: One Joseph A. Danino who signs
for Danino & Moscosa certifies that the guano belongs to the

Peruvian Government; and Her Britannic Majesty's Consul at Lima certifies that the said Joseph A. Danino appeared before him and "voluntarily declared that the foregoing signature is of his own handwriting, and also that the cargo above mentioned is truly and verily the property of the Peruvian Government." This was about equal to some of the Yankee attempts, that have been noticed, to cover cargoes. With the most perfect unconcern for the laws of nations, no one swore to anything. Mr. Danino certified, and the Consul certified that Mr. Danino had certified. *Voila tout!* We transferred to the Alabama such stores and provisions as we could make room for, and the weather being fine, we made a target of the prize, firing some shot and shell into her with good effect;* and at five P. M. we burned her and filled away on our course.

A few days afterward—on the 27th of April—being in latitude 11° 16′ S. and longitude 32° 07′ W., the weather being fine, and the wind light from the southeast, we descried, at three P. M., a large ship standing directly for us. Neither ship changed tack or sheet until we were within speaking distance. Nor had we shown the stranger any colors. We now hailed and ordered him to heave to whilst we should send aboard of him, hoisting our colors at the same time. We had previously seen the Yankee colors in the hands of one of his seamen, ready to be hoisted. The whole thing was done so quietly that one would have thought it was two friends meeting. The prize proved to be the *Tycoon* from New York for San Francisco. She had the usual valuable and assorted cargo. There was no claim of neutral property among the papers. The ship being only thirty-six days from New York, we received from her a batch of late newspapers; and a portion of her cargo consisting of clothing, the paymaster was enabled to replenish his storerooms with every variety of wearing apparel. We applied the torch to her soon after nightfall.

On the 2d of May we recrossed the equator into the northern hemisphere, took the northeast trade wind after the usual interval of calm and the usual amount of thunder, lightning, and rain, and with it ran up to our old toll gate at the crossing of the 30th parallel, where we had halted on our outward

* Although Semmes does not say so here, it was noticed that the *Alabama's* gunpowder had deteriorated from long storage, and some of the shells did not explode. ED.

passage and viséd the passports of so many travelers. The poor old *Alabama* was not now what she had been then. She was like the wearied foxhound, limping back after a long chase, footsore, and longing for quiet and repose. Her commander, like herself, was well-nigh worn down. Vigils by night and by day, the storm and the drenching rain, the frequent and rapid change of climate, now freezing, now melting or broiling, and the constant excitement of the chase and capture, had laid, in the three years of war he had been afloat, a load of a dozen years on his shoulders. The shadows of a sorrowful future, too, began to rest upon his spirit. The last batch of newspapers captured were full of disasters. Might it not be that after all our trials and sacrifices the cause for which we were struggling would be lost? Might not our federal system of government be destroyed, and state independence become a phrase of the past; the glorious fabric of our American liberty sinking, as so many others had done before it under a new invasion of Brennuses and Attilas? The thought was hard to bear.

We passed through our old cruising ground, the Azores, sighting several of the islands which called up reminiscences of the christening of our ship and of the sturdy blows she had struck at the enemy's whaling fleet in the first days of her career. Thence we stretched over to the coasts of Spain and Portugal and thence to the British Channel, making the Lizard on the 10th of June and being fortunate enough to get a channel pilot on board, just as night was setting in with a thick southwester brewing. By eleven P. M. we were up with the Start light, and at ten the next morning we made Cape La Hague on the coast of France. We were now boarded by a French pilot, and at thirty minutes past noon we let go our anchor in the port of Cherbourg.

This was to be the *Alabama*'s last port. She had run her career, her record had been made up, and in a few days more she would lay her bones beneath the waters of the British Channel and be a thing of the past. I had brought back with me all my officers except the paymaster, whom I had discharged at the island of Jamaica . . . and the young engineer who had been accidentally killed at Saldanha Bay. Many changes had taken place, of course, among my crew, as is always the case with sailors, but still a large proportion of my old men had come back with me. These were faithful and true and took more than an ordinary interest in their ship and their flag. There were harmony and mutual confidence between officers and men. Our discipline had been rigid, but mercy had always tempered justice, and the sailors understood and appreciated this. I had been successful with the health of my men beyond precedent. In my two ships, the *Sumter* and *Alabama*, I had had, first and last, say five hundred men under my command. The ships were small and crowded. As many as two thousand prisoners were confined for longer or shorter periods on board the two ships; and yet out of the total of twenty-five hundred men, *I had not lost a single man by disease*. I had skilful and attentive surgeons, I gave them *carte blanche* with regard to medicines and diet, and my first lieutenant understood it to be an important part of his duty to husband the strength of his men. The means which were resorted to by all these officers for preserving the health of the crew have been detailed. The reader has seen not only how their clothing was changed as we changed our latitude but how it was changed every evening when we were in warm climates. He has seen how sedulously we guarded against intemperance, at the same time that we gave the sailor his regular allowance of grog. And last, though by no means least, he has seen how we endeavored to promote a cheerful and hilarious spirit among them, being present at and encouraging them in their diversions.

Immediately upon anchoring, I sent an officer to call on the Port Admiral and ask leave to land my prisoners from the two last ships captured. This was readily granted, and the next day I went on shore to see him myself in relation to docking and repairing my ship. My arrival had, of course, been telegraphed to Paris, and indeed, by this time, had been spread all over Europe. The Admiral regretted that I had not gone into Havre or some other commercial port, where I would have found private docks. Cherbourg being exclusively a naval station, the docks all belonged to the Government, and the Government would have preferred not to dock and repair a belligerent ship. No positive objection was made, however, and the matter was laid over until the Emperor could be communicated with. The Emperor was then at Biarritz, a small watering place on the south coast, and would not be back in Paris for several days. It was my intention, if I had been admitted promptly into dock, to give my crew a leave of absence for a couple of months. They would have been discharged and dispersed in the first twenty-four hours after my arrival but for this temporary absence of the Emperor. The combat, therefore, which ensued, may be said to be due to the Emperor's accidental absence from Paris.

When the *Alabama* arrived in Cherbourg, the enemy's steamer *Kearsarge* was lying at Flushing. On the 14th of June, or three days after our arrival, she steamed into the harbor of Cherbourg, sent a boat on shore to communicate with the authorities, and, without anchoring, steamed out again, and took her station off the breakwater. We had heard a day or two before of the expected arrival of this ship, and it was generally understood among my crew that I intended to engage her. Her appearance, therefore, produced no little excitement on board. The object which the *Kearsarge* had in view in communicating with the authorities, was to request that the prisoners I had sent on shore might be delivered up to her. To this I objected on the ground that it would augment her crew, which she had no right to do in neutral waters and especially in the face of her enemy. Captain Winslow's request was refused, and the prisoners were not permitted to go on board of him. I now addressed a note to Mr. Bonfils, our agent, requesting him to inform Captain Winslow through the United States Consul that if he would wait until I could receive some coal on board—my supply having been nearly exhausted by my late cruising—I would come out and give him battle. This message was duly conveyed, and the defiance was understood to have been accepted.

We commenced coaling ship immediately, and making other preparations for battle, as sending down all useless yards and top hamper, examining the gun equipments, and overhauling the magazine and shell rooms. My crew seemed not only willing but anxious for the combat, and I had every confidence in their steadiness and drill, but they labored under one serious disadvantage. They had had but very limited opportunities of actual practice at target firing with shot and shell. The reason is obvious. I had no means of replenishing either shot or shell, and was obliged, therefore, to husband the store I had on hand for actual conflict. The stories that ran the round of the Federal papers at the time that my crew was composed mainly of trained gunners from the British practice-ship *Excellent* were entirely without foundation. I had on board some half dozen British seamen who had served in ships of war in former years, but they were in no respect superior to the rest of the crew. As for the two ships, though the enemy was superior to me both in size, stanchness of construction, and armament, they were of force so nearly equal that I cannot be charged with rashness in having offered battle. The *Kearsarge* mounted seven guns: two eleven-inch Dahlgrens, four 32-pounders, and a rifled 28-pounder. The *Alabama* mounted eight: one eight-inch, one rifled 100-pounder, and six 32-pounders. Though the *Alabama* carried one gun more than her antagonist, it is seen that the battery of the latter enabled her to throw more metal at a broadside—there being a difference of three inches in the bore of the shell-guns of the two ships.

Still the disparity was not so great but that I might hope to beat my enemy in a fair fight. But he did not show me a fair fight, for, as it afterward turned out, his ship was ironclad. It was the same thing as if two men were to go out to fight a duel, and one of them, unknown to the other, were to put a shirt of mail under his outer garment. The days of chivalry being past, perhaps it would be unfair to charge Captain Winslow with deceit in withholding from me the fact that he meant to wear armor in the fight. He may have reasoned that it was my duty to find it out for myself. Besides, if he had disclosed this fact to me and so prevented the engagement, the Federal Secretary of the Navy would have cut his head off to a certainty. A man who could permit a ship of war which had surrendered to be run off with by her crew *after they had been paroled*—see the case of the *Mercedita* described in a former chapter—and who could contrive, or connive at the sinking of the *Florida* to prevent the making of a reparation of honor to Brazil would not be likely to be very complacent toward an officer who showed any signs of *weakness* on the score of *honor* or *honesty*. Judging from the tone of the Yankee press, too, when it came afterward to describe the engagement, Winslow seemed to have gauged his countrymen correctly when he came to the conclusion that it would not do to reveal his secret to me. So far from having any condemnation to offer, the press, that chivalrous exponent of the opinions of a chivalrous people, was rather pleased at the Yankee trick. It was characteristic, "cute," "smart."

Appleton's *Encyclopedia of the War*, much more liberal and

fair than some of its congeners, thus speaks of Winslow's device: "Availing himself of an ingenious expedient for the protection of his machinery first adopted by Admiral Farragut in running past the rebel forts on the Mississippi in 1862, Captain Winslow had hung all his spare anchor cable over the midship section of the *Kearsarge* on either side; and in order to make the addition less unsightly, the chains were boxed over with inch deal boards, forming a sort of case which stood out at right-angles to the side of the vessel." One sees a twinge of honesty in this paragraph. The boxing stood out at right-angles to the side of the ship, and therefore the *Alabama* ought to have seen it. But unfortunately for the *Alabama*, the right-angles were not there. The forward and after ends of the "boxing," went off at so fine a point in accordance with the lines of the ship that the telescope failed to detect the cheat. Besides, when a ship is preparing for a fight, she does not care much about show. It is a fight, and not a review that she has on hand. Hence, we have another twinge, when the paragraphist remarks that the boxing was resorted to, to make the armor appear "*less unsightly!*" And, then, what about the necessity for protecting the machinery at all? The machinery of all the enemy's new sloops was below the waterline. Was the *Kearsarge* an exception? The plain fact is, without any varnish, the *Kearsarge*, though as effectually protected as if she had been armored with the best of iron plates, was to all appearance a wooden ship of war. But, to admit this would spoil the *éclat* of the victory and hence the effort to explain away the cheat, as far as possible.

In the way of crew, the *Kearsarge* had 162, all told—the *Alabama*, 149. I had communicated my intention to fight this battle to Flag-Officer Barron, my senior officer in Paris, a few days before, and that officer had generously left the matter to my own discretion. I completed my preparations on Saturday evening, the 18th of June, and notified the Port Admiral of my intention to go out on the following morning. The next day dawned beautiful and bright. The cloudy, murky weather of some days past had cleared off, and a bright sun, a gentle breeze, and a smooth sea were to be the concomitants of the battle. Whilst I was still in my cot, the Admiral sent an officer off to say to me that the ironclad frigate *Couronne* would accompany me a part of the way out to see that the neutrality of French waters was not violated. My crew had turned in

Officers on the deck of *The U.S. Kearsarge*

An unexploded shell from *The Alabama* lodged in the stern post of *The Kearsarge*

The forward pivot gun on *The Kearsarge*

early and gotten a good night's rest, and I permitted them to get their breakfasts comfortably—not turning them to until nine o'clock—before any movement was made toward getting under way beyond lighting the fires in the furnaces. I ought to mention that Midshipman Sinclair, the son of Captain Terry Sinclair of the Confederate Navy, whom I had sent with Low as his first lieutenant in the *Tuscaloosa*, being in Paris when we arrived, had come down on the eve of the engagement—accompanied by his father—and endeavored to rejoin me but was prevented by the French authorities. It is opportune also to state that in view of possible contingencies, I had directed Galt, my acting paymaster, to send on shore for safekeeping the funds of the ship and complete payrolls of the crew, showing the state of the account of each officer and man.

The day being Sunday and the weather fine, a large concourse of people—many having come all the way from Paris—collected on the heights above the town, in the upper stories of such of the houses as commanded a view of the sea, and on the walls and fortifications of the harbor. Several French luggers employed as pilot boats went out, and also an English steam yacht called the *Deerhound*. Everything being in readiness between nine and ten o'clock, we got under way and proceeded to sea through the western entrance of the harbor; the *Couronne* following us. As we emerged from behind the mole, we discovered the *Kearsarge* at a distance of between six and seven miles from the land. She had been apprised of our intention of coming out that morning and was awaiting us. The *Couronne* anchored a short distance outside the harbor. We were three quarters of an hour in running out to the *Kearsarge*, during which time we had gotten our people to quarters, cast loose the battery, and made all the other necessary preparations for battle. The yards had been previously slung in chains, stoppers prepared for the rigging, and preventer braces rove. It only remained to open the magazine and shell rooms, sand down the decks, and fill the requisite number of tubs with water. The crew had been particularly neat in their dress on that morning, and the officers were all in the uniforms appropriate to their rank. As we were approaching the enemy's ship, I caused the crew to be sent aft within convenient reach of my voice, and mounting a gun carriage, delivered them the following brief address. I had not spoken to them in this formal way since I had addressed them on the memorable occasion of commissioning the ship.

OFFICERS AND SEAMEN OF THE ALABAMA! You have, at length, another opportunity of meeting the enemy—the first that has been presented to you since you sank the *Hatteras!* In the meantime you have been all over the world, and it is not too much to say that you have destroyed and driven for protection under neutral flags, one half of the enemy's commerce, which, at the beginning of the war covered every sea. This is an achievement of which you may well be proud; and a grateful country will not be unmindful of it. The name of your ship has become a household word wherever civilization extends. Shall that name be tarnished by defeat? The thing is impossible! Remember that you are in the English Channel, the theater of so much of the naval glory of our race, and that the eyes of all Europe are at this moment, upon you. The flag that floats over you is that of a young Republic, who bids defiance to her enemies, whenever and wherever found. Show the world that you knew how to uphold it! Go to your quarters.

The utmost silence prevailed during the delivery of this address, broken only once in an enthusiastic outburst of *Never! never!* when I asked my sailors if they would permit the name of their ship to be tarnished by defeat. My official report of the engagement addressed to Flag-Officer Barron in Paris will describe what now took place. It was written at Southampton, England, two days after the battle.

SOUTHAMPTON, June 21, 1864

SIR: I have the honor to inform you that in accordance with my intention as previously announced to you, I steamed out of the harbor of Cherbourg between nine and ten o'clock on the morning of the 19th of June for the purpose of engaging the enemy's steamer *Kearsarge*, which had been lying off and on the port for several days previously. After clearing the harbor, we descried the enemy with his head off shore at the distance of about seven miles. We were three quarters of an hour in coming up with him. I had previously pivotted my guns to starboard and made all preparations for engaging the enemy on that side. When within about a mile and a quarter of the enemy, he suddenly wheeled and, bringing his head in shore, presented his starboard battery to me. By this time we were distant about one mile from each other, when I opened on him with solid shot to which he replied in a few minutes and the action became active on both sides. The enemy now pressed his ship under a full head of steam, and to prevent our passing each other too speedily, and to keep our respective broadsides bearing, it became necessary to fight in a circle; the two ships steaming around a common center and preserving a distance from each other of from three quarters to half a mile. When we got within good shell range we opened upon him with shell. Some ten or fifteen minutes after the commencement of the action, our spanker-gaff was shot away and our ensign came down by the run. This was immediately replaced by another at the mizzen-masthead. The firing now became very hot, and the enemy's shot and shell soon began to tell upon our hull, knocking down, killing, and disabling a number of men, at the same time, in different parts of the ship. Perceiving that our shell, though apparently exploding against the enemy's sides, were doing him but little damage, I returned to solid-shot firing, and from this time onward alternated with shot and shell.

After the lapse of about one hour and ten minutes, our ship was ascertained to be in a sinking condition, the enemy's shell having exploded in our side and between decks, opening large apertures through which the water rushed with great rapidity. For some few minutes I had hopes of being able to reach the French coast, for which purpose I gave the ship all steam and set such of the fore-and-aft sails as were available. The ship filled so rapidly, however, that before we had made much progress, the fires were extinguished in the furnaces, and we were evidently on the point of sinking. I now hauled down my colors to prevent the further destruction of life and dispatched a boat to inform the enemy of our condition. Although we were now but 400 yards from each other, the enemy fired upon me five times after my colors had been struck. It is charitable to suppose that a ship of war of a Christian nation could not have done this intentionally. We now directed all our exertions toward saving the wounded and such of the boys of the ship as were unable to swim. These were dispatched in my quarter-boats, the only boats remaining to me; the waist-boats having been torn to pieces. Some twenty minutes after my furnace fires had been extinguished, and when the ship was on the point of settling, every man, in obedience to a previous order which had been given the crew, jumped overboard and endeavored to save himself. There was no appearance of any boat coming to me from the enemy until after my ship went down. Fortunately, however, the steam-yacht *Deerhound* owned by a gentleman of Lancashire, England—Mr. John Lancaster—who was himself on board, steamed up in the midst of my drowning men and rescued a number of both officers and men from the water. I was fortunate enough myself thus to escape to the shelter of the neutral flag together with about forty others all told. About this time the *Kearsarge* sent one, and then, tardily, another boat. Accompanying, you will find lists of the killed and wounded, and of those who were picked up by the *Deerhound*; the remainder, there is reason to hope, were picked up by the enemy and by a couple of French pilot boats which were also fortunately near the scene of action. At the end of the engagement it was discovered by those of our officers who went alongside of the enemy's ship with the wounded that her midship section on both sides was thoroughly iron-coated; this having been done with chains constructed for the purpose, placed perpendicularly from the rail to the water's edge, the whole covered over by a thin outer planking which gave no indication of the armor beneath. This planking had been ripped off in every direction by our shot and shell, the chain broken and indented in many places and forced partly into the ship's side. She was effectually guarded, however, in this section, from penetration. The enemy was much damaged in other parts, but to what extent it is now impossible to say. It is believed he is badly crippled. My officers and men behaved steadily and gallantly, and though they have lost their ship, they have not lost honor. Where all behaved so well, it would be invidious to particularize, but I cannot deny myself the pleasure of saying that Mr. Kell, my first lieutenant, deserves great credit for the fine condition in which the ship went into action with regard to her battery, magazine and shell rooms, and that he rendered me great assistance, by his coolness and judgment as the fight proceeded. The enemy was heavier than myself, both in ship, battery, and crew; but I did not know until the action was over that she was also ironclad. Our total loss in killed and wounded is 30, to wit: 9 killed and 21 wounded.

It was afterward ascertained that as many as ten were drowned. As stated in the above despatch, I had the satisfaction of saving all my wounded men. Every one of them was passed carefully into a boat and sent off to the enemy's ship before the final plunge into the sea was made by the unhurt portion of the crew. Here is the proper place to drop a tear over the fate of a brave officer. My surgeon, D. H. Llewellyn, of Wiltshire, England, a grandson of Lord Herbert, lost his life by drowning. It was his privilege to accompany the wounded men in the boats to the *Kearsarge*, but he did not do so. He remained and took his chance of escape with the rest of his brethren in arms and perished almost in sight of his home after an absence of two years from the dear ones who were to mourn his loss. With reference to the drowning of my men, I desire to present a contrast to the reader. I sank the *Hatteras* off Galveston in a night engagement. When the enemy appealed to me for assistance, telling me that his ship was sinking, I sent him all my boats and saved every officer and man, numbering more than a hundred persons. The *Alabama* was sunk in open daylight—the enemy's ship being only 400 yards distant—and ten of my men were permitted to drown. Indeed, but for the friendly interposition of the *Deerhound*, there is no doubt that a great many more would have perished.

Captain Winslow has stated in his despatch to his Government that he desired to board the *Alabama*. He preserved a most respectful distance from her even after he saw that she was crippled. He had greatly the speed of me and could have laid me alongside at any moment, but so far from doing so, he was shy of me even after the engagement had ended. In a letter to the Secretary of the Federal Navy published by Mr. Adams in London a few days after the engagement, he says: "I have the honor to report that toward the close of the action between the *Alabama* and this vessel, all available sail was made on the former for the purpose of regaining Cherbourg. When the object was apparent, the *Kearsarge* was steered across the bow of the *Alabama* for a raking fire, but before reaching this point, the *Alabama* struck. Uncertain whether Captain Semmes was not making some ruse, the *Kearsarge* was stopped." This is probably the explanation of the whole of Captain Winslow's strange conduct at the time. He was afraid to approach us because of some ruse that we might be practising upon him. Before he could recover from his bewilderment and make up his mind that we were really beaten, my ship went down. I acquit him, therefore, entirely of any intention of permitting my men to drown, or even of gross negligence, which would be almost as criminal. It was his *judgment* which was entirely at fault. I had known and sailed with him in the old service and knew him *then* to be a humane and Christian gentleman. What the war may have made of him, it is impossible to say. It has turned a great deal of the milk of human kindness to gall and wormwood.

Chapter Twenty-Five—*1864*

---

*Other incidents of the battle between the Alabama
and the Kearsarge . . . The rescue of officers and seamen by the English Steam Yacht Deerhound . . .
The United States Government demands that they
be given up . . . British Government refuses compliance . . . The rescued persons not prisoners . . .
Inconsistency of the Federal Secretary of the Navy*

Notwithstanding my enemy went out chivalrously armored
to encounter a ship whose wooden sides were entirely without
protection, I should have beaten him in the first thirty minutes
of the engagement but for the defect of my ammunition,
which had been two years on board and become much
deteriorated by cruising in a variety of climates. I had directed
my men to fire low, telling them that it was better to fire too
low than too high, as the *ricochet* in the former case—the
water being smooth—would remedy the defect of their aims,
whereas it was of no importance to cripple the masts and
spars of a steamer. By Captain Winslow's own account, the
Kearsarge was struck twenty-eight times; but his ship being
armored, of course, my shot and shell, except in so far as
fragments of the latter may have damaged his spars and

377

rigging, fell harmless into the sea. The *Alabama* was not mortally wounded until after the *Kearsarge* had been firing at her *an hour and ten minutes.* In the meantime, in spite of the armor of the *Kearsarge,* I had *mortally wounded* that ship in the first thirty minutes of the engagement. I say "mortally wounded her" because the wound would have proved mortal but for the defect of my ammunition above spoken of. I lodged a rifled percussion shell near her stern post—*where there were no chains*—which failed to explode because of the defect of the cap. If the cap had performed its duty and exploded the shell, I should have been called upon to save Captain Winslow's crew from drowning, instead of his being called upon to save mine. On so slight an incident—the defect of a percussion cap—did the battle hinge. The enemy were very proud of this shell. *It was the only trophy they ever got of the Alabama!* We fought her until she would no longer swim, and then we gave her to the waves. This shell, thus imbedded in the hull of the ship, was carefully cut out along with some of the timber and sent to the Navy Department* in Washington to be exhibited to admiring Yankees. It should call up the blush of shame to the cheek of every Northern man who looks upon it. It should remind him of his ship going into action with *concealed* armor; it should remind him that his ship fired into a beaten antagonist *five* times, after her colors had been struck and when she was sinking; and it should remind him of the drowning of helpless men struggling in the water for their lives!

Perhaps this latter spectacle was something for a Yankee to gloat upon. The *Alabama* had been a scourge and a terror to them for two years. She had destroyed their *property!* Yankee property! Curse upon the "pirates," let them drown! At least this was the sentiment uttered by that humane and Christian gentleman to whom I have before had occasion to allude in these pages—Mr. William H. Seward—one of the chief Vandals who found themselves in the possession and control of the once glorious "Government of the States" during the war. This gentleman, in one of his dispatches to Mr. Adams, prompting him as to what he should say to the English Government on the subject of the rescue of my men by the *Deerhound,* remarks: "I have to observe upon these remarks of

---

* It is now in the museum of the Naval Academy at Annapolis. ED.

Killed   Peter Duncan   Fireman
         James Maw   Do
         John Roberts   Seaman
         Christian Pust   Fireman
         Christian Obdam   Seaman
         James King   Seaman

         Wounded

         David Williams   O.S
         Peter Hughes   Boatn Mate
         Martin King   Fireman
         Wm M. Gunley   Capt. Conswain
         Jas Mason   Fireman
         Saml Williams   "
         Thos Winter   "
         Robt Wright   "
         John Neil   Capt. M.T
         Jacob Berbor   Seaman

         Drowned

         S.H. Llewellyn
         Jas Hart   Seaman

Incomplete facsimile list of *The Alabama's* killed,
wounded, and drowned

A boat from *The Alabama* announces surrender

Earl Russell that it was the right of the *Kearsarge that the pirates should drown* unless saved by humane exertions of the officers and crew of that vessel, or by their own efforts *without the aid of the Deerhound.* The men were either already actually prisoners, or they were desperately pursued by the *Kearsarge.* If they had *perished* [by being permitted to be drowned, in cold blood after the action], the *Kearsarge would have had the advantage of a lawful destruction of so many enemies;* if they had been recovered by the *Kearsarge* with or without the aid of the *Deerhound*, then the voluntary surrender of those persons would have been perfected, and they would have been prisoners. In neither case would they have remained hostile Confederates."

No one who is not a seaman can realize the blow which falls upon the heart of a commander upon the sinking of his ship. It is not merely the loss of a battle—it is the overwhelming of his household, as it were, in a great catastrophe. The *Alabama* had not only been my battlefield but my home, in which I had lived two long years, and in which I had experienced many vicissitudes of pain and pleasure, sickness and health. My officers and crew formed a great military family, every face of which was familiar to me; and when I looked upon my gory deck toward the close of the action and saw so many manly forms stretched upon it with the glazed eye of death or agonizing with terrible wounds, I felt as a father feels who has lost his children—his children who had followed him to the uttermost ends of the earth in sunshine and storm and been always true to him.

A remarkable spectacle presented itself on the deck of the sinking ship after the firing had ceased and the boats containing the wounded had been shoved off. Under the order which had been given, "Every man save himself who can!" all occupations had been suspended and all discipline relaxed. One man was then as good as another. The *Kearsarge* stood sullenly at a distance, making no motion that we could see to send us a boat. The *Deerhound* and the French pilot boats were also at a considerable distance. Meantime, the water was rushing and roaring into the ship's side through her ghastly death wound, and she was visibly settling—lower and lower. There was no panic, no confusion, among the men. Each stood waiting his doom with the most perfect calmness. The respect and affection manifested for their officers was touching in the extreme. Several gathered around me and seemed anxious for my safety. One tendered me this little office of kindness and another, that. Kell was near me, and my faithful steward, Bartelli, also, was at my side. Poor Bartelli! he could not swim a stroke—which I did not know at the time, or I should have saved him in the boats—and yet he was calm and cheerful; seeming to think that no harm could befall him so long as he was at my side. He asked me if there were not some papers I wanted in the cabin. I told him there were and sent him to bring them. He had to wade to my stateroom to get them. He brought me the two small packages I had indicated, and, with tears in his eyes told me how the cabin had been shattered by the enemy's shot—our fine painting of the *Alabama* in particular being destroyed. Poor fellow! he was drowned ten minutes afterward.

Two of the members of my boat's crew being around me when the papers were brought, insisted that I should give them to them to take care of. They were good swimmers, they said, and would be sure to preserve them for me. I gave each a package—put up tightly between small slats—and they thrust them in the bosoms of their shirts. One of them then helped me off with my coat, which was too well laden with buttons to think of retaining, and I sat down whilst the other pulled off my boots. Kell stripped himself in like manner. The men with the papers were both saved. One swam to a French pilot boat, and the other to the *Deerhound*. I got both packages of papers. The seaman who landed on the French coast sought out Captain Sinclair, who was still at Cherbourg and delivered them to him. A writer in the London *Times* thus describes how I got the other package: "When the men came on board the *Deerhound*, they had nothing on but their drawers and shirts, having been stripped to fight; and one of them, with a sailor's devotedness, insisted on seeing his Captain, who was then lying in Mr. Lancaster's cabin in a very exhausted state, as he had been intrusted by Captain Semmes with the ship's papers, and to no one else would he give them up. The men were all very anxious about their Captain and were rejoiced to find that he had been saved. They appeared to be a set of first-rate fellows and to act well together in perfect union under the most trying circumstances."

The ship settled by the stern, and as the taffarel was about to be submerged, Kell and myself threw ourselves into the sea and swam out far enough from the sinking ship to avoid being drawn down into the vortex of waters. We then turned to get a last look at her and see her go down. Just before she disappeared, her main-topmast, which had been wounded, went by the board; and like a living thing in agony she threw her bow high out of the water and then descended rapidly, stern foremost, to her last resting place. A noble Roman once stabbed his daughter rather than she should be polluted by the foul embrace of a tyrant. It was with a similar feeling that Kell and I saw the *Alabama* go down. We had buried her as we had christened her, and she was safe from the polluting touch of the hated Yankee!

Great rejoicing was had in Yankeedom when it was known that the *Alabama* had been beaten. Shouts of triumph rent the air, and bonfires lighted every hill. But along with the rejoicing there went up a howl of disappointed rage that I had escaped being made a prisoner. The splendid victory of their ironclad over a wooden ship was shorn of half its brilliancy. Mr. Seward was in a furor of excitement; and as for poor Mr. Adams, he lost his head entirely. He even conceived the brilliant idea of demanding that I should be delivered up to him by the British Government. Two days after the action, he wrote to his chief from London as follows:

The popular excitement attending the action between the *Alabama* and the *Kearsarge* has been considerable. I transmit a copy of the *Times* of this morning, containing a report made to Mr. Mason by Captain Semmes. It is evidently intended for this meridian. The more I reflect upon the conduct of the *Deerhound*, the more grave do the questions to be raised with this Government appear to be. I do not feel it my duty to assume the responsibility of demanding, without instructions, the surrender of the prisoners. Neither have I yet obtained directly from Captain Winslow any authentic evidence of the facts attending the conflict. I have some reason to suspect that the subject has already been under the consideration of the authorities here.

Mr. Seward and Mr. Adams were both eminently civilians. The heads of both of them were muddled the moment they stepped from the Forum to the Campus Martius. Mr. Adams was now busy preparing another humiliation for the great American statesman. Some men learn wisdom by experience, and others do not. Mr. Adams seems to have been of the latter class. He had made a great many demands about the *Alabama*, which had been refused, and was now about to make another which was more absurd even than those that had gone before. The "instructions" coming from Mr. Seward in due time, the demand was made, and here is the reply of Lord Russell:

Secondly, [his lordship had been considering another point, which Mr. Adams had introduced into his dispatch, not material to the present question,] I have to state that it appears to her Majesty's Government that the commander of the private British yacht, the *Deerhound*, in saving from drowning some of the officers and crew of the *Alabama* after that vessel had sunk, performed a praiseworthy act of humanity, to which, moreover, he had been exhorted by the officer commanding the *Kearsarge*, to which vessel the *Deerhound* had in the first instance gone in order to offer to the *Kearsarge* any assistance which, after her action with the *Alabama*, she might stand in need of; and it appears further to her Majesty's Government that under all the circumstances of the case, Mr. Lancaster was not under any obligation to deliver to the captain of the *Kearsarge* the officers and men whom he had rescued from the waves. But however that may be, with regard to the demand made by you by instructions from your Government that those officers and men should now be delivered up to the Government of the United States as being escaped prisoners of war, her Majesty's Government would beg to observe that there is no obligation by international law, which can bind the government of a neutral state to deliver up to a belligerent prisoners of war who may have escaped from the power of such belligerent and may have taken refuge within the territory of such neutral. Therefore, even if her Majesty's Government had any power by law to comply with the above-mentioned demand, her Majesty's Government could not do so without being guilty of a violation of the duties of hospitality. In point of fact, however, her Majesty's Government have no lawful power to arrest and deliver up the persons in question. They have been guilty of no offence against the laws of England, and they have committed no act which would bring them within the provisions of a treaty between Great Britain and the United States for the mutual surrender of offenders, and her Majesty's Government are, therefore, entirely without any legal means by which, even if they wished to do so, they could comply with your above-mentioned demand.

This reasoning is unanswerable and adds to the many humiliations the Federal Government received from England during the war in connection with the *Alabama* through the bungling of its diplomatists. The *Deerhound*, a neutral vessel, was not only under no obligation in fact to deliver up the prisoners she had rescued from the water, but she could not lawfully have put herself under such obligation. The prisoners had rights in the premises as well as the *Deerhound*. The moment they reached the deck of the neutral ship by whatever means, they were entitled to the protection of the neutral flag, and any attempt on the part of the neutral master, whether by agreement with the opposite belligerent or not, to hand them over to the latter would have been an exercise of force by him and tantamount to an act of hostility against the prisoners. It would have been our right and our duty to resist any such attempt; and we would assuredly have done so if it had been made. It will be observed that Lord Russell does not discuss the question whether we were prisoners. It was not necessary to his argument; for even admitting that we were prisoners, hospitality forbade him to deliver us up.

But we were not prisoners. A person to become a prisoner must be brought within the power of his captor. There must be a manucaption, a possession, if even for a moment. I never was at any time during the engagement or after in the power of the enemy. I had struck my flag, it is true, but that did not make me a prisoner. It was merely an offer of surrender. It was equivalent to saying to my enemy, "I am beaten; if you will take possession of me I will not resist." Suppose my ship had not been fatally injured, and a sudden gale had sprung up and prevented the enemy from completing his capture by taking possession of her, and I had escaped with her, will it be pretended that she was his prize? There have been numerous instances of this kind in naval history, and no one has ever supposed that a ship under such circumstances would be a prize, or that any person on board of her would be a prisoner. Nor can the *cause* which prevents the captor from taking possession of his prize make any difference. If from any cause he is unable to take possession, he loses her. If she takes fire and burns up or sinks, she is equally lost to him, and if any one escapes from the burning or sinking ship to the shore, can it be pretended that he is a prisoner? And is there any difference between escaping to the shore and to a neutral flag? The folly of the thing is too apparent for argument, and yet the question was pressed seriously upon the British Government; and the head of Mr. Gideon Welles, the Secretary of the Federal Navy, was for a long time addled on the subject. I question, indeed, whether the head of the old gentleman has recovered from the shock it received, to this day. He afterward had me arrested, as the reader will see in due time, and conveyed to Washington a prisoner and did all in his power to have me tried by a military commission *in time of peace*, because I did not insist upon Mr. Lancaster's delivering me up to Captain Winslow! Will any one believe that this is the same Mr. Welles who approved of Captain Stellwagen's running off with the *Mercedita* after he had been paroled?

*   *   *

In the year 1862 . . . Admiral Buchanan of the Confederate States Navy in the engagement in Hampton Roads sunk the frigate *Congress*, and *before she could be taken possession of, the crew took to their boats and escaped*. Buchanan did not claim that the crew of the *Congress* that had thus escaped were his prisoners; he only claimed that Commander Smith and Lieutenant Pendergrast were his prisoners, *he having taken possession of them*, and they having escaped in violation of the *special parole* under which he had permitted them to return to their ship.

It thus appears that so far from its being the exception, it is the rule in naval combats for both ship and officers, and crew, to escape after surrender if possible. The enemy may prevent it by force if he can, but if the escape be successful, it is a valid escape. I have thus far been considering the case as though it were an escape with or from a ship which had not been fatally injured, and on board which the officers and crew might have remained if they had thought proper. If the escape be proper in such a case as this, how much more must it be proper when, as was the case with the *Alabama*, the officers and crew of the ship are compelled to throw themselves into the sea and struggle for their lives? Take my own individual case. The Federal Government complained of me because I threw my sword into the sea, which, as the Federal Secretary of the Navy said, no longer belonged to me. But what was I to do with it? Where was Mr. Welles' officer that he did not come to demand it? It had been tendered to him and *would* have belonged to him if he had had the ability or the inclination to come and take it. But he did not come. I did not betake myself to a boat and seek refuge in flight. I waited for him, or *his* boat, on the deck of my sinking ship until the sea was ready to engulf me. I was ready and willing to complete the surrender which had been tendered, but as far as was then apparent, the enemy intended to permit me to drown. Was I under these circumstances to plunge into the water with my sword in my hand and endeavor to swim to the *Kearsarge?* Was it not more natural that I should hurl it into the depths of the ocean in defiance and in hatred of the Yankee and his accursed flag? When my ship went down, I was a waif upon the waters. Battles and swords and all other things except the attempt to save life were at an end. I ceased from that moment to be the enemy of any brave man. A true sailor and above all one who had been bred to arms, when he found that he could not himself save me as his prisoner, should have been glad to have me escape from him with life, whether by my own exertions or those of a neutral. I believe this was the feeling which at the moment, was in the heart of Captain Winslow. It was reserved for William H. Seward to utter the atrocious sentiment which has been recorded against him in these pages. Mr. Seward is now an old man, and he has the satisfaction of reflecting that he is responsible for more of the woes which have fallen upon the American people than any other citizen of the once proud republic. He has worked from first to last for self, and he has met with the usual reward of the selfish—the contempt and neglect of all parties. He has need to utter the prayer of Cardinal Wolsey and to add thereto, "Forgive, O Lord! him who never did forgive."

Chapter Twenty-Six—*1864*

The Federal Government and the British Steam Yacht
Deerhound . . . Mr. Seward's dispatch and Mr. Lan-
caster's letter to the Daily News . . . Lord Russell's
reply to Mr. Adams on the subject of his complaint
against Mr. Lancaster . . . Presentation of a sword to
the author by the clubs in England . . . Presentation
of a flag by a lady

The howl that went up against Mr. Lancaster, the owner of
the *Deerhound*, for his humane exertions in saving my crew
and myself from drowning was almost as rabid as that which
had been raised against myself. Statesmen—or those who
should have been such—descended into the arena of coarse
and vulgar abuse of a private English citizen who had no
connection with them or their war and no sympathies that I
know of on the one side or the other. Mr. Welles, in one of
those patriotic effusions by which he sought to recommend
himself to the extreme party of the North, declared among
other things that he was "not a gentleman!" Poor Mr. Lancaster, to have thy gentility questioned by so competent a
judge as Mr. Gideon Welles! If these gentlemen had confined
themselves to mere abuse, the thing would not have been

386

so bad, but they gave currency to malicious falsehoods concerning Mr. Lancaster, as truths. Paid spies in England reported these falsehoods at Washington, and the too eager Secretary of State embodied them in his despatches. Mr. Adams and Mr. Seward have both since ascertained that they were imposed upon, and yet no honorable retraxit has ever been made. The following is a portion of one of Mr. Seward's characteristic despatches on his subject. It is addressed to Mr. Adams:

I have the honor to acknowledge the receipt of your dispatch of the 21st of June, No. 724, which relates to the destruction of the pirate ship *Alabama* by the *Kearsarge* off Cherbourg. This event has given great satisfaction to the Government, and it appreciates and commends the bravery and skill displayed by Captain Winslow and the officers and crew under his command. Several incidents of the transaction seem to demand immediate attention. The first is that this Government disapproves the proceedings of Captain Winslow in paroling and discharging the pirates who fell into his hands in that brilliant naval engagement, and in order to guard against injurious inferences which might result from that error, if it were overlooked, you are instructed to make the fact of this disapprobation and censure known to her Majesty's Government and to state at the same time that this Government, adhering to declarations heretofore made, does not recognize the *Alabama* as a ship of war of a lawful belligerent power.

Mr. Seward, when this dispatch was penned, had hopes that the "pirates" would be given up to him, and the *caveat* which he enters may give some indication of the course the Yankee Government intended to pursue toward the said "pirates" when they should come into its possession. It did not occur to the wily Secretary that if we were "pirates," it was as competent for Great Britain to deal with us as the United States; and that on this very ground his claim for extradition might be denied—a pirate being *hostis humani generis* and punishable by the first nation into whose power he falls. But these *mistakes* were common with Mr. Seward.

Laying aside, therefore, all his trash and nonsense about piracy, let us proceed with that part of his dispatch which relates to Mr. Lancaster:

Secondly, the presence and the proceedings of a British yacht, the *Deerhound*, at the battle require explanation. On reading the statements which have reached this Government, it seems impossible to doubt that the *Deerhound* went out to the place of conflict by concert and arrangement with the commander of the *Alabama*, and with at least a conditional purpose of rendering her aid and assistance. She did effectually render such aid by rescuing the commander and part of the crew of the *Alabama* from the pursuit of the *Kearsarge*, and by furtively and clandestinely conveying them to Southampton within British jurisdiction. We learn from Paris that the intervention of the *Deerhound* occurred after the *Alabama* had actually surrendered. The proceeding of the *Deerhound*, therefore, seems to have been directly hostile to the United States. Statements of the owner of the *Deerhound* are reported here to the effect that he was requested by Captain Winslow to rescue the drowning survivors of the battle, but no official confirmation of this statement is found in the reports of Captain Winslow. Even if he had made such a request, the owner of the *Deerhound* subsequently abused the right of interference by secreting the rescued pirates and carrying them away beyond the pursuit of the *Kearsarge*. Moreover, we are informed from Paris that the *Deerhound*, before going out, received from Semmes, and that she subsequently conveyed away to England, a deposit of money and other valuables of which Semmes in his long piratical career had despoiled numerous American merchantmen.

There was not one word of truth in this cock-and-a-bull story of concert between Mr. Lancaster and myself as to his going out to witness the combat, as to his receiving money or anything else from the *Alabama*, or as to any other subject whatever. We had never seen each other, or held the least communication together, until I was drawn out of the water by his boat's crew and taken on board his yacht after the battle.

It was quite natural that Mr. Seward's Yankee correspondents in London and Paris, and Mr. Seward himself, should suppose that money and stealings had had something to do with Mr. Lancaster's generous conduct. The whole American war on the Yankee side had been conducted on this principle of giving and receiving a "*consideration*" and on "*stealings*." Armies of hired vagabonds had roamed through the Southern

States, plundering and stealing—stealing not only gold and silver, but libraries, pianos, pictures, and even the jewelry and clothing of women and children! The reader has seen into what a mortal fright the lady-passengers on board the captured *Ariel* were thrown, lest the officers and crew of the *Alabama* should prove to be the peers of Yankee rogues, epauletted and unepauletted. These men even laid their profane hands on the sacred word of God, *if it would pay.* Here is a *morçeau* taken from the *Journal of Commerce* of New York, a Yankee paper quite moderate in its tone and a little given, withal, to religious sniffling. It shows how a family Bible was stolen from a Southern household and sold for a "consideration" in the North, without exciting so much as a word of condemnation from press or people:

An Old Bible Captured from a Rebel. H. Jallonack of Syracuse, New York, has exhibited to the editor of the *Journal* of that city a valuable relic—a Protestant Bible printed in German text 225 years ago, the imprint bearing date 1637. The book is in an excellent state of preservation, the printing perfectly legible, the binding sound and substantial, and the fastening a brass clasp. The following receipt shows how the volume came in Mr. Jallonack's possession:

NEW YORK, Aug. 21, 1862
Received of Mr. H. Jallonack $150 for a copy of one of the first Protestant Bibles published in the Netherlands, 1637, with the proclamation of the King of the Netherlands. This was taken from a descendant Hollander at the battle before Richmond, in the rebel service, by a private of the Irish Brigade.

JOSEPH HEIME, M. D., 4 Houston Street

"Semmes, in his long piratical career" scarcely equalled these doings of Mr. Seward's countrymen. He certainly did not send any stolen Bibles published in the Netherlands or elsewhere to the *Deerhound* to be sold to pious Jallonacks for $150 apiece.

But to return to Mr. Lancaster and the gross assault that was made upon him by the Secretary of State. Mr. Lancaster, being a gentleman of ease and fortune, spent a portion of his summers in yachting, as is the case with a large number of the better classes in England. Being in France with his family, he ordered his yacht, the *Deerhound*, to meet him at the port

of Cherbourg, where it was his intention to embark for a
cruise of a few weeks in the German Ocean. A day or two
before the engagement between the *Alabama* and the *Kearsarge*, a steam yacht under British colors was reported to me
as having anchored in the harbor. Beyond admiring the beautiful proportions of the little craft, we paid no further attention to her; and when she steamed out of Cherbourg on the
morning of the engagement, we had not the least conception
of what her object was. With this preface I will let Mr. Lancaster tell his own story. He had been assaulted by a couple
of Yankee correspondents in the London *Daily News*, a paper
in the interests, and reported to be in the pay of the Federal
Government. He is replying to those assaults, which, as the
reader will see, were the same that were afterward *rehashed*
by Mr. Seward in the dispatch already quoted.

THE DEERHOUND, THE ALABAMA, AND THE KEARSARGE

To THE EDITOR OF THE *Daily News*. SIR: As two correspondents of your journal, in giving their version of the fight
between the *Alabama* and the *Kearsarge*, have designated my
share in the escape of Captain Semmes and a portion of the
crew of the sunken ship as 'dishonorable,' and have moreover
affirmed that my yacht, the *Deerhound*, was in the harbor of
Cherbourg before the engagement, and proceeded thence on
the morning of the engagement in order to assist the *Alabama*,
I presume I may trespass upon your kindness so far as to ask
an opportunity to repudiate the imputation and deny the
assertion. They admit that when the *Alabama* went down,
the yacht, being near the *Kearsarge*, was hailed by Captain
Winslow and requested to aid in picking up the men who
were in the water; but they intimate that my services were
expected to be merely ministerial; or, in other words, that I
was to put myself under the command of Captain Winslow
and place my yacht at his disposal for the capture of the poor
fellows who were struggling in the water for their lives.

The fact is that when we passed the *Kearsarge* the captain
cried out, "For God's sake, do what you can to save them,"
and that was my warrant for interfering in any way for the
aid and succor of his enemies. It may be a question with
some, whether without that warrant, I should have been
justified in endeavoring to rescue any of the crew of the
Alabama; but my own opinion is that a man drowning in
the open sea cannot be regarded as an enemy at the time to
anybody, and is, therefore, entitled to the assistance of any

passerby. Be this as it may, I had the earnest request of Captain Winslow to rescue as many of the men who were in the water as I could lay hold of, but that request was not coupled with any stipulation to the effect that I should deliver up the rescued men to him as his prisoners. If it had been, I should have declined the task, because I should have deemed it dishonorable—that is, inconsistent with my notions of honor—to lend my yacht and crew for the purpose of rescuing those brave men from drowning only to hand them over to their enemies for imprisonment, ill-treatment, and perhaps execution.

One of your correspondents opens his letter by expressing a desire, to bring to the notice of the yacht clubs of England the conduct of the commander of the *Deerhound*, which followed the engagement of the *Alabama* and *Kearsarge*. Now that my conduct has been impugned, I am equally wishful that it should come under the notice of the yacht clubs of England, and I am quite willing to leave the point of honor to be decided by my brother yachtsmen, and indeed, by any tribunal of gentlemen. As to my legal right to take away Captain Semmes and his friends, I have been educated in the belief that an English ship is English territory, and I am, therefore, unable even now to discover why I was more bound to surrender the people of the *Alabama* whom I had on board my yacht than the owner of a garden on the south coast of England would have been if they had swum to such a place and landed there, or than the Mayor of Southampton was when they were lodged in that city; or than the British Government is, now that it is known that they are somewhere in England.

Your other correspondent says that Captain Winslow declares that "the reason he did not pursue the *Deerhound*, or fire into her was, that he could not believe at the time that anyone carrying the flag of the royal yacht squadron could act so dishonorable a part as to carry off the prisoners whom he had requested him to save from feelings of humanity." I was not aware then, and I am not aware now that the men whom I saved *were, or ever had been his* prisoners. Whether any of the circumstances which had preceded the sinking of the *Alabama* constituted them prisoners was a question that never came under my consideration, and one which I am not disposed to discuss even now. I can only say that it is a new doctrine to me that *when one ship sinks another in warfare, the crew of the sunken ship are debarred from swimming* for their lives and seeking refuge wherever they can find it; and it is a doctrine which I shall not accept unless backed by better authority than that of the master of the *Kearsarge*. What Captain Winslow's notion of humanity may be is a point beyond my knowledge, but I have good reason for believing that not many members of the royal yacht squadron would, from "motives of humanity" have taken Captain Semmes from the water in order to give him up to the tender mercies of Captain Winslow and his compatriots. Another reason assigned by your correspondent for that hero's forbearance may be imagined in the reflection that such a performance as that of Captain Wilkes who dragged two "enemies" or "rebels" from an English ship [the *Trent*,] would not bear repetition. (We have here the secret of the vindictiveness with which Mr. Seward pursued Mr. Lancaster. It was cruel of Lancaster to remind him of the "seven days" of tribulation through which Lord John Russell had put him.)

Your anonymous correspondent further says that "Captain Winslow would now have all the officers and men of the *Alabama* as prisoners had he not placed too much confidence in the honor of an Englishman, who carried the flag of the royal yacht squadron." This is a very questionable assertion; for why did Captain Winslow confide in that Englishman? Why did he implore his interference, calling out, "For God's sake, do what you can to save them?" I presume it was because he would not, or could not save them himself. The fact is that if the Captain and crew of the *Alabama* had depended for safety altogether upon Captain Winslow, not one half of them would have been saved. He got quite as many of them as he could lay hold of, time enough to deliver them from drowning.

I come now to the more definite charges advanced by your correspondents, and these I will soon dispose of. They maintain that my yacht was in the harbor of Cherbourg for the purpose of assisting the *Alabama*, and that her movements before the action prove that she attended her for the same object. My impression is that the yacht was in Cherbourg to suit my convenience and pleasure, and I am quite sure that when there, I neither did, nor intended to do anything to serve the *Alabama*. We steamed out on Sunday morning to see the engagement, and the resolution to do so was the result of a family council, whereat the question "to go out" or "not to go out" was duly discussed, and the decision in the affirmative was carried by the juveniles rather against the wish of both myself and my wife. Had I contemplated taking any part in the movements of the *Alabama*, I do not think I should have been accompanied with my wife and several young children.

One of your correspondents, however, says that he knows that the *Deerhound* did assist the *Alabama*, and if he does know this, he knows more than I do. As to the movements of the *Deerhound* before the action, all the movements with which I was acquainted, were for the objects of enjoying the summer morning and getting a good and safe place from which to watch the engagement. Another of your correspondents declares that since the affair it has been discovered that the *Deerhound* was a consort of the *Alabama*, and on the night before had received many valuable articles for safe keeping from that vessel. This is simply untrue. Before the engagement neither I nor any member of my family had any knowledge of, or communication with Captain Semmes, or any of his officers or any of his crew. Since the fight I have inquired from my Captain whether he or any of my crew had had any communication with the Captain or crew of the *Alabama* prior to meeting them on the *Deerhound* after the engagement, and his answer given in the most emphatic manner has been, "None whatever." As to the deposit of chronometers and other valuable articles, the whole story is a myth. Nothing was brought from the *Alabama* to the *Deerhound*, and I never heard of the tale until I saw it in an extract from your own columns.

After the fight was over, the drowning men picked up, and the *Deerhound* steaming away to Southampton, some of the officers who had been saved began to express their acknowledgments for my services, and my reply to them, which was addressed also to all who stood around, was "Gentlemen, you have no need to give me any special thanks. I should have done exactly the same for the other people, if they had needed it.' This speech would have been a needless and indeed an absurd piece of hypocrisy if there had been any league or alliance between the *Alabama* and the *Deerhound*. Both your correspondents agree in maintaining that Captain Semmes and such in his crew as were taken away by the *Deerhound* are bound in honor to consider themselves still as prisoners and to render themselves to their lawful captors as soon as practicable. This is a point which I have nothing to do with, and therefore I shall not discuss it. My object in this letter is merely to vindicate my conduct from misrepresentation; and I trust that in aiming at this, I have not transgressed any of your rules of correspondence and shall therefore be entitled to a place in your columns.   JOHN LANCASTER

"Mark how a plain tale shall put him down." There could not be a better illustration of this remark than the above reply proceeding from the pen of a gentleman, to Mr. Seward's charges against both Mr. Lancaster and myself. Mr. Adams having complained to Lord Russell of the conduct of Mr. Lancaster, the latter gentleman addressed a letter to his lordship containing substantially the defence of himself which he had prepared for the *Daily News*. In a day or two afterward, Lord Russell replied to Mr. Adams as follows:

FOREIGN OFFICE, JULY 26, 1864

Sir: With reference to my letter of the 8th inst., I have the honor to transmit to you a copy of a letter which I have received from Mr. Lancaster, containing his answer to the representations contained in your letter of the 25th ult., with regard to the course pursued by him in rescuing Captain Semmes and others on the occasion of the sinking of the *Alabama*; and I have the honor to inform you that I do not think it necessary to take any further steps in the matter. I have the honor to be, with the highest consideration, your most obedient, humble servant.   RUSSELL

The royal yacht squadron, as well as the Government, sustained their comrade in what he had done, and a number of officers of the Royal Navy and Army, approving of my course throughout the trying circumstances in which I had been placed—not even excepting the hurling of my sword into the sea under the circumstances related—set on foot a subscription for another sword to replace the one which I had lost, publishing the following announcement of their intention in the London *Daily Telegraph*:

JUNIOR UNITED SERVICE CLUB, S. W.
June 23, 1864

Sir: It will doubtless gratify the admirers of the gallantry displayed by the officers and crew of the renowned *Alabama* in the late action off Cherbourg, if you will allow me to inform them through your influential journal that it has been determined to present Captain Semmes with a handsome sword to replace that which he buried with his sinking ship. Gentlemen wishing to participate in this testimony to unflinching patri- otism and naval daring, will be good enough to communicate with the chairman, Admiral Anson, United Service Club, Pall Mall, or, sir, yours, &c.

BEDFORD PIM,
Commander R. N., Hon. Secretary

This design on the part of the officers of the British Navy and Army was afterward carried out by the presentation to me of a magnificent sword, which was manufactured to their order in the city of London with suitable naval and Southern devices. I could not but appreciate very highly this delicate mode on the part of my professional brethren of rebutting the slanders of the Northern press and people. I might safely rely upon the judgment of two of the principal naval clubs in England—the United Service and the Junior United Service on whose rolls were some of the most renowned naval and military names of Great Britain. The shouts of the multitude are frequently deceptive; the idol of an hour may be pulled down in the succeeding hour; but the approbation of my brethren in arms, who coolly surveyed my career and measured it by the rules which had guided the conduct of so many of their own soldiers by sea and by land, in whose presence my own poor name was unworthy to be mentioned, was indeed beyond all price to me.

To keep company with this sword, a noble English lady presented me with a mammoth Confederate flag, wrought with her own hands from the richest silk. There is not a spot on its pure white field, and the battle cross and the stars, when unfolded, flash as brightly as ever. These two gifts shall be precious heirlooms in my family to remind my descendants, that, in the words of Patrick Henry, "I have done my utmost to preserve their liberty."

> Furl that banner, for 't is weary;
> Round its staff 't is drooping dreary;
>   Furl it, fold it, it is best:
> For there's not a man to wave it,
> And there's not a sword to save it,
> And there's not one left to lave it
> In the blood which heroes gave it;
> And its foes now scorn and brave it;

Furl it, hide it—let it rest.

. . . .

Furl it! for the hands that grasped it,
And the hearts that fondly clasped it,
    Cold and dead are lying low;
And that banner—it is trailing!
While around it sounds the wailing
    Of its people in their woe.

. . . .

Furl that banner! true 'tis gory.
Yet 't is wreathed around with glory,
And 't will live in song and story,
    Though its folds are in the dust,
For its fame on brightest pages,
Penned by poets and by sages,
Shall go sounding down the ages—
    Furl its folds though now we must.

Mr. Mason, our Commissioner at the Court of London,
thanked Mr. Lancaster for his humane and generous conduct
in the following terms:

24 UPPER SEYMOUR STREET, PORTMAN SQUARE,
                    LONDON, June 21, 1864
Dear Sir: I received from Captain Semmes at Southampton,
where I had the pleasure to see you yesterday, a full report
of the efficient service rendered under your orders by the
officers and crew of your yacht, the *Deerhound*, in rescuing
him with thirteen of his officers and twenty-seven of his crew
from their impending fate after the loss of his ship. Captain
Semmes reports that finding the *Alabama* actually sinking,
he had barely time to dispatch his wounded in his own boats
to the enemy's ship, when the *Alabama* went down, and
nothing was left to those who remained on board but to
throw themselves into the sea. Their own boats absent, there
seemed no prospect of relief, when your yacht arrived in
their midst, and your boats were launched; and he impressively
told me that to this timely and generous succor, he with most
of his officers and a portion of his crew, were indebted for their
safety. He further told me that on their arrival on board of
the yacht, every care and kindness were extended to them
which their exhausted condition required, even to supplying all
with dry clothing. I am fully aware of the noble and disin-

terested spirit which prompted you to go to the rescue of the gallant crew of the *Alabama*, and that I can add nothing to the recompense already received by you and those acting under you, in the consciousness of having done as you would be done by; yet you will permit me to thank you, and through you, the captain, officers, and crew of the *Deerhound* for this signal service, and to say that in doing so I but anticipate the grateful sentiment of my country and of the Government of the Confederate States. I have the honor to be, dear sir, most respectfully and truly, your obedient servant,   J. M. MASON
JOHN LANCASTER, *Esq.*, *Hindley Hall, Wigan*

Subsequently upon my arrival in Richmond, in the winter of the same year, the Confederate Congress passed a joint resolution of thanks to Mr. Lancaster, a copy of which it requested the Secretary of the Navy to transmit to him. In the confusion incident to the downfall of the Confederacy, which speedily followed, Mr. Lancaster probably never received a copy of this resolution. Thus, with the indorsement of his own government, and with that of the yacht clubs of England, and of the Congress of the Confederate States, he may safely despise the malicious diatribes that were launched against him by a fanatical and infuriated people who were thirsting for an opportunity to wreak their vengeance upon the persons of the men whom he had saved.

Upon my landing in Southampton, I was received with great kindness by the English people, ever ready to sympathize with the unfortunate, and administer to the wants of the distressed. Though my officers and myself were not to be classed in this latter category, as my drafts on the house of Frazer, Trenholm & Co., of Liverpool, would have been accepted to any extent and were as good as cash in the market, there were many generous offers of pecuniary assistance made me. I cannot forbear to speak of one of these, as it came from a lady, and if, in doing so, I trespass upon the bounds of propriety, I trust the noble lady will forgive me. This is the only means left me of making her any suitable acknowledgment. This lady was Miss Gladstone, a sister of the Chancellor of the Exchequer, who wrote me a long letter full of sympathy and of those noble impulses which swell the heart of the true woman on such occasions. She generously offered me any aid of which my sailors or myself might be in need. Letters of condolence for my loss and congratulation upon my escape from the power of a ruthless enemy came in upon me in great profusion; and as for volunteers half the adventurous young spirits of England claimed the privilege of serving under me in my new ship. The career of the *Alabama* seemed to have fired the imagination of all the schools and colleges in England if I might judge by the number of ardent missives I received from the young gentlemen who attended them. Mr. Mason, Captain Bulloch, and the Rev. F. W. Tremlett came post-haste to Southampton to offer us sympathy and services. I became acquainted with the latter gentleman when I laid up the *Sumter* at Gibraltar and retired to London. He now came to insist that I should go again to my "English home" at his house, to recruit and have my wound cared for. As I had already engaged quarters at Millbrook, where I should be in excellent hands, and as duties connected with the welfare of my crew would require my detention in the neighborhood of Southampton for a week or two, I was forced to forego the pleasure for the present.

In connection with the gratitude due other friends, I desire to mention the obligations I am under to Dr. J. Wiblin, a distinguished surgeon and physician of Southampton, who attended my crew and officers whilst we remained there, without fee or reward. Previous to my engagement with the *Kearsarge* I had sent on shore through my paymaster, the ship's funds, and the books and papers necessary to a final settlement with my crew. The paymaster now recovered back these funds from the bankers with whom they had been deposited, paid off such of the officers and men as were with us at Southampton, and proceeded to Liverpool, where he was to pay off the rest of the survivors as fast as they should present themselves. Some of the crew were wounded and in French hospitals, where they were treated with marked kindness and consideration; some had been made prisoners and paroled by Captain Winslow with the approbation of Mr. Adams under the mistaken idea, as Mr. Seward afterward insisted, that they were prisoners of war, and some weeks elapsed, consequently, before they could all present themselves at the paymaster's table. This was finally accomplished however, and every officer and seaman received in full all the pay that was due him. The amounts due to those killed and drowned were paid in due time to their legal representatives; and thus were the affairs of the *Alabama* wound up.

Chapter Twenty-Seven—*1865*

The author makes a short visit to the Continent . . .
Returns to London and embarks on his return to the
Confederate States . . . Lands at Bagdad, near the
mouth of the Rio Grande . . . Journey through Texas
. . . Reaches Louisiana and crosses the Mississippi;
and in a few days more is at home, after an absence of
four years

I considered my career upon the high seas closed by the
loss of my ship and had so informed Commodore Barron,
who was our Chief of Bureau in Paris. We had a number of
gallant Confederate naval officers, both in England and
France, eager and anxious to go afloat—more than could be
provided with ships—and it would have been ungenerous in
me to accept another command. Besides, my health was
broken down to that degree that I required absolute quiet
for some months before I should again be fit for duty. I therefore threw off all care and responsibility as soon as I had
wound up the affairs of the *Alabama* and went up to enjoy the
hospitality of my friend Tremlett at Belsize Park in London.
Here we arranged for a visit of a few weeks to the Continent
and especially to the Swiss mountains, which was carried out

in due time. One other gentleman, an amiable and accomplished sister of my friend Tremlett, and two other ladies, connections or friends of the family, accompanied us.

We were absent six weeks; landing at Ostend, passing hurriedly through Belgium—not forgetting, however, to visit the battlefield of Waterloo—stopping a few days at Spa for the benefit of the waters, and then passing on to the Rhine; up that beautiful and historic river to Mayence, and thence to the Swiss lakes—drawing the first long breath at Geneva, where we rested a few days. . . .

In connection with this journey, I found a number of exceedingly patriotic, young, able bodied male Confederates of a suitable age for bearing arms traveling with or without their papas and mammas and boasting of the Confederacy! Most of these carpet knights had been in Europe during the whole war.

Returning to London in the latter days of September . . . I made my preparations for returning to the Confederate States; and on the 3d of October, 1864, embarked on board the steamer *Tasmanian* for Havana via St. Thomas. My intention was to pass into Texas through the Mexican port of Matamoras. My journey, by this route would occupy a little longer time and be attended, perhaps, with some discomfort, but I should avoid the risk of the blockade which was considerable. The enemy having resorted, literally, to the starving process as being the only one which was likely to put an end to the war, had begun to burn our towns, lay waste our corn fields, run off our Negroes and cattle, and was now endeavoring to seal, hermetically, our ports. He had purchased all kinds of steamers—captured blockade-runners and others—which he had fitted out as ships of war, and he now had a fleet little short of five hundred sail. Acting on the principle of abandoning his commerce he had concentrated all these before the blockaded ports in such swarms that it was next to impossible for a ship to run in or out without his permission. I preferred not to fall into the enemy's hands without the benefit of a capitulation. The very mention of my name had as yet some such effect upon the Yankee Government as the shaking of a red flag has before the bloodshot eyes of an infuriated bull. Mr. Seward gored and pawed and threw up the dust; and above all bellowed whenever the vision of the *Alabama* flitted across his brain; and the "sainted Abe" was in foreign affairs but his man Friday.

At St. Thomas we changed steamers, going on board the *Solent*—the transfer of passengers occupying only a few hours. The *Solent* ran down for the coast of Puerto Rico, where she landed some passengers; passed thence to the north side of St. Domingo, thence into the Old Bahama Channel, and landed us at Havana in the last days of October. Here we were compelled to wait a few days for a chance vessel to Matamoras, there being no regular packets. This enforced delay was tedious enough, though much alleviated by the companionship of a couple of agreeable fellow passengers who had embarked with me at Southampton, and who like myself were bound to Matamoras. One of these was Father Fischer, and the other, Mr. H. N. Caldwell, a Southern merchant. Father Fischer was a German by birth but had emigrated in early youth to Mexico, where he had become a priest. He was a remarkable man, of commanding personal appearance, and a well-cultivated and vigorous intellect. He spoke half a dozen modern languages—the English among the rest, with great precision and purity—and both Caldwell and myself became much attached to him. He afterward played a very important role in the affairs of Mexico, becoming Maximilian's confessor and one of his most trusted counsellors. He was imprisoned for a time after the fall of the Empire, but was finally released and has since made his way to Europe with important papers belonging to the late unfortunate monarch. . . .

No other vessel offering, we were compelled to embark in a small Yankee schooner still redolent of codfish though wearing the English flag to which she had recently been transferred. This little craft carried us safely across the Gulf of Mexico after a passage of a week, and landed us at a seashore village at the mouth of the Rio Grande, rejoicing in the dreamy Eastern name of Bagdad. So unique was this little village that I might have fancied it, as its name imported, really under the rule of Caliphs, but for certain signs of the Yankee which met my eye. The ubiquity of this people is marvelous. They scent their prey with the unerring instinct of the carrion bird. I had encountered them all over the world chasing the omnipotent dollar, notwithstanding the gigantic war they were carrying on at home; and here was this little village of Bagdad on the Texan border as full of them as an anthill is of ants; and the human ants were quite as busy as their insect prototypes. Numerous shanties had been con-

structed on the sands out of unplaned boards. Some of these
shanties were hotels, some billiard salons, and others grog-
shops. The beach was piled with cotton bales going out, and
goods coming in. The stores were numerous and crowded
with wares. Teamsters cracked their whips in the streets, and
horsemen, booted and spurred, galloped hither and thither.
The whole panorama looked like some magic scene which
might have been improvised in a night. The population was
as heterogeneous as the dwellings. Whites, blacks, mulattos,
and Indians were all mixed. But prominent above all stood
the Yankee. The shanties were his, and the goods were his.
He kept the hotels, marked the billiards, and sold the grog.

Pretty soon a coach drove up to the door of the *hotel* at
which we were stopping to take us to Matamoras, a distance
of thirty miles. Here was the Yankee again. the coach had
been built in Troy, New York. The horses were all Northern
horses—tall, strong, and gaunt, none of your Mexican mustangs. The Jehu was Yankee, a tall fellow with fisherman's
boots, and fancy top-hamper. The dried-up little Mexicans
who attended to the horses, harnessing and unharnessing them
on the road at the different relay stations evidently stood in
great awe of him. He took us into Matamoras "*on time*," and
at the end of his journey cracked his whip and drew up his
team at the hotel door with a flourish that would have done
honor to Mr. Samuel Weller, senior, himself.

As great a revolution had taken place in Matamoras as at
Bagdad. The heretofore quaint old Spanish town presented
the very picture of a busy commercial mart. House rent was
at an enormous figure; the streets as well as the stores were
piled with bales and boxes of merchandise, and everyone you
met seemed to be running somewhere, intent on business. Ox
and mule teams from the Texan side of the river were busy
hauling the precious staple of the Southern States, which put
all this commerce in motion, to Bagdad for shipment; and
anchored off that mushroom village, I had counted, as I
landed, no less than sixty sail of ships—nearly all of them
foreign. Fortunately for all this busy throng, Maximilian
reigned supreme in Mexico, and his Lieutenant in Matamoras,
General Mejia, gave security and protection to person and
property at the same time that he raised considerable revenue
by the imposition of moderate taxes.

Colonel Ford, the commandant at Brownsville, on the opposite side of the river came over to see me, and toward night-fall I returned with him to that place. We crossed the river in a skiff managed by a Mexican, and as my foot touched for the first time in four years the soil of my native South, I experienced in their full force the lines of the poet:

> Where shall that land, that spot of earth be found?
> Art thou a man?—a patriot?—look around;
> Oh! thou shalt find, howe'er thy footsteps roam,
> That land thy country, and that spot thy home!

There were no hotels at Brownsville, but I was comfortably lodged for the night with Colonel Beldon, the Collector of the port. The next morning I breakfasted with a large party at a neighboring restaurant who had assembled thither to welcome me back to my native land; and when the breakfast was over a coach and four which was to take me on my way to Shreveport, Louisiana, drew up at the door. An escort of cavalry had been provided to accompany me as far as King's Ranch, a point at which the road approaches the coast, and where it was supposed that some of the enemy's gunboats might attempt to ambuscade me. I found upon entering the coach, in which I was to be the only traveler, that my friends had provided for my journey in true Texan style; my outfit being a stout pair of gray blankets, which were to form my bed on the prairies for the next hundred miles, as we should have to travel that distance before we reached the shelter of a roof; a box containing a dozen bottles of excellent brandy, and cigars at discretion! As the driver cracked his whip, to put his mustangs in motion, and my escort clattered on ahead of me, the crowd who had gathered in the street to see me depart launched me upon the prairie with three hearty cheers such as only Texan throats can give.

It so happened that my *major-domo* for the journey, Sergeant——,was the same who had conducted my friend Colonel Freemantle over this route, some two years before. I found him the same invaluable traveling companion. His lunch-baskets were always well filled, he knew everybody along the road, was unsurpassed at roasting a venison steak before a campfire on a forked stick, and made a capital cup of coffee. I missed the Judge, whom Freemantle so humorously describes, but I found a good many judges on the road who might sit for his portrait. And now, for want of space, I must treat this journey as I did my European tour. We were fourteen days on the road, passing through San Patricio on the Nueces, Gonzales on the Guadalupe, Houston, Hempstead, Navasota, Huntsville, Rusk, Henderson, and Marshall, arriving on the 27th of November at Shreveport. I was received everywhere with enthusiasm by the warmhearted, brave Texans, the hotels being all thrown open to me free of expense, and salutes of artillery greeting my entrance into the towns. I was frequently compelled to make short speeches to the people merely that they might hear, as they said, "how the pirate talked;" and I fear I drank a good many more mint juleps than were good for me. At table I was always seated on the right hand of the "landlady," and I was frequently importuned by a bevy of blooming lasses to tell them "how I did the Yankees." Glorious Texas! what if you are a little too much given to the Bowie-knife and revolver, and what if grass-widows are somewhat frequent in some of your localities, you are all right at heart! Liberty burns with a pure flame on your prairies, and the day will yet come when you will be free. Your fate thus far, has been a hard one. In a single generation you have changed your political condition four times. When I first knew you, you were a Mexican province. You then became an independent state. In an evil hour you were beguiled into accepting the fatal embrace of the Yankee. Learning your mistake ere long, you united your fortunes with those of the Confederate States in the hope again to be free. You did what it was the power of mortals to do, but the Fates were adverse, and you have again been dragged down into worse than Mexican bondage. Bide your time! You are rapidly filling up with population. You will soon become an empire in yourself, and the day is not far distant when you may again strike for freedom!

At Shreveport I was hospitably entertained at the mansion of Colonel Williamson, serving on the staff of the commanding general of the Trans-Mississippi Department, Kirby Smith. The Mayor and a deputation of the Councils waited on me and tendered me a public dinner, but I declined. I remained with Colonel Williamson a couple of days, and the reader may imagine how agreeable this relaxation in comfortable quarters was to me after a journey of fourteen consecutive days and nights in a stagecoach through a rough, and comparatively wild country. Governor Allen was making Shreveport the temporary seat of government of Louisiana, and I had the pleasure of making his acquaintance and dining with him in company with General Smith and his staff. The Governor was not only a genial, delightful companion, but a gallant soldier who had rendered good service to the Confederacy at the head of his regiment. He had been terribly wounded and was still hobbling about on crutches. He seemed to be the idol of the people of his state. He was as charitable and kindhearted as brave, and the needy soldier, or soldier's wife, never left his presence without the aid they came to seek.

My object in taking Shreveport in my route instead of striking for the Red River some distance below was to meet my son, Major O. J. Semmes, who, I had been informed at Brownsville, was serving in this part of Louisiana. In the beginning of the war he withdrew from West Point, where he was within a year of graduating, and offered his sword to his state—Alabama. I had not see him since. He was now a major of artillery commanding a battalion in General Buckner's army stationed at Alexandria. Thither I now directed my course. The river being too low for boating, I was forced to make another land journey. The General kindly put an ambulance at my disposal, and my host, with the forethought of a soldier, packed me a basket of provisions. My friend and traveling companion, viz., the Jehu, who was to drive me, was an original. He was from Ohio and had served throughout the war as a private soldier in the Confederate army. He had been in a good many fights and skirmishes, and was full of anecdote. If he had an antipathy in the world, it was against the Yankee, and nothing gave him half so much pleasure as to "fight his battles o'er again." As I had a journey of four or five days before me—the distance being 140 miles over execrable roads—the fellow was invaluable to me. We passed through several of the localities where General Banks had been so shamefully beaten by General Dick Taylor—at Mansfield, Pleasant Hill, and Monett's Ferry. The fields were still strewn with the carcasses of animals; a few, unmarked hillocks here and there showed where soldiers had been buried; and the rent and torn timber marked the course of the cannon balls that had carried death to either side. The Vandals in their retreat had revenged themselves on the peaceful inhabitant and every few miles the charred remains of a dwelling told where some family had been unhoused and turned into the fields by the torch.

At Alexandria I was kindly invited by General Buckner to become his guest during my stay, and he sent a courier at once to inform my son, who was encamped a few miles below the town, of my arrival. The latter came to see me the same afternoon. I remained in the hospitable quarters of the General a week before the necessary arrangements could be made for my crossing the Mississippi. The enemy being in full possession of this river by means of his gunboats, it was a matter of some little management to cross in safety. The trans-Mississippi mails to Richmond had been sent over, however, quite regularly, under the personal superintendence of a young officer detailed for the purpose, and the General was kind enough to arrange for my crossing with this gentleman. The news of my passing through Texas had reached the enemy at New Orleans, as we learned by his newspapers, and great vigilance had been enjoined on his gunboats to intercept me, if possible. Our arrangements being completed, I left Alexandria on the 10th of December, accompanied by my son, who had obtained a short leave of absence for the purpose of visiting his home, and reached the little village of Evergreen the next day. Arrived at this point, we were joined by our companions of the mail service, and on the 13th we crossed both the Red and Mississippi Rivers in safety.

The journey through the the swamps leading to these rivers was unique. We performed it on horseback pursuing mere bridlepaths and cattletracks in single file like so many Indians. Our way sometimes led us through a forest of gigantic trees almost entirely devoid of undergrowth, and resembling very much, though after a wild fashion, the park scenery of England. At other times we would plunge into a dense, tangled brake, where the interlaced grape and other vines threatened every moment to drag us from our saddles. The whole was a drowned country and impassable during the season of rains. It was now low water, and as we rode along, the highwater marks on the trees were visible many feet above our heads. From this description of the country, the reader will see how impossible it was for artillery or cavalry, or even infantry, to operate on the banks of these rivers during a greater part of the year. Except at a few points, the enemy's gunboats were almost as secure from attack as they would have been on the high seas. Occasionally, we had to swim a deep bayou whose waters looked as black as those of the Stygian Lake; but if the bayou was wide as well as deep, we more frequently dismounted, stripped our horses, and surrounding them, and shouting at them made them take the water in a drove and swim over by themselves. We then crossed in skiffs, which the mailmen had provided for the purpose, and caught and resaddled our horses for a fresh mount.

We reached the bank of the Mississippi just before dark. There were two of the enemy's gunboats anchored in the river at a distance of about three miles apart. The enemy had converted every sort of a water craft into a ship of war, and now had them in such number that he was enabled to police the river in its entire length without the necessity of his boats being out of sight of each other's smoke. The officers of these river craft were mostly volunteers from the merchant service, whose commissions would expire with the war, and a greater set of predatory rascals was perhaps never before collected in the history of any government. They robbed the plantations and demoralized them by trade at the same time. Our people were hard pressed for the necessaries of life, and a constant traffic was being carried on with them by these armed river steamers, miscalled ships of war.

It would not do, of course, for us to attempt the passage of the river until after dark; and so we held ourselves under cover of the forest until the proper moment, and then embarked in a small skiff, sending back the greater part of our escort. Our boat was scarcely able to float the numbers that were packed into her. Her gunwales were no more than six inches above the water's edge. Fortunately for us, however, the night was still, and the river smooth, and we pulled over without accident. As we shot within the shadows of the opposite bank, our conductor, before landing, gave a shrill whistle to ascertain whether all was right. The proper response came directly, from those who were to meet us, and in a moment more, we leaped on shore among friends. We found spare horses awaiting us, and my son and myself slept that night under the hospitable roof of Colonel Rose. The next morning the colonel sent us to Woodville in his carriage, and in four or five days more we were in Mobile, and I was at home again after an absence of four years!

Chapter Twenty-Eight—*1865*

The author sets out for Richmond . . . Is two weeks in making the journey . . . An interview with President Davis; with General Lee . . . The author is appointed a Rear-Admiral and ordered to command the James River Squadron . . . Assumes command; condition of the fleet . . . Great demoralization . . . The enemy's armies gradually increasing . . . Lee's lines broken

I telegraphed my arrival immediately, to the Secretary of the Navy at Richmond, informing him of my intention to proceed to that capital after resting for a few days. The following reply came over the wires in the course of a few hours. "Congratulate you on your safe arrival. When ready to come on, regard this as an order to report to the Department." I did not, of course, dally long at home. The enemy was pressing us too hard for me to think of sitting down in inglorious ease so long as it was possible that I might be of service. At all events, it was my duty to present myself to the Government and see if it had any commands for me. Accordingly, on the 2d of January, 1865, I put myself *en route* for Richmond. I was two weeks making my way to the capital of the Confederacy, owing the many breaks which had been made in the roads by raiding parties of the enemy, and by Sherman's march through Georgia. Poor Georgia! She had suffered terribly during this Vandal march of conflagration and pillage, and I found her people terribly demoralized. I stopped a day in Columbia, the beautiful capital of South Carolina, afterward so barbarously burned by' a drunken and disorderly soldiery with no officer to raise his hand to stay the conflagration. Passing on, as soon as some temporary repairs could be made on a break in the road ahead of me, I reached Richmond, without further stoppage and was welcomed at his house by my friend and relative, the Hon. Thomas J. Semmes, a senator in the Confederate Congress from the state of Louisiana.

I had thus traveled all the way from the eastern boundary of Mexico to Richmond by land, a journey which perhaps has seldom been performed. In this long and tedious journey through the entire length of the Confederacy, I had been painfully struck with the changed aspect of things since I had left the country in the spring of 1861. Plantations were ravaged, slaves were scattered, and the country was suffering terribly for the want of the most common necessaries of life. Whole districts of country had been literally laid waste by the barbarians who had invaded us The magnificent valley of the Red River, down which I had traveled, had been burned and pillaged for the distance of a hundred and fifty miles. Neither Alaric nor Attila ever left such a scene of havoc and desolation in his rear. Demoniac Yankee hate had been added to the thirst for plunder. Sugar mills, sawmills, salt works, and even the grist-mills which ground the daily bread for families had been laid in ashes—their naked chimneys adding ghastliness to the picture. Reeling, drunken soldiers passed in and out of dwellings, plundering and insulting their inmates; and if disappointed in the amount of their plunder, or resisted, applied the torch in revenge. Many of these miscreants were foreigners incapable of speaking the English language. The few dwellings that were left standing looked like so many houses of mourning. Once the seats of hospitality and refinement and the centers of thrifty plantations with a contented and happy laboring population around them, they were now shut up and abandoned. There was neither human voice in the hall, nor neigh of steed in the pasture. The tenantless Negro cabins told the story of the war. The Yankee had liberated the slave and armed him to make war upon his former master. The slaves who had not been enlisted in the Federal armies were wandering purposeless about the country, in squads, thieving, famishing, and dying. This was the character of the war our *brethen* of the North—God save the mark —were making upon us.

To add to the heart-sickening features of the picture, our own people had become demoralized! Men generally seemed to have given up the cause as lost, and to have set themselves at work like wreckers to save as much as possible from the sinking ship. The civilians had betaken themselves to speculation and money getting, and the soldiers to drinking and debauchery. Such, in brief, was the picture which presented itself to my eyes as I passed through the Confederacy. The *Alabama* had gone to her grave none too soon. If she had not been buried with the honors of war with the howling winds of the British Channel to sing her requiem, she might soon have been handed over to the exultant Yankee to be exhibited at Boston as a trophy of the war.

My first official visit in Richmond was, of course, to the President. I found him but little changed in personal appearance since I had parted with him in Montgomery, the then seat of government, in April 1861. But he was evidently deeply impressed with the critical state of the country, though maintaining an outward air of cheerfulness and serenity. I explained to him briefly what he already knew too well, the loss of my ship. He was kind enough to say that though he deeply regretted her loss, he knew that I had acted for the best, and that he had nothing with which to reproach me. I dined with him on a subsequent day. There was only one other guest present. Mrs. Davis was more impressed with events than the President. With her womanly instinct, she already saw the handwriting on the wall. But though the coming calamity would involve her household in ruin, she maintained her self-possession and cheerfulness. The Congress, which was in session, received me with a distinction which I had little merited. Both houses honored me by a vote of thanks for my services and invited me to a privileged seat on the floor. The legislature of Virginia, also in session, extended to me the same honors.

As soon as I could command a leisure moment, I paid General Lee a visit at his headquarters near Petersburg and spent a night with him. I had served with him in the Mexican War. We discussed together the critical state of the country and of his army—we were near the end of January 1865 —and I thought the grand old chieftain and Christian gentle-man seemed· to foreshadow in his conversation—more by manner than by words—the approaching downfall of the cause for which we were both struggling. I had come to him, I told him, to speak of what I had seen of the people and of the Army in my transit across the country, and to say to him that unless prompt measures could be devised to put an end to the desertions that were going on among our troops, our cause must inevitably be lost. He did not seem to be at all sur-prised at the revelations I made. He knew all about the con-dition of the country, civil and military, but seemed to feel himself powerless to prevent the downward tendency of things. And he was right. It was no longer in the power of any one man to save the country. The body politic was already dead. The people themselves had given up the contest, and this being the case, no army could do more than retard the catas-trophe for a few months. Besides, his army was melting away. That very night—as I learned the next morning at the break-fast table—160 men deserted in a body! It was useless to attempt to shoot deserters when demoralization had gone to this extent.

After I had been in Richmond a few weeks, the President was pleased to nominate me to the Senate as a rear-admiral. My nomination was unanimously confirmed, and a few days afterward I was appointed to the command of the James River fleet. My commission ran as follows:

CONFEDERATE STATES OF AMERICA
NAVY DEPARTMENT, RICHMOND, February 10, 1865

REAR-ADMIRAL RAPHAEL SEMMES

Sir: You are hereby informed that the President has ap-pointed you, by and with the advice of the Senate, a *Rear-Admiral*, in the Provisional Navy of the Confederate States *"for gallant and meritorious conduct in command of the steam sloop Alabama."* You are requested to signify your acceptance or non-acceptance of this appointment.

S. R. MALLORY,
Secretary of the Navy

An old and valued friend, Commodore J. K. Mitchell, had been in command of the James River fleet, and I displaced him very reluctantly. He had organized and disciplined the fleet and had accomplished with it all that was possible, viz., the protection of Richmond by water. I assumed my command on the 18th of February 1865. My fleet consisted of three ironclad and five wooden gunboats. I found my old first lieutenant, Kell, who had preceded me to Richmond, and been made a commander, in command of one of the ironclads, but he was soon obliged to relinquish his command, on account of failing health. As reorganized, the fleet stood as follows:

Virginia, ironclad, flagship, four guns, Captain Dunnington.
Richmond, ironclad, four guns, Captain Johnson.
Fredericksburg, ironclad, four guns, Captain Glassel.
Hampton, wooden, two guns, Captain Wilson, late of the *Alabama*.
Nansemond, wooden, two guns, Captain Butt.
Roanoke, wooden, two guns, Captain Pollock.
Beaufort, wooden, two guns, Captain Wyatt.
Torpedo, wooden, one gun, Captain Roberts.

The fleet was assisted in the defence of the river by several shore batteries in command of naval officers: as Drury's Bluff; Battery Brooke; Battery Wood, and Battery Semmes—the whole under the command of my old friend, Commodore John R. Tucker.

I soon had the mortification to find that the fleet was as much demoralized as the army. Indeed, with the exception of its principal officers and about half a dozen sailors in each ship, its *personnel* was drawn almost entirely from the Army. The movements of the ships being confined to the headwaters of a narrow river, they were but little better than prison ships. Both men and officers were crowded into close and uncomfortable quarters without the requisite space for exercise. I remedied this as much as possible by sending squads on shore to drill and march on the riverbank. They were on half rations, and with but a scanty supply of clothing. Great discontent and restlessness prevailed. Constant applications were coming to me for leaves of absence—almost everyone having some story to tell of a sick or destitute family. I was obliged, of course, to resist all these appeals. The enemy was thundering at the gates, and not a man could be spared. Desertion was the consequence. Sometimes an entire boat's crew would run off, leaving the officer to find his way on board the best he might. The strain upon them had been too great. It was scarcely to be expected of men of the class of those who usually form the rank and file of ships' companies that they would rise above their natures and sacrifice themselves by slow but sure degrees in any cause, however holy. The visions of home and fireside and freedom from restraint were too tempting to be resisted. The general understanding that the collapse of the Confederacy was at hand had it influence with some of the more honorable of them. They reasoned that their desertion would be but an anticipation of the event by a few weeks.

To add to the disorder, the "Union element," as it was called, began to grow bolder. This element was composed mainly of Northern-born men who had settled among us before the war. In the height of the war, when the Southern States were still strong, and when independence was not only possible, but probable, these men pretended to be good Southerners. The Puritan leaven, which was in their natures, was kept carefully concealed. Hypocrisy was now no longer necessary. Many of these men were preachers of the various denominations and schoolmasters. These white-cravatted gentlemen now sprang into unusual activity. Every mail brought long and artfully written letters from some of these scoundrels, tempting my men to desert. Some of these letters came under my notice, and if I could have gotten hold of the writers, I should have been glad to give them the benefit of a short shift and one of my yardarms. If I had had my fleet upon the sea, it would have been an easy matter to restore its discipline, but my ships were, in fact, only so many tents into which entered freely all the bad influences of which I speak. I was obliged to perform guard-boat duty on the river and picket duty on shore, and these duties gave my men all the opportunities of escape that they desired.

With regard to the defence of Richmond by water, I felt quite secure. No fleet of the enemy could have passed my three ironclads, moored across the stream in the only available channel, with obstructions below me, which would hold it under my fire, and that of the naval batteries on shore by

which I was flanked. Indeed, the enemy, seeing the hopeless-
ness of approach by water, had long since given up the idea.
The remainder of the winter passed slowly and tediously
enough. A few months earlier, and I might have had something to occupy me. For a long time, there was no more than
a single ironclad in the lower James, the enemy being busy
with Charleston and Wilmington. An attack on City Point,
Grant's base of operations, and whence he drew all his supplies, would have been quite practicable. If the storehouses at
that place could have been burned, there is no telling what
might have been the consequences. But now, Charleston and
Wilmington having fallen, and the enemy having no further
use for his ironclad fleet on the coasts of North and South
Carolina, he had concentrated the whole of it on the lower
James under the command of Admiral Porter, who had chased
me so quixotically in the old frigate *Powhattan* in the commencement of the war. At first this concentration looked like
a preparation for an attempted ascent of the river, but if any
attempt of the kind was ever entertained by Porter he had the
good sense, when he came to view the situation, to abandon it.

I usually visited the Navy Department during this anxious
period once a week to confer with the Secretary on the state
of my fleet and the attitude of the enemy, and to receive any
orders or suggestions that the Government might have to
make. Mr. Mallory was kind enough on these occasions to
give me *carte blanche* and leave me pretty much to myself.
At length the winter passed, and spring set in. The winds
and the sun of March began to dry the roads and put them in
good order for military operations, and everyone anticipated
stirring events. As I sat in my twilight cabin on board the
Virginia and pored over the map of North Carolina, and
plotted upon it, from day to day, the approaches of Sherman,
the prospect seemed gloomy enough. Charleston and Wilmington had fallen. With the latter, we had lost our last
blockade-running port. Our ports were now all hermetically
sealed. The anaconda had at last wound his fatal folds around
us. With fields desolated at home and all supplies from abroad
cut off, starvation began to stare us in the face. Charleston
was evacuated on the 17th of February—General Hardee
having no more than time to get his troops out of the city and
push on ahead of Sherman to join General Joseph E. Johnston,
who had again been restored to command. Fort Ander-

son, the last defence of Wilmington, fell on the 19th of the same month. Sherman was about this time at Columbia, South Carolina, where he forever disgraced himself by burning, or *permitting to be burned*, it matters not which, that beautiful city which had already surrendered to his arms. The opportunity was too good to be lost. The Puritan was at last in the city of the cavalier. The man of ruder habits and coarser civilization was in the presence of the more refined gentleman whom he had envied and hated for generations. The ignoble passions of race hatred and revenge were gratified, and Massachusetts, through the agency of a brutal and debauched soldiery, had put her foot upon the neck of prostrate South Carolina! This was humiliation indeed! The coarse man of mills and manufactures had at last found entrance as a master into the halls of the South Carolina planter!

It was generally expected that Sherman would move upon Charlotte, North Carolina, one of the most extensive depots of the South, and thence to Danville, and so on to Richmond to unite his forces with those of Grant. There was nothing to oppose him. In ten days at the farthest, after burning Columbia, he could have affected a junction with Grant before Petersburg. But the "great commander" seemed suddenly to have lost his courage, and to the astonishment of every one, soon after passing Winsboro', North Carolina, which lies on the road to Charlotte, he swung his army off to the right and marched in the direction of Fayetteville! His old antagonist, Johnston, was endeavoring to gather together the broken remains of the Army of the Tennessee, and he was afraid of him. His object now was to put himself in communication with Schofield, who had landed at Wilmington and at Newbern with a large force, and establish a new base of operations at these points. He would be safe here, as his troops could be fed, and in case of disaster he could fall back upon the sea and upon Porter's gunboats. He effected the contemplated junction with Schofield at Goldsboro', North Carolina, on the 21st of March. He had not touched any of Lee's communications with his depots since leaving Winsboro'; the destruction of which communications Grant had so much at heart, and which had been the chief object of his—Sherman's—"great march." At Goldsboro' he was still 150 miles from Grant's lines, and he took no further part in the campaign.

His junction with Schofield had not been effected without

disaster. At Kinston, Bragg gained a victory over Schofield, utterly routing him and taking 1500 prisoners; and at Bentonsville, Johnston checked and gained some advantage over Sherman. As the reader is supposed to be looking over the map with me, we will now stick a pin in the point representing Goldsboro', and throw Sherman and Schofield out of view.

In the latter part of March, Sheridan, having overrun Early's small force in the valley of the Shenandoah, found himself at liberty to join General Grant. He brought with him from 10,000 to 12,000 excellent cavalry. Grant's army was thus swollen to 160,000 men. Adding Sherman's and Schofield's forces of 100,000, we have 260,000. In the meantime, Lee's half-starved, ragged army, had dwindled to 33,000. With this small number of men he was compelled to guard an intrenched line of forty miles in length, extending from the north side of the James River below Richmond, to Hatcher's Run south of Petersburg. As a mere general, he would have abandoned the hopeless task long ago, extricating his army and throwing it into the field, but *cui bono?* With Virginia in the enemy's possession, with a *beaten* people, and an army fast melting away by desertion, could the war be continued with any hope of success? If we could not defend ourselves before Richmond, could we defend ourselves anywhere? That was the question.

Grant's object was to force Lee's right in the vicinity of Hatcher's Run; but he masked this intention as much as possible by occasionally threatening the whole line. I had frequent opportunity from the deck of my flagship, to witness terrible artillery conflicts where nobody was killed. Suddenly, on a still night, all the enemy's batteries would be ablaze, and the heavens aroar with his firing. The expenditure of powder was enormous and must have gladdened the hearts of the Yankee contractors. I would sometimes be aroused from slumber and informed that a great battle was going on. On one or two occasions. I made some slight preparations for defence, myself, not knowing but Porter might be fool enough to come up the river under the inspiration of this powder burning and booming of cannon. But it all amounted to nothing more than Chinese grimaces and stink-pots resorted to to throw Lee off his guard and prevent him from withdrawing men from his left to reinforce his right.

The final and successful assault of Grant was not long delayed. The lines in the vicinity of Petersburg having been weakened by the necessity of withdrawing troops to defend Lee's extreme right, resting now on a point called the Five Forks, Grant, on the morning of Sunday, the 2d of April, made a vigorous assault upon them and broke them. Lee's army was uncovered, and Richmond was no longer tenable!

Chapter Twenty-Nine—*1865*

The evacuation of Richmond by the Army . . . The destruction of the James River fleet . . . The sailors of the fleet converted into soldiers . . . Their helpless condition without any means of transportation . . . The conflagration of Richmond and the entry of the enemy into the Confederate Capital . . . The author improvises a railroad train and escapes in it with his command to Danville, Va.

As I was sitting down to dinner about four o'clock on the afternoon of the disastrous day mentioned in the last chapter, on board my flagship, the *Virginia*, one of the small steamers of my fleet came down from Richmond, having on board a special messenger from the Navy Department. Upon being introduced into my cabin, the messenger presented me with a sealed package. Up to this time, I was ignorant, of course, of what had occurred at Petersburg. I broke the seal and read as follows:

CONFEDERATE STATES OF AMERICA
EXECUTIVE OFFICE, RICHMOND, VA., April 2, 1865
REAR-ADMIRAL RAPHAEL SEMMES
  Commanding James River Squadron

SIR: General Lee advises the Government to withdraw from this city, and the officers will leave this evening accordingly. I presume that General Lee has advised you of this, and of his movements and made suggestions as to the disposition to be made of your squadron. He withdraws upon his lines toward Danville this night; and unless otherwise directed by General Lee, upon you is devolved the duty of destroying your ships this night, and with all the forces under your command, joining General Lee. Confer with him, if practicable, before destroying them. Let your people be rationed as far as possible for the march, and armed and equipped for duty in the field. Very respectfully, your obedient servant,

S. R. MALLORY, *Secretary of the Navy*

This was rather short notice. Richmond was to be evacuated during the night, during which I was to burn my ships, accoutre and provision my men, and join General Lee! But I had become used to emergencies and was not dismayed. I signalled all my captains to come on board and communicated to them the intelligence I had received, and concerted with them the program of the night's work. It was not possible to attempt anything before dark without exciting the suspicions of the enemy, as we were no more than four or five miles from his lines; and I enjoined upon my commanders the necessity of keeping their secret until the proper moment for action should arrive. The sun was shining brightly, the afternoon was calm, and nature was just beginning to put on her spring attire. The fields were green with early grass, the birds were beginning to twitter, and the plowman had already broken up his fields for planting his corn. I looked abroad upon the landscape and contrasted the peace and quiet of nature, so heedless of man's woes, with the disruption of a great Government and the ruin of an entire people which were at hand!

So unsuspicious were the Government subordinates of what was going on that the flag-of-truce boats were still plying between Richmond and the enemy's headquarters, a few miles below us on the river, carrying backward and forward exchanged prisoners. As those boats would pass us, coming up the river, filled to overflowing with our poor fellows just released from Yankee prisons, looking wan and hollow-eyed, the prisoners would break into the most enthusiastic cheering as they passed my flag. It seemed to welcome them home. They little dreamed that it would be struck that night forever, and the fleet blown into the air; that their own fetters had been knocked off in vain, and that they were to pass henceforth under the rule of the hated Yankee. I was sick at heart as I listened to those cheers and reflected upon the morrow.

General Lee had failed to give me any notice of his disaster or of what his intentions were. As mine was an entirely independent command, he, perhaps, rightly considered that it was the duty of the Executive Government to do this. Still, in accordance with the expressed wishes of Mr. Mallory, I endeavored to communicate with him; sending an officer on shore to the signal station at Drury's Bluff for the purpose. No response came, however, to our telegrams, and night having set in, I paid no further attention to the movements of the Army. I plainly saw that it was a case of *sauve qui peut*, and that I must take care of myself. I was to make another *Alabama*-plunge into the sea and try my luck. Accordingly, when night drew her friendly curtain between the enemy and myself, I got all my ships under way and ran up to Drury's Bluff. It was here I designed to blow up the iron-clads, throw their crews on board the wooden gunboats, and proceed in the latter to Manchester, opposite Richmond, on my way to join General Lee. Deeming secrecy of great importance to the Army in its attempted escape from its lines, my first intention was to sink my fleet quietly instead of blowing it up, as the explosions would give the enemy notice of what was going on. The reader may judge of my surprise when an hour or two after dark, I saw the whole horizon on the north side of the James glowing with fires of burning quarters, *materiel* &c., lighted by our own troops as they successively left their intrenchments! Concealment on my part was no longer necessary or indeed practicable.

I now changed my determination and decided upon burning my fleet. My officers and men worked like beavers. There were a thousand things to be done. The sailor was leaving the homestead which he had inhabited for several months. Arms had to be served out, provisions gotten up out of the hold, and broken into such packages as the sailors could carry. Hammocks had to be unlashed. and the blankets taken out and rolled up as compactly as possible. Haversacks and canteens had to be improvised. These various operations occupied us until a late hour. It was between two and three o'clock in the morning before the crews of the ironclads were all safely embarked on board the wooden gunboats, and the ironclads were well on fire. My little squadron of wooden boats now moved off up the river by the glare of the burning ironclads. They had not proceeded far before an explosion like the shock of an earthquake took place, and the air was filled with missiles. It was the blowing up of the *Virginia*, my late flagship. The spectacle was grand beyond description. Her shell-rooms had been full of loaded shells. The explosion of the magazine threw all these shells with their fuses lighted into the air. The fuses were of different lengths, and as the shells exploded by twos and threes, and by the dozen, the pyrotechnic effect was very fine. The explosion shook the houses in Richmond and must have waked the echoes of the night for forty miles around.

There are several bridges spanning the James between Drury's Bluff and the city, and at one of these we were detained an hour, the draw being down to permit the passage of some of the troops from the north side of the river, who had lighted the bonfires of which I have spoken. Owing to this delay, the sun—a glorious, unclouded sun, as if to mock our misfortunes—was now rising over Richmond. Some windows which fronted to the east were all aglow with his rays, mimicking the real fires that were already breaking out in various parts of the city. In the lower part of the city, the School-ship *Patrick Henry* was burning, and some of the houses near the Navy Yard were on fire. But higher up was the principal scene of the conflagration. Entire blocks were on fire here, and a dense canopy of smoke, rising high in the still morning air, was covering the city as with a pall. The rearguard of our army had just crossed as I landed my fleet at Manchester, and the bridges were burning in their rear. The Tredegar Iron Works were on fire, and continual explosions of loaded shell stored there were taking place. In short, the scene cannot be described by mere words, but the reader may conceive a tolerable idea of it if he will imagine himself to be looking on Pandemonium broken loose.

The population was in a great state of alarm. Hundreds of men and women had sought refuge on the Manchester side in the hope of getting away by some means or other, they knew not how. I was, myself, about the most helpless man in the whole crowd. I had just tumbled on shore, with their bags and baggage, 500 sailors, incapable of marching a dozen miles without becoming footsore, and without any means whatever of transportation being provided for them. I had not so much as a pack mule to carry a load of provisions. I was on foot, myself, in the midst of my men. A current of horsemen belonging to our retreating column was sweeping past me, but there was no horse for me to mount. It was every man for himself, and devil take the hindmost. Some of the young cavalry rascals—lads of eighteen or twenty— as they passed, jibed and joked with my old salts, asking them how they liked navigating the land, and whether they did not expect to anchor in Fort Warren pretty soon? The spectacle presented by my men was, indeed, rather a ludicrous one; loaded down as they were with pots, and pans, and mess-kettles, bags of bread, and chunks of salted pork, sugar, tea, tobacco, and pipes. It was as much as they could do to stagger under their loads—marching any distance seemed out of the question. As I reviewed my "troops" after they had been drawn up by my captains who were now all become colonels, I could not but repeat to myself Mr Mallory's last words— "You will join General Lee in the field with all your forces."

Yes; here were my "forces," but where the devil was General Lee, and how was I to join him? If I had had the Secretary of the Navy on foot by the side of me, I rather think this latter question would have puzzled him.

But there was no time to be lost—I must do something. The first thing, of course, after landing my men, was to burn my wooden gunboats. This was done. They were fired and shoved off from the landing and permitted to float down the stream. I then put my column in motion, and we marched a distance of several squares, blinded by the dust kicked up by those vagabonds on horseback. When we came in sight of the railroad depot, I halted and inquired of some of the fugitives who were rushing by, about the trains.

"The trains!" said they in astonishment at my question; "the last train left at daylight this morning—it was filled with the civil officers of the Government."

Notwithstanding this answer, I moved my command up to the station and workshops to satisfy myself by a personal inspection. It was well that I did so, as it saved my command from the capture that impended over it. I found it quite true that the last train had departed; and also that all the railroad men had either run off in the train or hidden themselves out of view. There was no one in charge of anything, and no one who knew anything. But there was some material lying around me; and with this I resolved to set up railroading on my own account. Having a dozen and more steam engineers along with me from my late fleet, I was perfectly independent of the assistance of the alarmed railroad men who had taken to flight.

A pitiable scene presented itself upon our arrival at the station. Great numbers had flocked thither in the hope of escape; frightened men, despairing women, and crying children. Military patients had hobbled thither from the hospitals; civil employees of the Government, who had missed the last train by being a little too late, had come to remedy their negligence; and a great number of other citizens who were anxious to get out of the presence of the hated Yankee had rushed to the station, they scarcely knew why. These people had crowded into and on the top of a few straggling passenger cars that lay uncoupled along the track in seeming expectation that some one was to come in due time and take them off. There was a small engine lying also on the track, but there was no fire in its furnace, no fuel with which to make a fire, and no one to manage it. Such was the condition of affairs when I deployed my forces upon the open square, and grounded arms—the butts of my rifles not ringing on the ground quite as harmoniously as I could have desired. Soldiering was new to Jack; however, he would do better by-and-by.

My first move was to turn all these wretched people I have described out of the cars. Many plaintive appeals were made to me by the displaced individuals, but my reply to them all was that it was better for an unarmed citizen to fall into the hands of the enemy than a soldier with arms in his hands. The cars were then drawn together and coupled, and my own people placed in them. We next took the engine in hand. A body of my marine sappers and miners were set at work to pull down a picket fence in front of one of the dwellings and chop it into firewood. An engineer and firemen were detailed for the locomotive, and in a very few minutes we had

the steam hissing from its boiler. I now permitted as many of
the frightened citizens as could find places to clamber upon the
cars. All being in readiness, with the triumphant air of a man
who had overcome a great difficulty and who felt as if he
might snap his fingers at the Yankees once more, I gave the
order to go ahead. But this was easier said than done. The
little locomotive started at a snail's pace and drew us creep-
ingly along until we reached a slightly ascending grade, which
occurs almost immediately after leaving the station. Here it
came to a dead halt. The firemen stirred their fires, the engineer turned on all his steam, the engine panted and struggled and screamed, but all to no purpose. We were effectually
stalled. Our little iron horse was incompetent to do the work
which had been required of it. Here was a predicament!

We were still directly opposite the city of Richmond and
in full view of it, for the track of the road runs some distance
up the riverbank before it bends away westward. Amid
flames and smoke and tumult and disorder, the enemy's hosts
were pouring into the streets of the proud old capital. Long
lines of cavalry and artillery and infantry could be seen moving like a huge serpent through the streets and winding their
way to State House Square. As a crowning insult, a regiment
of Negro cavalry, wild with savage delight at the thought of
triumphing over their late masters, formed a prominent feature in the grand procession. Alongside the black savage
marched the white savage—worthy compeers! nay, scarcely;
the black savage under the circumstances was the more worthy
of respect of the two. The prophecy of Patrick Henry was
fulfilled; the very halls in which he had thundered forth the
prophecy were in possession of the "stranger," against whom
he had warned his countrymen!

My temporary safety lay in two circumstances: first, the
enemy was so drunk with his success that he had no eyes for
any one but himself and the population of the proud city
of Richmond which he was seeking to abase; and secondly,
the bridges leading across the river were all on fire. Whilst I
was pondering what was best to be done, whether I should
uncouple a portion of the train and permit the rest to escape,
an engineer came running to me to say that he had discovered
another engine, which the absconding railroad people had
hidden away in the recesses of their workshops. The new
engine was rolled out immediately, steam raised on it in a

few minutes, and by the aid of the two engines, we gave our train, with the indifferent fuel we had, a speed of five or six miles per hour until we reached the first wood pile. Here getting hold of some better fuel, we fired up with better effect and went thundering with the usual speed on our course.

It was thus, after I had, in fact, been abandoned by the Government and the Army that I saved my command from capture. I make no charges—utter no complaints. Perhaps neither the Government nor the Army was to blame. The great disaster fell upon them both so suddenly that perhaps neither could do any better; but the naked fact is that the fleet was abandoned to shift for itself, there being not only no transportation provided for carrying a pound of provisions or a cooking utensil, but not even a horse for its Admiral to mount. As a matter of course, great disorder prevailed in all the villages and at all the waystations by which we passed. We had a continual accession of passengers until not another man could be packed upon the train. So great was the demoralization that we picked up "unattached" generals and colonels on the road in considerable numbers. The most amusing part of our journey, however, was an attempt made by some of the railroad officials to take charge of our train after we had gotten some distance from Richmond. Conductors and engineers now came forward and insisted upon regulating our affairs for us. We declined the good offices of these gentlemen and navigated to suit ourselves. The president, or superintendent of the road, I forget which, even had the assurance to complain afterward to President Davis at Danville of my usurping his authority! Simple civilian! discreet railroad officer! to scamper off in the manner related and then to complain of my usurping his authority! My railroad cruise ended the next day—April 4th—about midnight, when we reached the city of Danville and blew off our steam, encamping in the cars for the remainder of the night. Our escape had been narrow in more respects than one. After turning Lee's flank at the Five Forks, the enemy made a dash at the Southside Railroad; Sheridan with his cavalry tearing up the rails at the Burksville Junction just *one hour and a half* after we had passed it.

Chapter Thirty—*1865*

An interview with President Davis and Secretary Mallory . . . The command is organized as a brigade of artillery . . . Brigade marches to Greensboro, North Carolina . . . Capitulation between General Joseph E. Johnston and Sherman . . . Dispersion of Johnston's troop . . . The author returns home and is arrested . . . Conclusion

My memoirs are drawing to a close, for the career of the Confederacy, as well as my own, is nearly ended. I found at Danville, President Davis and a portion of his cabinet—the Secretary of the Navy among the rest. Here was temporarily established the seat of Government. I called on the President and Secretary, who were staying at the same house, at an early hour on the morning after my arrival and reported for duty. They were both calm in the presence of the great disaster which had befallen them and the country. Mr. Mallory could scarcely be said now to have a portfolio, though he still had the officers and clerks of his Department around him. It was at once arranged between him and the President, that my command should be organized as a brigade of artillery and assigned to the defences around Danville. The question

426

of my rank being discussed, it was settled by Mr. Davis that I should act in the capacity of a brigadier-general. My grade being that of a rear admiral, I was entitled to rank relatively with the officers of the Army as a major-general, but it was folly, of course, to talk of rank in the circumstances in which we were placed, and so I contented myself by saying pleasantly to the President that I would waive the matter of rank to be discussed hereafter if there should ever be occasion to discuss it. "That is the right spirit," said he with a smile playing over his usually grave features.

I did not see him afterward. He moved soon to Charlotte, North Carolina, and a few weeks afterward he fell into the hands of the enemy. The reader knows the rest of his history; how the enemy gloated over his captivity; how he was reviled and insulted by the coarse and brutal men into whose power he had fallen; how lies were invented as to the circumstances of his capture to please and amuse the Northern multitudes, eager for his blood; and finally, how he was degraded by imprisonment and the manacles of a felon! His captors and he were of different races—of different blood. They had nothing in common. He was the Cavalier, endowed by nature with the instincts and refinement of the gentleman. They were of the race of the Roundheads to whom all such instincts and refinements were offensive. God has created men in different molds, as he has created the animals. It was as natural that the Yankee should hate Jefferson Davis as that the cat should arch its back and roughen its fur, upon the approach of the dog. I have said that the American war had its origin in money and that it was carried on throughout "for a consideration." It ended in the same way. The "long-haired barbarian"—see Gibbon's *Decline and Fall of the Roman Empire*—who laid his huge paw upon Jefferson Davis to make him prisoner was paid in money for the gallant deed. A President of the United States had degraded his high office by falsely charging Mr. Davis with being an accomplice in the murder of President Lincoln and offered a reward for his apprehension; thus gratifying his malignant nature by holding him up to the world as a common felon. All men now know this charge to be false, the libeller among the rest. Gentlemen retract false charges when they know them to be such. The charge made by Andrew Johnson against Jefferson Davis has not been retracted.

Upon leaving the presence of the President and Secretary of the Navy, I sought out my old friend, Captain Sydney Smith Lee of the Navy, the Assistant Secretary, who had accompanied Mr. Mallory, and arranged with him, and afterward with General Cooper, the Adjutant-General of the Army, the transformation of my sailors into soldiers. There were a great many other naval officers besides those under my command, fugitives in Danville, and the President and Secretary had been kind enough to authorize me to employ such of them in my new organization as I might desire. But the difficulty was not in the want of officers; it was the want of men. Already my command of five hundred had dwindled down to about four hundred on my retreat from Richmond and since my arrival in Danville. I broke these into skeleton regiments, so as to conform to the Brigade organization, and appointed Dunnington, late captain of my flagship, the colonel of one of them, and Johnston, late captain of the *Richmond*, colonel of the other. My youngest son, who had been a midshipman on board the school ship at Richmond, and who had retreated thence with the school on the night before the surrender, was ordered by Captain Lee to report to me, and I assigned him to a position on my staff with the rank of a second lieutenant. Mr. Daniel, my secretary, became my other aide-de-camp, and Captain Butt, late commander of the *Nansemond*, was appointed Assistant Adjutant-General.

We remained in the trenches before Danville ten days; and anxious and weary days they were. Raiding parties were careering around us in various directions, robbing and maltreating the inhabitants, but none of the thieves ventured within reach of our guns. Lee abandoned his lines on the 3d of April, and surrendered his army, or the small remnant that was left of it, to Grant on the 9th at Appomattox Court-House. The first news we received of his surrender came to us from the stream of fugitives which now came pressing into our lines at Danville. It was heartrending to look upon these men, some on foot, some on horseback, some nearly famished for want of food, and others barely able to totter along from disease. It was, indeed, a rabble rout. Hopes had been entertained that Lee might escape to Lynchburg or to Danville and save his army. The President had entertained this hope and had issued a proclamation of encouragement to the people, before he left Danville. But the fatal tidings came at last, and when they did come, we all felt that the fate of the Confederacy was sealed.

A new impetus was given to desertions, and before I reached Greensboro', North Carolina, to which point I was now removed by the orders of General Joseph E. Johnston, my command had dwindled to about 250 men. Commissioned officers slunk away from me one by one, and became deserters! I was ashamed of my countrymen. Johnston, by reason of his great personal popularity, was enabled to gather around him the fragments of several armies, whilst Grant had been pressing Lee; and but for Lee's disaster would soon have been able to hold Sherman in check very effectually. But the moment the news of Lee's surrender reached him, there was a stampede from his army. It melted away like a hillock of snow before the sunshine. Whole companies deserted at a time. Still, many true men remained with him, and with these he stood so defiantly before Sherman that the latter was glad to enter into negotiations with him for the *dispersion* of his troops. The reader will be pleased to pay attention to this expression. Johnston *dispersed* his troops under the capitulation which will presently be spoken of. He never surrendered them as *prisoners* to the enemy. The country is familiar with what occurred at Greensboro' between Johnston and Sherman, and I do not propose to rehearse it here. Sherman, yielding to the impulses of Johnston's master mind, entered into an agreement with the latter which would have achieved more fame for him in the future than all his victories if he had had the courage and ability to stand up to his work. This agreement was that the Southern States should be regarded as *ipso facto*, on the cessation of the war, restored to their rights in the Union. The stroke was one of a statesman. It is in times of great revolutions that genius shows itself. The Federal Government at the time that this convention was made was prostrate beneath the foot of the soldier, and a military man of genius might have governed it with the crook of his finger. If such a one had arisen, he might have applied the scourge to the back of the Northern people and they would have yelped under it as submissively as any hound. They *had* yelped under the scourging of Abraham Lincoln. But Sherman was not the man to conceive the emergency or to avail himself of it. He, on the contrary, permitted himself to be scourged by a creature like Stanton, the Federal Secretary of War, and if he did not yelp under the scourging, he at least submitted to it with most admirable docility. Stanton insolently rejected the convention which had been entered into between the two generals, and, reminding Sherman that he was nothing but a soldier, told him to attend to his own business. Stanton knew his man, and Sherman did afterward attend to his own business; for he now entered into a purely military convention with Johnston.

The main features of that convention were that Johnston should disperse his army, and Sherman should, in consideration thereof, guarantee it against molestation by the Federal authorities. It was in the interval between these two conventions, that my camp was astounded one morning, by the report that Abraham Lincoln, President of the United States, was dead. He had gone to a small theater in the city of Washington on the evening of Good Friday and had been shot by a madman! It seemed like a just retribution that he should be cut off in the midst of the hosannas that were being shouted in his ears for all the destruction and ruin he had wrought upon twelve millions of people. Without any warrant for his conduct, he had made a war of rapine and lust against eleven sovereign states, whose only provocation had been that they had made an effort to preserve the liberties which had been handed down to them by their fathers. These states had not sought war but peace, and they had found, at the hands of Abraham Lincoln, destruction. As a Christian, it was my duty to say, "Lord, have mercy upon his soul!" but the devil will surely take care of his memory.

The last days of April and the first days of May were employed by General Johnston in dispersing his army according to agreement. Commissioners appointed by the two Generals to arrange the dispersion and provide the dispersed troops with the guaranties that had been agreed upon, met in the village of Greensboro' on the 1st of May, 1865. On the previous evening I had called at the headquarters of General Johnston, where I had met Beauregard, Wade Hampton, Wheeler, D. H. Hill, and a host of other gallant spirits who formed the galaxy by which he was surrounded. He was kind enough to give me precedence in the matter of arranging for my departure with the Federal Commissioner. Accordingly, on the morning of the 1st of May, accompanied by my staff, I rode into Greensboro' and alighted at the Britannia Hotel, where the Commissioners were already assembled. They were Brevet Brigadier-General Hartsuff on the part of the Federals, and Colonel Mason on the part of the Confederates. Each guaranty of non-molestation had been prepared beforehand in a printed form and signed by Hartsuff, and only required to be filled up with the name and rank of the party entitled to receive it and signed by myself to be complete. Upon being introduced to General Hartsuff, we proceeded at once to business. I produced the muster-roll of my command duly signed by my Assistant Adjutant-General; and General Hartsuff and myself ran our eyes over the names together, and when we had ascertained the number, the General counted out an equal number of blank guaranties, and handing them to me said: "You have only to fill up one of these for each officer and soldier of your command with his name and rank, and sign it and hand it to him. I have already signed them myself. You can fill up the one intended for yourself in like manner."

"With regard to the latter," I replied, "I prefer, if you have no objection, to have it filled up and completed here in your presence."

"Oh! that makes no difference," he replied.

"Very well," said I, "if it makes no difference, then you can have no objection to complying with my request."

He now called an aide-de-camp, and desiring him to be seated at the table where we were, told him to fill up my guaranty after my dictation. I gave him my titles separately, making him write me down a "Rear-Admiral in the Confederate States Navy, and a Brigadier-General in the Confederate States Army, commanding a brigade." When he had done this, he handed me the paper; I signed it and put it in my pocket, and turning to the General said, "I am now satisfied." The following is a copy of the paper:

GREENSBORO', NORTH CAROLINA, May 1, 1865

In accordance with the terms of the Military Convention entered into on the 26 day of April 1865, between General Joseph E. Johnston, commanding the Confederate Army, and Major-General W. T. Sherman, commanding the United States Army, in North Carolina, *R. Semmes, Rear-Admiral, and Brigadier-General, C. S. Navy, and C. S. Army, commanding brigade,* has given his solemn obligation not to take up

arms against the Government of the United States until
properly released from this obligation; and is permitted to
return to his home, not to be disturbed by the United States
authorities so long as he observes this obligation and obeys
the laws in force where he may reside.   R. SEMMES
                                    Rear-Admiral C. S. Navy, and
                                    Brigadier-General C. S. Army
WM. HARTSUFF
          Brevet Brigadier-General U. S. Army
                    Special Commissioner

It was well I took the precautions above described in dealing with the enemy, for when I was afterward arrested, the
Yankee press, howling for my blood, claimed that I had not
been paroled at all! that I had deceived the paroling officer,
and obtained my parole under false pretences; the said paroling officer not dreaming, when he was paroling one Brigadier-
General Semmes that he had the veritable "pirate" before
him. I dispersed my command on the same afternoon, and
with my son and half a dozen of my officers, a baggage
wagon, and the necessary servants, made my way to Montgomery, Alabama, and at that point, took steamer for my
home in Mobile, which I reached in the latter days of May.

Andrew Johnson, the Vice-President of the United States,
had succeeded Mr. Lincoln as President. He was a Southern
man, born in the State of North Carolina, and a citizen of
Tennessee. He had been elected to the Senate of the United
States a short time before the breaking out of the war. He had
belonged to the Democratic Party and had arisen from a
very low origin—his father having belonged to the common
class of laborers, and he having learned the trade of a tailor,
which he practised after he had grown to man's estate. Gifted
by nature with a strong intellect, he studied the law and
afterward embarked in politics. The word "embark" ex-
presses my idea precisely, for from this time onward he became a mere politician. As a rule it requires an unscrupulous
and unprincipled man to succeed in politics in America. Honorable men do sometimes, of course, make their way to high
places; but these form the exceptions, not the rule. Andrew
Johnson succeeded in politics. In the earlier stages of our
troubles he spoke and wrote like a Southern man, demanding,
in behalf of the South some security for the future in the

way of additional guaranties. But when these were all denied, and it became evident that his state would secede, and that he would be stripped of his Senatorial honors, so recently won, if he abided by his former record and went with his state, he abjured his record, and abandoned his state. Like all renegades, he became zealous in the new faith which he had adopted and proved himself so good a Radical that President Lincoln sent him back to Tennessee as a satrap to govern with a rod of iron, under military rule, the Sovereign State for which he had so recently demanded additional securities.

Still growing in favor with his new party, he was elected Vice-President upon the re-election of Mr. Lincoln in the fall of 1864. The Presidential mantle having fallen upon him by the tragical death of Mr. Lincoln, he retained the Cabinet of his predecessor, and made his zeal still more manifest to his party by insisting on the necessity of making treason odious—the same sort of treason enjoined upon the states by Jefferson in his Kentucky Resolutions of 1798 and 1799, which formed the basis of the creed of the Democratic Party to which Mr. Johnson had belonged—and punishing "traitors." A grand jury in Norfolk, Va., found an indictment for treason against General Lee, and but for the interposition of General Grant, he would have been tried under Mr. Johnson's administration; and probably tried by a packed jury that would have hanged him. Mr. Davis was already in close and ignominious confinement, as has been related. Captain Wirz, of the late Confederate States Army, who had been for a short time in charge of the prison at Andersonville, was tried by a Military Commission in the city of Washington under the shadow of the President's chair, convicted, and executed, notwithstanding he was a paroled *prisoner of war.* Another Military Commission *in time of peace* had convicted and executed a woman—Mrs. [Anna] Surratt—on the false charge, as is now admitted by the whole country, that she was an accomplice in Mr. Lincoln's assassination. Mr. Johnson signed her death warrant.

It was under these circumstances that on the night of the 15th of December, 1865, or seven months and a half after I had received the guaranty of General Sherman at Greensboro', North Carolina, that I should not be molested by the United States authorities, that a lieutenant of the Marine Corps with a guard of soldiers, surrounded my house and arrested me on an order signed by Mr. Gideon Welles without the process of any court. I was torn from my family under guard—the thieving soldiery committing some petty thefts about my premises—and hurried off to Washington. Arrived here, I was imprisoned, first in the Navy Yard and then in the Marine Barracks. I was kept a close prisoner with a sentinel at my door for nearly four months; the gentlemen about the barracks however, doing everything in their power to render my confinement more endurable. It was the intention of the Government to throw me, as it had thrown Wirz, as a sop to the extreme Radicals of the New England states, whose commerce I had destroyed; and I was only saved by the circumstances which will be presently related. But before I relate these circumstances, I deem it pertinent to give to the reader the following letter* addressed by me to President Johnson from my place of confinement, charging his Government with a breach of faith in arresting me.

To His Excellency Andrew Johnson
President of the United States

Sir: Being satisfied that you are anxious to arrive at a correct decision in my case—one that shall accord, at the same time, with the honor and dignity of the United States and with justice to myself—I venture to address you the following brief exposition of the law and the facts of the case.

On the 26th day of April, 1865, the following military convention was entered into at Greensboro', N. C., between General Joseph E. Johnston, commanding the Confederate States Armies in North Carolina, and Major-General W. T. Sherman, commanding the United States Army in the same state, viz:

1. All acts of war on the part of the troops under General Johnston's command to cease from this date.

2. All arms and public property to be deposited at Greensboro' and delivered to an ordnance officer of the United States Army.

3. Rolls of all the officers and men to be made in duplicate, one copy to be retained by the commander of the troops, and the other to be given to an officer to be designated by General

---

* In this long letter, which Semmes himself calls tedious, he is very much the lawyer arguing his own case. Ed.

Sherman. Each officer and man to give his individual obligation in writing not to take up arms against the Government of the United States until properly released from this obligation.

4. The side-arms of officers and their private horses and baggage to be retained by them.

5. This being done, all the officers and men will be permitted to return to their homes, not to be disturbed by the United States authorities so long as they observe their obligation and the laws in force where they may reside.

[Signed]   W. T. SHERMAN, *Major-General*
        Commanding U. S. Forces in North Carolina
[Signed]   "JOSEPH E. JOHNSTON, *General*
        Commanding C. S. Forces in North Carolina

Here, Mr. President, was a solemn military convention entered into by two generals, who had opposing armies in the field, in which convention the one and the other general stipulated for certain terms—General Johnston agreeing to lay down his arms and disband his forces, and General Sherman agreeing, *in consideration thereof*, that the forces thus disbanded shall proceed to their homes and there remain undisturbed by the United States authorities. I beg you to observe the use of the word "undisturbed," one of the most comprehensive words in our language. I pray you also to remark the formalities with which this convention was drawn. We were treated as officers commanding armies, representing, of course, if not a *de jure*, at least a *de facto* government. Our proper military titles were acknowledged. I was myself styled and treated on the muster-rolls, and other papers drawn up by both parties, a brigadier-general and a rear-admiral. The honors of war usual upon surrenders, upon terms, were accorded to us in our being permitted to retain our side-arms, private horses, and baggage. In short, the future historian, upon reading this convention, will be unable to distinguish it in any particular from other similar papers agreed upon by armies of recognized governments.

At the date of, and some weeks prior to the ratification of this convention, I commanded a brigade of artillery, forming a part of the army of General Johnston. I was, of course, included in the terms of the convention. I complied with those terms under orders received from General Johnston by turning over my arms to the proper officer and disbanding my forces. The convention was approved by the Government of the United States. Your Excellency may recollect that the first convention entered into between General Johnston and General Sherman, which provided, among other things, for the return of the Southern States to their functions under the Constitution of the United States, was disapproved by the Government on the ground that General Sherman, in undertaking to treat of political matters, had transcended his authority. The armistice which had been declared between the two armies was dissolved and hostilities were renewed. A few days afterward, however, new negotiations were commenced, and the convention with which we have to do was the second convention entered into by those Generals, and which was a substantial readoption of the military portion of the first convention. It was this latter convention which was formally approved both by General Grant, the Commander-in-Chief, under whose orders General Sherman acted, and by the Executive at Washington.

Confiding in the good faith of the Government pledged in a solemn treaty as above stated, I returned to my home in Alabama and remained there for the space of seven months, engaging in civil pursuits as a means of livelihood for my dependent family and yielding a ready obedience to the laws. I had, in fact, become an officer of the law, having established myself as an attorney. It would have been easy for me at any time within these seven months to pass out of the country if I had had any doubt about the binding obligation of the Greensboro' convention or of the good faith of the Government. But I had no doubt on either point, nor have I any doubt yet, as I feel quite sure that when you shall have informed yourself of all the facts of the case, you will come to the conclusion that my arrest was entirely without warrant and order my discharge. While thus remaining quietly at my home in the belief that I was "not to be disturbed by the United States authorities," I was, on the 15th of December, 1865, in the nighttime, arrested by a lieutenant and two sergeants of the Marine Corps under an order signed by the Secretary of the Navy, and placed under guard; a file of soldiers in the meantime surrounding my house. I was informed by the officer making the arrest that I was to proceed to Washington in his custody, there to answer to a charge, a copy of which he handed me. This charge, and the protest which I filed the next day with the Commanding General of the Department of Alabama, against my arrest, your Excellency has already seen. The question for you then to decide, Mr. President, is the legality of this arrest. Can I, in violation

of the terms of the military convention already referred to
and under which I laid down my arms, be held to answer for
any act of war committed anterior to the date of the convention? I respectfully submit that I cannot be so held, either
during the continuance of the war, (and the political power
has not yet proclaimed the war ended,) or after the war shall
have been brought to a close by proclamation, and the
restoration of the writ of *habeas corpus*, without a flagrant
violation of faith on the part of the United States. If it be
admitted that I might be tried for any act *dehors* the war,
and having no connection with it—as, for instance, for a
forgery—it is quite clear that I cannot be arrested or arraigned
for any act manifestly of war and acknowledged as such, (as
the act, for instance, for which I was arrested,) whether such
act be in consonance with the laws of war or in violation
thereof; and this for the simple reason that the military convention was a *condonation* and an *oblivion* of all precedent
acts of war of what nature soever those acts might be.

I am "not to be disturbed" says the military convention.
Disturbed for what? Why, manifestly, for any act of war
theretofore committed against the United States. This is the
only commonsense view of the case; and if the convention
did not mean this, it could mean nothing; and I laid down
my arms, not upon terms, as I had supposed, but without
terms. If I was still at the mercy of the conqueror, and my
arrest asserts as much, I was in the condition of one who
had surrendered *unconditionally*, but it has been seen that
I did not surrender unconditionally, but upon terms—terms
engrafted upon a treaty ratified and approved by the conqueror's Government. Nor is it consistent with good faith
to qualify or restrain those terms, so as to make them in-
applicable to acts of war that may be claimed to have been
in violation of the laws of war; for this would be to refine away
all the protection which has been thrown around me by treaty,
and put me in the power of the opposite contracting party,
who might put his own construction upon the laws of war.
This very attempt, Mr. President, has been made in the case
before you. I claim to have escaped after my ship had sunk
from under me in the engagement off Cherbourg, and I had
been precipitated into the water, the enemy not having taken
possession of me according to the laws and usages of war, as
your Excellency may read in almost every page of naval
history; the Secretary of the Navy claiming the contrary. The
true, and the only just and fair criterion, is, was the act for

which the arrest was made an act of war? If so, there is an
end of the question, and I must be discharged, for, as before
remarked, the convention, if it is anything, is an oblivion of
all acts of war of whatever nature.

But it may be said that although I cannot be tried by a
military tribunal during the war, I may yet be tried by a civil
tribunal after the war. Let us look at this question also. I
was undoubtedly amenable to the civil tribunals of the
country as well after as before the convention for any offence
of a purely civil nature not founded upon an act of war—to
instance, as before, the crime of forgery. If I had committed
a forgery in North Carolina, I could not, upon arraignment,
plead the military convention in bar of trial. Why not?
Because that convention had reference only to acts of war.
I was treated with, in my capacity of a soldier and a seaman.
But, does it follow that I may be tried for treason? And if
not, why not? The Attorney-General tells you that treason
is a civil offence, and in his opinion triable exclusively by
the civil courts, and he hopes you will give him plenty of
occupation in trying "many whom the sword has spared."
(See his letter to you of the 4th of January, 1866.) But does
not that officer forget that treason is made up of acts of war;
and is it not apparent that you cannot try me for an act of
war? The Constitution of the United States, which the Attorney-General says he loves even better than blood, declares
that treason against the United States shall consist only in
levying war against them, or in adhering to their enemies,
giving them aid and comfort—all of which adherence, giving
of aid and comfort, &c., are equally acts of war. There is no
constructive treason in this country. Thus I can neither be
tried by a military tribunal during the war, nor a civil tribunal after the war, for any act of war, or for treason which
consists only of acts of war.

But it may further be said that this convention of which I
am claiming the protection is not a *continuing* convention
and will expire with the war, when, as Mr. Speed thinks, you
may hand me over to the civil tribunals. Whence can such
a conclusion be drawn? Not from the terms of the convention,
for these contradict the conclusion; not by implication merely
but in *totidem verbis*. The terms are, "not to be disturbed *so
long as they shall observe their obligation and the laws in force
where they may reside.*" A misuse of terms, Mr. President,
sometimes misleads very clever minds. And I presume it is by
a misuse of terms that the Attorney-General has fallen into

this error. (See his letter to your Excellency, before referred to.) That officer, while he admits that PAROLE protects the party paroled from trial during the war, yet contends that it does not protect him from trial by a civil tribunal for treason, after the war. As I have shown that treason can only consist of acts of war, and that the military convention is an oblivion of all acts of war, the Attorney-General, when he says that a paroled party may be tried for treason at the end of the war, (the parole being no longer a protection to him,) must mean that the parole will have died with the war. This is entirely true of a *mere parole*, for a parole is only a promise on the part of a prisoner of war that if released from imprisonment, he will not take up arms again unless he is exchanged. This parole is as frequently given by prisoners of war who have surrendered unconditionally, as by those who have surrendered upon terms. There cannot be any parole, then, without a prisoner of war, and the status of prisoner of war ceasing, the parole ceases—*cessante ratione cessat et ipsa lex*. Thus far the Attorney-General is quite logical, but by confounding in his mind the certificates given to the officers and men of General Johnston's army, stating the terms of the Greensboro' convention and guaranteeing those officers and men against molestation in accordance with those terms, with PAROLES, it is easy to see how the mistake I am exposing can have been made. But the convention made between General Johnston and General Sherman was not a mere release of prisoners on parole; nor, indeed, had it anything to do with prisoners, for none of the officers and men of General Johnston's army ever were prisoners, as may be seen at a glance by an inspection of the terms of the convention. It was a treaty between commanding generals in the field, in which the word *parole* is not once used, or could be used with propriety; a treaty in which mutual stipulations are made, one in consideration of another, and there is no limit as to time set to this treaty.

On the contrary, it was expressly stated that the guaranties contained in it were to continue and be in force so long as the parties to whom the guaranties were given should perform their part of the treaty sipulations. It was made, not in contemplation of a continuation of the war, but with a view to put an end to the war, and the guaranties were demanded by us as *peace guaranties*. It did, in effect, put an end to the war and pacify the whole country; General Taylor in Alabama and Mississippi, and General Buckner and others in

Texas, following the lead of General Johnston. Are we to be told now by an Attorney-General of the United States, that the moment the object of the convention, to wit, the restoration of peace, was accomplished, the convention itself became a nullity, its terms powerless to protect us, and that General Johnston's army surrendered, in fact, without any terms whatever? You cannot sustain such an opinion, Mr. President. It will shock the common sense and love of fair play of the American people. But to show still further that it was the intention of the parties that this should be a continuing convention, the words used were, "not to be disturbed by the United States Authorities," these words being co-extensive with the whole power of the Government. We were not only "not to be disturbed" by General Sherman or any other military commander or authority but by any authority whatever, civil or military. Nor will it do to say that General Sherman, being merely a military man, had no authority to speak for the civil branch of the Government, for his action, as we have seen, was approved by the Administration at Washington.

One more remark, Mr. President, and I will forbear to trespass further on your time and patience. The act of war for which I was arrested was well known to the Department of the Government making the arrest ten months before the convention was entered into at Greensboro'. It was also well known to the same Department that about the middle of February, 1865, I was assigned to the command of the James River Squadron near Richmond with the rank of a rear-admiral; being thus promoted and employed by my Government after the alleged illegal escape off Cherbourg. If the Federal Government then entertained the design which it has since developed of arresting and trying me for this alleged breach of the laws of war, was it not its duty, both to itself and to me, to have made me an exception to any military terms it might have been disposed to grant to our armies? I put it to you, Mr. President, as a man and a magistrate, to say, and I will rest my case on your answer, whether it was consistent with honor and fair dealing, for this Government first to entrap me by means of a military convention, and then, having me in its power, to arrest me and declare that convention null and void, for the course recommended to you by Mr. Speed comes to this—nothing more, nothing less.

I have thus laid before you, tediously I fear, and yet as concisely as was consistent with clearness, the grounds upon which I claim at your hands, who are the guardian of the honor of a great nation, my discharge from arrest and imprisonment. I have spoken freely and frankly, as it became an American citizen to speak to the Chief Magistrate of the American Republic. We live in times of high party excitement, when men unfortunately are but too prone to take counsel of their passions; but passions die, and men die with them, and after death comes history. In the future, Mr. President, when America *shall* have a history, my record and that of the gallant Southern people will be engrafted upon and become a part of your history, the pages of which you are now acting; and the prayer of this petition is that you will not permit the honor of the American name to be tarnished by a perfidy on those pages. In this paper I have stood strictly upon legal defences; but should those barriers be beaten down, conscious of the rectitude of my conduct throughout a checkered and eventful career, when the commerce of half a world was at my mercy, and when the passions of men, North and South, were tossed into a whirlwind by the current events of the most bloody and terrific war that the human race had ever seen, I shall hope to justify and defend myself against any and all charges affecting the honor and reputation of a man and a soldier. Whatever else may be said of me, I have, at least, brought no discredit upon the American name and character.

I am, very respectfully, &c.,
RAPHAEL SEMMES

WASHINGTON CITY, January 15, 1866

At the time of my arrest, there was a newspaper called the *Republican* published in the city of Washington in the interests of President Johnson. There had been some little struggle between Congress and the President as to who should take the initiative in the wholesale hanging of "traitors" which had been resolved upon. The *Republican* speaking for President Johnson declares in the article which will be found below, *his* readiness to act. He is only waiting, it says, for Congress to move in the matter. Here is the article:

WHY DON'T CONGRESS ACT?

As long ago as last October, the President of the United States commenced an earnest effort to initiate the trials of prominent traitors, beginning with the arch-traitor Jefferson

Davis. It is now a historical record, and officially in the
possession of the Congress of the United States, that, upon
application to the Chief Justice of the Supreme Court to
know at what time, if any, the United States Court for the
District of Virginia would be ready to try certain high crimes
against the National Government, the President received an
answer from Chief-Justice Chase, that the Court would not
sit in that district, while that territory was under military control, and suggested the propriety of delaying action in the
matter, until Congress acted. Congress assembled. The President referred the whole subject, respectfully, to the consideration of Congress in his annual message, and subsequently,
in answer to a resolution of inquiry, he sent, by special message, the correspondence alluded to above, between himself
and Chief-Justice Chase.

All the facts were thus legitimately laid before the legisla-
tive branch of the Government *three and a half months ago!*
The President, some time in November last, stopped the work
of pardoning, except in a few cases where the applications
were accompanied by the most positive evidence of good intentions toward the Government. From among those who
have applied for pardon, the President has reserved for trial
about *five hundred* of the military and political leaders of the
rebel Government—a sufficient number to begin with at least.
This number, as classified by the President, we published, by
permission, some time since.

Now, in view of the above statement of facts, what has
Congress done? Has Congress passed any law directing how
the rebels shall be tried? No. Has Congress passed any resolution requesting the President to order a military court for
the trial of Davis & Co.? No. Has Congress agitated the subject at any time, in any manner, looking to a trial of the cases
referred to? No.

But what have Congressmen done in their individual capacity? Many of them, from day to day, have spoken sneeringly
of the President, because he has not done what he began to
do, but which the Chief Justice of the Supreme Court prevented, by refusing to hold the court, and which the Congress
of the United States has wholly neglected, or *purposely
ignored.* The people, through the press of the country, and
in private communication, are beginning to inquire why
Congress don't act. Governors of States, ignorant of the facts,
are haranguing the people about the *indisposition* or *neglect*
of the *President* to try traitors. Why don't Congress act?

The President is ready, and has been ready from the beginning, to co-operate with Congress in any constitutional measure by which traitors can be tried, to the end that treason may thereby be made odious. We repeat the question with which we commenced, and which is echoed by the people everywhere, "Why don't Congress act?"

There is an old adage which says, "When rogues fall out, honest men get their rights." Fortunately for the "traitors" of the South, Andrew Johnson and the Congress quarreled. Johnson undertook to reconstruct the Southern States in *his* interests, and Congress claimed the right to reconstruct them in *its* interests. The Constitution of the United States was equally disregarded by them both. Johnson had no more respect for it than Congress. His mode of reconstruction equally violated it with that of Congress. It was a struggle between usurpers, which should be master—that was all. Johnson, with a single stroke of the pen, struck down all the State governments, called conventions of the people, and told the conventions what they should do. Congress might go a little farther, but its violation of the Constitution could not well be more flagrant. The breach widened from day to day, and the quarrel at last became bitter. Neither party, opposed by the other, could afford to become the hangman of the Southern people, and the very little program, which, according to the *Republican* newspaper, had been arranged between the rogues, naturally fell to the ground.

Johnson finding that his quarrel with Congress had ruined him with his party, now set about constructing a new one— a Johnson party. His scheme was to ignore both the Democratic and the Republican Parties. If he could succeed in reconstructing the Southern States to the exclusion of Congress, he might hope to get the votes of those states in the next Presidential election. But to conciliate these states, it would not do to hang "five hundred of the military and political leaders of the rebel Government" as a mere "beginning." He must pursue a different policy. He now issued first one amnesty proclamation and then another—doling out amnesty grudgingly in broken doses—until he had issued three of them. By the last of these proclamations, the writer of these pages, who was true to his state, was "graciously pardoned" by Andrew Johnson, who had not only been a traitor to his state, but had betrayed, besides, two political parties. A glorious opportunity presented itself for him to show himself a statesman. He has proved a charlatan instead. He cowered in his struggle with Congress, and that body has shorn him of his prerogatives, and reduced him to the mere position of a clerk. This is the second act of the drama, the first act of which was the secession of the Southern States. The form of government having been changed by the revolution, there are still other acts of the drama to be performed.

Appendix

Semmes' account of the battle between the Alabama and the *Kearsarge* is brief and inadequate—perhaps because he lost his ship. The account written by the *Alabama's* executive officer, John McIntosh Kell, is much better. He wrote it for the *Century* Magazine.

In his book, *Semmes of the Alabama,* (New York, 1938) W. Adolphe Roberts, compares the two versions:

The best authority on how the *Alabama* came to fight the *Kerarsarge*, as well as the emotional reasons behind Semmes's act, is not Semmes himself. It is Kell. The Captain, of course, gives an account of what he did, but his words do not impress [one] as being entirely candid. He treats the occurrence as a chapter in history, and is careful to place all the official documents on record. As to what was passing in his mind, he is profoundly reticent. He raises controversial questions which it should have been possible for him to clarify, but he snarls them by the violence of his partisanship. From the military point of view, he was a good loser. Politically, he was a rancorous one.

Kell . . . deals with his subject curtly. But every line has the ring of truth and stand up under investigation. Kell was no intellectual giant. He had a poor sense of the dramatic. His devotion to Semmes amounted to hero worship. He was . . . the perfect subordinate. His nationalism was unreasoned,

445

and therefore more inflexible than that of Semmes. Yet the man was so fundamentally honest, so simple in a noble sense, that he would have been incapable of suppressing a fact or coloring anything with the object of putting his cause in a better light. The little that he tells about Semmes and the *Alabama* at Cherbourg is worth all the pages of bombast written by others.

Kell's Account of the
Battle Between the
Alabama and the *Kearsarge*

On the 11th of June, 1864, we entered the port of Cherbourg and applied for permission to go into dock. There being none but national docks, the Emperor had first to be communicated with before permission could be granted, and he was absent from Paris. It was during this interval of waiting, on the third day after our arrival, that the *Kearsarge* steamed into the harbor for the purpose . . . of taking on board the prisoners we had landed from our last two prizes. Captain Semmes, however, objected to this on the ground that the *Kearsarge* was adding to her crew in a neutral port. The authorities conceding this objection valid, the *Kearsarge* steamed out of the harbor without anchoring. During her stay we examined her closely with our glasses, but she was keeping on the opposite side of the harbor out of the reach of a very close scrutiny, which accounts for our not detecting the boxing to her chain armor. After she left the harbor Captain Semmes sent for me to his cabin, and said: "I am going out to fight the *Kearsarge*; what do you think of it?" We discussed the battery, and especially the advantage the *Kearsarge* had over us in her 11-inch guns. She was built for a vessel of war, and we for speed, and though she carried one gun less, her battery was more effective at point-blank range. While the *Alabama* carried one more gun, the *Kearsarge* threw more metal at a broadside; and while our heavy guns were more effective at long range, her 11-inch guns gave her greatly the advantage at close range. She also had a slight advantage in her crew,

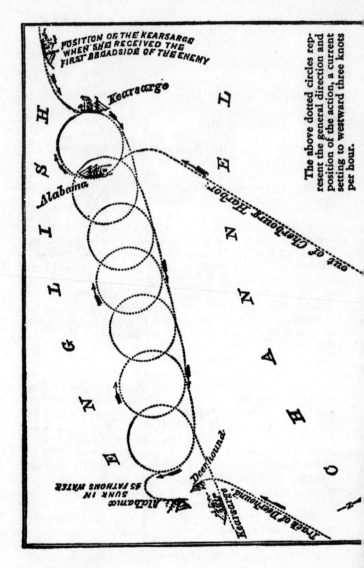

POSITION OF THE KEARSARGE WHEN SHE RECEIVED THE FIRST BROADSIDE OF THE ENEMY

Kearsarge

Alabama

Out of Cherbourg Harbor

The above dotted circles represent the general direction and position of the action, a current setting to westward three knots per hour.

Track of Deerhound.

Track of Kearsarge

The Alabama SUNK IN 45 FATHONS WATER

448

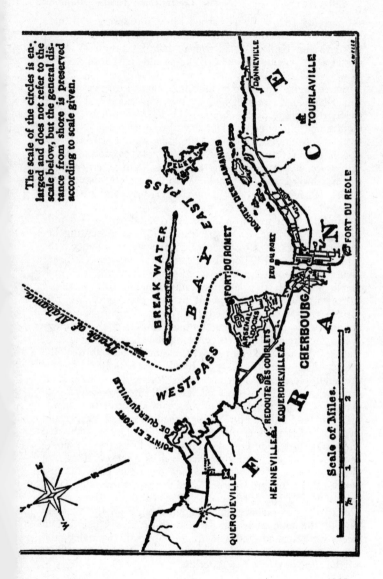

The scale of the circles is enlarged and does not refer to the scale below, but the general distance from shore is preserved according to scale given.

PELEE

BREAK WATER

EAST PASS

B A Y

WEST PASS

Strait of Alabama

POINTE ET FORT DE QUERQUEVILLE

QUERQUEVILLE

F

FORT DU ROMET

ROCHES DE FLAMANDS

FEU DU PORT

ARSENAL DOCKS

REDOUTE DES COUPLETS

EQUERDREVILLE

HENNEVILLE

CHERBOURG

R   A   N

FORT DU REOLE

C

TOURLAVILLE

DANNEVILLE

E

Scale of Miles.

½   1   2   3

she carrying 162, while we carried 149. Considering well these advantages, Captain Semmes communicated through our agent to the United States consul that if Captain Winslow would wait outside the harbor, he would fight him as soon as we could coal ship.

Accordingly, on Sunday morning, June 19th, between 9 and 10 o'clock, we weighed anchor and stood out of the western entrance of the harbor, the French ironclad frigate *Couronne* following us. The day was bright and beautiful with a light breeze blowing. Our men were neatly dressed, and our officers in full uniform. . . . As we rounded the breakwater we discovered the *Kearsarge* about seven miles to the northward and eastward. We immediately shaped our course for her, called all hands to quarters, and cast loose the starboard battery. . . .

In about forty-five minutes we were somewhat over a mile from the *Kearsarge*, when she headed for us, presenting her starboard bow. At a distance of a mile we commenced the action with our 100-pounder pivot-gun from our starboard bow. Both ships were now approaching each other at high speed, and soon the action became general with broadside batteries at a distance of about five hundred yards. To prevent passing, each ship used a strong port helm. Thus the action was fought around a common center, gradually drawing in the circle. At this range we used shell upon the enemy. Captain Semmes, standing on the horse-block abreast the mizzen-mast with his glass in hand, observed the effect of our shell. He called to me and said: "Mr. Kell, use solid shot; our shell strike the enemy's side and fall into the water." We were not at this time aware of the chain armor of the enemy, and attributed the failure of our shell to our defective ammunition. After using solid shot for some time, we alternated shell and shot. The enemy's 11-inch shells were now doing severe execution upon our quarter-deck section. Three of them successively entered our 8-inch pivot-gun port: the first swept off the forward part of the gun's crew; the second killed one man and wounded several others; and the third struck abreast of the gun-carriage and spun around on the deck till one of the men picked it up and threw it overboard. Our decks were now covered with the dead and the wounded, and the ship was careening heavily to starboard from the effects of the shot holes on her waterline.

Captain Semmes ordered me to be ready to make all sail possible when the circuit of fight should put our head to the coast of France; then he would notify me at the same time to pivot to port and continue the action with the port battery, hoping thus to right the ship and enable us to reach the coast of France. The evolution was performed beautifully, righting the helm, hoisting the head-sails, hauling aft the fore try-sail sheet, and pivoting to port, the action continuing almost without cessation.

This evolution exposed us to a raking fire, but strange to say, the *Kearsarge* did not take advantage of it. The port side of the quarter-deck was so encumbered with the mangled trunks of the dead that I had to have them thrown overboard in order to fight the after pivot-gun. I abandoned the after 32-pounder and transferred the men to fill up the vacanices at the pivot-gun under the charge of young Midshipman Anderson, who in the midst of the carnage filled his place like a veteran. At this moment the chief engineer came on deck and reported the fires put out, and that he could no longer work the engines. Captain Semmes said to me, "Go below, sir, and see how long the ship can float." As I entered the wardroom the sight was indeed appalling. There stood Assistant-Surgeon Llewellyn at his post, but the table and the patient upon it had been swept away from him by an 11-inch shell, which opened in the side of the ship an aperture that was fast filling the ship with water.

It took me but a moment to return to the deck and report to the captain that we could not float ten minutes. He replied to me, "Then, sir, cease firing, shorten sail, and haul down the colors; it will never do in this nineteenth century for us to go down, and the decks covered with our gallant wounded." The order was promptly executed, after which the *Kearsarge* deliberately fired into us five shot.* I ordered the men to

---

* In Captain Winslow's letter (dated Cherbourg, June 21st, 1864) to the Secretary of the Navy, he says: "Toward the close of the action between the *Alabama* and this vessel, all available sail was made on the former for the purpose of again reaching Cherbourg. When the object was apparent the *Kearsarge* was steered across the bow of the *Alabama* for a raking fire; but before reaching this point the *Alabama* struck. Uncertain whether Captain Semmes was using some ruse, the *Kearsarge* was stopped"—and, I may add,

stand to their quarters and not flinch from the shot of the enemy; they stood every man to his post most heroically. With the first shot fired upon us after our colors were down, the quartermaster was ordered to show a white flag over the stern, which order was executed in my presence. When the firing ceased, Captain Semmes ordered me to dispatch an officer to the *Kearsarge* to say that our ship was sinking and to ask that they send boats to save our wounded, as our boats were disabled. The dinghy, our smallest boat, had escaped damage. I dispatched Master's-mate Fullam with the request. No boats appearing, I had one of our quarter-boats lowered, which was slightly injured, and I ordered the wounded placed in her. Dr. Galt, the surgeon who was in charge of the magazine and shell-room division, came on deck at this

---

continued his fire, for by his own words he thought Captain Semmes was making some ruse. The report that the *Alabama* fired her guns after the colors were down and she had shortened sail is not correct. There was a cessation in the firing of our guns when we shifted our battery to port, after which we renewed the action.

Almost immediately afterward the engineer reported the fires put out, when we ceased firing, hauled down the colors, and shortened sail. There was no gun fired from the *Alabama* after that. Captain Winslow may have thought we had surrendered when we ceased firing and were in the act of shifting the battery; but the idle report that junior officers had taken upon themselves to continue the action after the order had been given to cease firing is not worthy of notice. I did not hear the firing of a gun, and the discipline of the *Alabama* would not have permitted it.—J. McI. K.

In the letter from which Captain Kell quotes Captain Winslow does not speak of "continuing his fire." But in his detailed report (dated July 30th, 1864) Captain Winslow says of the *Alabama*, after she had winded and set sail: "Her port broadside was presented to us with only two guns bearing, not having been able, as I learned afterward, to shift over but one. I saw now that she was at our mercy, and a few more guns well directed brought down her flag. I was unable to ascertain whether it had been hauled down or shot away; but a white flag having been displayed over the stern our fire was reserved. Two minutes had not more than elapsed before she again opened on us with the two guns on the port side. This drew our fire again, and the *Kearsarge* was immediately steamed ahead and laid across her bows for raking. The white flag was still flying, and our fire was again reserved. Shortly after this her boats were seen to be lowering, and an officer in one of them came alongside and informed us the ship had surrendered and was fast sinking."

moment and was at once put in charge of the boat with orders to "take the wounded to the *Kearsarge*." They shoved off just in time to save the poor fellows from going down in the ship.

I now gave the order for every man to jump overboard with a spar and save himself from the sinking ship. To enforce the order, I walked forward and urged the men overboard. As soon as the decks were cleared, save of the bodies of the dead, I returned to the stern-port, where stood Captain Semmes with one or two of the men and his faithful steward, who, poor fellow was doomed to a watery grave, as he could not swim. The *Alabama*'s stern-port was now almost at the water's edge. Partly undressing, we plunged into the sea and made an offing from the sinking ship, Captain Semmes with a life-preserver and I on a grating.

The *Alabama* settled stern foremost, launching her bows high in the air. Graceful even in her death struggle, she in a moment disappeared from the face of the waters. The sea now presented a mass of living heads, striving for their lives. Many poor fellows sank for the want of timely aid. Near me I saw a float of empty shell boxes, and called to one of the men, a good swimmer, to examine it; he did so and replied, "It is the doctor, sir, dead." Poor Llewellyn! he perished almost in sight of his home. The young midshipman, Maffitt, swam to me and offered his life preserver. My grating was not proving a very buoyant float, and the whitecaps breaking over my head were distressingly uncomfortable. Maffitt said: "Mr. Kell, take my life preserver, sir; you are almost exhausted." The gallant boy did not consider his own condition, but his pallid face told me that his heroism was superior to his bodily suffering, and I refused it. After twenty minutes or more I heard near me some one call out, "There is our first lieutenant," and the next moment I was pulled into a boat in which was Captain Semmes stretched out in the stern-sheets, as pallid as death. He had received during the action a slight contusion on the hand, and the struggle in the water had almost exhausted him. There were also several of our crew in the boat, and in a few moments we were alongside a little steam yacht, which had come among our floating men, and by throwing them ropes had saved many lives. Upon reaching her deck, I ascertained for the first time that she was the yacht *Deerhound*, owned by Mr. John Lancaster of England. In looking about I saw two French pilot boats engaged in saving our crew, and finally two boats from the *Kearsarge*. To my surprise I found on the yacht Mr. Fullam, whom I had dispatched in the dinghy to ask that boats be sent to save our wounded. He reported to me that our shot had literally torn the casing from the chain armor of the *Kearsarge*, indenting the chain in many places, which explained Captain Semmes's observation of the effect of our shell upon the enemy, "that they struck the sides and fell into the water."

Captain Winslow, in his report states that his ship was struck twenty-five or thirty times, and I doubt if the *Alabama* was struck a greater number of times. I may not, therefore, be bold in asserting that had not the *Kearsarge* been protected by her iron cables, the result of the fight would have been different. Captain Semmes felt the more keenly the delusion to which he fell a victim (not knowing the the *Kearsarge* was chainclad) from the fact that he was exceeding his instructions in seeking an action with the enemy; but to seek a fight with an ironclad he conceived to be an unpardonable error. However, he had the satisfaction of knowing she was classed as a wooden gunboat by the Federal Government; also that he had inspected her with most excellent glasses, and so far as outward appearances showed she displayed no chain armor. At the same time it must be admitted that Captain Winslow had the right unquestionably to protect his ship and crew. In justice to Captain Semmes I will state that the battle would never have been fought had he known that the *Kearsarge* wore an armor of chain beneath her outer covering. Thus was the *Alabama* lost by an error, but . . . a most pardonable one, and not until Father Neptune claimed her as his own did she lower her colors.

The 11-inch shells of the *Kearsarge* did fearful work, and her guns were served beautifully, being aimed with precision, and deliberate in fire. She came into action magnificently. Having the speed of us, she took her own position and fought gallantly. But she tarnished her glory when she fired upon a fallen foe. It was high noon of a bright, beautiful day with a moderate breeze blowing to waft the smoke of battle clear, and nothing to obstruct the view at five hundred yards. The very fact of the *Alabama* ceasing to fire, shortening sail, and hauling down her colors simultaneously, must have attracted the attention of the officer in command of the *Kearsarge*. Again, there is no reason given why the *Kearsarge* did not steam immediately into the midst of the crew of the *Alabama*, after their ship had been sunk, and, like a brave and generous foe save the lives of her enemies, who had fought nobly as long as they had a plank to stand upon. Were it not for the timely presence of the kind-hearted Englishman and the two French pilot boats, who can tell the number of us that would have rested with our gallant little ship beneath the waters of the English Channel? I quote the following from Mr. John Lancaster's letter to the London *Daily News*: "I presume it was because he [Captain Winslow] would not or could not save them himself. The fact is that if the captain and crew of the *Alabama* had depended for safety altogether upon Captain Winslow, not one half of them would have been saved."*

* In his report of June 21st, 1864, Captain Winslow said:

It was seen shortly afterward that the *Alabama* was lowering her boats, and an officer came alongside in one of them to say that they had surrendered and were fast sinking, and begging that boats would be dispatched immediately for the saving of life. The two boats not disabled were at once lowered, and as it was apparent the *Alabama* was settling, this officer was permitted to leave in his boat to afford assistance. An English yacht, the *Deerhound*, had approached near the *Kearsarge* at this time, when I hailed and begged the commander to run down to the *Alabama*, as she was fast sinking and we had but two boats, and assist in picking up the men. He answered affirmatively, and steamed toward the *Alabama*, but the latter sank almost immediately.

The following is an extract from Mr. John Lancaster's log, dated "Steam yacht *Deerhound*, off Cowes":

Sunday, June 19th, 9 A. M. Got up steam and proceeded out of Cherbourg Harbor. Half-past ten, observed the *Alabama* steaming out of the harbor toward the Federal steamer *Kearsarge*. Ten minutes past eleven, the *Alabama* commenced firing with her starboard battery, the distance between the contending vessels being about one mile. The *Kearsarge* immediately replied with her starboard guns. A very sharp, spirited fire was kept up, shot sometimes being varied by shells. In maneuvering, both vessels made seven complete

When Mr. Lancaster approached Captain Semmes and said, "I think every man has been picked up; where shall I land you?" Captain Semmes replied, "I am now under the English colors, and the sooner you put me with my officers and men on English soil, the better." The little yacht moved rapidly away at once, under a press of steam, for South-hampton. Armstrong, our second lieutenant, and some of our men who were saved by the French pilot boats, were taken into Cherbourg. Our loss was 9 killed, 21 wounded and 10 drowned.

It has been charged that an arrangement had been entered into between Mr. Lancaster and Captain Semmes, previous to our leaving Cherbourg, that in the event of the *Alabama* being sunk the *Deerhound* would come to our rescue. Captain Semmes and myself met Mr. Lancaster for the first time when rescued by him, and he related to us the circumstance that was the occasion of his coming out to see the fight. Having his family on board, his intention was to attend church with his wife and children, when the gathering of the spectators on the shore attracted their attention, the report having been widely circulated that the *Alabama* was to go out that morning and give battle to the *Kearsarge*. The boys were clamorous to see the fight, and after a family discussion as to the propriety of going out on the Sabbath to witness a naval combat, Mr. Lancaster agreed to put the question to vote at the breakfast table, where the youngsters carried their point by a majority. Thus many of us were indebted for our lives to that inherent trait in the English character, the desire to witness a passage at arms.

That evening we landed in Southhampton and were re-

circles at a distance of from a quarter to half a mile. At 12 a slight intermission was observed in the *Alabama's* firing, the *Alabama* making head-sail and shaping her course for the land, distant about nine miles. At 12:30, observed the *Alabama* to be disabled and in a sinking state. We immediately made toward her, and in passing the *Kearsarge* were requested to assist in saving the *Alabama's* crew. It was 12:50, when within a distance of two hundred yards, the *Alabama* sunk. We then lowered our two boats, and with the assistance of the *Alabama's* whaleboat and dinghy, succeeded in saving about forty men, including Captain Semmes and thirteen officers. At 1 P. M. we started for Southampton.

ceived by the people with every demonstration of sympathy and kindly feeling. Thrown upon their shores by the chances of war, we were taken to their hearts and homes with that generous hospitality which brought to mind with tenderest feeling our own dear Southern homes in *ante-bellum* times.

Index

459

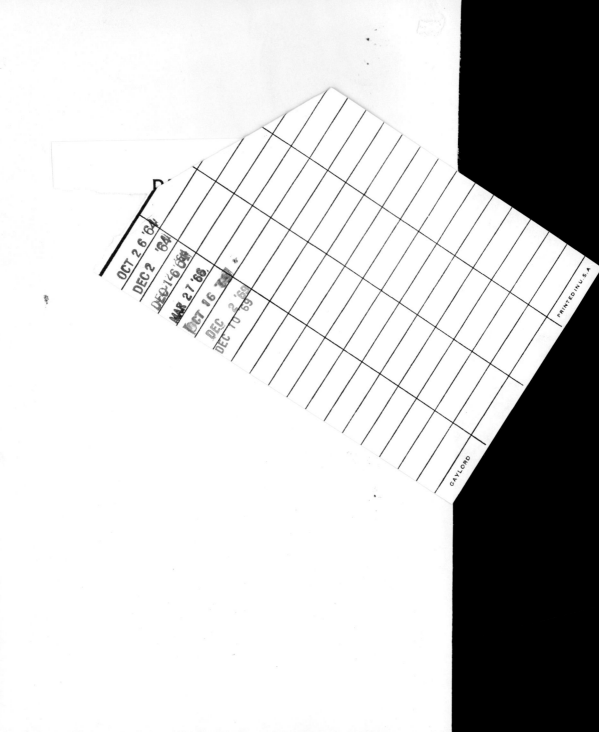